National Geographic Picture Atlas of

Our Fifty States

National Geographic Picture Atlas of

Our Fifty States

National Geographic Picture Atlas of

Our Fifty States

Published by
The National Geographic Society

Gilbert M. Grosvenor
President and
Chairman of the Board

Michela A. English
Senior Vice President

Robert L. Breeden
Executive Adviser to
the President for Publications
and Educational Media

Prepared by
The Book Division

William R. Gray
Director

Margery G. Dunn
Senior Editor

Charles O. Hyman
National Geographic
Book Service

Staff for this Book

Margaret Sedeen
Editor

Greta Arnold
Linda B. Meyerriecks
Illustrations Editors

David M. Seager
Art Director

Melanie Patt-Corner
Chief Researcher

Charlotte Golin
Designer

Susan C. Eckert
Map Coordinator

Mary B. Dickinson
Catherine Herbert Howell
Edward Lanouette
Writer-Editors

H. Robert Morrison
Melanie Patt-Corner
Jean Kaplan Teichroew
Contributing Writers

Ratri Banerjee
Susan C. Eckert
James B. Enzinna
Patricia F. Frakes
Lise S. Sajewski
Penelope A. Timbers
Anne E. Withers
Editorial Researchers

Karen Dufort Sligh
Jean C. Stringer
Illustrations Assistants

Sandra F. Lotterman
Elizabeth G. Jevons
Karen F. Edwards
Teresita Cóquia Sison
Marilyn J. Williams
Staff Assistants

Richard S. Wain
Production Project Manager

Lewis R. Bassford
Heather Guwang
Production

George V. White
Director
John T. Dunn
Associate Director
Vincent P. Ryan
Manager
and R. Gary Colbert
Manufacturing and
Quality Management

Maps by Publications Art
John D. Garst, Jr.
Virginia L. Baza
Sharon M. Atkins
Peter J. Balch
Sven M. Dolling
Gary M. Johnson
Carl Mehler
Joseph F. Ochlak
William T. Spicer

Dianne L. Hardy
Indexer

Sue Appleby Purcell
Educational Consultant

State Flowers and State Birds
painted by
Robert Hynes

State Flags painted by
Marilyn Dye Smith
and Robert Hynes

Cover photography:
Michel Tcherevkoff
Eagle photograph:
Tom and Pat Leeson

First edition: 239,000 copies
264 pages, 315 illustrations,
80 maps

Contents

Our Fifty States

6 a.m.
Hawaii-Aleutian Time

7 a.m.
Alaska Time

8 a.m.
Pacific Time

The fifty United States make up the fourth largest country in the world, both in area and in population. The country's 3,618,770 square miles (9,372,614 sq km) span six time zones and a wide diversity of geography and climate. From the woods of Maine to the mountains of California, from arctic Alaska to tropical Hawaii, almost 250,000,000 Americans form a colorful kaleidoscope of cultures.

Each standard time zone is about 900 miles (1,450 km) wide. Time zones are based on a system that uses lines of longitude as borders. But the borders bend or zigzag so that neighboring areas can share the same time.

Regional colors match the colors of state maps within each regional section of the atlas.

ALASKA

Olympia
WASHINGT

Salem

OREGON

Sacramento
★

Carson
City
★
NEVAD

CALIFORNIA

★ Juneau

	New England
	Mid-Atlantic States
	Appalachian Highlands
	The Southeast
	Great Lakes States
	The Heartland
	The Southwest
	Mountain States
	Pacific Coast States
	Alaska, Hawaii, and Distant Shores

HAWAII

★
Honolulu

Hawaii and the Aleutian Islands share the same time zone.

9 a.m.
Mountain Time

10 a.m.
Central Time

11 a.m.
Eastern Time

MONTANA

★ Helena

Boise

IDAHO

NORTH DAKOTA

★ Bismarck

MINNESOTA

Lake Superior

MAINE

★ Augusta

SOUTH DAKOTA

★ Pierre

St. Paul ★

WISCONSIN

Lake Michigan

MICHIGAN

Lake Huron

VERMONT

Montpelier ★

NEW
HAMPSHIRE

★ Concord

Salt Lake
City ★

WYOMING

Cheyenne ★

NEBRASKA

Madison
★

Lansing
★

Lake Ontario

Albany ★

NEW YORK

Lake Erie

★ Boston

MASSACHUSETTS

★ Providence

Hartford ★
CONNECTICUT

RHODE
ISLAND

UTAH

Denver ★

COLORADO

Lincoln ★

IOWA

Des Moines
★

ILLINOIS

INDIANA

OHIO

Columbus
★

PENNSYLVANIA

Harrisburg ★

★ Trenton

NEW JERSEY

★ Dover

DELAWARE

ARIZONA

★ Santa Fe

KANSAS

Topeka ★

MISSOURI

Jefferson
City ★

Springfield
★

Indianapolis
★

WEST
VIRGINIA

Charleston
★

Annapolis
Washington, ⊗
D. C. ★
MARYLAND

Richmond ★

VIRGINIA

★ Phoenix

NEW MEXICO

OKLAHOMA

★ Oklahoma
City

ARKANSAS

Frankfort
★

KENTUCKY

Nashville ★

TENNESSEE

Raleigh
★

NORTH CAROLINA

Little
Rock ★

MISSISSIPPI

ALABAMA

Columbia
★

SOUTH
CAROLINA

★ Atlanta

TEXAS

LOUISIANA

Jackson
★

Montgomery
★

GEORGIA

Baton Rouge
★

Austin ★

★ Tallahassee

FLORIDA

0   KILOMETERS   300

0   STATUTE MILES   300

America's Many Faces

"*E Pluribus Unum*" is the Latin phrase on the Great Seal of the United States—"From Many, One." When Benjamin Franklin, Thomas Jefferson, and John Adams proposed this motto to the Continental Congress in 1776, they meant that one indivisible nation, the United States of America, was being formed from 13 separate colonies. Today we can see other meanings as well in the words, meanings perhaps undreamed of by those first congressional delegates. From many countries of the world, millions upon millions of immigrants have come to the shores of this country to make one people.

Just as the face of the American people is one of great diversity, so is the face of the land. This essay will present scenes and portraits of both. Wherever we live, to explore the whole expanse of our country brings an understanding of how the American land is part of all of us and how we all are part of the land. Each region of the country offers wonders and surprises and its own particular kind of beauty.

Alaska is a place where you can sense the wildness and spaciousness of much of the land before Europeans arrived. Imagine what it would be like to travel a distance greater than that from New York to the Mississippi River and see mountains, rivers, glaciers, marshes, forests, endless tundra plains, and multitudes of birds and other animals. This is the primeval wilderness that characterizes most of Alaska.

One of the northernmost mountain systems on Earth, the Brooks Range lies within the Arctic Circle and sweeps across Alaska from the Canadian border to the Chukchi Sea. On the North Slope of the Brooks, rolling tundra overlies permafrost that begins from a few inches to a few feet below the surface and reaches down hundreds of feet. Some tundra plants hug the ground to avoid harsh winds. In the briefest of summers, they grow and flower. The tundra and the mountains are migration grounds for moose and caribou herds. Also making their homes on the tundra or on the mountain slopes are musk oxen, Dall's sheep, wolves, arctic foxes, grizzly bears, polar bears, and, in spring and summer, millions of migrant birds.

Thick spruce forests, some perched on high bluffs, line the banks of the Yukon River in its middle stretch. Where the Yukon turns south-westward, leaving behind its canyon walls, it flows through marshy land. The arctic tern, one of the world's champion long-distance commuters, summers here and in autumn migrates as far away as South America and Antarctica.

At a great fan-shaped delta, the Yukon River empties into the Bering Sea. In spring and summer, the delta's thousands of square miles resound with the quacking of ducks, the yodeling of tundra swans, and the calls of millions of other birds. Grizzly bears range through the northern uplands, feasting on salmon and berries. When winter comes, bears sleep in their dens. Quiet descends, except for the rush of the wind, the scratches of moose pawing through the snow for plants to eat, or the low croak of a soaring raven.

To the south, the Aleutian Islands stretch for hundreds of miles in a rampart of windswept, fogbound mountain peaks. Nutrient-rich waters off the Aleutians and other parts of southern Alaska support what may be the greatest concentration of marine mammals in the world. Fur seals, sea otters, sea lions, and walruses thrive here. Humpback whales feed here during the summer, and in the fall head southwestward across 3,000 miles of open ocean to Hawaii.

Being home to humpbacks for half of each year is not all that Alaska and Hawaii have in common. In both states, volcanoes rumble. Both states protect their wildlife populations, but, unlike Alaska's huge refuges, some of Hawaii's are tiny—rocky, sandy islets in the vast Pacific, where seabirds in the tens of thousands nest and raise their offspring, and where the endangered Hawaiian monk seal finds haven.

In the western United States, the Cascade Range, the Sierra Nevada, and the Coast Ranges give this part of the country a high profile characterized by rolling seas of evergreen forest, mountain glaciers and snowfields, rocky cliffs plunging headlong into the ocean, and deep bays and sounds.

Between the Pacific mountain ranges and the Rocky Mountains is the Basin and Range, a region of deserts and plateaus and valleys separated by mountain ranges. Here, on Nevada's high,

In the southern Colorado Rocky Mountains, a frigid lake mirrors mountain peaks once veined with precious ores of gold and silver.

rocky slopes grow groves of bristlecone pines, some of the oldest living trees on Earth. These stunted, gnarled, grotesquely beautiful pines have survived through centuries of storm and drought. Wind-driven ice polishes their wood. The miracle of the bristlecone is its ability to keep a spark of life glowing in a thin strip of bark and a few branches, needles, and roots long after the rest of the tree has died.

In the Grand Canyon, the Colorado River has cut a window into the continent's history. The layers of exposed rock can be read like a book. Once shale lay on top, on the canyon rim. Now eroded, the shale marked the time when dinosaurs ruled the Earth. Today's top layers are limestone, rich in fossils of sponges, fish, and corals that lived in seas some 200 million years ago, when the floating plates of Earth's crust formed the supercontinent of Pangaea. There was no Grand Canyon yet, nor a Colorado River. Where today canyon walls plunge nearly a mile (1.6 km) to the river, the story told by the rocks is one of Earth turning itself inside out in geologic upheavals, faulting, erosion, and sea flooding. The bottom rocks, nearly two billion years old, are themselves the roots of ancient mountains.

Cresting the North American continent, the Rocky Mountains reach from New Mexico to Alaska's Brooks Range. In Wyoming, in the Teton Range of the central Rockies, peaks rise steeply from the valley floor through forests of pine, fir, and spruce, to alpine meadows bright with wildflowers, past glaciers even now shaping the landscape in slow motion, to stark, granite pinnacles. Here, along the banks of the Snake River, aspen and willow provide beavers with their favorite food. River otters, ospreys, and eagles dine on trout. In winter, solitary moose browse in willow thickets, and elk herds graze by night on meadow grasses.

Eastward from the Rocky Mountains, the land slopes down to the plains and prairies of the mid-continent. Little more than a century ago, tallgrass prairie spread for hundreds of miles. Now it has dwindled to a precious few thousand acres, mostly in Kansas.

A tallgrass prairie rolls in waves, like a sea. It rustles in the wind. Its intermingled life-forms weave an intricate web. The plant that dominates is big bluestem, a grass whose total ex-

tent, top to bottom, can be greater than the height of three men. Above the prairie sod, big bluestem can stand ten feet (3 m) in height. Its roots reach down at least twelve feet (3.7 m), finding soil nutrients and protection from harsh weather. From spring to fall, patches of flowers brighten the grassland. Their blossoms lure insects that find meals of nectar or flower parts and help the flowers to reproduce by carrying pollen from one flower to another. Birds and mammals eat the fruits that flowers produce and deposit the undigested seeds where they may sprout into the growth of a new season. Other plants depend on wind to scatter their seeds, and hang on to the seeds until the wind is high enough to carry them away. Still others, with sticky seeds, owe the distribution of their species to animals that accidentally pick up the seeds, carry them off, and later drop them. The seeds may grow, or they may be eaten by birds.

A busy, hidden world thrives under the prairie sod, inhabited by tiny creatures without which the grasses, flowers, shrubs, and animals from deer to mice could not exist here. A kind of microscopic fungus helps the root hairs of plants to absorb nutrients from the soil. In exchange, the plants feed some of their own carbohydrates to the fungus. There are bacteria that live in the root hairs and enable the plants to get the nitrogen essential to growth. Larger creatures such as the larvae of June bugs, cicadas, and click beetles feed on roots. This underground world is a densely populated place, with hundreds of microscopic inhabitants in a handful of soil.

East of the grasslands, past the valleys of the Mississippi and Ohio Rivers, the flanks of the Appalachian Mountains begin their rise. The green-clad Appalachian peaks descend eastward to the Piedmont and the Atlantic Coastal Plain. In these parts of the country, wild places are fewer and smaller than in the West, but their rewards are as great.

In southern Georgia, in the mysterious depths of the Okefenokee Swamp, the bellows of bull alligators can take us back to prehistoric times and remind us of the alligator's ancient

Newborn babies in a Dallas, Texas, hospital take a ride to visit their parents. Every day in this hospital at least 40 new Texans are born.

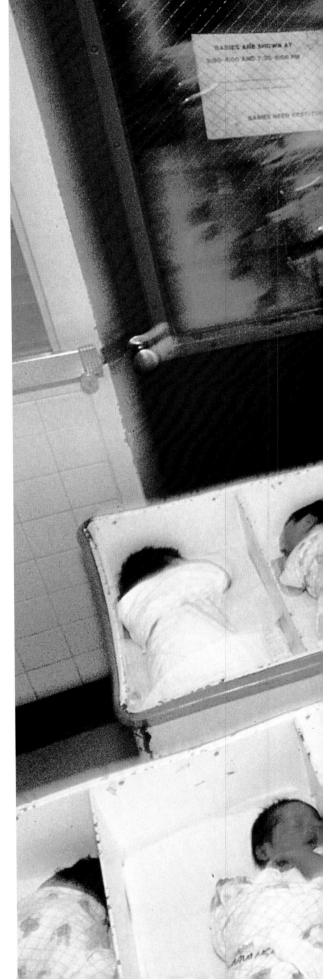

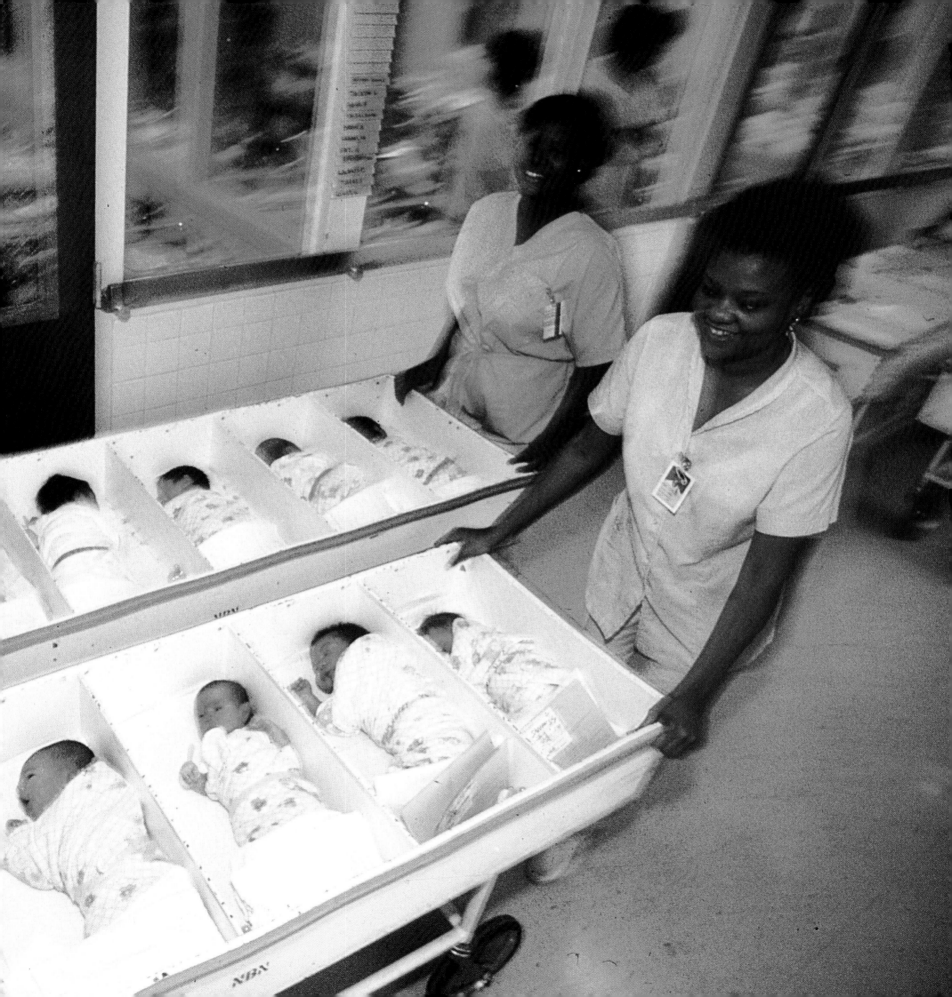

relative, the dinosaur. Soaring bald cypress trees sink their great knobby roots in thick peat, a legacy of ages of decaying plant life. The swamp water flows slowly, drifting to its outlets, the St. Marys River and the Suwannee River. Waterbirds nest deep in the swamp and often flock to the vast expanses of marsh and water known here as prairies. River otters, black bears, muskrats, bats, bobcats, foxes, and some 40 other species of animals live in the swamp or on the drier uplands of Okefenokee.

Just as there are layers in rock that reveal the geological past, so there are layers in the story of human existence. Those of us alive today in the United States are actors in the latest chapter of a history that began on this continent thousands of years ago. What happened in the first chapter? Who were the first Americans?

Anthropologists and archaeologists debate this question heatedly. For many years, most believed that the earliest humans to enter North America crossed a land bridge between Siberia and Alaska about 12,000 years ago. But in the 1970s, scientists made some intriguing—and still disputed—discoveries. For instance, there are signs that some 16,000 years ago, at a place now called Meadowcroft, in southwestern Pennsylvania, people had made a shelter under a sandstone cliff. These people lived by hunting deer and small animals and by gathering plants to eat and, perhaps, to make baskets. For many generations people used this rock-shelter as a temporary home and as a base camp. Other sites have been excavated in South America where such things as tools, uneaten mastodon meat, a human footprint, and vivid rock paintings suggest that people had ranged that far by 13,000 years ago. Even if this turns out to be true, no one knows how they got there. Did they travel in boats or on rafts? Or did they walk, in small migratory bands, moving southward perhaps a few miles a year all the way from Alaska?

That is exactly what some early Americans did. They trickled, step by step, following mammoths, elephants, bison, caribou, and other beasts. They quarried stone for spearpoints to

The energy of big cities everywhere radiates from this special-effects view of New York, the heart of our country's most populous metropolitan area.

kill their game and for tools to butcher it. They gathered plants for food, medicine, and clothing. They shared their domain with lions, cheetahs, saber-toothed cats, and huge bears. This was late in the Ice Age, when glaciers still held enough seawater to keep ocean levels low and to expose a vast, ice-free area of Alaska's continental shelf. We call this dry land Beringia or the Bering Land Bridge, but people slowly crossing it from Asia would have had no sense of being on anything like a bridge. At its widest, Beringia covered a thousand miles (1,600 km). It was largely a rolling plain crossed by great rivers and dotted with groves of willow and patches of prairie grasses, sedge, and sagebrush. Spring flowers brightened the tundra then as now.

These hunters, as well as others who may have traveled along the coasts and hunted sea mammals, were the ancestors of the American Indians. They were the first immigrants. They are the people who really discovered America.

In time their descendants fanned out across the continent. When Christopher Columbus sailed into the New World, at the end of the 15th century, there were some two million people— Indians and other native groups—living on the continent north of Central America. Today, five centuries later, the population of the United States alone, at almost 250,000,000, is more than a hundred times greater.

One reason for this growth is that Americans have traditionally been a people on the move. When the first census was taken in 1790, colonists and settlers from Europe made up most of the population. At that time the census counted the number of Americans at a little over 3,900,000. Indians were not included, but historians say that, by then, there were only about 600,000 in the entire area of today's contiguous 48 states. The black population numbered more than 700,000. Most were slaves, tragic and unwilling immigrants, but several thousand were free blacks, many of whom had worked for money as indentured servants. The movement of Europeans to the United States soon took on the proportions of a flood. By 1860 more than five million new Americans had arrived, mostly from western Europe. The greatest growth occurred in the late 19th and early 20th centuries, when more than 22 million newcomers, many from

southern and eastern Europe, arrived on the shores of America.

The face of our country is always changing. Demographers, people who study the characteristics of populations, tell us that a nation's population changes because of three things: births, deaths, and migration. Demographers can tell us, for instance, that every 8 seconds a baby is born somewhere in the United States. Every 15 seconds someone dies. Every 35 seconds a new immigrant arrives in the United States. And every 3 minutes an American emigrates. A demographic portrait reveals many things—about ourselves, our families, our neighbors, our work, the places we live.

Today we Americans live farther west and farther south than ever before. States in the West and South saw rapid population growth from 1980 to 1990. States in the Northeast and Midwest grew slowly or saw their populations fall. The westward movement of the population center of the 50 states reflects our history. As settlers migrated across the Appalachian Mountains, populated the Midwest, and made homes from the plains to the Pacific coast, the country's population center shifted westward, following them. Today it lies about 95 miles (152 km) southwest of St. Louis, Missouri. (For more information, see pages 172 and 173.)

More than half of the people in the United States live in metropolitan areas of one million or more. This is a group that has grown steadily. In 1950 it was less than one-third of the population. When you include smaller metropolitan areas, you find that almost 80 percent of Americans are dwellers in cities or suburbs.

In 1950, 15 percent of Americans lived on farms. This is a group that has declined steadily, and today includes fewer than 2 of every 100 people. Around the country, rural areas have lost population because of the decline in family farms and because of a loss of mining jobs.

When people give up living on farms or in small towns, where do they go? Most do not go to big cities. They go to the suburbs. City people, too, often choose to move to the suburbs. Today,

The 1,250,000 crushed beverage cans awaiting shipment here testify to a rising American awareness of the importance of recycling our resources.

of all the kinds of places that we Americans live in, it is the outermost fringes of suburban areas that see the strongest growth. Demographers predict that this trend will continue.

When people move, they usually go where the jobs are. The fact that Florida attracts large numbers of retirees means that other people are needed to open and work in stores, dry-cleaning and repair shops, health-care facilities, or restaurants to serve the senior citizens. Where the tourism industry is thriving, such as in Las Vegas, Nevada, that creates jobs in areas from construction to popcorn vending. In Austin, the capital of Texas, employers such as the state government, the University of Texas, and high-tech industries helped to give Texas a 1990 population that was almost 20 percent greater than its 1980 population. But several other states beat that figure: Nevada grew by 50 percent; Alaska, 37 percent; Arizona, 35 percent; Florida, 33 percent; California, 26 percent. Across the United States as a whole, there are at least 10 percent more people than there were in 1980.

Of these some 23 million new Americans, more than a third are immigrants. People have come from China, Korea, the Philippines, India, Iran, Vietnam, and other parts of Asia. They have come from Mexico, Cuba, El Salvador, the Dominican Republic, Guatemala, and Colombia, as well as other Latin American countries. Most of the immigration in the decade of the 1980s was Asian and Hispanic, but newcomers also arrived from Europe, Africa, and Canada.

Another group that has grown in size is the Native American population. Since 1960, the number of people identifying themselves as American Indian has more than tripled. Experts believe that many who once concealed their ethnic identity now proudly call themselves Indian, take a new pleasure in their heritage, and feel optimistic about their future.

The United States has been called a melting pot, a nation of nations, a world nation. One of the strengths of our country has always been its diversity. As we head into the 21st century, we are a people united, yet more diverse than ever.

"In God's wildness lies the hope of the world," wrote naturalist John Muir, an ardent defender of trees such as these California redwoods.

The Maps in Your Atlas

An atlas is a collection of maps. Maps show many things, such as where places are, how big they are, and their distance from other places. In your Picture Atlas you will find maps of the fifty United States and the territories, as well as maps of regions. Each map is full of information. Notes on the maps point out places of geographical or historical importance. Some map symbols represent natural features, while others show man-made features.

The state maps in your atlas, like this sample map of Washington, are general reference maps, sometimes called political maps. They present each state as if you were looking straight down on it. These maps emphasize state boundaries and man-made features, such as cities, towns, and highways.

Physical features—mountains, lakes, and rivers—are also shown. Some rivers, such as the Gila in Arizona (page 179), are drawn with dashed and dotted blue lines. This is a cartographer's way of showing that the rivers are intermittent and may dry up in certain seasons. Dashed blue outlines also mark salt lakes and dry lakes, such as the Bonneville Salt Flats and Sevier Lake in Utah (page 213). A bar scale with each map lets you measure distance in both miles and kilometers.

The maps of regions in your atlas are physical maps. They show features of Earth's surface. Except for Alaska and Hawaii, each region is a group of contiguous states with physical similarities, and sometimes with surprising differences. These maps are also paintings. Because of their three-dimensional quality, as well as the perspective, or angle, from which each region is seen, not everything is visible. A river may disappear behind a mountain, or a city could be hidden by a high peak.

Each state in your atlas has photographs; illustrations of the state flag, flower, and bird; a text article; and a fact box with the state's area and population, the three largest cities with their population, information about the economy, and the date of statehood. The categories of mining, agriculture, and industry appear in order of economic value to that state. Within each category, products are listed in order of value.

This is a pictorial map of the Mid-Atlantic region. Your atlas contains a similar map for each region of the United States. These maps show the main physical features, such as mountains, lakes, rivers, and shorelines. Studying these maps will help you understand the unity and diversity of each region. You can also see that a mountain range can be a barrier or that major cities are often·on rivers or protected bays.

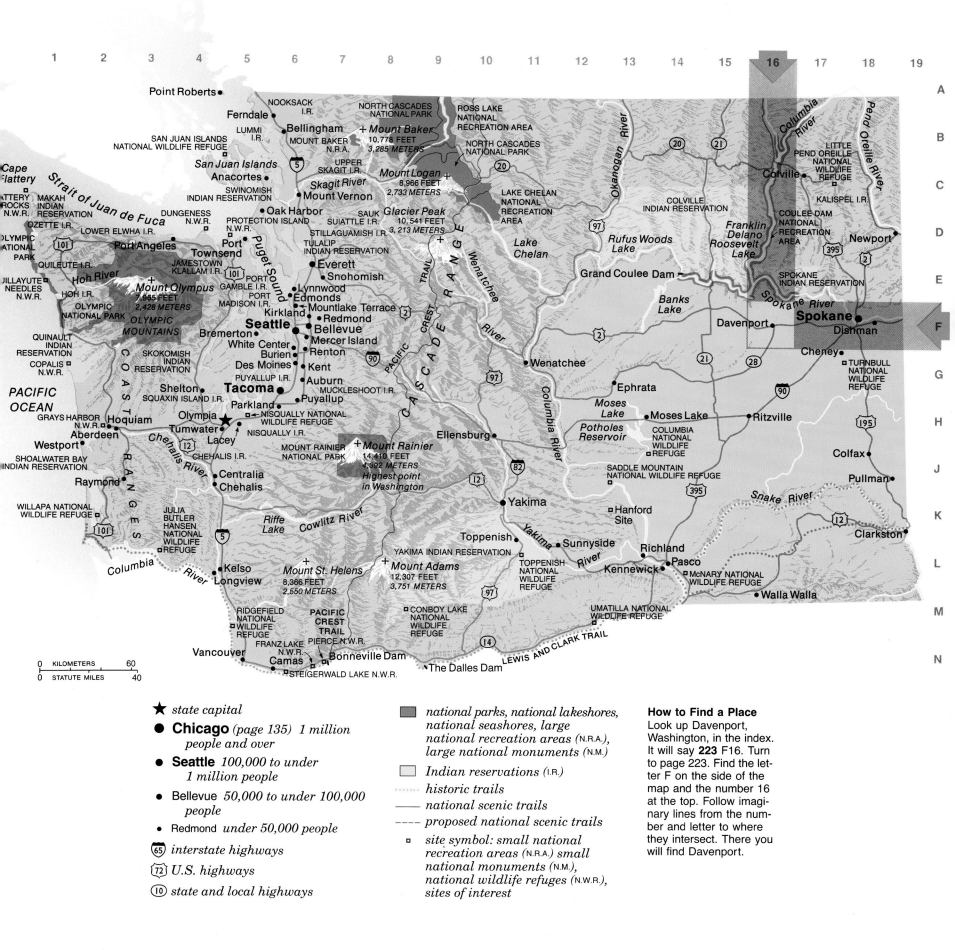

Point Roberts

NOOKSACK
I.R.

Ferndale

LUMMI
I.R.

SAN JUAN ISLANDS
NATIONAL WILDLIFE REFUGE

Bellingham
MOUNT BAKER
N.R.A.

+ Mount Baker
10,778 FEET
3,285 METERS

NORTH CASCADES
NATIONAL PARK

ROSS LAKE
NATIONAL
RECREATION AREA

NORTH CASCADES
NATIONAL PARK

Columbia
River

20

21

LITTLE
PEND OREILLE
NATIONAL
WILDLIFE
REFUGE

Cape
Flattery

BATTERY
ROCKS
N.W.R.

San Juan Islands

Anacortes

UPPER
SKAGIT I.R.

Mount Logan
8,966 FEET
2,733 METERS

20

Colville

Pend Oreille River

MAKAH
INDIAN
RESERVATION

SWINOMISH
INDIAN RESERVATION

Skagit River

Mount Vernon

97

LAKE CHELAN
NATIONAL
RECREATION
AREA

KALISPEL I.R.

OZETTE I.R.

DUNGENESS
N.W.R.

Oak Harbor

SAUK
SUIATTLE I.R.

Glacier Peak
10,541 FEET
3,213 METERS

COLVILLE
INDIAN RESERVATION

COULEE DAM
NATIONAL
RECREATION
AREA

OLYMPIC
NATIONAL
PARK

LOWER ELWHA I.R.

PROTECTION ISLAND
N.W.R.

STILLAGUAMISH I.R.

Rufus Woods
Lake

Franklin
Delano
Roosevelt
Lake

Newport

QUILEUTE I.R.

Port Angeles

Port
Townsend

TULALIP
INDIAN RESERVATION

395

2

JILLAYUTE
NEEDLES
N.W.R.

Hoh River

JAMESTOWN
KLALLAM I.R.

101

Everett

Lake
Chelan

SPOKANE
INDIAN RESERVATION

HOH I.R.

Mount Olympus
7,965 FEET
2,428 METERS

PORT
GAMBLE I.R.

101

Snohomish

Grand Coulee Dam

OLYMPIC
NATIONAL PARK

OLYMPIC
MOUNTAINS

PORT
MADISON I.R.

Lynnwood
Edmonds
Mountlake Terrace

2

Spokane River

QUINAULT
INDIAN
RESERVATION

Kirkland

Banks
Lake

Spokane

Dishman

COPALIS
N.W.R.

Seattle

Bellevue

Redmond

Davenport

Bremerton

White Center

Mercer Island

Cheney

PACIFIC
OCEAN

GRAYS HARBOR
N.W.R.

Hoquiam

Burien

Renton

90

2

28

TURNBULL
NATIONAL
WILDLIFE
REFUGE

Des Moines

Kent

21

SKOKOMISH
INDIAN
RESERVATION

Shelton

Tacoma

Auburn

MUCKLESHOOT I.R.

Wenatchee

97

Ephrata

90

Westport

Parkland

Puyallup

195

SQUAXIN ISLAND I.R.

Moses
Lake

Aberdeen

Olympia

NISQUALLY NATIONAL
WILDLIFE REFUGE

Moses Lake

Ritzville

SHOALWATER BAY
INDIAN RESERVATION

Tumwater

Lacey

NISQUALLY I.R.

Potholes
Reservoir

COLUMBIA
NATIONAL
WILDLIFE
REFUGE

Colfax

Raymond

Chehalis River

CHEHALIS I.R.

MOUNT RAINIER
NATIONAL PARK

Mount Rainier
14,410 FEET
4,392 METERS
Highest point
in Washington

Ellensburg

82

12

Pullman

WILLAPA NATIONAL
WILDLIFE REFUGE

JULIA
BUTLER
HANSEN
NATIONAL
WILDLIFE
REFUGE

Centralia

Chehalis

SADDLE MOUNTAIN
NATIONAL WILDLIFE REFUGE

12

395

101

Riffe
Lake

Cowlitz River

12

Yakima

Hanford
Site

Clarkston

5

Snake River

Kelso

Mount St. Helens
8,366 FEET
2,550 METERS

Mount Adams
12,307 FEET
3,751 METERS

Toppenish

Yakima

Richland

Longview

YAKIMA INDIAN RESERVATION

Sunnyside

River

Pasco

McNARY NATIONAL
WILDLIFE REFUGE

Columbia

River

RIDGEFIELD
NATIONAL
WILDLIFE
REFUGE

PACIFIC
CREST
TRAIL

CONBOY LAKE
NATIONAL
WILDLIFE
REFUGE

TOPPENISH
NATIONAL
WILDLIFE
REFUGE

97

Kennewick

UMATILLA NATIONAL
WILDLIFE REFUGE

Walla Walla

Vancouver

FRANZ LAKE
N.W.R.

PIERCE N.W.R.

Camas

Bonneville Dam

14

LEWIS AND CLARK TRAIL

STEIGERWALD LAKE N.W.R.

The Dalles Dam

KILOMETERS 60

STATUTE MILES 40

★ state capital

● **Chicago** (page 135) 1 million
people and over

● **Seattle** 100,000 to under
1 million people

● Bellevue 50,000 to under 100,000
people

• Redmond under 50,000 people

🛡 interstate highways

🛡 U.S. highways

🛡 state and local highways

national parks, national lakeshores,
national seashores, large
national recreation areas (N.R.A.),
large national monuments (N.M.)

Indian reservations (I.R.)

.... historic trails

—— national scenic trails

---- proposed national scenic trails

▫ site symbol: small national
recreation areas (N.R.A.) small
national monuments (N.M.),
national wildlife refuges (N.W.R.),
sites of interest

How to Find a Place
Look up Davenport,
Washington, in the index.
It will say **223** F16. Turn
to page 223. Find the letter F on the side of the
map and the number 16
at the top. Follow imagi-
nary lines from the num-
ber and letter to where
they intersect. There you
will find Davenport.

District of Columbia

Our Nation's Capital

The founders of the United States wrestled with the problem of where the capital of the young nation should be. Finally, in 1790, they agreed on a location somewhere on the Potomac River. They left the exact choice of a site to President George Washington. It is his memory we honor when we call the city Washington, D. C.

George Washington chose a site on the fall line that divides the Piedmont from the Atlantic Coastal Plain. He directed surveyors to lay out a square ten miles (16 km) on each side for the new capital. The city was to stand on both sides of the Potomac at the head of navigation, partly in Maryland and partly in Virginia. Those states ceded the land to the government, but in 1846 Virginia asked for its portion back.

To design the city, President Washington selected Pierre Charles L'Enfant, a French engineer who had served as a volunteer in the Revolutionary War. The chief surveyor, Maryland's Andrew Ellicott, and his assistant, a self-taught black mathematician and astronomer named Benjamin Banneker, used positions of

During World War I, when Woodrow Wilson was President, sheep were put to work cropping the south lawn of the White House to free men for the war effort.

the stars to determine the District's latitude and longitude and to lay out its boundaries.

Today L'Enfant's ideas can be seen in the traffic circles and broad thoroughfares of the city, lined with stately buildings and memorials built in the architectural styles of ancient Greece and Rome. Toward one end of Pennsylvania Avenue stands the domed Capitol Building, toward the other the White House, where Presidents have worked and lived with their families since 1800. During the War of 1812, British troops marched on Washington and set fire to both buildings.

L'Enfant designed the Mall to be a "Grand Avenue . . . bordered with gardens," and so it is. On the Mall stand museums administered by the Smithsonian Institution. These include the Museum of American History, where you can see what life was like in the past. Among the enormous collections here are a green-and-gold 1920s locomotive, gowns of America's First Ladies, one of George Washington's uniforms, and Thomas Edison's phonograph.

George Washington had hoped that the capital city would become part of an important trade route, by way of the Ohio River, to the interior of the country. In 1828 work was begun on the Chesapeake and Ohio Canal to bypass falls and rapids on the Potomac River, but financial problems and competition from railroads eventually put the canal out of business.

Today government is the chief business of the city. Some 370,000 people, city residents and suburbanites, work directly for the federal government, and hundreds of thousands more work for organizations such as research firms, publishers, and trade associations that want to be near the government. Many Washington workers are lawyers. Their numbers are equal to almost a tenth of the city's population.

Washington is the heart of a metropolitan area of almost four million people, but its status as a federal district makes it unique. It is the only American city whose residents have no voting members of Congress. Congressional committees oversee the District government. Today residents campaign not only for full representation in Congress but also for statehood. The state would be called New Columbia.

For all its grandeur and importance, the District of Columbia is a city on a human scale. There are no skyscrapers. A 19th-century law limited buildings to a height that could be reached by the fire-fighting equipment of the day, and lawmakers have kept the restrictions so as not to dwarf the Capitol. A Washingtonian once remarked that "it's almost as if you could hold the city in the palm of your hand."

Throughout the city are multitudes of parks. In one, Rock Creek Park, a walk through thick native forests can lead your imagination back to the days before European settlement, when Algonquian Indians quarried stone there for tools. If you stand on a street corner just southeast of the Capitol, at a spot where sewer workers unearthed some dinosaur fossils, you might picture the giant creatures that reigned over the area more than a hundred million years ago.

The residents of today's District of Columbia are a varied group. A large number, such as those who work for embassies, are foreign citizens. Immigrants from Africa, Asia, and Latin America have arrived to make the city their home. During the early 19th century, the city was a mecca for free blacks. After the Civil War, former slaves migrated there from the South and, after World War II, so did black farm workers. In those years Washington's black citizens lived isolated and segregated in what one histo-

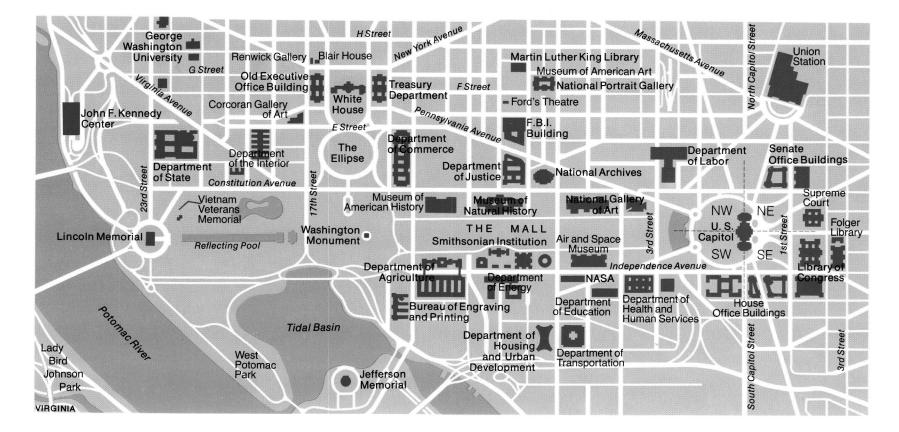

George Washington University
Renwick Gallery
Blair House
H Street
New York Avenue
Massachusetts Avenue
North Capitol Street
Union Station
Martin Luther King Library
Museum of American Art
National Portrait Gallery
G Street
Old Executive Office Building
White House
Treasury Department
F Street
Ford's Theatre
Virginia Avenue
Corcoran Gallery of Art
Pennsylvania Avenue
F.B.I. Building
John F. Kennedy Center
E Street
The Ellipse
Department of Commerce
Department of Justice
National Archives
Department of Labor
Senate Office Buildings
Department of State
Department of the Interior
Constitution Avenue
23rd Street
17th Street
Department of Justice
National Gallery of Art
Supreme Court
Folger Library
Vietnam Veterans Memorial
Museum of American History
Museum of Natural History
3rd Street
NW NE
U.S. Capitol
1st Street
Lincoln Memorial
Washington Monument
Reflecting Pool
THE MALL
Smithsonian Institution
Air and Space Museum
SW SE
Library of Congress
Department of Agriculture
Department of Energy
NASA
Independence Avenue
Department of Education
Department of Health and Human Services
House Office Buildings
Bureau of Engraving and Printing
Potomac River
Tidal Basin
Department of Housing and Urban Development
Department of Transportation
South Capitol Street
3rd Street
Lady Bird Johnson Park
West Potomac Park
Jefferson Memorial
VIRGINIA

rian has called a "secret city." Their city is secret no longer. Two-thirds of Washington's people are black, and from their ranks come local and national leaders in government, business, medicine, law, and the arts. Every year millions of people in the District of Columbia are not Washingtonians at all, but residents of the fifty states and many foreign countries—tourists who come to experience the living history of the capital of the United States of America.

Area: *69 sq mi (178 sq km)*
Population: *606,900*
Important Economic Activities: *federal government, tourism, printing and publishing*
Founded: *site chosen October 1790; became the United States capital June 1800*

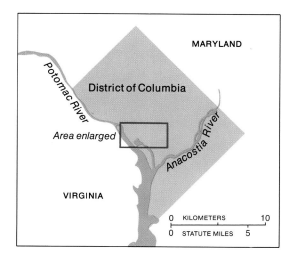

MARYLAND
Potomac River
District of Columbia
Anacostia River
Area enlarged
VIRGINIA

0 KILOMETERS 10
0 STATUTE MILES 5

In the heart of the District of Columbia stand buildings that house the federal government and the nation's treasures.

American Beauty Rose

Wood Thrush

1

2

3

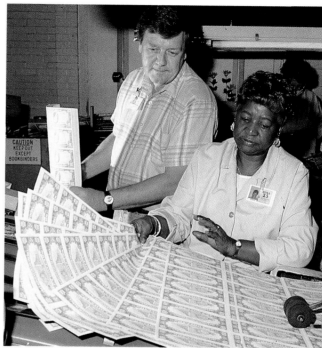

4

District of Columbia

1 *In dusk's soft glow, the 555-foot (169-m) Washington Monument and the domed Jefferson Memorial rise beyond the White House, home to every President except George Washington.*

2 *At the Vietnam Veterans Memorial, a youngster leans forward to kiss the name of his grandfather, killed in action in the Vietnam War.*

3 *The* Spirit of St. Louis, *flown in 1927 by Charles Lindbergh on the first solo flight across the Atlantic Ocean, hangs in the Air and Space Museum.*

4 *Workers at the Bureau of Engraving and Printing examine new sheets of bills.*

5 *Surgeons operate at Howard University Hospital, part of the largest mostly black university in the United States.*

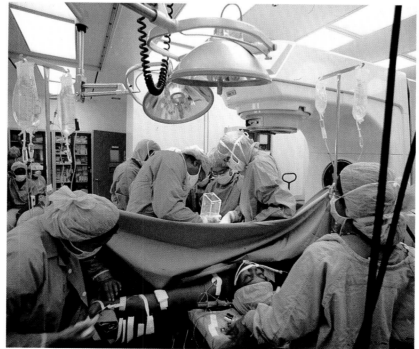

5

New England

The sunlight of a new day first touches the United States mainland on the treeless, mile-high (1.6-km) summit of Mount Katahdin, a solitary mountain of resistant rock called a monadnock that makes up part of the Appalachian Mountains in northern Maine. Lakes and streams glisten near Katahdin's foot. They are part of the Allagash Wilderness Waterway, a 92-mile-long (148-km) run of untamed rivers and lakes that each year lures thousands of canoeists to some of the nation's deepest, wildest woods.

Here, too, with Katahdin as its centerpiece, spreads a remarkable wilderness, a 200,000-acre (81,000-ha) state park bought and donated to the people of Maine by a former governor of the state, Percival Proctor Baxter. Today Baxter State Park serves those who truly savor the wilds. Camping is primitive and strictly regulated. Roads are unpaved. No motorboats, motorcycles, or luxury motor homes disturb the solitude, for this is the lair of the loon and the moose . . . and of those who revel in the lonely splendor of woods and lakes and streams.

Sloping from the mountains toward the ocean, northern New England ends in a burst of bays and inlets and islands, a shoreline as gingerbready as the woodwork on some of the graceful old houses along the coast. There are no deltas here, no great swamps, no sweeps of sandy dune to hint that the ocean waits nearby. The pointed firs march to the very lip of cliffs and headlands that in many places drop sheer to the waves.

Glaciers helped to chisel the shore here, shoving soil and rocks southward. At one time ice covered Mount Washington half a mile (0.8 km) deep. Then, as the glaciers slowly melted and receded, sea levels rose some 400 feet (122 m), transforming Maine's coastal hills into islands and their valleys into myriad fingerlike fjords and deepwater channels.

Whenever the ice paused for any length of time, it piled up sand and soil and boulders along its leading edge, like a giant conveyor belt. You can see here how far south the glaciers reached during the Ice Age. Cape Cod and its island satellites are long, sandy ridges called terminal moraines. They were left behind when the ice began its retreat about 12,000 years ago.

Most New Englanders live near the coast, or along rivers whose flowing waters turned the waterwheels that ran early mills and factories. Today these same rivers produce electric power for homes and industries throughout the region.

In this region the Connecticut River splits the Appalachian Mountains into two major ranges, the White Mountains east of the river and the Green Mountains to the west. In the northwest, the mountains border the fertile pastures and orchards around Lake Champlain. Glaciers were not the only builders of this lake or its valley. Millions of years ago, as Earth's crust shifted, a long, narrow slab of bedrock slipped and tilted toward the west, creating a crease between the Appalachians and neighboring western mountains that filled with water, forming today's sparkling, 107-mile-long (172-km) lake.

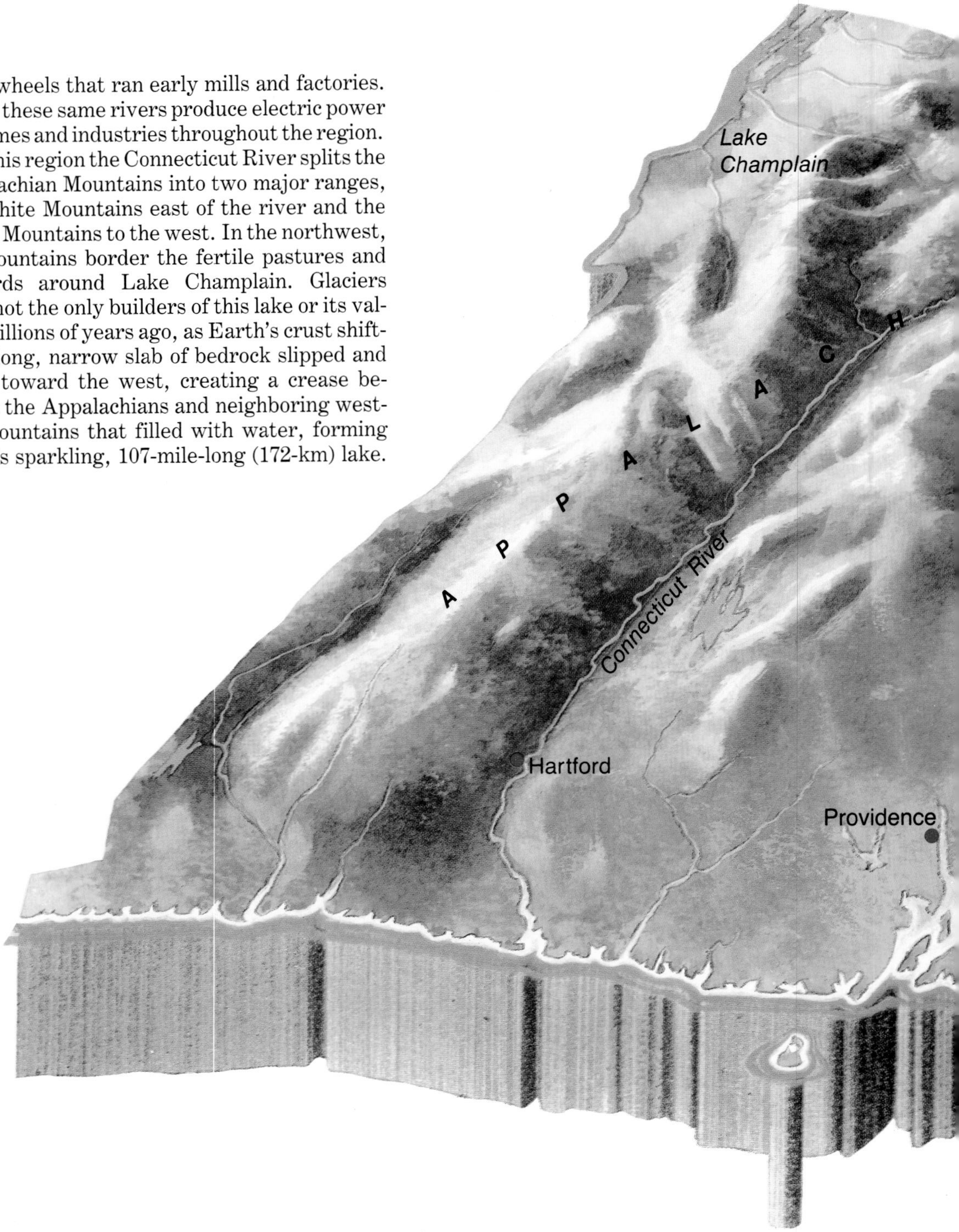

Lake Champlain

APPALACH

Connecticut River

Hartford

Providence

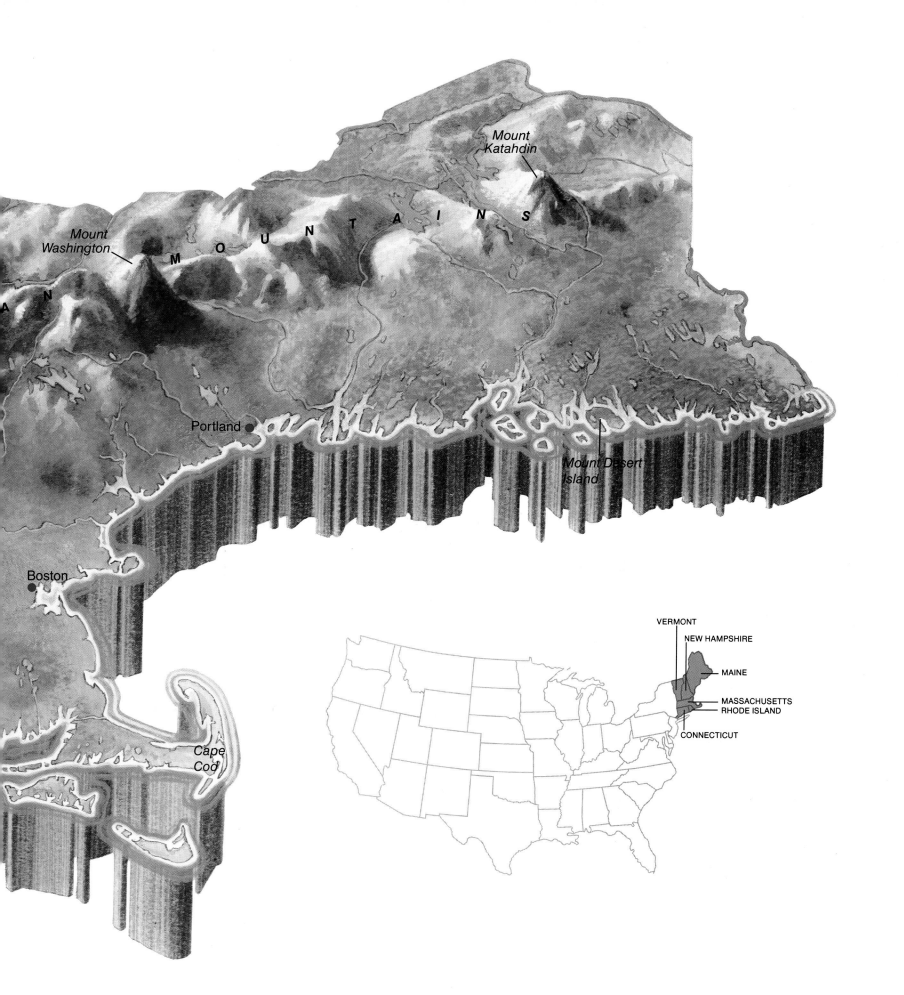

Mount
Katahdin

M O U N T A I N S

Mount
Washington

A

Portland

Mount Desert
Island

Boston

VERMONT

NEW HAMPSHIRE

MAINE

MASSACHUSETTS
RHODE ISLAND

CONNECTICUT

Cape
Cod

Vermont

The forested Green Mountains run the length of Vermont and are part of a chain that reaches southward into Massachusetts and north into Canada. The 250-mile (402-km) Vermont range is unbroken, except for deep gaps cut by the Winooski and Lamoille Rivers, and, in Canada, the Missisquoi River.

Streams flowing down the eastern slopes empty into the Connecticut River and help support a rich agricultural valley. The westward-flowing rivers drain into Lake Champlain, which forms part of the border with New York. Vermont is the only state in New England without direct access to the sea, but, at the southern tip of the lake, commercial and pleasure boats work their way to New York City on a canal connected to the Hudson River.

Outdoor Vermont is a year-round asset. Forests cover nearly 80 percent of the state. In fall the leaves flare into brilliance, and thousands of visitors travel the state, admiring autumn's "last hurrah" before the snows descend. When that happens, skiers from near and far swoosh down the powdery slopes or glide along the smooth trails of more than 50 ski resorts.

In the early spring, when the days begin to warm up but the nights are still freezing, sap flows in the sugar maples. From maple groves, called sugar bushes, comes Vermont's sweetest product, maple syrup. A sugar maker, as this kind of farmer is known, boils down the sap of about 4 trees, some 40 gallons, to make one gallon of syrup. Each spring sugar makers tap millions of trees to obtain the half million gallons of syrup Vermont produces every year.

Then, when summer arrives, cool, crisp nights and warm days bring out campers, hikers, and fishermen. Many visitors are French Canadians, and, for them, people in northern Vermont often put up signs in French.

Vermont, with about the same number of people as Boston, Massachusetts, has the smallest population of any state east of the Mississippi River. Montpelier, a regional industrial and insurance center, is the smallest state capital in the United States. Nearly three-quarters of all Vermonters live on farms or in small towns scattered throughout the state. Since 1980, Vermont's population has increased, though not enough to make it a crowded place. Some outsiders are attracted by life in the small communities or by the prospect of employment in a computer factory or another high-tech company around Burlington.

Even though Vermont is rural, it is not agricultural. Only about 15 percent of the land is level and fertile enough for crops. The rest has soil too thin and rocky. Most of the good cropland is in the Connecticut River Valley and around Lake Champlain and its islands.

There are about half as many cows as there are Vermonters, and many herds graze on mountain pastures. Their milk earns more than three-fourths of the state's agricultural income. The state is also famous for its cheese. Manufacturing, too, helps keep the state's economy going. Vermont's extensive forests provide wood for the paper industry and timber for making furniture and toys.

Sons of the superintendent at Bennington's E.Z. Waist Company pose for a 1915 advertisement for knit union suits guaranteed to make "the child happy and comfortable."

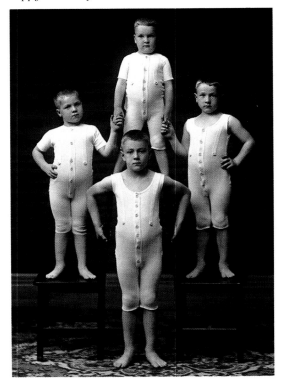

Vermont's economy also benefits from its geology. The mountains began to form some 440 million years ago, when the forces of plate tectonics folded, cracked, and thrust the land upward. Molten rock, or magma, slowly cooled and crystallized. Much of the cooled rock became granite. The largest granite quarry in the world is east of Montpelier. Stone for buildings and memorial markers has been sliced from this quarry and polished in nearby Barre for more than a century.

Marble, which forms when limestone crystallizes, is found along the western edges of the Green Mountains and in the world's largest underground quarry, near the town of Danby. The dome, pillars, and walls of the Thomas Jefferson Memorial in Washington, D. C., are made of Vermont's white marble.

Vermonters are grateful for their economic stability, but they worry about endangering the environment. Around 1970 the state government addressed this issue, and Vermont became one of the first states to get rid of roadside commercial billboards and to legislate refunds for can and bottle returns.

The number of Vermont farms is declining. Writer Saul Bellow, a summer visitor to the state, tells of seeing abandoned farms "in the backlands of Vermont," where he discovers "old foundations, heaps of red brick," and "pairs of lilac bushes that once grew beside the driveway." Farming the rocky soil is hard, and the land has become valuable. In some areas farms are taxed on their potential worth as commercial land. But the state has passed laws to help farmers and to help protect its open land. Since 1988, Vermont towns have been required to participate in regional planning.

Area: *43rd largest state, 9,614 sq mi (24,900 sq km)*
Population: *562,758; ranks 48th*
Major Cities: *Burlington, 39,127; Rutland, 18,230; South Burlington, 12,809*
Manufacturing: *electronics, metal products, machinery, paper products, food products, transportation equipment, lumber and wood products, stone, glass, and clay products*
Agriculture: *milk, cattle, hay, maple products*
Mining and Quarrying: *granite, marble*
Other Important Activities: *tourism, printing and publishing*
Statehood: *the 14th state; admitted March 4, 1791*

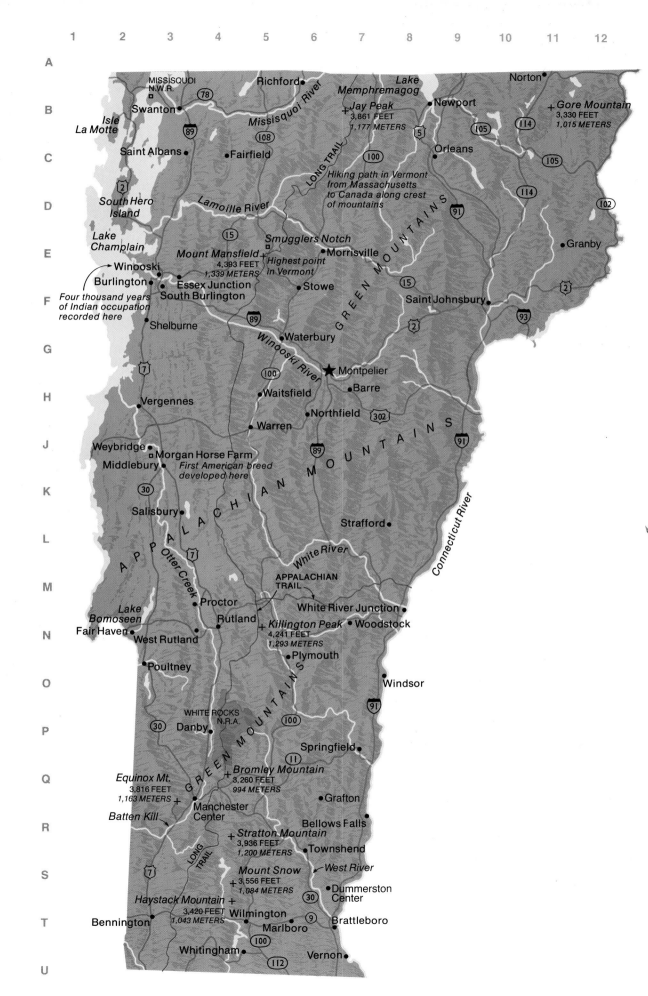

1 2 3 4 5 6 7 8 9 10 11 12

A
B
C
D
E
F
G
H
J
K
L
M
N
O
P
Q
R
S
T
U

MISSISQUOI N.W.R.
Richford
Lake Memphremagog
Norton
78
Swanton
Missisquoi River
Jay Peak
3,861 FEET
1,177 METERS
Newport
Gore Mountain
3,330 FEET
1,015 METERS
Isle La Motte
89
105
114
108
Saint Albans
Fairfield
LONG TRAIL
100
Orleans
105
South Hero Island
Hiking path in Vermont from Massachusetts to Canada along crest of mountains
5
114
Lake Champlain
Lamoille River
15
Smugglers Notch
Morrisville
GREEN MOUNTAINS
91
102
Granby
Winooski
Mount Mansfield
4,393 FEET
1,339 METERS
Highest point in Vermont
Burlington
Essex Junction
South Burlington
Stowe
15
2
Four thousand years of Indian occupation recorded here
Shelburne
89
Waterbury
Saint Johnsbury
93
Winooski River
100
Montpelier
2
Vergennes
Waitsfield
Barre
Northfield
302
Weybridge
Morgan Horse Farm
First American breed developed here
Warren
89
91
Middlebury
30
Salisbury
APPALACHIAN MOUNTAINS
Strafford
Otter Creek
7
White River
Connecticut River
APPALACHIAN TRAIL
Proctor
White River Junction
Lake Bomoseen
Rutland
Killington Peak
4,241 FEET
1,293 METERS
Woodstock
Fair Haven
West Rutland
Plymouth
Poultney
Windsor
WHITE ROCKS N.R.A.
91
30
Danby
100
GREEN MOUNTAINS
Springfield
11
Equinox Mt.
3,816 FEET
1,163 METERS
Bromley Mountain
3,260 FEET
994 METERS
Grafton
Batten Kill
Manchester Center
Bellows Falls
LONG TRAIL
Stratton Mountain
3,936 FEET
1,200 METERS
Townshend
7
Mount Snow
3,556 FEET
1,084 METERS
West River
Haystack Mountain
3,420 FEET
1,043 METERS
Wilmington
30
Dummerston Center
Bennington
Marlboro
9
Brattleboro
Whitingham
100
Vernon
112

KILOMETERS 30
STATUTE MILES 20

Vert mont. The words mean "green mountain" in French and hark back to 1609 when explorer Samuel de Champlain saw the tree-covered hills. The words give the state its name and are a reminder that part of French-speaking Canada is near.

The Long Trail runs the ridges of the Green Mountains. Near Mount Mansfield, Smugglers Notch cuts a gap in the mountains. During the War of 1812, while Britain and the U. S. quarreled, the notch provided a route for Vermonters to trade goods illegally with their British neighbors a few miles to the north.

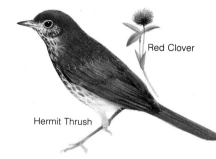

Red Clover

Hermit Thrush

1

2

Vermont

1 *Fall colors cast their spell over the village of Grafton. Small towns such as this give rural Vermont an air of tranquillity.*

2 *Children play around the trunk of a sugar maple tree in the Green Mountains. Sap collected in buckets each spring makes maple sugar, syrup, and candy.*

3 *A teacher monitors her class in Granby's one-room schoolhouse. The state constitution, adopted in 1777, requires every Vermont town to have a public school.*

4 *Workers at the Rock of Ages quarry, near Barre, anchor a pulley. Torches have replaced the drills that once cut these blocks.*

5 *Pies for an apple pie festival crowd church pews in Dummerston Center.*

3

4

5

New Hampshire

Every March, on the first Tuesday, citizens in small towns across New Hampshire observe a New England custom that dates back to colonial days, when spring thaws made dirt roads impassable. They hold a town meeting before the mud season sets in, to vote on local laws and decide how much their property taxes will be. They determine what they can pay their teachers and police, how many library books they can buy, and how much salt they can afford to spread over winter's icy roads.

Usually in March, says New Hampshire writer Donald Hall, winter "goes into hibernation, sleeping off the balmy months of peeper-sing until the red leaf wakes it again and the white season returns." But summer is short in the northern part of the state and in the mountains. Winter can last seven months and bring an average of more than eight feet (2.4 m) of snow.

New Hampshire is the most mountainous of the New England states. Mount Washington, the highest peak in the Northeast, looms over the Presidential Range, part of the White Mountains that cut across northern New Hampshire. In warm weather, people hike, drive, or take a historic cog railway to Mount Washington's summit. In winter the trip is like going to the Arctic, with hurricane-force winds frequently pummeling the peak. At such times the crews working at the weather observatory and at the television transmitter are alone.

From the northern mountains flow New Hampshire's most important rivers. The Connecticut begins in a boggy area only a few hundred yards from Canada. After it flows southward through small lakes named for it, it forms the border with Vermont. In the Connecticut and Merrimack River Valleys, dairy cows graze rich pastures below wooded hills.

On a hilltop in the valley of the Merrimack stands the Shaker village of Canterbury, founded in 1792 and now a museum. Leading a self-sufficient, communal, monastic life, Shaker brothers and sisters built a meetinghouse, dwellings, and barns. They cleared rocky fields where they pastured sheep, cattle, and oxen and grew crops. The Shakers believed that their "gift to be simple" was the way to worship God.

With its small towns and covered bridges, New Hampshire looks rural, but it really is high-

Great-granddad's Big Wheel: This monster machine at the 1896 Concord Bicycle Parade weighed in at almost 2,000 pounds (908 kg) and was billed as the world's largest tricycle.

ly industrialized. Manufacturing is the mainstay of its economy. In the early 19th century, Manchester businessmen began to develop the Amoskeag Mills. Amoskeag's massive red-brick mills eventually stretched for a mile and a half (2.4 km) along the Merrimack River below their original power source, the Amoskeag Falls. Amoskeag became the largest cotton textile producer in the world. Every couple of months the mills wove enough cloth to encircle the globe. Immigrants from Canada, Ireland, Poland, and Greece came to work in Manchester.

Once the center of New Hampshire's economy, the mills suffered from competition from other mills, outmoded technology, and a bitter strike over low wages. The mill owners declared bankruptcy on Christmas Eve, 1935.

Grandchildren of people who lost their mill jobs benefited from the development of high-tech industries that produce computers and electronic equipment. Prosperity spread throughout the southeast, particularly around Manchester, Portsmouth, and Nashua. Between 1980 and 1990 the population of New

Hampshire grew by almost 20 percent, more than any other eastern state except Florida. A little more than half of New Hampshire's residents live in urban areas, and about 85 percent of the total live in the southern half of the state. Some people feel that southern New Hampshire is actually a suburb of Boston. Many who live here commute to work in Boston and enjoy the best of both worlds: small-town life with a big-city paycheck and no state income tax.

In northern New Hampshire, cut off from the rest of the state by the White Mountains, small towns depend on the forest products industry. Paper companies own more than a half million acres of land, and Berlin is the only northern industrial city. Workers at its mill have produced paper and pulp for more than a century. Forests of spruce, white pine, ash, birch, oak, and other species cover about 86 percent of New Hampshire. Most of this is second growth. By the early 1900s, most New Hampshire forests had been cleared by farmers or logged by lumber barons. In 1911 conservationists managed to control timber harvesting and establish the White Mountain National Forest, which today covers about one-eighth of the state. In the wild north woods, where they have room to range, live deer, moose, bobcats, and black bears.

New Hampshire's seacoast, only 18 miles (29 km) long, is the shortest in the nation. Portsmouth, with its deepwater harbor, is the state's oldest settlement. Since its founding in 1630, Portsmouth has been known for shipbuilding. There in 1800 the United States Navy opened its first shipyard, the site of the first World War I submarine launching. Today the shipyard builds and repairs submarines.

Area: *44th largest state, 9,279 sq mi (24,032 sq km)*
Population: *1,109,252; ranks 40th*
Major Cities: *Manchester, 99,567; Nashua, 79,662; Concord, 36,006*
Manufacturing: *machinery, scientific instruments, electronics, rubber and plastics, paper products, food products, metal products, lumber and wood products*
Mining and Quarrying: *sand and gravel, granite*
Agriculture: *milk, greenhouse and nursery products, apples, cattle, hay*
Other Important Activities: *tourism*
Statehood: *the ninth state; ratified the Constitution on June 21, 1788*

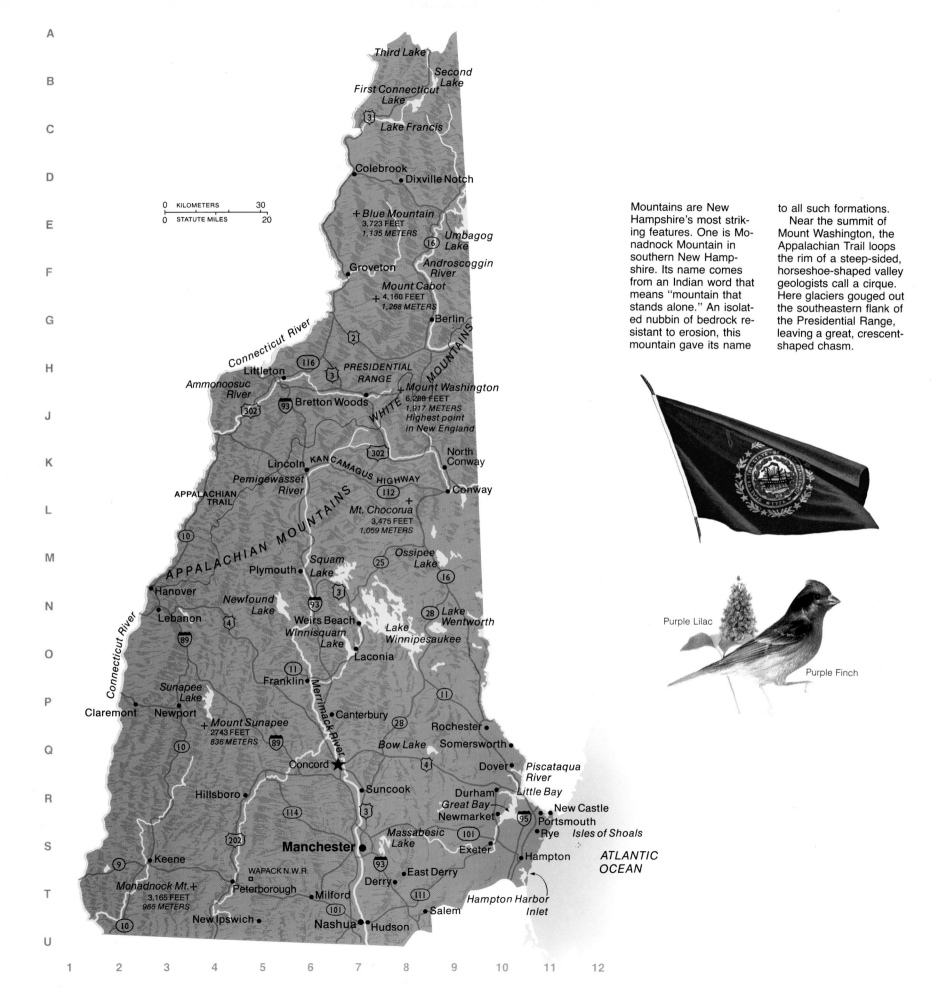

Mountains are New Hampshire's most striking features. One is Monadnock Mountain in southern New Hampshire. Its name comes from an Indian word that means "mountain that stands alone." An isolated nubbin of bedrock resistant to erosion, this mountain gave its name to all such formations.

Near the summit of Mount Washington, the Appalachian Trail loops the rim of a steep-sided, horseshoe-shaped valley geologists call a cirque. Here glaciers gouged out the southeastern flank of the Presidential Range, leaving a great, crescent-shaped chasm.

Purple Lilac

Purple Finch

1

2

3

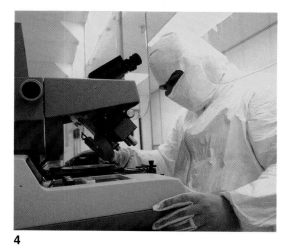

4

5

New Hampshire

1 *A skier takes wing on Wildcat Mountain. Skiing in winter, hiking in summer, and breathtaking views year-round keep the White Mountains busy in all seasons.*

2 *Mount Washington Observatory, a climate research station, wears a coat of snow and ice. The station lies in the path of some of the world's most ferocious winds.*

3 *Portsmouth, a primary builder of clipper ships in the 1800s, hosts a tall ship, the Simón Bolívar, which hails from Venezuela.*

4 *A technician performs experiments at a microelectronics plant in Nashua, a center of high-tech industry.*

5 *Clean, simple lines in the attic of a Shaker dwelling in Canterbury reflect the religious sect's enduring values of symmetry, order, and painstaking workmanship.*

Maine

On West Quoddy Head, a cape in northeastern Maine, the Algonquian Indians say they "live at the sunrise" because here morning sunlight first strikes the shoreline of the 50 states. West Quoddy Head is just one of hundreds of points of land along the Maine coast. To trace every curve, cove, inlet, and island shore would take a journey of 3,478 miles (5,596 km), farther than from New York City to San Francisco.

Along the coast from Passamaquoddy Bay to Kittery are beaches, rocky cliffs, and bay after bay, cove after inlet after estuary. Rivers that flow into the estuaries are tidal, mixing fresh water and salt water as the ocean tides rise and fall in their ceaseless six-hour rhythm. Tidewater reaches as far inland as Bangor and Augusta, where ships have traveled the Kennebec and Penobscot Rivers since the early 1800s.

Maine's coastline was shaped during the Ice Age. When the glaciers melted, they released water that had been locked away as ice for thousands of years. The ocean began to rise, drowning the coastline. The 1,100 or so coastal islands that, under glaciers, were part of the mainland are now the tops of partly submerged hills. The largest is Mount Desert Island.

Once there were some 20 Algonquian tribes in the Maine region. Today there remain only the Penobscot and the Passamaquoddy, with a population of some 6,000. English colonists settled here in the 1620s. Descendants of those settlers and of Scotch-Irish immigrants make up most of Maine's present population.

The northern half of Maine, bordered by Canada, is home to many French Canadians, the state's next largest ethnic group. In the 18th century, Acadians, people of French descent from Nova Scotia, settled in the valley of the St. John River. Other French Canadians migrated from Quebec after the Civil War to work in the growing lumber and textile industries. Today, throughout much of northern Maine, French is the dominant language and French-Canadian workers have moved south, making Waterville, Lewiston, and other industrial cities bilingual.

Timberlands provide much of the raw material for the state's industries. Maine has more forestland than any other New England state. Pine, birch, maple, and oak cover nearly 90 percent of Maine. Timber companies own almost

Using a spiked wheel gauge, a worker at a logging camp near Flagstaff Lake during the 1930s measures the length of a log. Each revolution of the ten spokes marked five feet (1.5 m).

half the state's woodlands, mostly in the sparsely populated northern region.

White pines were once Maine's greatest forest resource. By the middle of the 19th century most had been cut down to make masts for sailing ships. Today's white pines are mostly second- and third-growth trees. From the forests come paper bags, cardboard boxes, wood pulp, and paper. Canoes, ice-cream sticks, skis, and more toothpicks than from any other state also originate in the north woods.

Northeastern Maine is the richest agricultural area. This is potato country, where 90 percent of the state's most valuable farm crop is grown. Until 1962 Maine produced the greatest number of potatoes in the United States. Today Idaho, Washington, Wisconsin, and Oregon offer strong competition. In 1958 Maine had 26,000 potato farms. In 1990 there were only 700.

Until New England's economic boom of the

1980s took hold, most young adults moved away from Maine to find work. Bygone prosperity is most visible in the inland region, where an abandoned paper or textile mill may be a town's main feature. Increased automation put many workers out of a job, and foreign competition closed many of the mills. Even so, the population of Maine has climbed slowly but steadily.

Since precolonial times most of the people have lived along rivers or where they could reap the bounty of the ocean. Today more than half live on the coast or within a short drive of it. For some, lobstering is a productive occupation, although it can be hard, uncertain work. Maine's yearly catch of some 22 million pounds (10 million kg) is the largest in the country.

Other coastal Mainers grow blueberries. During the short picking season at the end of summer, a grower may need hundreds of temporary workers. Sometimes, if the crop is slow to ripen, schools delay opening so that students can work in the fields. The Passamaquoddies are among the world's leading blueberry packers. During the 1980s other kinds of workers, from cabinetmakers to computer-software designers, helped populate southern coastal towns.

To protect their forests, lakes, rivers, and wetlands from development, the people of Maine have voted millions of dollars to buy land, preserving precious wildlife habitat and wild country. Even today there are places in the state that arouse feelings similar to those of New England writer Henry David Thoreau when he traveled in Maine in the 1840s and 1850s. North of Bangor, he wrote, "the country is virtually unmapped and unexplored, and there still waves the virgin forest of the New World." Most Mainers hope to keep it that way.

Area: *39th largest state, 33,265 sq mi (86,156 sq km)*
Population: *1,227,928; ranks 38th*
Major Cities: *Portland, 64,358; Lewiston, 39,757; Bangor, 33,181*
Manufacturing: *paper products, electronics, transportation equipment, lumber and wood products, leather, food products, machinery, textiles*
Mining and Quarrying: *sand and gravel, stone*
Agriculture: *potatoes, eggs, milk, blueberries, cattle, greenhouse and nursery products, apples*
Other Important Activities: *tourism, printing and publishing, fishing*
Statehood: *the 23rd state; admitted March 15, 1820*

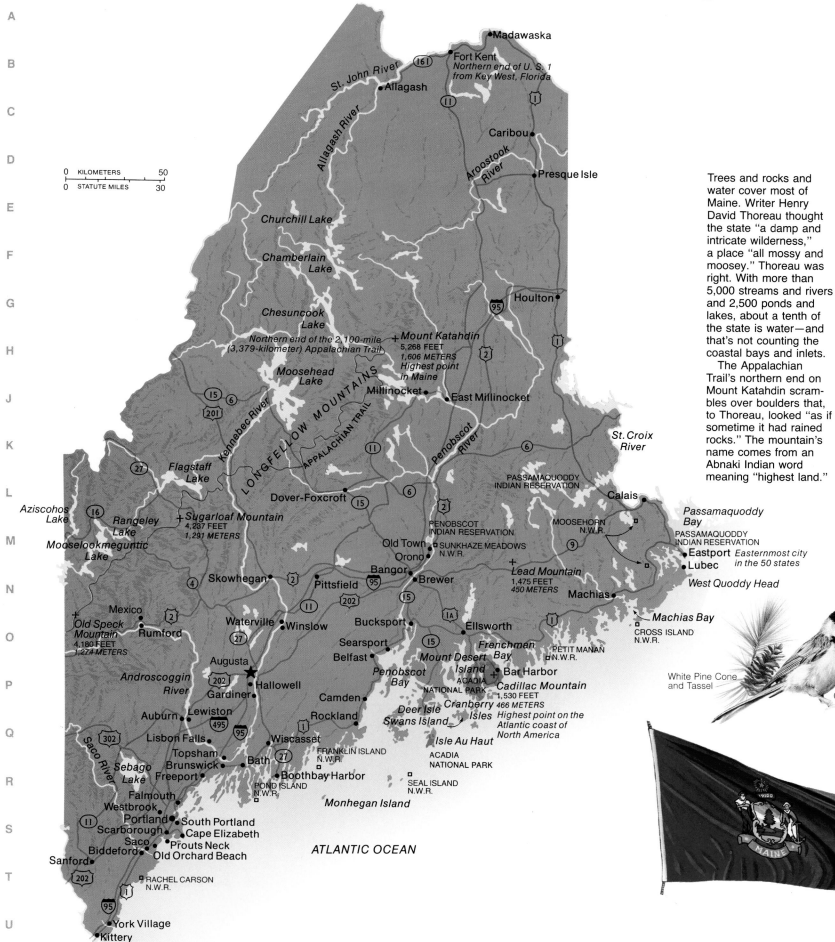

1 2 3 4 5 6 7 8 9 10 11 12 13 14 15

A
B
C
D
E
F
G
H
J
K
L
M
N
O
P
Q
R
S
T
U

•Madawaska

St. John River
Fort Kent
Northern end of U. S. 1
from Key West, Florida
161

•Allagash
11

11

Allagash River
Caribou

Aroostook River
•Presque Isle

Churchill Lake

Chamberlain Lake

Houlton
95

Chesuncook Lake

Northern end of the 2,100-mile
(3,379-kilometer) Appalachian Trail
+ Mount Katahdin
5,268 FEET
1,606 METERS
Highest point
in Maine
2

Moosehead Lake
Millinocket • •East Millinocket

Kennebec River
LONGFELLOW MOUNTAINS
15
6
201
APPALACHIAN TRAIL
Penobscot River
St. Croix River

Flagstaff Lake
11
6
27
PASSAMAQUODDY
INDIAN RESERVATION
Calais

Dover-Foxcroft
15
6
2

Aziscohos Lake
16
Rangeley Lake
+ Sugarloaf Mountain
4,237 FEET
1,291 METERS
PENOBSCOT
INDIAN RESERVATION
MOOSEHORN
N.W.R.
Passamaquoddy Bay

Mooselookmeguntic Lake
Old Town • •SUNKHAZE MEADOWS
N.W.R.
9
PASSAMAQUODDY
INDIAN RESERVATION
Eastport Easternmost city
in the 50 states
Lubec

Mexico
4
Orono
Bangor
Brewer
+ Lead Mountain
1,475 FEET
450 METERS
Machias
West Quoddy Head

Old Speck Mountain
4,180 FEET
1,274 METERS
2
Skowhegan
2
Pittsfield
95
15
1A
Machias Bay
CROSS ISLAND
N.W.R.

Rumford
11
202
Bucksport
Ellsworth
PETIT MANAN
N.W.R.

Waterville • Winslow
Searsport
15
Frenchman Bay
1

Androscoggin River
27
Belfast
Mount Desert Island
Bar Harbor
ACADIA
NATIONAL PARK
+ Cadillac Mountain
1,530 FEET
466 METERS
Highest point on the
Atlantic coast of
North America

Augusta
202
Hallowell
Penobscot Bay
Camden

Gardiner
Rockland
Cranberry Isles

Auburn Lewiston
495
95
Wiscasset
Deer Isle
Swans Island
Isle Au Haut

Lisbon Falls
1

Saco River
302
Topsham
Brunswick
Bath
27
FRANKLIN ISLAND
N.W.R.
ACADIA
NATIONAL PARK

Sebago Lake
Freeport
•Boothbay Harbor
SEAL ISLAND
N.W.R.

Falmouth
POND ISLAND
N.W.R.

Westbrook
Monhegan Island
ATLANTIC OCEAN

11
Portland
Scarborough •South Portland
Saco Cape Elizabeth

Biddeford •Prouts Neck
Sanford •Old Orchard Beach

202
RACHEL CARSON
N.W.R.

1
95
•York Village
•Kittery

0 KILOMETERS 50
0 STATUTE MILES 30

Trees and rocks and water cover most of Maine. Writer Henry David Thoreau thought the state "a damp and intricate wilderness," a place "all mossy and moosey." Thoreau was right. With more than 5,000 streams and rivers and 2,500 ponds and lakes, about a tenth of the state is water—and that's not counting the coastal bays and inlets.

The Appalachian Trail's northern end on Mount Katahdin scrambles over boulders that, to Thoreau, looked "as if sometime it had rained rocks." The mountain's name comes from an Abnaki Indian word meaning "highest land."

White Pine Cone and Tassel
Chickadee

Maine

1 *Newly dug potatoes are gathered for storage near Presque Isle. Most Maine potatoes are now harvested mechanically. The result: larger farms and fewer workers.*

2 *Lobster traps crowd a pier on Mount Desert Island. Lobstermen lower the baited traps into coastal waters where lobsters crawl inside to eat the bait of rotting fish. Colored buoys mark the location of the traps and identify their owners.*

3 *A moose and her calf dine on aquatic plants at the edge of a pond in Maine's dense and remote north woods.*

4 *Waving kerchiefs and shaking bells, morris dancers at West Quoddy Head seek to banish winter and wake up the earth.*

5 *A truck in Maine's north woods carries spruce and fir logs destined to become paper and pulp at one of the state's mills.*

1

2

3

4

5

Massachusetts

Bostonians of 1902 show off their office equipment: typewriter, telephone, and electric light. Christopher Sholes judged his typewriting invention a blessing, "especially to womankind."

The Puritan settlers of Massachusetts stood at the forefront of education in their new country. To them, literacy was important because "one chiefe project of that ould deluder, Satan [is] to keepe men from the knowledge of the Scriptures." In 1635, five years after establishing the Massachusetts Bay Colony, settlers opened the first public school, Boston Latin. The following year Harvard was founded as the nation's first college. Graduates became clergymen and community leaders and helped spread education throughout Massachusetts. By the mid-1600s, the colony called for all towns with 50 or more families to build an elementary school, and towns with 100 families, a secondary school. This was the first time any government provided education paid for by the citizens.

About a hundred years after it was first settled, Boston had become the largest city in the Colonies and the cornerstone of New England. Today about half of the state's population lives in the Boston metropolitan area, where there are some 68 colleges and universities. The site of Harvard University, Cambridge alone counts 26 bookstores, more per square mile than anywhere else in the country.

In the 19th century, Boston entrepreneurs financed railroads, factories, and ironworks throughout the region. Ships leaving Boston's harbor traded around the globe. Immigrants began to arrive, at first mostly Irish, later French Canadians, and Italians, Germans, and other Europeans. They supplied labor for the textile mills in Lowell, the shoe factories in Beverly, and the sawmills, gristmills, and tanneries that sprang up in towns throughout the state. Even today the population of Massachusetts is ethnically diverse. A third of the people are either foreign-born or are children of at least one parent from another country.

Massachusetts has no coal, oil, or gas, and no metal ores worth mining. When the state's textile and shoe factories closed down and moved south in the 1950s and 1960s, they often were replaced by space research laboratories and electronics companies because Massachusetts had a large pool of skilled, well-educated workers.

Along Route 128, a highway that arcs through Boston's western suburbs, the electronics industry joined forces with universities such as Harvard and the Massachusetts Institute of Technology to develop computers and software products, solar energy devices, and laboratories dedicated to studying artificial intelligence. Researchers in biotechnology companies strive to solve the mysteries of cancer and other diseases, and genetic engineers work to devise advanced medical treatments.

South of Boston a hook of land called Cape Cod reaches 65 miles (105 km) into the Atlantic Ocean. Until around 1850 many towns on the cape, as well as in southeastern Massachusetts and on the islands of Nantucket and Martha's Vineyard, flourished as whaling and trading ports. The largest town was New Bedford. There foresighted merchants built textile mills and factories, making it a successful manufacturing city. Today descendants of the immigrants who worked in New Bedford's factories make up the country's largest community of Portuguese Americans. The whaling industry

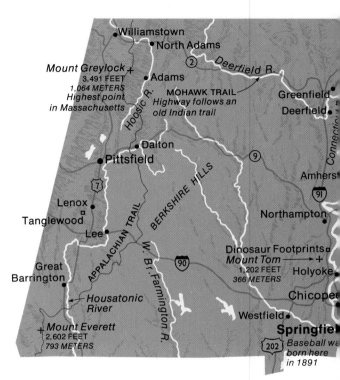

declined as whales became scarce and kerosene replaced whale oil as lamp fuel. Tourism and fish processing became the main sources of income. Much of Massachusetts has thin, rocky soil, but sandy bogs in the southeast produce nearly half of the country's cranberries.

West of Boston and the state's coastal lowlands rise rolling mountains threaded by the fertile Connecticut River Valley. Indians had long planted crops alongside the Connecticut River, and 17th-century colonists soon realized that the rich soil and mild climate would make good farming country. The river itself served as a highway. By the early 19th century, vessels hailing from Connecticut River towns carried on a lively trade of crops, lumber products, and farm animals with cities along the East Coast and as far away as the West Indies.

One of the most thinly populated parts of Massachusetts, the Berkshire Hills, is an extension of Vermont's Green Mountains. The Berkshires'

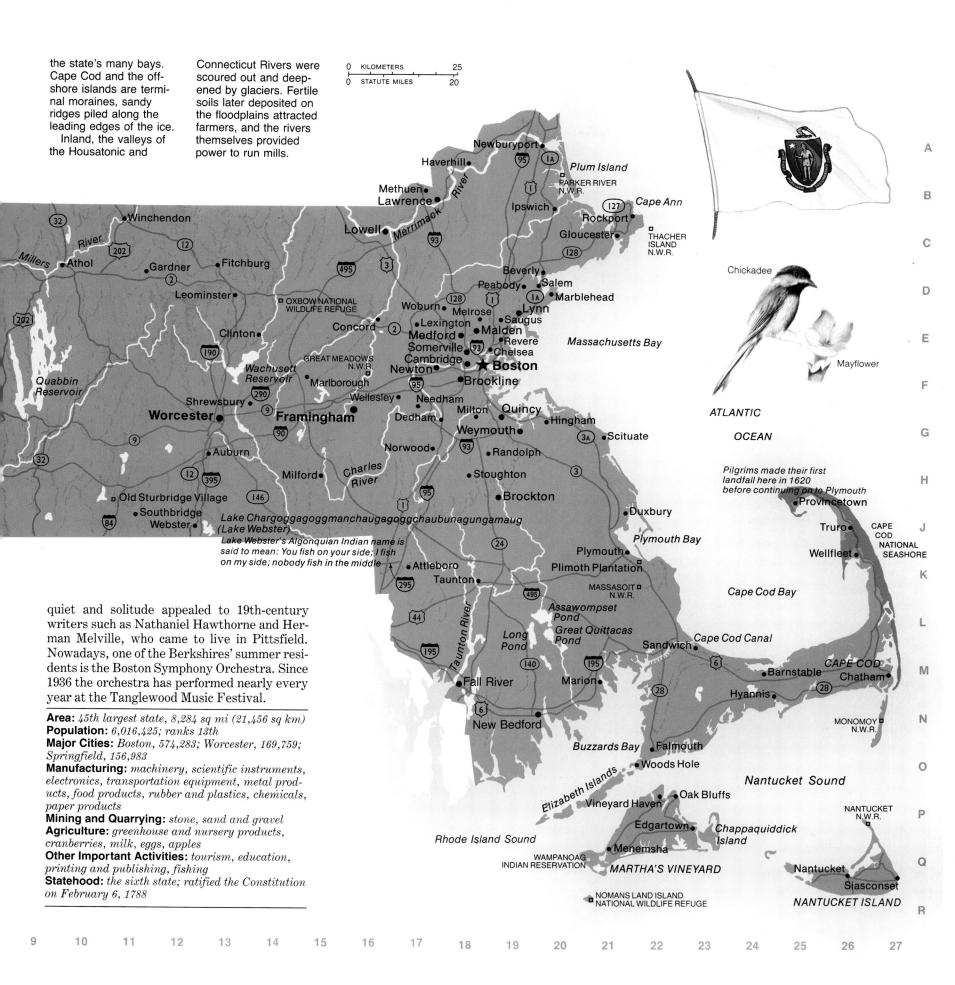

the state's many bays. Cape Cod and the offshore islands are terminal moraines, sandy ridges piled along the leading edges of the ice.

Inland, the valleys of the Housatonic and Connecticut Rivers were scoured out and deepened by glaciers. Fertile soils later deposited on the floodplains attracted farmers, and the rivers themselves provided power to run mills.

quiet and solitude appealed to 19th-century writers such as Nathaniel Hawthorne and Herman Melville, who came to live in Pittsfield. Nowadays, one of the Berkshires' summer residents is the Boston Symphony Orchestra. Since 1936 the orchestra has performed nearly every year at the Tanglewood Music Festival.

Area: *45th largest state, 8,284 sq mi (21,456 sq km)*
Population: *6,016,425; ranks 13th*
Major Cities: *Boston, 574,283; Worcester, 169,759; Springfield, 156,983*
Manufacturing: *machinery, scientific instruments, electronics, transportation equipment, metal products, food products, rubber and plastics, chemicals, paper products*
Mining and Quarrying: *stone, sand and gravel*
Agriculture: *greenhouse and nursery products, cranberries, milk, eggs, apples*
Other Important Activities: *tourism, education, printing and publishing, fishing*
Statehood: *the sixth state; ratified the Constitution on February 6, 1788*

Chickadee

Mayflower

ATLANTIC OCEAN

Pilgrims made their first landfall here in 1620 before continuing on to Plymouth

Lake Chargoggagoggmanchaugagoggchaubunagungamaug (Lake Webster)

Lake Webster's Algonquian Indian name is said to mean: You fish on your side; I fish on my side; nobody fish in the middle

Massachusetts

1 *Snow dusts the evergreen ridges of Mount Greylock in the Berkshire Hills while autumn lingers on lower slopes and valleys.*

2 *Cranberries spread a crimson carpet on a bog flooded for harvest. Shaken from low-growing vines, the berries bob to the surface and are skimmed into holding pens with long-handled scrubbers.*

3 *Boston's Faneuil Hall stands amid stores, restaurants, and offices overlooking Boston Harbor. A market and meeting place for patriots in Revolutionary times, Faneuil Hall today is a popular gathering spot for tourists and residents alike.*

4 *Commercial fishermen sort through a catch off Cape Cod. Fishing, one of the state's economic mainstays since earliest colonial times, has declined sharply in recent years because of overfishing.*

5 *Cape Cod, named by navigator Bartholomew Gosnold after he explored the area in 1602, presents an arm of glacial sand and gravel to pounding Atlantic waves.*

1

2

3

4

5

Connecticut

While exploring Long Island Sound in 1614, Dutch sea captain Adriaen Block sailed into the wide mouth of the Connecticut River. There he found numerous Algonquian Indians grouped in settlements near the river and along the shore of what is now Connecticut. But it was the English, not the Dutch, who began to settle the area nearly 20 years later. They had been attracted by reports of the Connecticut River Valley's fertility. Today much of the state's tobacco, apples, and potatoes grow there, even though agriculture is not a big source of income for Connecticut. About 21 percent of the state's people live in rural areas, and 79 percent live in and around cities.

The Connecticut River Valley's chief city, Hartford, rises on the fall line at the head of river navigation. Since the 17th century, when the Dutch began trading with the Indians, Hartford has thrived on both industry and business. It has been an insurance center for almost 200 years, first providing financial protection against fires, and later extending coverage to sailing ships and their cargoes. Hartford pioneered in many kinds of insurance that we now take for granted: the first American accident insurance, the first to offer American farmers protection against hail damage, the first American automobile insurance. Today the state is home to more than a thousand insurance companies.

On either side of the Connecticut River Valley rise low hills where the soil is thin and rocky. Glaciers left so many boulders here that, over the years, landowners have fenced their fields and pastures with some 25,000 miles (40,225 km) of stone walls. Crushed stone is an important product for Connecticut, especially because it has no coal or oil or other valuable minerals.

Even without many natural resources Connecticut has developed into a rich industrial state. A knack for making things has been a tradition. Here, in the early 1800s, Eli Whitney devised mass-production machinery and produced muskets with interchangeable parts. Samuel Colt assembled the first successful repeating pistol, and Charles Goodyear succeeded in strengthening rubber by vulcanizing it. Other innovators turned their talents to producing clocks, bicycles, cigars, silk thread, and combs. Over the years Yankee ingenuity replaced dy-

Sailors practice escape maneuvers at the New London Submarine Base in 1938. The diving bell carries them down 100 feet (30.5 m), and they slowly ascend a rope while breathing oxygen from a tank.

ing industries with vital ones. Today high-tech companies that produce computer chips and fiber-optic equipment have taken the place of old brass, rubber, and clothing factories.

Running the length of Connecticut's shore is the coastal lowland. Here the early towns with their spacious harbors enjoyed success with fishing. But it took other maritime activities to make them truly prosperous. Shipbuilding, a major industry at Mystic seaport during the mid-1800s, promoted trade with the rest of the world. During their heyday, Mystic shipyards launched more than 300 vessels. Steamers and clipper ships in turn brought raw materials that spurred Connecticut's growth as an industrializing state. Today Mystic is a re-created seaport, where restored sailing ships recall New England's seafaring past.

Around the 1850s, many of Connecticut's coastal towns thrived on whaling. Chief among

them was New London, near the mouth of the Thames River. The whaling industry declined within a few decades, but New London's importance did not. The United States Coast Guard established its academy there in 1910. Today, in addition, shipyards and major ferry terminals serving Long Island Sound keep New London a busy and important seaport.

One of the most densely populated areas of Connecticut is the coastline along the western reaches of Long Island Sound. Fishing towns on the sound flourished in the mid-1800s as factories grew, demanding more workers. People from agricultural towns flocked to a more lucrative way of life, as did French-Canadian and European immigrants. Today New Haven and Bridgeport have large populations of Italian and Irish ancestry. New Haven is also the home of Yale University, founded in 1701 by Connecticut clergymen. Stamford is a center for corporate headquarters, burgeoning in the 1980s as many companies fled crowded New York City's high prices and taxes.

Connecticut's economy has been linked to warfare and defense since colonial days, when its shipyards built vessels for the British Navy. In more recent years, Connecticut has produced everything from firearms to helicopters and submarines. For most of the 1980s the state's economy boomed, in part because its defense industry did. Now, as the country's defense budget shrinks, thousands of workers may lose their jobs. Some defense contractors, their ingenuity again challenged, are examining ways their specialized skills can be used by other government agencies or in civilian businesses.

Area: *48th largest state, 5,018 sq mi (12,997 sq km)*
Population: *3,287,116; ranks 27th*
Major Cities: *Bridgeport, 141,686; Hartford, 139,739; New Haven, 130,474*
Manufacturing: *transportation equipment, machinery, metal products, scientific instruments, chemicals, electronics, food products, metals, paper products, rubber and plastics*
Mining and Quarrying: *stone, sand and gravel*
Agriculture: *greenhouse and nursery products, eggs, milk, tobacco, cattle*
Other Important Activities: *insurance, printing and publishing, fishing*
Statehood: *the fifth state; ratified the Constitution on January 9, 1788*

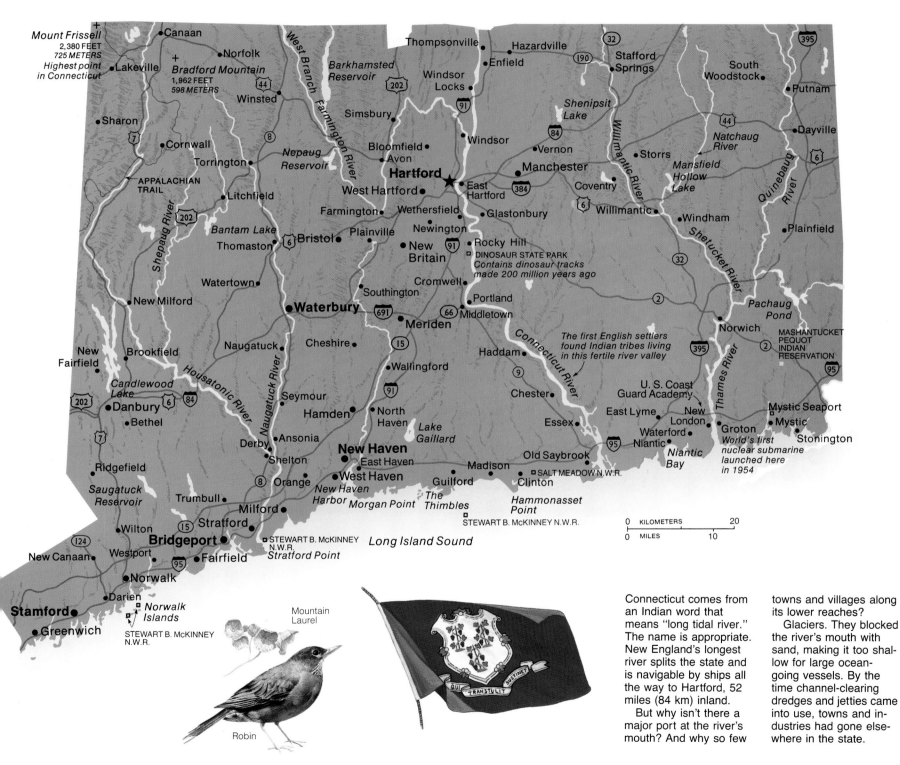

1　2　3　4　5　6　7　8　9　10　11　12　13　14　15　16　17　18

A
B
C
D
E
F
G
H
J
K
L
M
N
O

Mount Frissell
2,380 FEET
725 METERS
Highest point
in Connecticut

•Canaan

•Lakeville

•Norfolk

+Bradford Mountain
1,962 FEET
598 METERS

West Branch

Thompsonville•

Hazardville•

•Enfield

32

190

Stafford
Springs

395

•Sharon

Winsted•

44

Barkhamsted
Reservoir

202

Windsor
Locks

91

South
Woodstock

•Putnam

•Cornwall

Torrington•

8

Simsbury•

Shenipsit
Lake

84

Willimantic River

•Storrs

Natchaug
River

44

•Dayville

6

APPALACHIAN
TRAIL

202

•Litchfield

Nepaug
Reservoir

Farmington

Bloomfield•
•Avon

Hartford★

West Hartford•

Windsor•

•Vernon

Manchester•

East
Hartford

384

Coventry•

Mansfield
Hollow
Lake

Windham•

Shetucket River

•Plainfield

Shepaug River

Bantam Lake

6

•Bristol

Thomaston•

Plainville•

Wethersfield•

Newington•

Rocky Hill•

New
Britain

91

6

Willimantic•

32

Quinebaug River

Watertown•

•New Milford

Southington•

Cromwell•

DINOSAUR STATE PARK
Contains dinosaur tracks
made 200 million years ago

Portland•

2

Pachaug
Pond

Waterbury

691

Meriden•

Middletown•

66

Norwich•

395

2

MASHANTUCKET
PEQUOT
INDIAN
RESERVATION

New
Fairfield

Brookfield•

Housatonic River

Naugatuck•

Cheshire•

15

Haddam•

The first English settlers
found Indian tribes living
in this fertile river valley

U.S. Coast
Guard Academy

95

Candlewood
Lake

202

•Danbury

6

84

Seymour•

Wallingford•

9

Chester•

East Lyme•

New
London

Mystic Seaport

•Bethel

Hamden•

91

North
Haven

Lake
Gaillard

Essex•

Waterford•

Groton•

•Mystic

7

Derby•

•Ansonia

New Haven

Niantic•

World's first
nuclear submarine
launched here
in 1954

•Stonington

•Ridgefield

Shelton•

East Haven•

Old Saybrook•

95

Niantic
Bay

Saugatuck
Reservoir

8

Orange•

New Haven
Harbor

Madison•

Clinton•

SALT MEADOW N.W.R.

Trumbull•

Milford•

Guilford•

The
Thimbles

Hammonasset
Point

•Wilton

Stratford•

15

Morgan Point

STEWART B. McKINNEY N.W.R.

New Canaan•

Bridgeport•

STEWART B. McKINNEY
N.W.R.
Stratford Point

Long Island Sound

0　KILOMETERS　20

Westport•

95

•Fairfield

0　MILES　10

Norwalk•

124

Stamford•

•Darien

□Norwalk
Islands

•Greenwich

STEWART B. McKINNEY
N.W.R.

Mountain
Laurel

Robin

Connecticut comes from an Indian word that means "long tidal river." The name is appropriate. New England's longest river splits the state and is navigable by ships all the way to Hartford, 52 miles (84 km) inland.

But why isn't there a major port at the river's mouth? And why so few towns and villages along its lower reaches?

Glaciers. They blocked the river's mouth with sand, making it too shallow for large ocean-going vessels. By the time channel-clearing dredges and jetties came into use, towns and industries had gone elsewhere in the state.

QUI TRANSTULIT SUSTINET

1

2

3

4

5

Connecticut

1 *A worker checks a jet engine at an assembly plant in Hartford. Connecticut industries today turn out everything from plastic Wiffle balls to submarines.*

2 *A Wampanoag Indian holds his son at a tribal gathering in Portland. Wampanoag helped* Mayflower *Pilgrims celebrate their first Thanksgiving in the New World.*

3 *Cadets drill at the U. S. Coast Guard Academy on the Thames River in New London. Only 300 new students are accepted into the academy each year.*

4 *Oysters are netted by hand near the mouth of the Connecticut River. Connecticut's coastal waters provide an ideal combination of temperature, salinity, and habitat for oyster cultivation.*

5 *Herbs and edible flowers fresh from a farm in Coventry go into salads, vinegars, soups, and breads sold at the farm.*

Rhode Island

The full and official name of the country's smallest state is The State of Rhode Island and Providence Plantations. The state has 35 islands scattered within its largest body of water, Narragansett Bay. The bay's largest island, also called Rhode Island, may have been named for the Greek island of Rhodes. Some people also refer to the island as Aquidneck, an Indian word meaning "longest island."

The Providence Plantations part of the state's name comes from its origin as a refuge for religious dissenters. It was founded in 1636 by Roger Williams, a minister who disagreed with the Puritan government of the Massachusetts Bay Colony. Williams insisted that people should not be persecuted by civil authorities for religious beliefs. He was banished from the Bay Colony, and made his way to Indian friends near Narragansett Bay. Learning the language of the Narragansett, Williams received land from them and became an intermediary between the Indians and the English. He established a farming community on a long arm of the bay, naming it in honor of "God's merciful providence unto me in my distresse." Other settlers followed Williams, and soon the English Parliament granted the colony a charter as "Rhode Island and Providence Plantations." Eventually, Williams drew up America's first document calling for the separation of church and state, one of the nation's guiding principles.

Rhode Island was the first of the 13 Colonies to declare independence, yet, because it feared too powerful a central government, it was last to ratify the U. S. Constitution. Instead, Rhode Island waited to sign until the Bill of Rights was ready to be added in 1790.

Only a few months after Rhode Island became a state, industrialization began. In Pawtucket a 22-year-old English machinist named Samuel Slater designed the first water-powered cotton mill in the United States, a factory in which children worked the spinning machinery. The genius of Slater and other men launched the New England textile industry. Dozens of mill villages sprang up in the valley of the Blackstone River, and the industry spread rapidly. Rhode Island also manufactured textile machinery. Although machinery making and textiles still figure in the economy, other manufactured products have

Six feet (2 m) of seawater flooded downtown Providence after a 1938 hurricane, marooning office workers and submerging automobiles and trolley cars in front of the Biltmore Hotel.

become more important.

Opportunities for factory jobs in the 19th and 20th centuries attracted immigrants from Canada, Europe, the Caribbean, and Southeast Asia, and contributed to Rhode Island's present ethnic diversity. Because the majority of job seekers came from Catholic countries, Rhode Island has the highest proportion of Roman Catholics of any state in the country.

Rhode Island is also the most densely populated state after New Jersey. More than 80 percent of all Rhode Islanders live in urban areas in the east, with about two-thirds living in and around the state capital, Providence.

The least populated parts of Rhode Island are the rocky, forested hills in the west-central and northwest parts of the state. Although very little of this land is farmed now, miles of stone walls in the forests recall a time when it was.

About a third of the state is covered by lakes,

ponds, reservoirs, swamps, and rivers. Eastern and southern Rhode Island are coastal lowlands, with sandy beaches, salt ponds, rocky cliffs, and islands. Narragansett Bay reaches far inland, extending a deepwater channel to Providence.

The state of Rhode Island measures only 37 miles (60 km) from east to west, but it has 400 miles (644 km) of coastline along Narragansett Bay and around the islands. Newport, the site of sailboat races and music festivals, occupies part of the island of Rhode Island.

Before the Revolutionary War, Newport was a major point of entry to the Colonies and one of the busiest ports on the East Coast. Then the British occupied its harbor, ruining the prosperous shipping trade. In the 1730s the town had already become a summer resort as southern plantation owners came north to escape heat and humidity. By the end of the 19th century, industrial titans from New York were summering in Newport and building mansions called "cottages" along the rocky cliffs. One of them, The Breakers, was Cornelius Vanderbilt's grand Italian Renaissance villa, a palace with silver faucets and 70 rooms, 33 of them for servants.

With its reputation for religious tolerance, Rhode Island became a haven for persecuted Quakers and Jews in the 17th and 18th centuries. Touro Synagogue, the oldest Jewish temple in North America, was dedicated in Newport in 1763. It was to this synagogue that President George Washington gave his pledge of religious freedom, stating that the country's new government would give "to bigotry no sanction, to persecution no assistance." This proclamation is read to the congregation every year.

Area: *the smallest state, 1,212 sq mi (3,140 sq km)*
Population: *1,003,464; ranks 43rd*
Major Cities: *Providence, 160,728; Warwick, 85,427; Cranston, 76,060*
Manufacturing: *jewelry and silverware, metal products, scientific instruments, metals, machinery, electronics, textiles, rubber and plastics, food products, chemicals*
Agriculture: *greenhouse and nursery products, milk, eggs, potatoes, apples*
Mining and Quarrying: *sand and gravel, stone*
Other Important Activities: *tourism, printing and publishing, fishing*
Statehood: *the 13th state; ratified the Constitution on May 29, 1790*

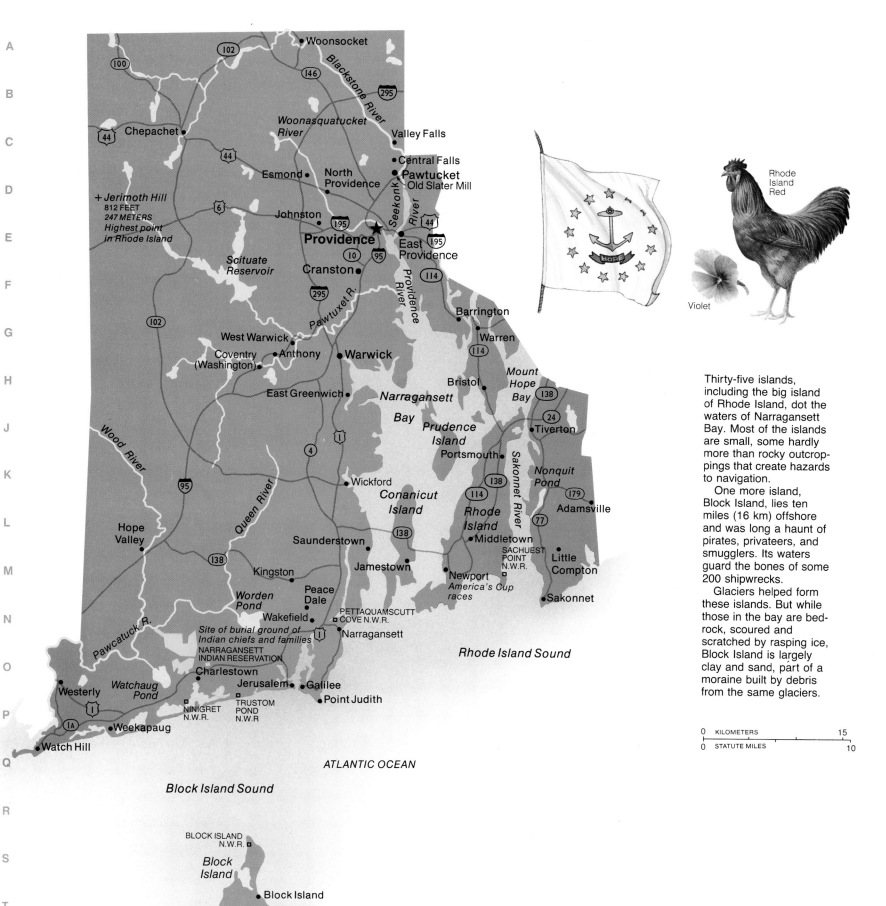

1 2 3 4 5 6 7 8 9 10 11 12 13

A
B
C
D
E
F
G
H
J
K
L
M
N
O
P
Q
R
S
T

Woonsocket

102

100

146

Blackstone River

295

Chepachet

44

Woonasquatucket River

Valley Falls

44

Central Falls

Esmond

North Providence

Pawtucket

Old Slater Mill

+ Jerimoth Hill
812 FEET
247 METERS
Highest point
in Rhode Island

6

Johnston

Seekonk River

195

44

Providence

195

Scituate Reservoir

10

95

East Providence

Cranston

Providence River

114

295

Pawtuxet R.

Barrington

102

Warren

West Warwick

114

Coventry (Washington)

Anthony

Warwick

Mount Hope Bay

138

Bristol

24

East Greenwich

Narragansett Bay

Tiverton

Wood River

Prudence Island

Portsmouth

Nonquit Pond

4

1

Conanicut Island

138

Rhode Island

114

Sakonnet River

179

Adamsville

Hope Valley

Queen River

Saunderstown

138

Middletown

77

Little Compton

95

Kingston

Jamestown

SACHUEST POINT N.W.R.

138

Peace Dale

Newport
America's Cup races

Sakonnet

Worden Pond

Wakefield

PETTAQUAMSCUTT COVE N.W.R.

Site of burial ground of
Indian chiefs and families

1

Narragansett

Rhode Island Sound

NARRAGANSETT
INDIAN RESERVATION

Charlestown

Watchaug Pond

Jerusalem

Galilee

Pawcatuck R.

Westerly

NINIGRET
N.W.R.

TRUSTOM
POND
N.W.R

Point Judith

1

1A

Weekapaug

Watch Hill

ATLANTIC OCEAN

Block Island Sound

BLOCK ISLAND
N.W.R.

Block
Island

Block Island

Rhode Island Red

Violet

Thirty-five islands, including the big island of Rhode Island, dot the waters of Narragansett Bay. Most of the islands are small, some hardly more than rocky outcroppings that create hazards to navigation.

One more island, Block Island, lies ten miles (16 km) offshore and was long a haunt of pirates, privateers, and smugglers. Its waters guard the bones of some 200 shipwrecks.

Glaciers helped form these islands. But while those in the bay are bedrock, scoured and scratched by rasping ice, Block Island is largely clay and sand, part of a moraine built by debris from the same glaciers.

0   KILOMETERS   15
0   STATUTE MILES   10

1

2

3

4

Rhode Island

1 *Southeast Light crowns the heights of Block Island, a resort of Victorian houses and hotels set amid rolling, treeless moors.*

2 *A silversmith pursues his calling in Providence, where artisans have worked with gold and silver since 1794.*

3 *Spinnaker sails ballooning, sailboats compete in an international race off Newport, a historic seaport and yachting center.*

4 *The Cliff Walk winds past many of Newport's summer "cottages," palaces built by wealthy industrialists during the Gilded Age of the late 1800s. Several are open in season for public tours.*

Mid-Atlantic States

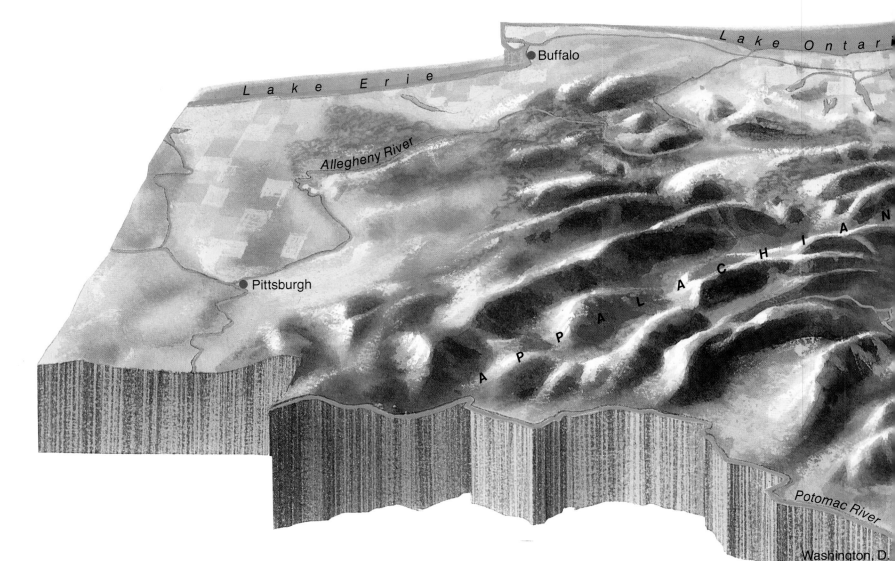

In the Mid-Atlantic region, wooded ridges of the Appalachian Mountains and their foothills, the Piedmont, give way to patterns of farmland along the Atlantic Coastal Plain.

The oldest mountains in North America, the Appalachians began to rise about 300 million years ago. When they were young, they were as tall as today's Rockies, but time and weather have since worn down the Appalachians, smoothing their ragged edges. Rivers on the western slopes, such as the Allegheny, join others and flow eventually to the Gulf of Mexico.

Rivers on the eastern slopes carry eroded rock and soil as sediment to the Atlantic Coastal Plain and into the Atlantic Ocean. Where they cross the Piedmont, the Delaware, Susquehanna, and Potomac Rivers have cut deep, narrow valleys through the hard rock. Waterfalls and rapids mark their passage until they cross a geologic boundary known as a fall line and reach the softer sediments of the Coastal Plain.

At river confluences, such as the site of Pittsburgh, and along the fall line rise some of the country's largest cities, including Baltimore and Philadelphia. On the fall line early settlers found waterpower to run their mills, sheltered inland harbors, and flat terrain to build roads linking the cities together. Today the Mid-Atlantic region is home to some 43 million people, about one-sixth of the nation's population.

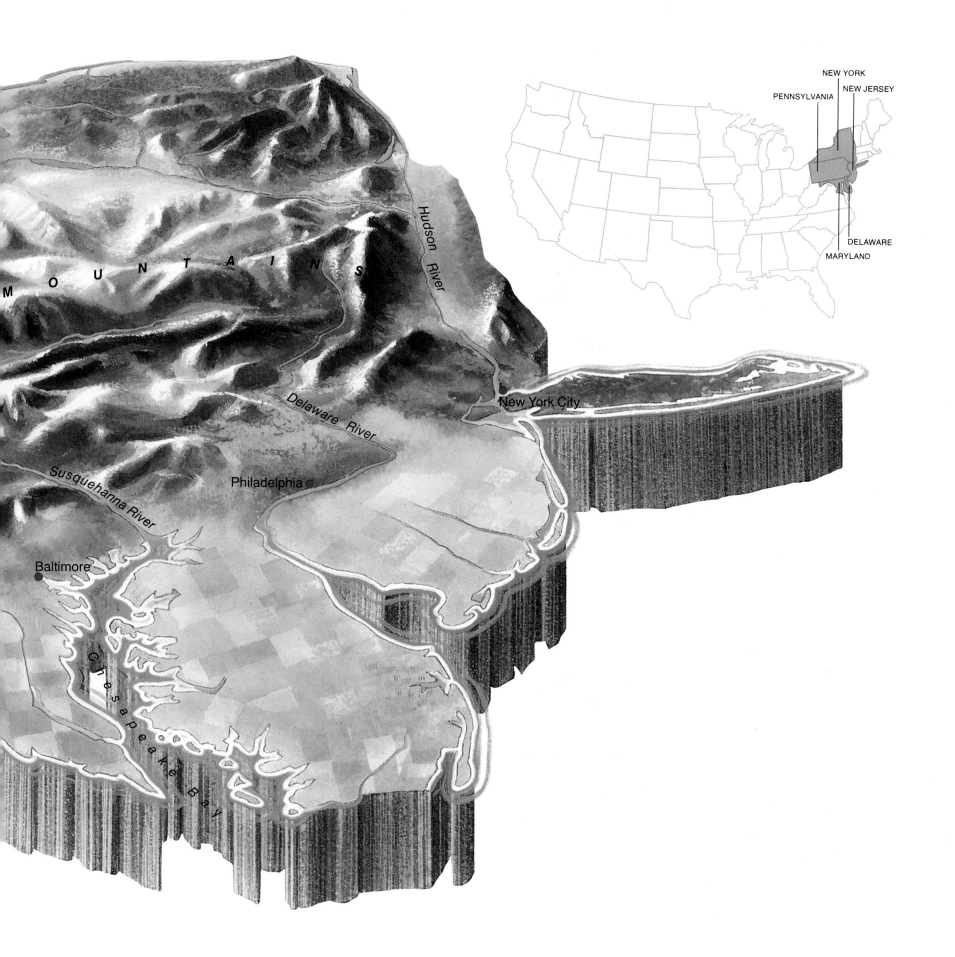

M O U N T A I N S

Hudson River

Delaware River

Susquehanna River

Philadelphia

New York City

Baltimore

Chesapeake Bay

NEW YORK

NEW JERSEY

PENNSYLVANIA

DELAWARE

MARYLAND

New York

New York has been a major gateway to the United States ever since its earliest days as a Dutch colony. A colonial governor in 1644 claimed to distinguish 18 languages spoken by the inhabitants. Of the millions upon millions of immigrants who have entered the country, many stayed in New York City, transforming it into one of the world's largest and most exciting

Niagara Falls has always attracted more than its share of death-defying daredevils. This tightrope walker balances below the falls around 1890.

cities, a center of commerce and culture.

Other people only paused in New York, passing through the state on their way westward. New York City's deep, sheltered harbor, one of the world's biggest and finest, took in thousands of newcomers each year. Through Ellis Island, within sight of the Statue of Liberty, passed more than 16 million immigrants between 1892 and 1954, when the center closed. One of three Americans today has an ancestor or relative who entered the United States at Ellis Island.

Today New York City is headquarters to a

hundred of the nation's 500 largest companies, including giant firms such as Woolworth and RCA. The city's tallest building, the World Trade Center with its twin towers, is home to dozens of corporations. About half a million people work in the city's banks, brokerage houses, and insurance companies. The Wall Street area, a financial center since just after the Revolutionary War, houses the New York and American Stock Exchanges. Here millions of shares of stock in thousands of companies are bought and sold each day. The city is also a leading producer of clothes, books, jewelry, and machinery.

People from all over the world come to New York City to enjoy its art galleries, theaters, concert halls, and museums, including the Metropolitan Museum of Art, the nation's largest art museum. The state has produced hundreds of artists, musicians, and writers, from filmmaker Woody Allen and painter Winslow Homer to the performers who have made Broadway synonymous with show business.

The state's other large population centers include Buffalo, which, thanks to its access to Great Lakes shipping, has huge steel mills, auto assembly and chemical plants, and flour mills. Rochester manufactures optical and photographic equipment, electronic instruments, and copying machines. Syracuse, Utica, and Schenectady, astride the Mohawk Valley transportation corridor, produce electrical machinery and paper products. Albany, the capital, leads in government jobs, and Binghamton assembles computers and business machines.

Almost as varied as New York's people is its geography. The state's terrain ranges from the Great Lakes Lowland to the Adirondack Upland and the great fertile valleys carved by the Hudson and Mohawk Rivers. Much of the state is mountainous and covered by forests. About 135 native tree species grow in the forests. Among them are commercially important trees such as firs, beech, oaks, pines, and sugar maples.

Glaciers left their mark on the state, scooping out and filling the Great Lakes and the long, narrow trenches of the Finger Lakes. As the last glaciers retreated about 10,000 years ago, they left behind a great ridge of rocks and soil that became Long Island. Blocks of melting ice left dimples in the soil that became some of the state's

At the end of the last ice age, melting ice created the Niagara River, which over the ages cut through a high cliff to form Niagara Falls

8,000 or so lakes. When melting glaciers filled the Great Lakes, the overflow formed the Niagara River and deepened the channel of the St. Lawrence River.

Today New York has about 50,000 farms and is important in the production of dairy products. Large truck farms supply cities with vegetables. Orchards around Lake Ontario, Lake Erie, and the Finger Lakes grow cherries, apples, and other fruit. In the spring, cool air from the lakes delays blossoms, lessening the chances of frost damage. In the autumn, air warmed by the lakes lengthens the growing season, prolonging the ripening process. Wineries in the region produce some of the nation's finest wines from grapes grown in local vineyards.

The St. Lawrence Seaway connects the Great Lakes to the Atlantic Ocean

Massena
ST. REGIS INDIAN RESERVATION
Lake Champlain
Plattsburgh
Ogdensburg
Potsdam
St. Lawrence River
Thousand Islands
Lake Placid
Whiteface Mountain
4,867 FEET
1,483 METERS
Saranac Lake
Tupper Lake
Watertown
Black River
Mount Marcy
5,344 FEET
1,629 METERS.
Highest point in New York
Ticonderoga
Lake George
LAKE ONTARIO
ADIRONDACK MOUNTAINS
Hudson River
Oswego
Glens Falls
Irondequoit
reece
Rochester
ERIE CANAL
Genesee River
Oneida Lake
ONEIDA INDIAN RESERVATION
Rome
Saratoga Springs
MONTEZUMA NATIONAL WILDLIFE REFUGE
Syracuse
Oneida
Utica
Mohawk River
Amsterdam
Geneva
Auburn
ONONDAGA INDIAN RESERVATION
NEW YORK STATE THRUWAY
Rotterdam
Schenectady
Finger Lakes
Glaciers dug deep basins for lakes
Great Sacandaga Lake
APPALACHIAN MOUNTAINS
Cooperstown
Troy
Albany
Ithaca
NORTH COUNTRY TRAIL
Chenango River
Susquehanna River
Hornell
Corning
Elmira
Chemung R.
Susquehanna River
Binghamton
CATSKILL MOUNTAINS
Kingston
Hyde Park
Poughkeepsie
Delaware River
Newburgh
Middletown
West Point
U. S. Military Academy
APPALACHIAN TRAIL
Peekskill
New City
LONG ISLAND SOUND
Montauk Point
White Plains
Port Chester
Yonkers
New Rochelle
Riverhead
Sag Harbor
Mount Vernon
Glen Cove
MORTON NATIONAL WILDLIFE REFUGE
WERTHEIM NAT. WILDLIFE REF.
Southampton
New York City
Levittown
Brentwood
Deer Park
LONG ISLAND
Staten Island
Hempstead
Babylon
FIRE ISLAND NATIONAL SEASHORE
GATEWAY NATIONAL RECREATION AREA
ATLANTIC OCEAN

The only state that reaches from the Atlantic Ocean to the Great Lakes, New York became a gateway to the United States. Tiny Ellis Island, in the harbor of New York City, received hopeful immigrants who helped build the nation's ethnic diversity.

The Mohawk River Valley made a highway through the Appalachians, a route to the Great Lakes that the Erie Canal later followed. The Adirondacks are part of the Canadian Shield, a platform of the continent's oldest rock.

Eastern Bluebird

Rose

EXCELSIOR

Area: *30th largest state, 49,108 sq mi (127,190 sq km)*
Population: *17,990,455; ranks second*
Major Cities: *New York, 7,322,564; Buffalo, 328,123; Rochester, 231,636*
Manufacturing: *scientific instruments, machinery, chemicals, electronics, food products, clothing, transportation equipment, metal products, paper products, metals, rubber and plastics, stone, clay, and glass products, jewelry*
Agriculture: *greenhouse and nursery products, cattle, milk, hay, apples, corn, onions, eggs, grapes*
Mining and Quarrying: *stone, oil and gas, sand and gravel, zinc*
Other Important Activities: *finance, insurance, tourism, printing and publishing*
Statehood: *the 11th state; ratified the Constitution on July 26, 1788*

1

2

3

New York

1 *Visitors don slickers for a spray-filled view of Niagara Falls as it tumbles 182 feet (55 m) over a ledge on the American side of the Niagara River. Water spilling over the limestone rim here eats away the falls at a rate of about an inch (2.3 cm) a year.*

2 *New York City's financial district weaves a carpet of light across Manhattan Island. Twin towers of the World Trade Center (left) rise 110 stories above the Hudson River just north of Battery Park.*

5

4

---

3 *Iroquois Indians meet opponents at a lacrosse championship game in Syracuse. Ancestors of these players sometimes substituted the game for war, settling disputes in a contest that could last three days.*

4 *Cider and freshly picked apples and tomatoes prove a mouth-watering temptation to shoppers at a farmers' market in Ithaca.*

5 *Steam wreathes a racehorse after a workout at the track in Saratoga Springs.*

Pennsylvania

Pennsylvania's rivers flow every which way. Nearly 4,500 streams and rivers crisscross the mountains and valleys that make up most of the state. From the mountains near the New York border, streams flow in three directions. Some small ones run northwestward and empty into Lake Erie. Larger streams drain southeastward, emptying into the Susquehanna River and Chesapeake Bay. The waters of still others feed into the Ohio, which joins the Mississippi and ultimately reaches the Gulf of Mexico.

Glaciers advancing and retreating across the landscape thousands of years ago helped set the course of some of Pennsylvania's rivers. They planed away uplands and rerouted rivers by plugging old channels and creating new ones.

Nearly all of Pennsylvania lies in the Appalachian Highlands, a region of plateaus, valleys, and parallel mountain ranges. Corn and hay flourish in the rich soils of southeastern Pennsylvania, as do poultry and dairy farms.

Today most Pennsylvanians live in cities and towns. Philadelphia has ranked as the state's largest city since colonial days. More than a third of all Pennsylvanians live in and around Philadelphia, making it the fifth largest city in the United States after New York, Los Angeles, Chicago, and Houston.

Since its founding by William Penn, Pennsylvania has welcomed people from many lands and many religions. Early settlers included English, Welsh, French, Swedish, and Dutch colonists. Later came Irish immigrants, as well as newcomers from southern and eastern Europe. Some German groups became known as "Pennsylvania Dutch." The word comes from a misinterpretation of *Deutsch*, the German word for "German." Many of them settled in Lancaster County. These Amish and Mennonite farmers maintain neat, prosperous farms. Often these farms are run on religious principles, with horse-drawn equipment and without modern conveniences such as telephones and electricity.

World War II brought the migration of black families from the South in search of factory jobs. Most recently Hispanics and Asians have come, seeking peace, freedom, and a better way of life than was possible in their strife-torn homelands.

Pennsylvania is heavily industrialized. The state counts some 17,000 companies turning out

Young boys were common in coal mines around 1905, before laws were passed to protect children. This youngster worked underground 10 to 12 hours a day, driving mules that pulled coal carts.

300 products ranging from steel rails to nylon bristles. Even so, about three-fifths of its land is forested. Beech, maple, birch, and evergreens flourish in the mountains; hickory, oak, and black walnut in the lowlands. Pennsylvania has more publicly owned parks and forestlands than all the other northeastern states combined.

In the days before railroads and highways, Pennsylvania's waterways served as thoroughfares. Philadelphia, because of its location on the Delaware River some 90 miles (145 km) from the Atlantic, became America's largest freshwater port, shipping food and manufactured goods throughout the eastern states and abroad. Later, Erie became a port vital to Great Lakes shipping. Pittsburgh, a town that grew where the Allegheny and Monongahela Rivers join to form the Ohio River, provided access to the West.

In 1794 Pennsylvania completed America's first turnpike, a stone-paved toll road linking Philadelphia and Lancaster. Travelers paid to travel on the road. The toll collector first received their fee, then turned a pike, or gate, to let them through. A century and a half later, the Pennsylvania Turnpike became the nation's first limited-access highway, a direct descendant of the old Philadelphia-to-Lancaster road.

By the 1850s discoveries of coal, oil, and limestone, and ready access to iron ore shipped across the Great Lakes, had turned Pennsylvania into an industrial powerhouse. In 1859 the nation's first commercial oil well came into production near Titusville, marking the birth of the petroleum industry.

During World War II, Pennsylvania ranked second among the states in industrial production. Pittsburgh's steelmaking furnaces produced so much smoke and soot that motorists drove with headlights on—at noon. Today most of the smog is gone, and the old steel mills are closed. Pittsburgh has a gleaming new downtown laced with parks and promenades. Despite the decline of the steel and coal industries, Pennsylvania still ranks as a major mining and manufacturing state, turning out about a seventh of all the steel made in the United States.

In recent years the state has also diversified its industry, creating jobs in research and high technology. Tourism, too, has become a billion-dollar business. More than 300 lakes, many of them a gift of ancient glaciers, attract boaters and fishermen, and some of the East's most spectacular waterfalls spill down the cliffs and gorges of the Pocono Mountains.

Area: *33rd largest state, 45,308 sq mi (117,348 sq km)*
Population: *11,881,643; ranks fifth*
Major Cities: *Philadelphia, 1,585,577; Pittsburgh, 369,879; Erie, 108,718*
Manufacturing: *food products, chemicals, machinery, metal products, electronics, metals, transportation equipment, paper products, stone, clay, and glass products, scientific instruments, clothing*
Mining and Quarrying: *coal, oil and gas, stone, sand and gravel*
Agriculture: *milk, cattle, greenhouse and nursery products, mushrooms, eggs, broilers, hogs, fruits, hay, corn*
Other Important Activities: *tourism, printing and publishing*
Statehood: *the second state; ratified the Constitution on December 12, 1787*

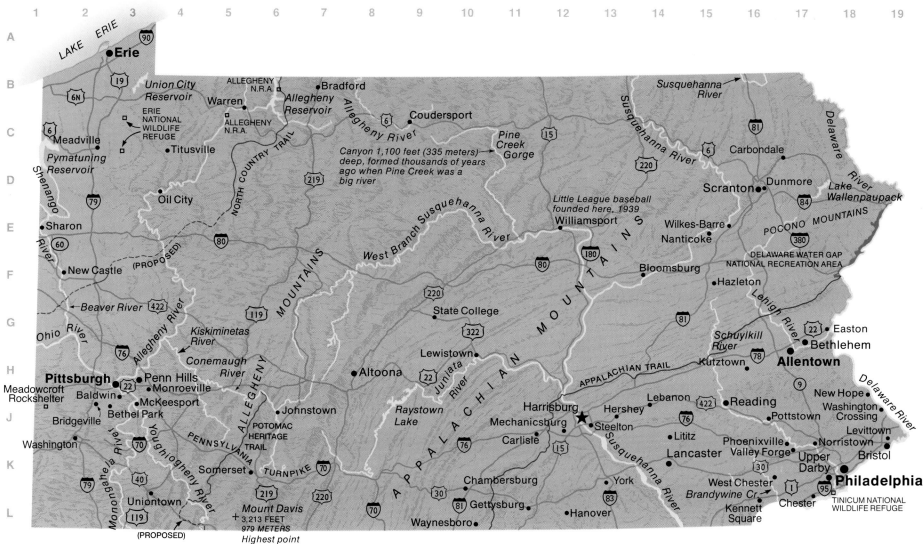

LAKE ERIE

Erie

90

19

6N

6

Meadville

Pymatuning
Reservoir

Shenango
River

79

60

Sharon

New Castle

(PROPOSED)

Beaver River 422

Ohio River

76

Allegheny River

Kiskiminetas
River

Conemaugh
River

Meadowcroft
Rockshelter

Pittsburgh

Penn Hills

22 Monroeville

Baldwin

McKeesport

Bridgeville

Bethel Park

Washington

70

79

40

Monongahela River

Youghiogheny River

119

Uniontown

(PROPOSED)

Somerset

PENNSYLVANIA

TURNPIKE

Johnstown

219

POTOMAC
HERITAGE
TRAIL

70

220

Mount Davis
+ 3,213 FEET
979 METERS
Highest point
in Pennsylvania

Union City
Reservoir

ERIE
NATIONAL
WILDLIFE
REFUGE

Titusville

ALLEGHENY
N.R.A.

ALLEGHENY
N.R.A.

Warren

Bradford

Allegheny
Reservoir

Allegheny River

6

Coudersport

NORTH COUNTRY TRAIL

Oil City

219

80

119

MOUNTAINS

Canyon 1,100 feet (335 meters)
deep, formed thousands of years
ago when Pine Creek was a
big river

Pine
Creek
Gorge

West Branch Susquehanna River

15

220

Williamsport

180

80

State College

322

Lewistown

Altoona

22

Juniata River

Raystown
Lake

76

ALLEGHENY MOUNTAINS

Little League baseball
founded here, 1939

Susquehanna River

Wilkes-Barre

Nanticoke

Bloomsburg

Hazleton

APPALACHIAN MOUNTAINS

Susquehanna
River

Carbondale

Scranton

84

Dunmore

6

81

Lake
Wallenpaupack

POCONO MOUNTAINS

380

DELAWARE WATER GAP
NATIONAL RECREATION AREA

Lehigh River

Delaware River

22 Easton

Bethlehem

Schuylkill
River

81

Kutztown

APPALACHIAN TRAIL

78

Allentown

9

New Hope

Washington
Crossing

Harrisburg

Hershey

Mechanicsburg

Steelton

Carlisle

15

76

Chambersburg

30

81 Gettysburg

Waynesboro

Hanover

Lebanon

422 Reading

76

Lititz

York

83

Lancaster

Phoenixville
Valley Forge

30

West Chester

Brandywine Cr.

Kennett
Square

Pottstown

Norristown

Upper
Darby

Levittown

Bristol

1

95 **Philadelphia**

Chester

TINICUM NATIONAL
WILDLIFE REFUGE

Delaware River

0 KILOMETERS 60

0 STATUTE MILES 40

The only Mid-Atlantic
state that doesn't touch
the ocean, Pennsylvania
nevertheless has a major
port, Philadelphia, on the
Delaware River. Colliding
continental plates
pushed the state's moun-
tains into an S-shaped
curve millions of years
ago and thrust up a pla-
teau that glaciers and
meltwater later carved
into a jumble of valleys
and flat-topped hills.

Stone Age hunters and
gatherers roamed near a

glacier in the southwest
corner 16,000 years ago,
hunting elk and deer and
living beneath an over-
hanging ledge now
named Meadowcroft
Rockshelter.

Mountain
Laurel

Ruffed
Grouse

1

Pennsylvania

1 *The seven stallion paddocks of a horse farm wheel across a hilltop near York, along the frozen Susquehanna River.*

2 *Glowing yellow, a railway rail slides from the forge of the Bethlehem Steel mill in Steelton. Completed in 1867, the plant is the nation's oldest steel mill.*

3 *Independence Hall thrusts its belfry above a park in downtown Philadelphia. In this hall, in 1776, the Continental Congress signed the Declaration of Independence, affirming "that all men are created equal."*

4 *A mummer in feathered regalia struts her stuff in a New Year's Day parade, a Philadelphia tradition dating to 1876.*

5 *Chocolate-covered pretzels have long been a Christmas tradition among the Amish and Mennonites. America's first pretzel bakery opened in Lititz in 1861.*

2

3

4

5

New Jersey

Tucked between New York City and Philadelphia, New Jersey ranks as one of the nation's most heavily industrialized states, a thriving center of trade and manufacturing that has few equals. Towns and cities, especially in the northern part of the state, crowd close together along the land traversed by America's busiest toll road, the New Jersey Turnpike. Each year the superhighway carries more than 190 million cars, buses, and trucks past railroad yards, tank farms, and industrial sites. Along parts of this corridor live 12,000 people per square mile (4,630 per sq km). The population density of New Jersey varies widely from region to region, but the average is almost 993 people per square mile (383 per sq km). This is higher than in any other state, even higher than in densely populated India or Japan.

Nearly 90 percent of all New Jerseyans live in and around large cities such as Newark, Jersey City, Paterson, and Elizabeth. Each workday thousands of them commute to out-of-state jobs in New York City and Philadelphia. As early as the 1830s some New Jerseyans commuted to New York every day. Today tunnels and bridges link the state to various parts of New York City, and four bridges span the Delaware River to Philadelphia.

New Jersey's farms and factories produce a prodigious outflow of goods—everything from orchids and blueberries to aspirin, trucks, turbines, and telephones. Manufacturing produces a fifth of the state's revenues. Even in colonial days New Jersey's corn, wheat, and vegetables found ready markets in New York and Philadelphia, leading Benjamin Franklin to describe the state as "a cider barrel tapped at both ends."

But this is only part of New Jersey. More than half the state is made up of open land, with farms, woods, marshes, and some of the finest white-sand beaches on the East Coast.

Kittatinny Mountain, a 35-mile-long (56-km) ridge of the Appalachians, lies across the state's northwestern corner. Flanking it is a highland region of low, flat-topped summits largely covered with forests of oak, maple, and ash. Many of the state's 800 or so lakes and ponds nestle in the highlands near Kittatinny Mountain.

Glacial rocks and rubble and steep slopes discourage large-scale vegetable farming here, so

The renowned Diving Horse, a Texas cow pony named Lorgah, is caught in action with two quick flashes. Lorgah made her 1958 plunge to fame from a 40-foot (12-m) tower in Atlantic City.

most farmers stick to dairying and raising poultry. The foothills are horse country, lush, rolling pastures nourished by limestone soils.

The Delaware River forms New Jersey's western boundary. In the north it has cut a dramatic, twisting pathway through Kittatinny Mountain, the Delaware Water Gap. Along its southern reaches, below Trenton, the river is tidal and navigable, and rivals the Mississippi in the amount of commerce it carries.

In the foothills east of the mountain, real estate developers have discovered rural areas close to New York City. Here town-house developments now rub shoulders with dairy farms. Here you can also find towns with white-spired churches and village greens remindful of their early New England settlers.

Across the state, facing the open Atlantic, 127 miles (204 km) of lagoons and barrier beaches reach from Sandy Hook in the north to Cape May on the lower reaches of Delaware Bay. This stretch is known as the Jersey Shore. Beach communities range from comfortable old towns like Bay Head and the exuberant Victorian restorations of Cape May, where Presidents Lincoln, Grant, Pierce, Buchanan, and Harrison vacationed, to the honky-tonk hustle of Asbury Park and Atlantic City's boardwalk, gambling casinos, and Miss America contests. Each year the Jersey Shore draws millions of tourists and vacationers, despite concerns over beaches polluted by industrial and other wastes. And each fall and spring tens of thousands of herons, ducks, terns, and other birds visit Brigantine, Barnegat, and other shoreside areas.

A few miles inland lies the largest tract of protected land between Boston and Washington, D. C., the one-million-acre (405,000-ha) Pine Barrens. Early settlers called the region barren because its sandy soil was not good for farming. Stretching from Cape May north to Toms River, the barrens are made up of swamps and salt marshes, stands of pine, cedar, and oak, cranberry bogs, and tracts of cultivated blueberries. The people of the barrens live mostly in towns and villages, but there are places where the population density is only ten per square mile (four per sq km).

Beneath the Pine Barrens, and nourishing its swamps, streams, marshes, and wildlife, lies a little-known natural wonder, the Cohansey Aquifer. This underground maze of tunnels and caverns is thought to hold the greatest supply of fresh, clean water in the East north of Florida, about equal to a thousand-square-mile (2,590-sq-km) lake 75 feet (23 m) deep.

Between the Pine Barrens and the Delaware River lies the heartland of New Jersey's farming district. The fertile, loamy soils of the region rank among the most productive and valuable in the United States. Almost 60 kinds of fruits and vegetables grow here. Much of the food is trucked to New York City and Philadelphia as well as other eastern cities. Although much farmland has been converted to build offices, shopping malls, and suburbs in recent years, New Jersey still has some 8,300 farms.

Glaciers, in places up to a mile (1.6 km) thick, helped shape the face of New Jersey. Moving south some 20,000 years ago, they covered the northern part of the state, above a line between Phillipsburg and Perth Amboy. They piled up rocks and soil that formed the hills and ridges in the north, and gouged depressions that filled with water. These became lakes and wetlands such as the Great Swamp near Morristown.

Untouched by glaciers, the southern part of New Jersey remains a relatively smooth coastal plain fringed with bays, inlets, and sandbars.

American Goldfinch

Violet

Area: *the 46th largest state, 7,787 sq mi (20,169 sq km)*

Population: *7,730,188; ranks ninth*

Major Cities: *Newark, 275,221; Jersey City, 228,537; Paterson, 140,891*

Manufacturing: *chemicals, food products, scientific instruments, electronics, machinery, metal products, rubber and plastics, paper products, clothing, stone, clay, and glass products, metals, transportation equipment, furniture*

Agriculture: *greenhouse and nursery products, vegetables, milk, blueberries, eggs, soybeans, cattle*

Mining and Quarrying: *stone, sand and gravel*

Other Important Activities: *tourism, printing and publishing, fishing*

Statehood: *the third state; ratified the Constitution on December 18, 1787*

High Point
1,803 FEET
550 METERS
Highest point in New Jersey

DELAWARE WATER GAP NATIONAL RECREATION AREA

KITTATINNY MOUNTAIN

APPALACHIAN TRAIL

23

Wanaque Reservoir

Hopatcong

Lake Hopatcong

80

Dover

287

Montclair

Morristown

GREAT SWAMP NATIONAL WILDLIFE REFUGE

Bloomfield

East Orange

Irvington

Ridgewood

Paramus

Paterson

Clifton

Hackensack

Passaic

Hudson River

Union City

Hoboken

Jersey City

Newark

Elizabeth

Bayonne

Phillipsburg

78

Passaic River

Plainfield

Raritan River

95

Woodbridge

Perth Amboy

202

New Brunswick

Edison

Sayreville

DELAWARE AND RARITAN CANAL

Sandy Hook

GATEWAY NATIONAL RECREATION AREA

Hopewell

Princeton

1

9

Red Bank

Eatontown

Long Branch

Mercerville

Trenton

White Horse

NEW JERSEY TURNPIKE

195

Neptune

Asbury Park

Lakewood

Point Pleasant

Bay Head

Delaware River

Willingboro

Pennsauken

Camden

Cherry Hill

Haddonfield

The first dinosaur skeleton found in North America, 1858

206

70

Chatsworth

PINE BARRENS

Toms River

72

GARDEN STATE PARKWAY

Barnegat Bay

9

ATLANTIC OCEAN

295

Glassboro

ATLANTIC CITY EXPRESSWAY

Mullica River

EDWIN B. FORSYTHE NATIONAL WILDLIFE REFUGE (BARNEGAT)

SUPAWNA MEADOWS NATIONAL WILDLIFE REFUGE

40

49

Vineland

Great Egg Harbor River

Beach Haven

Great Bay

EDWIN B. FORSYTHE NATIONAL WILDLIFE REFUGE (BRIGANTINE)

Bridgeton

Millville

Maurice River

PINE BARRENS

9

Atlantic City

Ventnor City

Ocean City

47

Delaware Bay

Every fall millions of migrating birds gather here to cross Delaware Bay

Avalon

Cape May

Wildwood

Cape May

KILOMETERS 0 — 30
STATUTE MILES 0 — 20

1

New Jersey

1 *A meandering stream reflects a soggy, boggy part of the Pine Barrens. Early settlers mined the region for bog iron to make nails, kettles, and cannonballs.*

2 *Near Vineland, a Korean-American youngster joyfully hefts a whopping radish on his family's vegetable farm.*

2

3

5

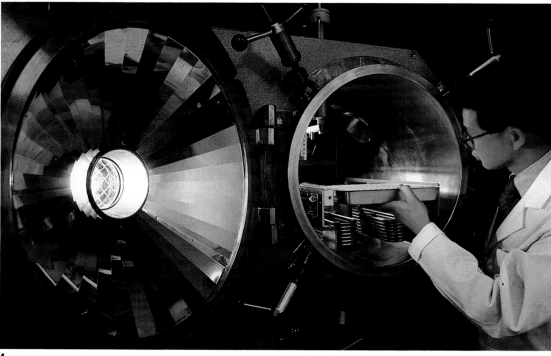

4

3 *Planes, trains, ships, and trucks come together in Newark, a major shipping center. Cranes stack truck-size containers on the decks of ships bound for distant ports.*

4 *A worker at a laboratory near Elizabeth examines cancer-fighting interferon. New Jersey has about a thousand plants producing medicines and chemicals.*

5 *A lifeguard team battles the surf to launch a boat near Asbury Park in an annual tournament that draws many contestants, such as these from the Barnegat Bay area.*

Maryland

Chesapeake Bay slices Maryland nearly in two. Hills and mountains rise west of the bay. So do the gentle streams and broad, limestone-rich valleys of the Piedmont. In the foothills lie suburban communities that reach from Baltimore to the nation's capital, Washington, D. C. Just at the edge of the Piedmont, on the Atlantic Coastal Plain, stands the city of Baltimore. East of the bay spreads Maryland's share of the Delmarva Peninsula, a mostly flat, marsh-fringed stretch of land known as the Eastern Shore.

The bay itself is a submerged river valley, or estuary, the United States' largest. It formed after the Ice Age thousands of years ago, as the land gradually sank and sea levels rose, flooding the mouth of the Susquehanna River. Although Maryland has only 31 miles (50 km) of coast on the Atlantic Ocean, the myriad coves, creeks, and indentations on the bay side give the state nearly 4,000 miles (6,440 km) of shoreline.

Chesapeake Bay plays an important part in Maryland life, especially in the Tidewater region surrounding it. More than 2.3 million people live within 20 miles (32 km) of the bay and its tributaries, a number that may reach 12 million by the end of the century.

Despite problems with silting, flooding, and pollution, the bay remains a paradise for boaters, bird-watchers, sport fishermen, and those who like to feast on fish, crabs, and oysters. In a good year the bay provides about 90 million pounds of blue crabs, about half the nation's catch, and nearly all its soft-shell crabs. Tonging and dredging for oysters is hard work and always has been. Soaring expenses, state government regulation, growing competition from Louisiana and Venezuela, and pollution have driven many a waterman from the bay.

Ever since colonial days the bay has served as an avenue of commerce between North America, Europe, and the Caribbean. Colonial planters shipped tobacco, lumber, and livestock to London from sheltered bay-side landings. From the Caribbean came sugar and slaves, sugar to be made into rum, slaves to till the fields of sotweed, as tobacco was sometimes called.

The bay provides direct access to Baltimore, one of the nation's busiest ports and Maryland's most industrial city. Today, as in times past, people of many ethnic backgrounds live in Balti-

Around 1920 a book wagon makes house-to-house deliveries from the Washington County Free Library at Hagerstown. Established in 1902, it was the first county library in the United States.

more. Many Italians live in a 12-block area near the waterfront. Greek families live in a nearby neighborhood, as do Hispanics. Poles and other East Europeans often prefer an eastern part of the city. Brick row houses with gleaming marble doorsteps are a common sight in many of these older Baltimore neighborhoods.

About three-fourths of all Marylanders live in the densely populated corridor between Baltimore and Washington, D. C. Even 30 years ago a newspaper noted that "Baltimore and Washington are reaching out for each other like octopuses, sending out tentacles of freeways, sewage lines, and industrial zones." Those tentacles have long since met and entangled.

Even so, much of Maryland remains rural. Forests cover about 40 percent of the state—spruce, white pine, hemlock, and maple in the western mountains and foothills. Farms and orchards fill the broad, fertile valleys between the mountains. In the lowlands to the east spread forests of yellow pine, cedar, and cypress.

Farmers still grow tobacco on the western shore of Chesapeake Bay. Across the bay raising poultry vies with trapping crabs and harvesting oysters as a way to earn a living. On the ocean side of Delmarva lies Ocean City, a major resort teeming with vacationers and holiday crowds during the summer months. South of Ocean City lies Assateague Island, a long, thin barrier island with few inhabitants other than nesting shorebirds and wild ponies.

The state capital, Annapolis, hugs the bay. Annapolis's State House, begun in 1772, ranks as the nation's oldest state capitol building in continuous use. And briefly, from November 1783 until the following August, it served as the nation's capitol. The treaty that ended the Revolutionary War was ratified here in 1784.

Birds depend on the bounty of Chesapeake Bay. Thousands of ducks nest and raise their broods in the wetlands fringing the bay. Up to three million Canada geese winter over each year, and bald eagles, protected by law from hunters, have begun to make a comeback.

Area: *the 42nd largest state, 10,460 sq mi (27,092 sq km)*
Population: *4,781,468; ranks 19th*
Major Cities: *Baltimore, 736,014; Rockville, 44,835; Frederick, 40,148*
Manufacturing: *food products, scientific instruments, chemicals, transportation equipment, metals, electronics, machinery, metal products, paper products, rubber and plastics, stone, clay, and glass products, clothing, lumber and wood products*
Agriculture: *broilers, milk, greenhouse and nursery products, soybeans, cattle, corn, vegetables, eggs*
Mining and Quarrying: *stone, coal, sand and gravel*
Other Important Activities: *tourism, printing and publishing, fishing*
Statehood: *the seventh state; ratified the Constitution on April 28, 1788*

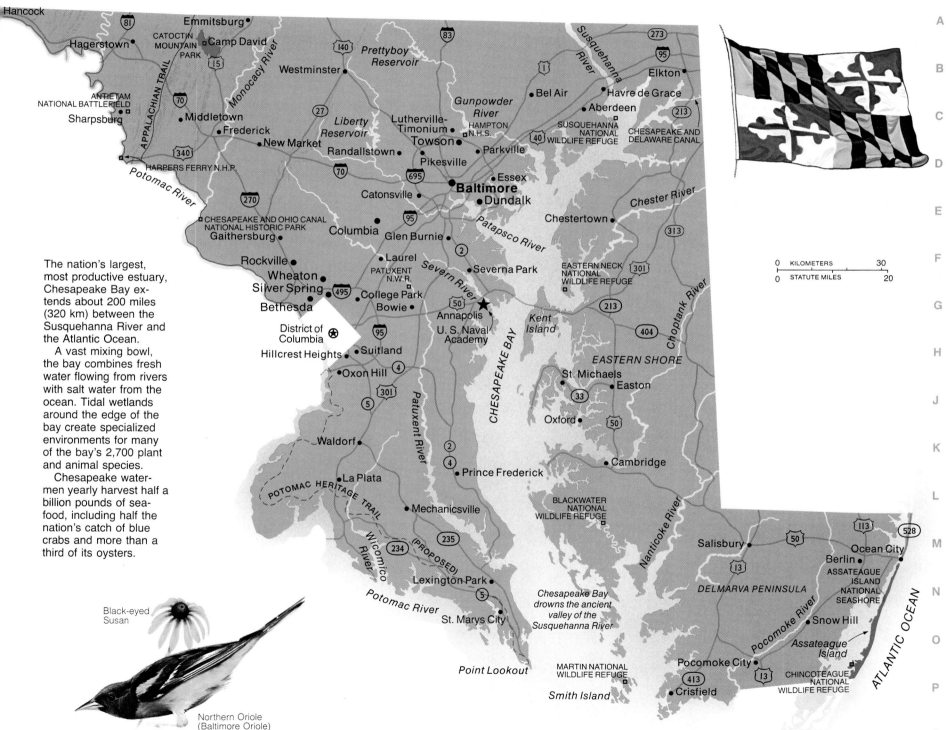

The nation's largest, most productive estuary, Chesapeake Bay extends about 200 miles (320 km) between the Susquehanna River and the Atlantic Ocean.

A vast mixing bowl, the bay combines fresh water flowing from rivers with salt water from the ocean. Tidal wetlands around the edge of the bay create specialized environments for many of the bay's 2,700 plant and animal species.

Chesapeake watermen yearly harvest half a billion pounds of seafood, including half the nation's catch of blue crabs and more than a third of its oysters.

Chesapeake Bay drowns the ancient valley of the Susquehanna River

Black-eyed Susan

Northern Oriole (Baltimore Oriole)

KILOMETERS 30
STATUTE MILES 20

EASTERN SHORE

DELMARVA PENINSULA

CHESAPEAKE BAY

ATLANTIC OCEAN

Hancock
Emmitsburg
Hagerstown
CATOCTIN MOUNTAIN PARK
Camp David
Prettyboy Reservoir
Elkton
ANTIETAM NATIONAL BATTLEFIELD
Sharpsburg
Middletown
Westminster
Gunpowder River
Bel Air
Havre de Grace
Aberdeen
SUSQUEHANNA NATIONAL WILDLIFE REFUGE
CHESAPEAKE AND DELAWARE CANAL
Frederick
Liberty Reservoir
Lutherville-Timonium
HAMPTON N.H.S.
HARPERS FERRY N.H.P.
New Market
Randallstown
Towson
Parkville
Potomac River
Pikesville
Chester River
Catonsville
Baltimore
Essex
Dundalk
Chestertown
CHESAPEAKE AND OHIO CANAL NATIONAL HISTORIC PARK
Columbia
Glen Burnie
Patapsco River
EASTERN NECK NATIONAL WILDLIFE REFUGE
Gaithersburg
Rockville
Laurel
PATUXENT N.W.R.
Severn River
Severna Park
Choptank River
Wheaton
Silver Spring
College Park
Annapolis
Kent Island
Bethesda
Bowie
U.S. Naval Academy
District of Columbia
Hillcrest Heights
Suitland
St. Michaels
Easton
Oxon Hill
Oxford
Waldorf
Patuxent River
Prince Frederick
Cambridge
La Plata
POTOMAC HERITAGE TRAIL
Mechanicsville
BLACKWATER NATIONAL WILDLIFE REFUGE
Nanticoke River
Salisbury
Ocean City
Wicomico River
(PROPOSED)
Berlin
ASSATEAGUE ISLAND NATIONAL SEASHORE
Lexington Park
Potomac River
Snow Hill
Assateague Island
St. Marys City
Pocomoke River
Point Lookout
MARTIN NATIONAL WILDLIFE REFUGE
Pocomoke City
Smith Island
Crisfield
CHINCOTEAGUE NATIONAL WILDLIFE REFUGE

1

2

Maryland

1 *A cook in the town of Oxford prepares a dish of soft-shell clams steamed and dipped in a tangy sauce. Most Maryland clams are shipped to northeastern states.*

2 *Twin spans of the 4.4-mile (7-km) Chesapeake Bay Bridge link the once isolated Eastern Shore with the rest of Maryland.*

3 *Forsaking modern farm equipment, an Amish boy hitches his plow to a four-horse-power team near Mechanicsville. Religious beliefs lead Amish people to seek simplicity in their daily lives and to shun contraptions of the modern world.*

3

4

5

4 Annapolis reaches for the Severn River on radiating streets laid out in 1696. Filling its circle (background), the capitol once housed the Continental Congress. One street runs from Church Circle (foreground) to the green-roofed buildings of the United States Naval Academy.

5 Hats aloft! Graduating Naval Academy cadets celebrate by flinging away their "middie" caps at the climax of commencement exercises. No longer midshipmen, they will now wear the hats of commissioned officers.

Delaware

Delaware is a small state, "a jewel among states," Thomas Jefferson called it. Only Rhode Island is smaller. The state lies mostly on the Atlantic Coastal Plain, where it forms a flat, low-lying strip of land extending 96 miles (154 km) along the Delmarva Peninsula, which Delaware shares with Maryland and Virginia. Here the land seldom rises more than 80 feet (24 m) above sea level. Only Florida lies lower.

But not all of Delaware is flat. Its northernmost reach, a strip only 10 miles (16 km) at its widest, is an edge of the rolling foothills of the Appalachian Mountains, the Piedmont. Here the Delaware River forms the boundary between New Jersey and Delaware as it flows into Delaware Bay to meet the sea. This part of the state lies along a busy transportation corridor between northern and southern states, and has become heavily industrialized.

Swamps and marshlands rich in plants and insects dot Delaware's Atlantic Coastal Plain, making it a haven for deer, otters, and muskrats, as well as a stopover for migrating ducks and geese. Cypress Swamp spreads across some 30,000 acres (12,150 ha) along the southern border, and contains the northernmost stand of cypress trees in the United States. Salt marshes and estuaries line much of Delaware Bay, providing nesting sites for birds and breeding grounds for mollusks and shellfish. In 1971 Delaware became the first state to enact strict seashore protection laws; they forbid construction of oil refineries, steel mills, and other polluting industries within two miles (3 km) of the coast.

Beyond the mouth of Delaware Bay, from Cape Henlopen to Fenwick Island, lie 28 miles (45 km) of sandy Atlantic Ocean beaches. These are long, thin barrier islands that enclose shallow bays and lagoons. Each summer Delaware's beaches attract vacationers from Washington, D. C., Baltimore, and other eastern cities.

Small as it is, Delaware is almost two states rolled into one, a major commercial and industrial center in the north, where 70 percent of the people live and work, and a thinly populated farming state elsewhere. As a local newspaperman observed: "Delaware is a northern state with a southern exposure. And it's a southern state with a northern exposure."

As to Delaware's northern exposure, it was

In 1935 the world's first synthetic fiber, nylon, was invented in a Du Pont lab. By 1950 Du Pont machines at the plant in Seaford were spinning the sturdy nylon threads by the mile.

along the banks of Brandywine Creek, near Wilmington, that Éleuthère Irénée du Pont in 1802 decided to locate his gunpowder mills. Since then his enterprise has expanded globally and is regarded as one of the world's leading chemical companies. Many other chemical companies operate in Delaware and, with Du Pont, produce plastics, synthetic fibers, and agricultural and industrial chemicals.

Many large companies of all kinds have "paper offices" in Delaware because the state has licensed them to do business, and the legal papers originate in and are stored in Delaware offices. In fact, the incorporation of companies, whether they actually locate in the state or as far away as Asia, has become big business in Delaware. Each year the process brings in about a fifth of the state's income in legal fees and taxes. About half of the largest companies in the U. S. call themselves Delaware corporations. Liberal tax

laws, lawyers and judges experienced in corporate law, and rules that enable businesses to operate without much outside interference have attracted more than 170,000 companies to sign on as Delaware corporations.

In 1981 the state eased credit restrictions and banking regulations, a move that has since spurred an influx of banks, credit card operations, and other financial services.

As for Delaware's southern exposure, commerce gives way to farming in the lower two-thirds of the state. Here the pace of life is slower and more relaxed than in Wilmington. As one writer noted: "This is a small-town state, where peace, quiet, and good neighbors are surplus commodities." The sandy, loamy soil produces abundant corn and soybeans which, in turn, feed the some 217 million chickens that Delaware farmers raise each year.

Delaware gets its name from Lord De La Warre, a governor of colonial Virginia who financed a voyage of exploration along this part of North America's coast. In 1631 the first colonists, from the Netherlands, built a whaling settlement at Zwaanendael ("swan valley"), now Lewes, but Indians massacred the group. In 1638 Swedes arriving near present-day Wilmington introduced log cabins to the New World. The Dutch and the English fought over the territory but eventually England prevailed, and in 1682 the Duke of York gave Delaware to William Penn as part of his Pennsylvania colony. During the Revolutionary War the territory became the "Delaware State."

Area: *the 49th largest state, 2,044 sq mi (5,294 sq km)*
Population: *666,168; ranks 46th*
Major Cities: *Wilmington, 71,529; Dover, 27,630; Newark, 25,098*
Manufacturing: *chemicals, food products, rubber and plastics, paper products, scientific instruments, transportation equipment, electronics, clothing, metal products*
Agriculture: *broilers, soybeans, vegetables, greenhouse and nursery products, corn, milk, eggs, wheat, hogs*
Mining and Quarrying: *sand and gravel, magnesium*
Other Important Activities: *finance, tourism, printing and publishing, fishing*
Statehood: *the first state; ratified the Constitution on December 7, 1787*

Brandywine Creek →

Highest point in Delaware
+ 442 FEET
135 METERS

Talleyville

A

(41)

(95) Claymont

Elsmere • Wilmington

B

Marshallton •

0 KILOMETERS 20
0 STATUTE MILES 10

• Newark

C

• Brookside • New Castle

(40)

D

(301) Lums Pond • Delaware City

CHESAPEAKE AND
DELAWARE CANAL

E

Middletown •

F

Noxontown Pond

(13)

Delaware River

G

H

Smyrna •

Clayton •

Leipsic River

BOMBAY HOOK
NATIONAL
WILDLIFE REFUGE

(300)

J

★ Dover

Delaware Bay

K

Wyoming •

• Camden

• Kitts Hammock

L

(13)

M

DELMARVA
PENINSULA

N

Harrington •

Milford •

(1)

O

PRIME HOOK
NATIONAL
WILDLIFE REFUGE

Cape Henlopen

P

(404)

Bridgeville •

• Milton

Lewes

(9)

Rehoboth Beach

Q

(18)

• Dewey Beach

Seaford •

Georgetown •

Rehoboth Bay

ATLANTIC
OCEAN

R

Nanticoke River

Indian River Bay

(1)

S

Laurel •

(113)

Bethany Beach •

(24)

Cypress Swamp
Ancient wetlands,
home to rare plants
and animals

Selbyville •

Fenwick Island

T

1 2 3 4 5 6 7 8 9

WASH.

British until 1818

MAINE

Oregon Territory
1846

OREG.

MONT.

N. DAK.

VT.
N.H

IDAHO

S. DAK.

MINN.

WIS.

N.Y.

MASS.
R.I.
CONN.

WYO.

MICH.

PA.

N.J.

NEV.

UTAH

NEBR.

IOWA

OHIO

MD.
DEL.

Mexican Cession
1848

COLO.

Louisiana Purchase
1803

ILL. IND.

W. VA.
KY.

VA.

CALIF.

Treaty line of 1819

KANS.

MO.

The United States
1783

N.C.

ARIZ.

OKLA.

TENN.

ARK.

Area of
Original
13 Colonies
1775

S.C.

N. MEX.

TEX.

MISS. ALA.

GA.

Gadsden Purchase
1853

Texas Annexation
1845

LA.

FLA.

Spanish until
1806/1819

Florida Purchase
1819

Peach
Blossom

Blue Hen
Chicken

On December 7, 1787,
Delaware became the
first state to join the
Union. It led a parade of
states and territories
(above) that, in 60 years,
would reach from the At-
lantic to the Pacific.

Delaware is also the
only state to have a
rounded boundary—an
arc formed by a 12-mile
(19-km) radius drawn
from the old courthouse
in New Castle. The long,
straight boundary, sur-
veyed in the 1760s by
English astronomers
Charles Mason and Jere-
miah Dixon, later be-
came part of the Mason-
Dixon Line that divided
the slave states from the
nonslave states.

1

Delaware

1 *Founded by Swedish settlers in 1638, Wilmington today mixes old with new as part of a downtown renewal plan. Delaware's largest city, long a leader in corporate law and the chemical industry, has also become an important credit card center.*

2 *An antique train chugs past Granogue, a du Pont family estate built in 1923. "Château country" is what Delawareans call the rolling countryside northwest of Wilmington dotted with du Pont mansions.*

2

3

4

3 *Hoisting shellfish from the bottom of Rehoboth Bay, a clammer grapples with a heavy bull rake to haul in a load of bivalves prized for their salty flavor.*

4 *Youngsters share a giggle in the Touch and Discover Room at Winterthur, a du Pont estate near Wilmington, now a museum famous for its gardens and furnishings.*

Appalachian Highlands

Like giant ripples on the land, the Appalachian Mountains sweep along the eastern United States for some 2,000 miles (3,200 km) from central Alabama to Maine and on into Canada. Many mountain ranges make up the Appalachian system. Here the Blue Ridge Mountains form the range's eastern front. Behind them, other mountains roll westward to forested interior highlands bordered by rivers.

Along the Blue Ridge, foothills called the Piedmont slope eastward, then step down onto the Atlantic Coastal Plain fringed with low wetlands and long, thin islands. The barrier islands of the Outer Banks, once sand ridges that were flooded when ocean levels rose after the Ice Age, act as a buffer between the mainland and the open ocean. Shallow sounds and lagoons between the islands and the shore also provide food and shelter for fish and wildlife.

Many dams also dot the region. You can see them where rivers widen into long, narrow lakes. These man-made lakes, or reservoirs, attract boaters and fishermen and provide flood control. Water from the lakes spilling through some dams turns turbines that produce electricity for homes and factories in the region.

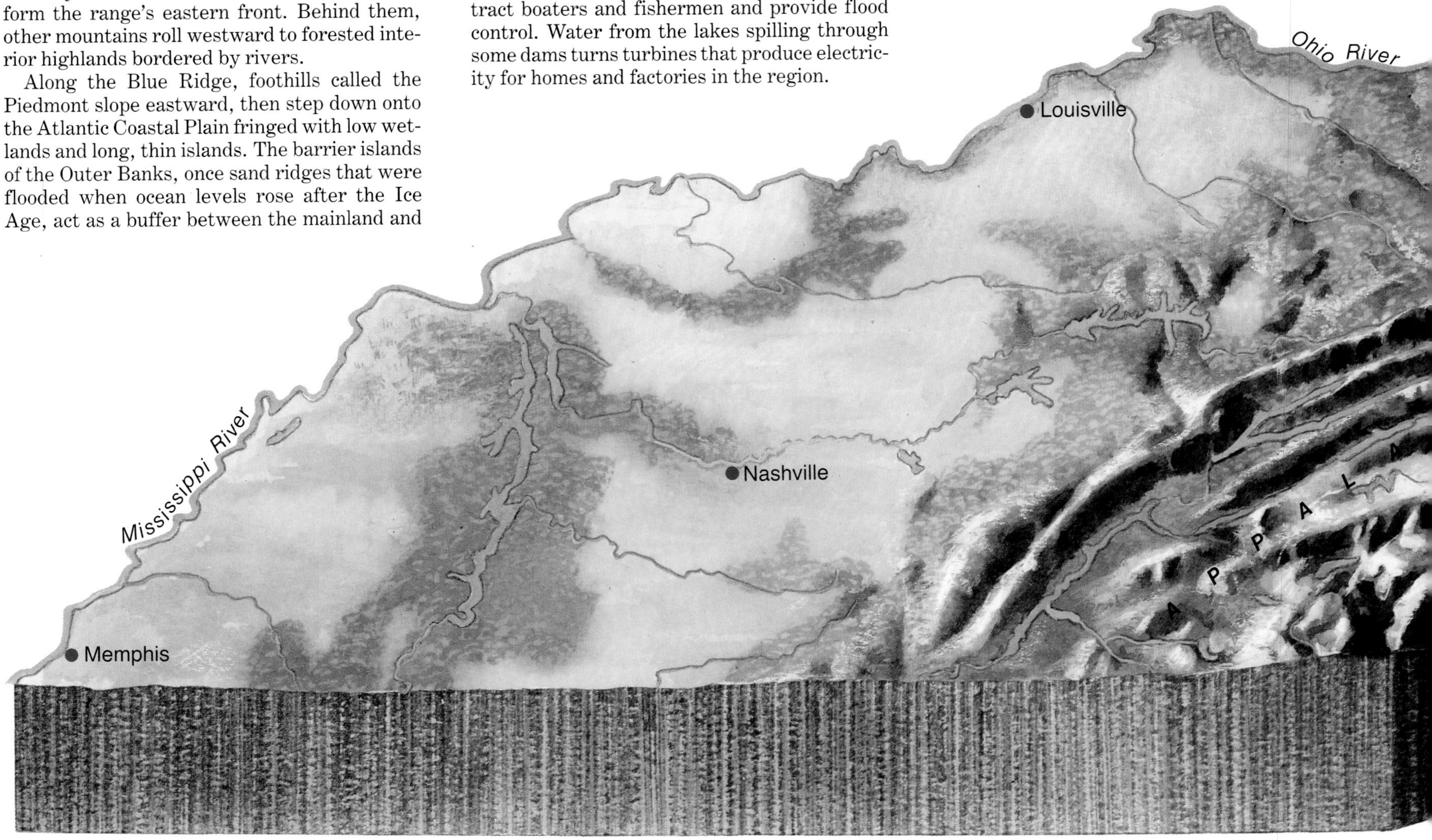

Ohio River

Louisville

Mississippi River

Nashville

Memphis

A P P A L A

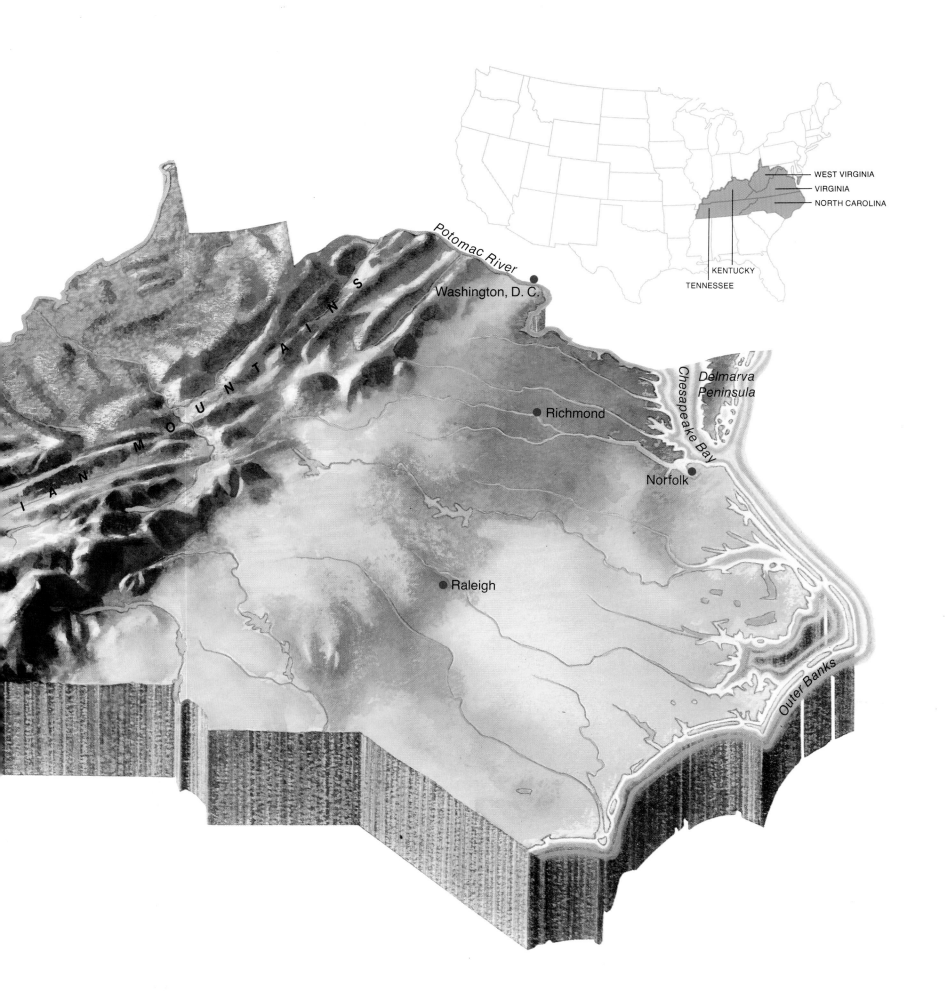

Potomac River

Washington, D. C.

Richmond

Norfolk

Raleigh

Delmarva Peninsula

Chesapeake Bay

Outer Banks

APPALACHIAN MOUNTAINS

WEST VIRGINIA

VIRGINIA

NORTH CAROLINA

KENTUCKY

TENNESSEE

Kentucky

Folk musician and maker of musical instruments John Jacob Niles, in his workshop near Lexington around 1940, puts finishing touches on a dulcimer of an unusual shape.

Kentucky is a land of rivers. Much of its border is formed by rivers. This gives the state a shape like a camel trying to get up, one local humorist observed. Kentucky has more than a thousand miles (1,600 km) of navigable waterways for recreation and commerce. Its major cities, located on rivers, were founded in the days when rivers were highways for flatboats and steamboats.

The Appalachian Mountains and the Cumberland Plateau make up much of eastern Kentucky. Here the land is a scramble of heavily forested peaks, ridges, and deep, narrow valleys settled mostly by Scotch-Irish pioneers. Rugged terrain and lack of good roads for many years kept much of eastern Kentucky shut off from the outside world. But such isolation also helped preserve the ballads of the settlers and kept alive skills such as quilting and basketry.

Even though the giant oaks, hickories, and poplars that once grew in Kentucky have long

ago been logged, and many mountainsides have been torn apart to dig out coal, the land still retains much of its wild beauty.

Waterfalls tumble from the heights. Cumberland Falls, near Corbin, is one of the largest east of the Rocky Mountains. When the water is high and the moon is full, the mist of the falls creates a moonbow. Kentucky streams have carved cliffs, palisades, and natural bridges. Rivers have gnawed winding passageways called gaps through the mountains. One is historic Cumberland Gap, Daniel Boone's route when he blazed his pioneering Wilderness Road in 1775. Boone and his wife, Rebecca, are buried in a cemetery in Frankfort, the state capital.

Kentucky mines coal and has ever since the 1850s. Today the state ranks as one of the nation's leading producers of soft, or bituminous, coal. Most of it comes from huge deposits in the eastern mountains and in western coalfields near the Ohio River. Geologists estimate that Kentucky and neighboring Tennessee have enough coal to mine for a thousand years.

Nowadays most of the coal is strip-mined, dug out by huge power shovels and bulldozers that tear away the trees, earth, and rocks covering the deposits. Such methods provide cheap coal, but they also pollute streams and destroy farmland, forests, and animal habitats.

A 1977 federal law requires mine owners to reclaim land by restoring its shape and replanting it. But lands stripped before 1977 still lie mostly unreclaimed, giant scars on the land.

In recent years Kentucky has also become a major producer of marijuana. For impoverished farmers and unemployed mine workers of eastern Kentucky, illegal marijuana growing can be tempting. The average tobacco plot earns about $2,000 a year; 50 well-tended marijuana plants can bring in more than $50,000.

West of the mountains lies Kentucky's Bluegrass region, with some of the world's finest horse farms. Gently rolling fields and pastures lie covered with lush grass and laced with white fences. Although bluegrass is really green, it gets its name from the tiny bluish flowers that bloom briefly each May. Limestone bedrock beneath the turf nourishes the rich grass with lime and calcium needed to build strong bones and muscles in fine horses. Farmers in the region

also grow large crops of tobacco, corn, and hay.

Lexington serves as the commercial and cultural hub of the Bluegrass region, while Louisville reigns as the site for America's best known horse race, the Kentucky Derby.

Louisville, a major Ohio River port with a waterfront rebuilt in steel, glass, and concrete, turns out trucks, farm equipment, household appliances, and air-pollution equipment. It also produces bourbon whiskey, a leading state export. Factories in Lexington manufacture electric typewriters, paper and food products, and heating equipment.

South-central Kentucky has one of the world's great natural wonders, Mammoth Cave. This longest of all known cavern systems extends some 330 miles (530 km) in five underground levels that have yet to be fully explored. Over millions of years water, seeping through cracks in the limestone bedrock, created a labyrinth of tunnels and chambers. In these dark recesses live fish, shrimp, crayfish, and other creatures. Over the ages these animals have adapted to their environment by losing sight or skin color, or both, and developing sensitive organs on their bodies that help them feel their way around in the blackness.

Kentucky's western tip, the part that jogs south between the Mississippi River and Kentucky Lake, is known as the Jackson Purchase. It was named for Andrew Jackson, who helped buy this bottomland from the Chickasaw Indians in 1818, before he became President of the U. S.

One part of the Purchase can't be reached by road from Kentucky. It's a pom-pom-shaped dot of land barely three miles (5 km) across that a loop of the Mississippi River cuts off from the rest of the state. To get there by car, you have to drive through neighboring Tennessee.

Area: *37th largest state, 40,410 sq mi (104,659 sq km)*
Population: *3,685,296; ranks 23rd*
Major Cities: *Louisville, 269,063; Lexington, 225,366; Owensboro, 53,549*
Manufacturing: *transportation equipment, machinery, electronics, food products, chemicals, metals, metal products, rubber and plastics, paper products, stone, clay, and glass products, clothing*
Mining and Quarrying: *coal, oil and gas, stone*
Agriculture: *horses, cattle, tobacco, milk, soybeans, corn*
Other Important Activities: *tourism, printing and publishing*
Statehood: *the 15th state; admitted on June 1, 1792*

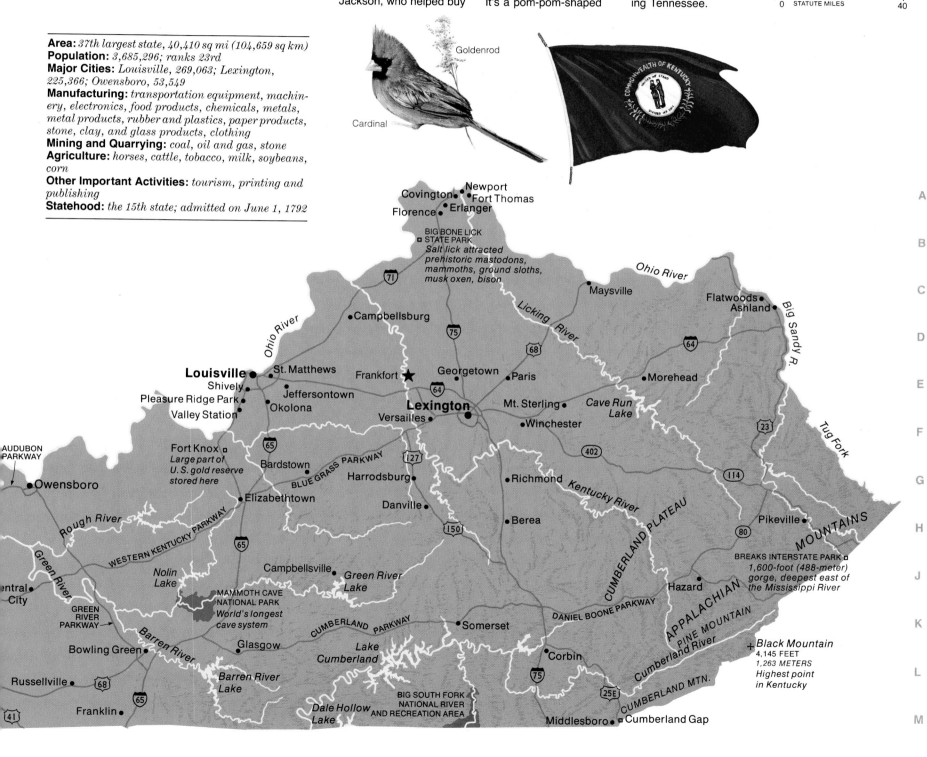

KILOMETERS 0 — 60
STATUTE MILES 0 — 40

Goldenrod

Cardinal

Newport
Covington
Fort Thomas
Florence
Erlanger

Ohio River

BIG BONE LICK STATE PARK
Salt lick attracted prehistoric mastodons, mammoths, ground sloths, musk oxen, bison

Maysville
Flatwoods
Ashland
Big Sandy R.

71

Campbellsburg

Licking River

75

68

64

Ohio River

Louisville
St. Matthews
Shively
Pleasure Ridge Park
Valley Station
Jeffersontown
Okolona

Frankfort
Georgetown
Paris
Morehead

Versailles
Lexington
Mt. Sterling
Cave Run Lake

64

Winchester

23

Tug Fork

AUDUBON PARKWAY

Owensboro

Fort Knox
Large part of U.S. gold reserve stored here

65

Bardstown

BLUE GRASS PARKWAY

127

Harrodsburg

Danville

402

Richmond

Kentucky River

114

CUMBERLAND PLATEAU

Pikeville

MOUNTAINS

Rough River

WESTERN KENTUCKY PARKWAY

65

Elizabethtown

Berea

150

80

BREAKS INTERSTATE PARK
1,600-foot (488-meter) gorge, deepest east of the Mississippi River

Green River

ntral City

GREEN RIVER PARKWAY

Nolin Lake

Campbellsville
Green River Lake

MAMMOTH CAVE NATIONAL PARK
World's longest cave system

CUMBERLAND PARKWAY

Somerset

DANIEL BOONE PARKWAY

Hazard

APPALACHIAN

PINE MOUNTAIN

Bowling Green

Barren River

Glasgow

Lake Cumberland

Corbin

75

Cumberland River

CUMBERLAND MTN.

Black Mountain
4,145 FEET
1,263 METERS
Highest point in Kentucky

Russellville

68

65

Barren River Lake

Dale Hollow Lake

BIG SOUTH FORK NATIONAL RIVER AND RECREATION AREA

25E

CUMBERLAND MTN.

41

Franklin

Middlesboro
Cumberland Gap

A B C D E F G H J K L M N

8 9 10 11 12 13 14 15 16 17 18 19 20 21 22 23 24 25 26

1

2

Kentucky

1 *Hoofs pounding, nostrils flaring, colts head for the homestretch at Keeneland Race Course near Lexington.*

2 *Rolling pastures surround a gabled barn at Calumet Farm near Lexington. The farm has owned eight Kentucky Derby winners, twice as many as any other stable.*

3 *Seamstresses at an underwear factory near Danville gather around to greet a colleague's new baby.*

4 *Draped along the Levisa Fork of the Big Sandy River, Pikeville presides over the state's richest coal-producing region.*

5 *The Tower, a staircase bathed in light, rises 138 steps to challenge visitors exploring Mammoth Cave's passageways.*

3

5

4

West Virginia

West Virginia has its ups and downs. No other eastern state has such rugged land, crisscrossed with hills, mountains, and steep, narrow valleys. Except along river floodplains, very little of its land is flat. West Virginians joke that if you smoothed out the bumps and wrinkles of their state, it would cover more ground than Texas.

West Virginia has quirky boundaries. It has two panhandles and borders that jiggle along rivers and meandering mountain ridges. The skinny northern panhandle resulted when colonial mapmakers, plotting the area of William Penn's Pennsylvania grant from the English king, drew Pennsylvania's western boundary a few miles shy of the Ohio River. The eastern panhandle, reaching to Harpers Ferry, came about during the Civil War, when pro-Union counties in western Virginia broke away from secessionist eastern Virginia in 1861.

Geography had a hand in the breakup. The counties east of the Appalachian Mountains, with their lush fields and plantations worked by slaves, turned east to trade with Europe and the other coastal states. Westerners, on the other hand, could carve out only small, hardscrabble farms amid the thin soils and rough terrain of the mountains. Poor roads and lack of communications left them feeling cut off and ignored by eastern lawmakers. So the westerners turned west to trade, along westward-flowing rivers such as the Ohio and Kanawha. Eventually they grew apart from the flatlanders, quarreling over taxes, slavery, and education.

For a few months the people of West Virginia called their new state Kanawha. The word comes from an Indian term meaning "place of the white stone" and probably refers to the vast salt deposits found in the area. But the name didn't stick, and in 1863 the country's 35th state joined the Union as West Virginia.

Minerals always have been important to West Virginia. Mining and manufacturing today account for nearly half the state's output of goods and services, a bigger percentage than in any other state. Immense seams of soft coal lie under approximately half the state and have been mined since the mid-1800s.

But coal has proved a fickle friend, bringing the state economic bumps and valleys to match its geographical ones. In the peak year, 1949,

In the 1930s, going to the movies could cost a quarter or, on special days, as little as a dime, and helped viewers briefly escape the hardships of the Depression outside the theater doors.

West Virginia's mines produced about 170 million tons of coal and employed 100,000 miners. Then hard times appeared. Some steel mills and factories have shut down, so they don't need coal to stoke their furnaces. Other mills produce steel more efficiently and use less coal. Giant shovels, draglines, and robot rock choppers can rip apart a mountain to get at the buried coal, so there are fewer jobs for miners. Now West Virginia mines produce about the same amount of coal as in 1949 but employ only 25,000 miners.

Underground coal mining is very dangerous. Miners continually face the possibility of explosions and accidents. Black lung disease, caused by long years of inhaling coal dust, kills thousands of miners every year. Worries about acid rain, stream pollution, and ozone holes in the atmosphere caused by burning fossil fuels, such as coal and oil, may also threaten production of high-sulfur coal.

To help weather these economic storms, West Virginia over the last few decades has modernized some of its old steel and glassmaking factories and has also developed new industries. Most of the state's newer jobs, such as banking, insurance, and transportation, are concentrated around its biggest cities. Even so, nearly two-thirds of all West Virginians live in rural areas, on farms and in small communities tucked away in hills and hollows.

Coal is not West Virginia's only important mineral. The state has a lot of salt, too. Long before the first white settlers arrived, Indians hunted deer, bison, and other game attracted to the salt at Great Buffalo Lick near the Kanawha River. Indians traded the salt, and in 1797 Elisha Brooks began selling it to other settlers to make butter and cure meat. Nowadays large chemical companies in the Kanawha and Ohio River Valleys use much of the salt to make chlorine, dyes, paints, plastics, and other products. Charleston, the capital, has a chemical industry that is one of the largest in the United States.

West Virginia also produces oil and gas, and quarries pottery clays. Silica-rich sandstone, found in the eastern panhandle and in several north-central counties, has made the state a major producer of fine glassware. Also, if you have a bag of marbles made in the United States, you can bet they came from West Virginia.

Today about three-quarters of the state is forested. Although the ancient oaks, poplars, and chestnuts have long since fallen to the ax, botanists still consider West Virginia a plant paradise brimming with everything from azaleas and honeysuckles to rarer plants such as coltsfoot, sundew, and bog rosemary.

Area: *41st largest state, 24,232 sq mi (62,758 sq km)*
Population: *1,793,477; ranks 34th*
Major Cities: *Charleston, 57,287; Huntington, 54,844; Wheeling, 34,882*
Mining and Quarrying: *coal, stone, sand and gravel, oil and gas, clay*
Manufacturing: *chemicals, metals, stone, clay, and glass products, metal products, machinery, food products, scientific instruments, electronics*
Agriculture: *cattle, broilers, milk, apples, turkeys, hay, greenhouse and nursery products, hogs*
Other Important Activities: *tourism, printing and publishing*
Statehood: *the 35th state; admitted on June 20, 1863*

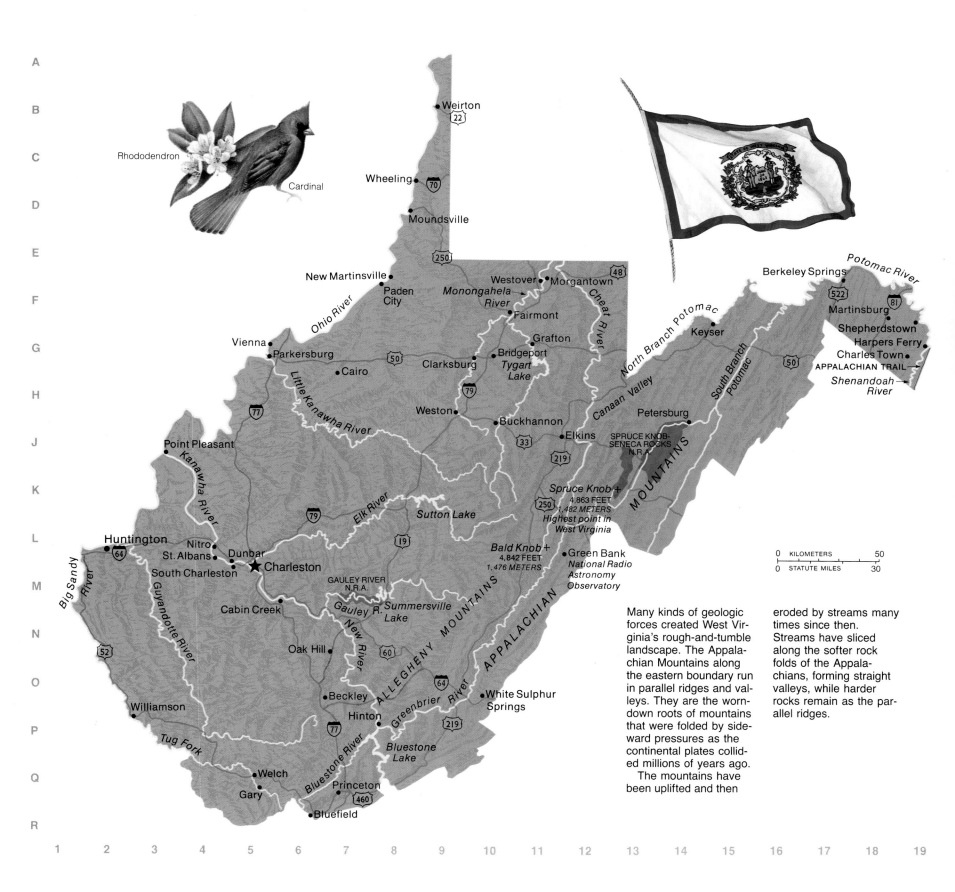

Rhododendron

Cardinal

Weirton
🛡22

Wheeling
🛡70

Moundsville

🛡250

New Martinsville
Paden City
Westover • Morgantown
Monongahela River
Fairmont
🛡48
Cheat River
Berkeley Springs
Potomac River
🛡522
🛡81
Martinsburg
Shepherdstown
Harpers Ferry
Charles Town
APPALACHIAN TRAIL →
Shenandoah River

Ohio River
Vienna
Parkersburg
Cairo
🛡50
Clarksburg
Grafton
Bridgeport
Tygart Lake
North Branch Potomac
Keyser
🛡50
South Branch Potomac

🛡77
Little Kanawha River
🛡79
Weston
Buckhannon
Canaan Valley
Petersburg

Point Pleasant
Kanawha River
🛡33
Elkins
🛡219
SPRUCE KNOB-SENECA ROCKS N.R.A.

MOUNTAINS

Spruce Knob +
4,863 FEET
1,482 METERS
Highest point in West Virginia
🛡250

Elk River
Sutton Lake
🛡79

Huntington
🛡64
Nitro
St. Albans • Dunbar
South Charleston
★ Charleston
🛡19
Bald Knob +
4,842 FEET
1,476 METERS
• Green Bank
National Radio Astronomy Observatory

Big Sandy River
Guyandotte River
Cabin Creek
GAULEY RIVER N.R.A.
Gauley R.
Summersville Lake
New River
🛡60
APPALACHIAN
ALLEGHENY MOUNTAINS

🛡52
Oak Hill
🛡64
• White Sulphur Springs

Williamson
Beckley
Hinton
Greenbrier River
🛡219

🛡77
Bluestone River
Bluestone Lake

Tug Fork

Welch
Gary
Princeton
🛡460

Bluefield

KILOMETERS 0 — 50
STATUTE MILES 0 — 30

Many kinds of geologic forces created West Virginia's rough-and-tumble landscape. The Appalachian Mountains along the eastern boundary run in parallel ridges and valleys. They are the worn-down roots of mountains that were folded by side-ward pressures as the continental plates collided millions of years ago.

The mountains have been uplifted and then eroded by streams many times since then. Streams have sliced along the softer rock folds of the Appalachians, forming straight valleys, while harder rocks remain as the parallel ridges.

1

2

3

4

5

West Virginia

1 *Turning an electronic ear to the stars, radio telescopes along a ridge at Green Bank were among the first to listen, in vain so far, for messages from outer space.*

2 *A miner checks a timber shoring along a coal seam at a mine in Bald Knob while his partner operates a digging machine called a continuous miner.*

3 *Looking much as it did before the Civil War, Harpers Ferry sits amid slopes of the Blue Ridge Mountains at the confluence of the Shenandoah and Potomac Rivers.*

4 *Hot stuff: A worker prepares to tong recycled glass into a furnace at a marble factory in Paden City. West Virginia's three marble factories turn out more than a million of these "glassies" every day.*

5 *Flame azaleas explode into sunbursts of color along a hiking trail in the Allegheny Mountains near White Sulphur Springs.*

Virginia

Without Virginia the United States would be a very different country from the one we know. In 1607 Virginia became the site of the first permanent English settlement in America, Jamestown. Twelve years later the Jamestown settlers established the House of Burgesses, colonial America's first legislative assembly.

As the years rolled by, events crucial to the survival of an independent and united country took place in Virginia: in 1781 the British surrender at Yorktown; in 1865, at Appomattox, the end of the Civil War.

Equally important was the state's contribution of leaders and ideas to a new, young country. Virginians helped lead the American Revolution. They helped draw up the Constitution and the Bill of Rights, upon which the United States government is based. Four of our first five presidents were Virginians: George Washington, Thomas Jefferson, James Madison, and James Monroe.

Virginia is a state of elegant landscapes. In the west are forested mountains and sweeping valleys, in the east, rolling farmlands. Along the coast stretch wild and sandy seashores. The poet Walt Whitman in 1864 wrote: "How full of breadth the scenery, everywhere distant mountains, everywhere convenient rivers."

Four of Virginia's "convenient rivers," the Potomac, Rappahannock, York, and James, flow into Chesapeake Bay. The river mouths made convenient harbors for arriving colonists, and the rivers themselves became convenient highways for shipping tobacco from the flourishing riverside plantations.

The region of the low, sandy plain surrounding the bay is called the Tidewater because its rivers and inlets feel the pull of ocean tides. Much of this area is farming country, with fruits and vegetables trucked to nearby cities.

Hampton Roads, the deepwater harbor formed where the James River empties into the bay, today ranks as one of the country's busiest ports and is home base to almost 150 warships and 110,000 sailors and marines. Cities around the harbor export coal, tobacco, and other goods, while workers at Newport News shipyards turn out vessels ranging from tugboats to nuclear-powered aircraft carriers.

Southside Virginia, as the region south of the

Hampton Institute, founded after the Civil War to educate freed slaves to "lead their people," held classes that ranged from math to bricklaying. Booker T. Washington was a Hampton graduate.

James River is known, also contains the Great Dismal Swamp. George Washington called the 750-square-mile (1,943-sq-km) wetland a "glorious paradise." Now part of it is a wildlife refuge. More than 200 kinds of birds, including hummingbirds, orioles, tanagers, and a dozen warbler species, are found here.

Across the bay lies Virginia's Eastern Shore, part of the Delmarva Peninsula shared with Delaware and Maryland. Much of the peninsula is sparsely populated. Scores of inlets indent the bay side of the Eastern Shore, while on the ocean side barrier beaches, lagoons, and small offshore islands provide a home for wild ponies and snow geese.

West of the Tidewater extends the Piedmont, the rolling foothills of the Appalachian Mountains. A sharp drop-off called the fall line divides the Piedmont from the Atlantic Coastal Plain. Here rivers spill over falls onto the plain. Cities such as Alexandria, Fredericksburg, Richmond, and Petersburg grew along the fall line, where they tapped the power of fast rivers to run mills and factories and served as off-loading points for goods to be moved inland. Richmond,

the state capital, was also the capital of the Confederacy during much of the Civil War.

The Blue Ridge Mountains rise along the western edge of the Piedmont. Roaming the wooded areas are deer and black bears. In the autumn the bears like to raid apple orchards.

Between the Blue Ridge and the Allegheny Mountains lies the Shenandoah Valley. Shenandoah, an Indian word poetically translated as "daughter of the stars," is a fitting name for one of the country's most scenic and fertile valleys. Here farmers raise poultry, livestock, and dairy cattle. Each spring apple blossoms flower over large tracts of land. Limestone makes the valley soil fertile, and water seeping through the limestone bedrock in the nearby mountains has hollowed out caverns and rock formations.

Although Virginia was an agricultural state through most of its history, today its economy depends much less on tobacco and other farm products. Manufacturing and high-tech industries have grown rapidly, because of the state's central location along the eastern seaboard, its extensive transportation network, and the mushrooming growth of the federal government. Many federal facilities are located in Virginia, including the Central Intelligence Agency, centers for space research, and—in the Pentagon building—the headquarters of the Department of Defense and the U. S. Army, Navy, and Air Force. The Pentagon is the world's largest office building, and some 25,000 people work there. Federal and state government agencies account for about a fifth of the state's income.

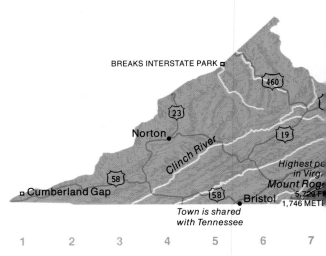

BREAKS INTERSTATE PARK ▫

460

23

Norton ⦁

19

Clinch River

58

▫ Cumberland Gap

58 ⦁ Bristol

Highest po
in Virg
Mount Rog
5,729 F
1,746 METE

*Town is shared
with Tennessee*

1   2   3   4   5   6   7

Virginia is a state divided by Chesapeake Bay. The Delmarva Peninsula, which fronts on the Atlantic Ocean, is linked at its tip to the rest of the state by a 23-mile-long (37-km) combination bridge and tunnel.

In the west, the Appalachian Trail and Skyline Drive share the crest of the Blue Ridge Mountains overlooking the Shenandoah Valley. Here, near Front Royal, archaeologists have unearthed a Paleo-Indian settlement occupied from more than 11,000 years ago until about 8,500 years ago. Dark spots in the earth show where the Indians built shelters.

Area: *36th largest state, 40,767 sq mi (105,586 sq km)*
Population: *6,187,358; ranks 12th*
Major Cities: *Virginia Beach, 393,069; Norfolk, 261,229; Richmond, 203,056*
Manufacturing: *tobacco products, chemicals, transportation equipment, food products, electronics, scientific instruments, paper products, rubber and plastics, lumber and wood products, clothing*
Mining and Quarrying: *coal, stone*
Agriculture: *cattle, broilers, milk, tobacco, turkeys*
Other Important Activities: *federal government, tourism, printing and publishing, fishing*
Statehood: *tenth state; ratified the Constitution on June 25, 1788*

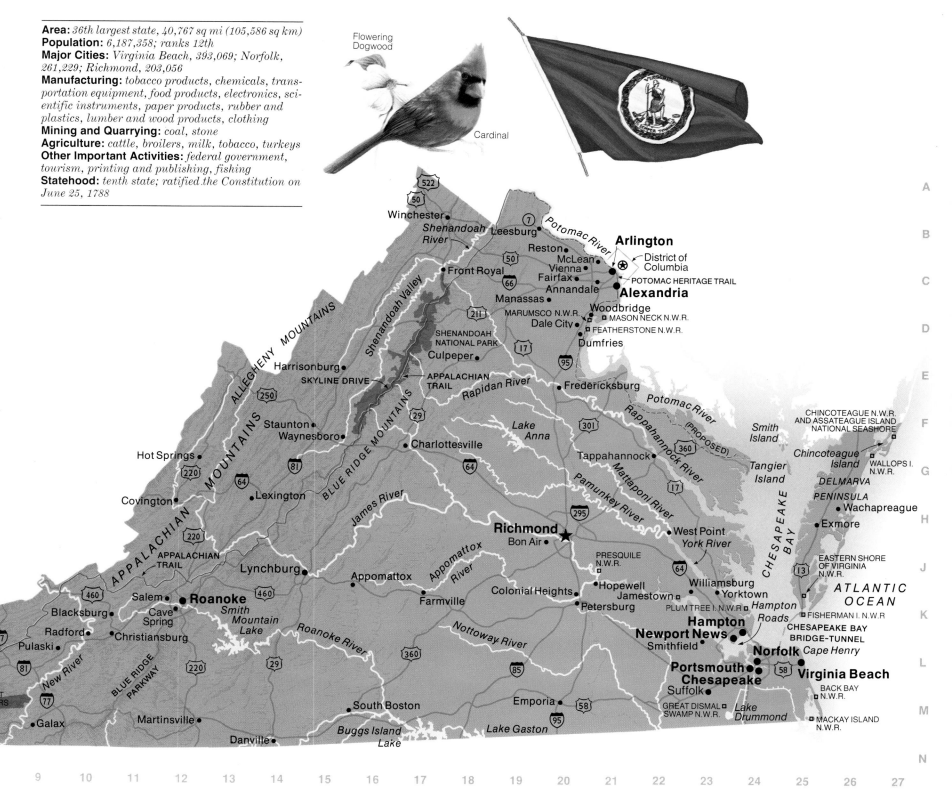

Flowering Dogwood

Cardinal

KILOMETERS 0 — 60
STATUTE MILES 0 — 40

Winchester
522
50
7
Potomac River
Shenandoah River
Leesburg
Reston
Arlington
District of Columbia
McLean
50
Vienna
Front Royal
Fairfax
66
Annandale
POTOMAC HERITAGE TRAIL
Manassas
Alexandria
211
Woodbridge
MARUMSCO N.W.R.
MASON NECK N.W.R.
Dale City
FEATHERSTONE N.W.R.
17
Dumfries
95
SHENANDOAH NATIONAL PARK
Culpeper
Harrisonburg
250
SKYLINE DRIVE
APPALACHIAN TRAIL
Fredericksburg
Potomac River (PROPOSED)
ALLEGHENY MOUNTAINS
Rapidan River
301
360
Smith Island
CHINCOTEAGUE N.W.R. AND ASSATEAGUE ISLAND NATIONAL SEASHORE
Staunton
29
Lake Anna
Rappahannock River
Tangier Island
Chincoteague Island
WALLOPS I. N.W.R.
Waynesboro
Charlottesville
17
Tappahannock
DELMARVA PENINSULA
Hot Springs
81
64
Pamunkey River
Mattaponi River
Wachapreague
220
Lexington
295
West Point
York River
Exmore
Covington
BLUE RIDGE MOUNTAINS
James River
Richmond
Bon Air
PRESQUILE N.W.R.
64
EASTERN SHORE OF VIRGINIA N.W.R.
13
APPALACHIAN TRAIL
220
Lynchburg
Appomattox
Appomattox River
Williamsburg
Jamestown
Yorktown
ATLANTIC OCEAN
460
Hopewell
Colonial Heights
PLUM TREE I. N.W.R.
Hampton Roads
FISHERMAN I. N.W.R.
Salem
Roanoke
460
Farmville
Petersburg
Hampton
CHESAPEAKE BAY BRIDGE-TUNNEL
Blacksburg
Cave Spring
Smith Mountain Lake
Newport News
Cape Henry
Radford
Christiansburg
Roanoke River
Smithfield
Norfolk
7
Pulaski
360
Nottoway River
85
Portsmouth
Chesapeake
58
Virginia Beach
81
220
29
Suffolk
BACK BAY N.W.R.
Galax
Martinsville
South Boston
Emporia
58
GREAT DISMAL SWAMP N.W.R.
Lake Drummond
Danville
Buggs Island Lake
Lake Gaston
95
MACKAY ISLAND N.W.R.

A B C D E F G H J K L M N

9 10 11 12 13 14 15 16 17 18 19 20 21 22 23 24 25 26 27

1

2

3

Virginia

1 *Using a centuries-old technique called pound netting, fishermen of Tangier Island in Chesapeake Bay haul in a catch. Stakes driven into the bottom of the bay hold nets that guide fish into corral-like traps.*

2 *Wisps of fog streak the lowlands of the Shenandoah Valley. Grain fields and apple orchards flourish in this valley, known to Indians, pioneers, and Civil War soldiers.*

3 *A nuclear-powered submarine, looking like a big brother to a flock of balloons, slides down the ways at Newport News.*

4

5

---

4 *A worker checks Smithfield hams hung to cure for six months. These hams are considered delicacies, noted for their robust, tangy flavor.*

5 *The Governor's Palace at Williamsburg, restored to regal splendor after burning to the ground in 1781, was home to seven royalist governors and two elected ones—Patrick Henry and Thomas Jefferson.*

Tennessee

A worker in a Chattanooga hosiery mill in the late 1940s inspects nylon stockings for flaws. During World War II, nylon was used for parachutes, tent fabric, tire cords, and other wartime needs.

Tennessee is three states rolled into one, a long, narrow strip of land reaching from the rumpled ridges of the Great Smoky Mountains to the Mississippi River. Signs near the borders used to welcome motorists to the Three States of Tennessee—East, Middle, and West. That's because geography made each region so different from the other two.

Eastern Tennessee is ruggedly beautiful, a land of mountains row upon row to the horizon. It's hard to imagine, but 300 million years ago these rounded peaks may have thrust as high as the Himalaya. Time and erosion have since done. their work, smoothing ragged summits, building soil, and draping slopes and valleys with forests. Each spring a host of trees and shrubs mounts extravagant displays of blossoms.

Amid these mountains, Tennessee shares Great Smoky Mountains National Park with neighboring North Carolina. The 520,004-acre (210,602-ha) park, the nation's most popular, lies within a day's drive of nearly half the people

in the United States. The Smokies get their name from the bluish haze that sometimes hangs over the peaks and valleys, wisps of water vapor and evaporating plant oils. Indians knew the region as the Place of Blue Smoke. Black bears roam these mountains, as do deer, skunks, and wild boars.

Valleys and hollows lace the mountains, some of them so hidden and isolated that few people ever visit them. When the U. S. government wanted to make atomic bombs during World War II, it picked a secret site that it named Oak Ridge. Until after the war, very few outsiders ever found out about this town of 75,000 scientists and workers. No map showed it; officially it did not exist. Today people in Oak Ridge work in energy research, in the production of nuclear weapons, and in a multibillion-dollar effort to clean up the hazardous wastes from nearly half a century of nuclear weapons production.

Since the war, industry has grown in East Tennessee because of abundant electrical power created by dozens of hydroelectric dams along the winding Tennessee River and its tributaries. Factories in Alcoa produce and recycle aluminum, while Chattanooga turns out steel and textiles, including yarns, clothing, and hosiery.

There is also a dark side to some of East Tennessee's mountains. Remote, hard-to-reach valleys that once concealed illegal whiskey makers, called moonshiners, now harbor marijuana growers. Today illegal marijuana ranks as Tennessee's largest cash crop.

Middle Tennessee, a large, oval-shaped basin surrounded by a rim of highlands, lies west of the mountains and the Cumberland Plateau. Its principal city, Nashville, presides both as the state capital and world capital of country music. More than 200 music publishing and record companies jam a 14-block area of Nashville known as Music Row. Thousands of songwriters and performers, many working as clerks and waiters, crowd into the city, hoping to strike it rich.

Limestone bedrock underlies much of Middle Tennessee, giving the state some of its most fertile farmland. Tobacco, vegetables, and tomatoes flourish here. So do beef and dairy cattle and the Tennessee walking horse, prized for its smooth, easy-riding gait.

Since 1980 industry has come to Middle Ten-

nessee in a big way with the opening of the General Motors Saturn subcompact car factory in Spring Hill and a Nissan plant in Smyrna. Japanese companies have invested in factories and distribution centers that make and sell everything from auto seats and oil filters to television sets and musical instruments.

West Tennessee, an area of fertile flatlands, lies between the Tennessee and Mississippi Rivers. This is mostly farming country dotted with small towns. Memphis, on the Mississippi River, is the financial and commercial hub of most of the lower Mississippi Valley. It is the world's largest cash cotton market, a producer of furniture and steel, and a center of biomedical research and telecommunications.

During the 1920s, Memphis musicians helped to popularize jazz and the blues. Beale Street is the home of the Memphis blues, based on black folk tunes. The street has been restored, and parks and museums grace the city's riverfront.

In the northwest corner of the state lies

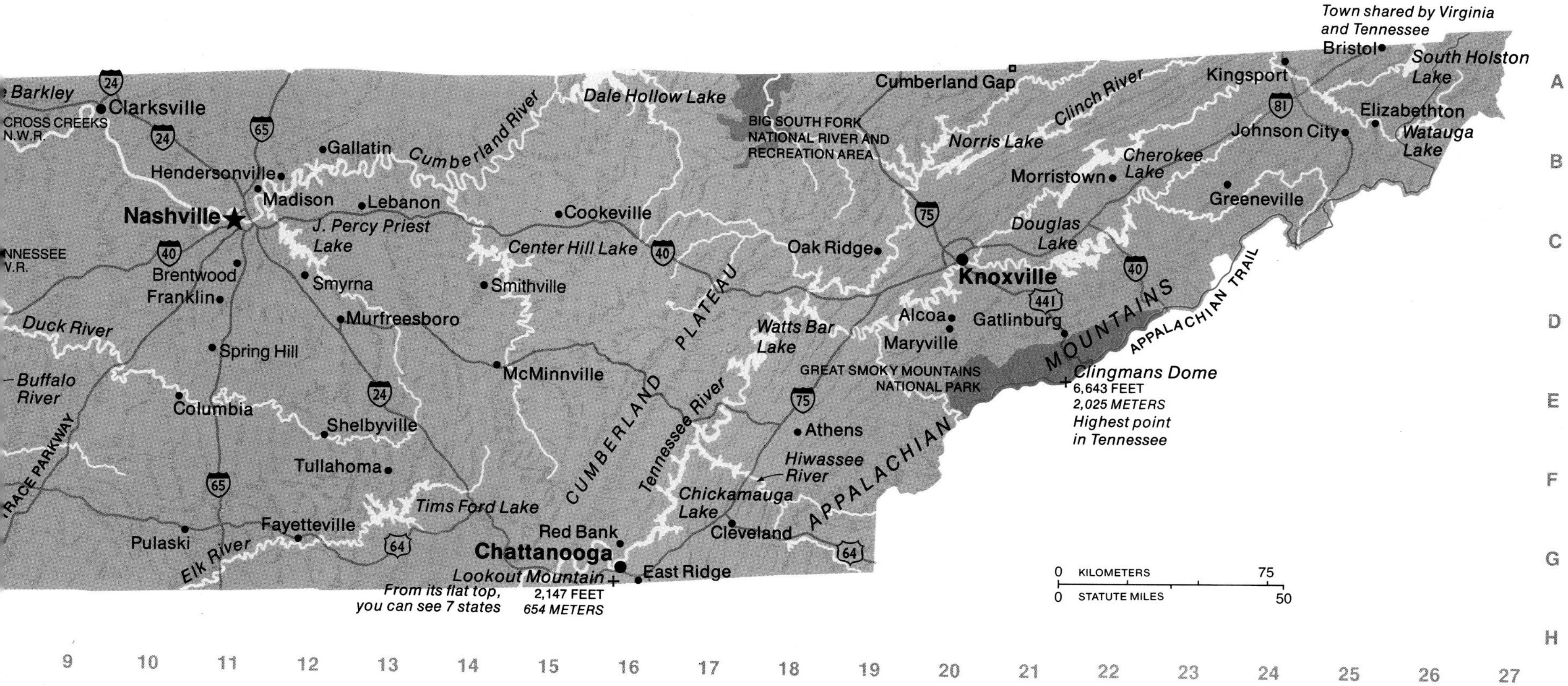
Town shared by Virginia and Tennessee
Bristol
South Holston Lake
Kingsport
Cumberland Gap
Dale Hollow Lake
Barkley
Clarksville
CROSS CREEKS N.W.R.
Clinch River
Elizabethton
Johnson City
Watauga Lake
BIG SOUTH FORK NATIONAL RIVER AND RECREATION AREA
Norris Lake
Cherokee Lake
Morristown
Greeneville
Gallatin
Cumberland River
Hendersonville
Madison
Lebanon
Nashville
Cookeville
J. Percy Priest Lake
Douglas Lake
Center Hill Lake
Oak Ridge
NNESSEE N.W.R.
Brentwood
Franklin
Smyrna
Smithville
Knoxville
PLATEAU
Murfreesboro
Duck River
Alcoa
Gatlinburg
Watts Bar Lake
Maryville
MOUNTAINS
APPALACHIAN TRAIL
Spring Hill
McMinnville
Buffalo River
GREAT SMOKY MOUNTAINS NATIONAL PARK
Clingmans Dome
6,643 FEET
2,025 METERS
Highest point in Tennessee
Columbia
Tennessee River
CUMBERLAND
Athens
Shelbyville
APPALACHIAN
Hiwassee River
Tullahoma
TRACE PARKWAY
Chickamauga Lake
Tims Ford Lake
Fayetteville
Cleveland
Pulaski
Red Bank
Elk River
Chattanooga
East Ridge
Lookout Mountain
2,147 FEET
654 METERS
From its flat top, you can see 7 states
0 KILOMETERS 75
0 STATUTE MILES 50
A
B
C
D
E
F
G
H
9 10 11 12 13 14 15 16 17 18 19 20 21 22 23 24 25 26 27

Tennessee's only large natural lake, Reelfoot. A series of violent earthquakes in 1811 and 1812 created the lake, sloshing water from the Mississippi River into a low-lying area nearby. Today more than 50 kinds of fish swim among the cypress stumps of Reelfoot's shallow water, and the forests around it provide shelter for some 240 bird species, including 200 or so bald eagles that winter here.

Area: *34th largest state, 42,144 sq mi (109,152 sq km)*
Population: *4,877,185; ranks 17th*
Major Cities: *Memphis, 610,337; Nashville, 510,784; Knoxville, 165,121*
Manufacturing: *chemicals, food products, transportation equipment, machinery, electronics, metal products, rubber and plastics, paper products, clothing, stone, clay, and glass products, textiles*
Agriculture: *cattle, milk, soybeans, cotton, greenhouse and nursery products, tobacco*
Mining and Quarrying: *coal, stone, zinc*
Other Important Activities: *tourism, printing and publishing*
Statehood: *the 16th state; admitted June 1, 1796*

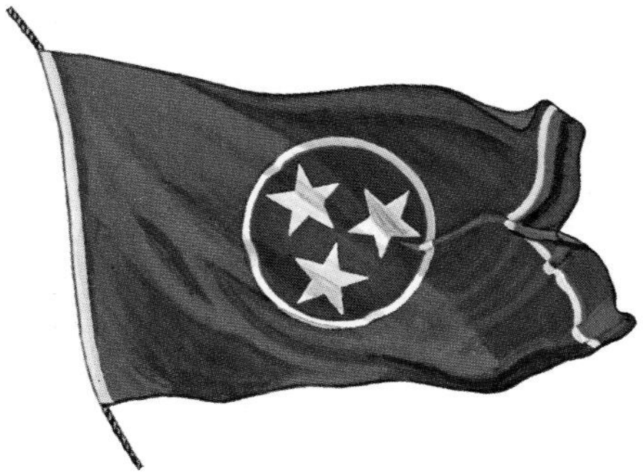

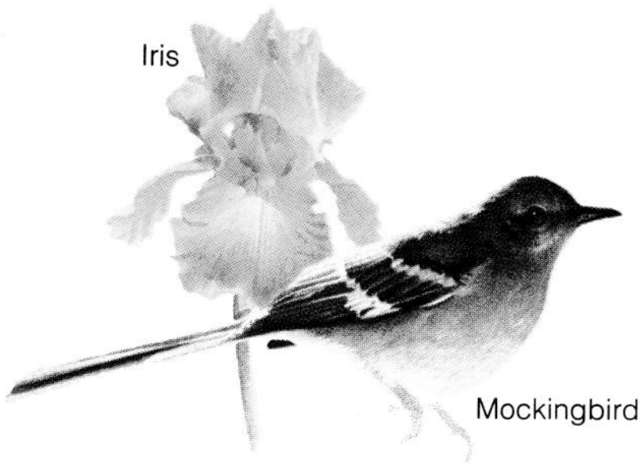
Iris
Mockingbird

No, there are not two Tennessee Rivers in Tennessee. It's the same river. But, from its source in the Appalachian Mountains of eastern Tennessee, the river flows out of the state near Chattanooga before turning north and entering western Tennessee.

Almost all of Tennessee's lakes are reservoirs, created by dams built to control floods and to supply power to the turbines that make electricity. Lakes such as Watts Bar and Douglas in eastern Tennessee are easy to see. They are where the rivers widen out behind dams built across their channels.

1

2

Tennessee

1 *Cumberland Gap, here a spillway for clouds beneath Pinnacle Overlook, also provided a route through the Appalachian Mountains for westward-bound settlers.*

2 *A bluegrass band plucks a tune at the Smithville jamboree, an annual country music contest that takes place in July.*

3 *The University of Tennessee's stadium rises beside the Tennessee River in Knoxville. Over 40,000 students attend classes on several campuses throughout the state.*

3

5

4

4 *A white-gloved worker checks the finish on a new car at a Nissan plant in Smyrna. Japan has invested nearly four billion dollars in Tennessee in nearly a hundred facilities that employ about 20,000 people.*

5 *Processing cotton in Memphis, women mix raw cotton in a hopper. A conveyor belt carries it to a ginning machine, an [en]gin[e] that combs out the seeds.*

North Carolina

A girl tending spools in a spinning mill in 1908 was one of more than 1.7 million youngsters from 10 to 15 years of age working in American factories, fields, and mines.

There was "gold in them thar hills," but the hills weren't in California. They were near Charlotte, North Carolina, in the foothills of the Appalachian Mountains that slant across the western part of the state. Here, in 1799, young Conrad Reed found a big, glittery rock that his family used as a doorstop for their cabin. Years passed before the Reeds learned that the glitter in their doorstop was gold. Other people soon found the deposit from which the rock had come, and until 1848, when gold was discovered in California, North Carolina was the country's biggest gold producer.

North Carolina has some 300 different kinds of minerals that were formed millions of years ago. Minerals mined today include mica, used to insulate electrical appliances; limestone for building; lithium, an important ingredient for making glass and aluminum; kaolin clay, used in the manufacture of dishes; and phosphate rock, used in making fertilizers. The state even has rubies, emeralds, and sapphires.

North Carolina has few deep, natural harbors. Most of the rivers trend north to south. In the days before roads, this limited the rivers'

usefulness as highways into the interior. Along the coast are extensive swamps and marshy areas that discouraged early settlement.

Such geographic conditions meant that very few colonists came to North Carolina directly by ship from Europe. Most came from other colonies, people looking for new lands to farm. Not until Wilmington was founded in 1730 did North Carolina have a port of any size of its own.

A string of long, thin barrier islands known as the Outer Banks fringes much of North Carolina's Atlantic coast. Points of land called capes jut seaward from the islands on the bulge of the continent. Cape Hatteras, Cape Lookout, and Cape Fear are often swept by storms and hurricanes. Over the years the shifting sands and shoals of the Outer Banks have claimed some 2,000 vessels. In 1903, on the treeless, windswept dunes of the Outer Banks near Kitty Hawk, Orville and Wilbur Wright launched their *Flyer*, the world's first successful airplane.

It was near here, on Roanoke Island, that the famous Lost Colony of English settlers landed in 1587, and disappeared altogether by the time a second expedition reached them. Some historians think the colonists may have become part of an Indian tribe. Today the Lumbee Indians, who have spoken English for at least two centuries, claim that some of their ancestors were members of the missing colony.

Many of the Native Americans living in North Carolina are Cherokee. The Cherokee were among the Indians driven west along the Trail of Tears between 1830 and 1840. Some took refuge in the Great Smoky Mountains, and today their descendants live on a reservation in the western part of the state. A Cherokee myth explains the origin of the Smokies. The Great Buzzard, flying over the land, dipped too close to the ground, where his wings brushed out the valleys and pushed up the mountains.

Between the barrier islands and the mainland stretch broad, shallow expanses of water called sounds. The sounds, the rivers feeding into them, and the edges of the ocean provide food and shelter for shrimp, blue crabs, sea trout, and flounder. The northern part of this area, known as the Tidewater, includes the Great Dismal Swamp, which reaches into Virginia.

Farther inland, on drier ground, lie farms

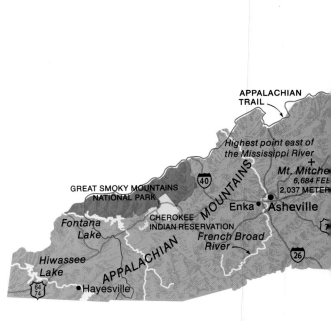

once given over to cotton and now heavily planted in tobacco. Today no other state turns out more tobacco products than North Carolina.

West of the Tidewater lies the Piedmont, a 200-mile-wide (320-km) swath of rolling hills largely covered with oaks, maples, and other hardwoods used to make furniture.

Beyond the Piedmont rise the forested slopes of the Appalachian chain, rugged country that includes the Blue Ridge and Great Smoky Mountains. Most of North Carolina's largest cities are located in the Piedmont, where abundant streams and reservoirs provide hydroelectric power to run mills and factories. In the days before electricity, the same streams powered textile factories run by waterwheels.

In recent years many North Carolina textile plants have shut down because of competition from foreign countries. Even so, the state has some 1,300 textile mills that make about half the nation's hosiery and many of its sheets, towels, and synthetic fabrics. Greensboro has the world's largest mill for weaving denim.

A major road and railroad building effort in

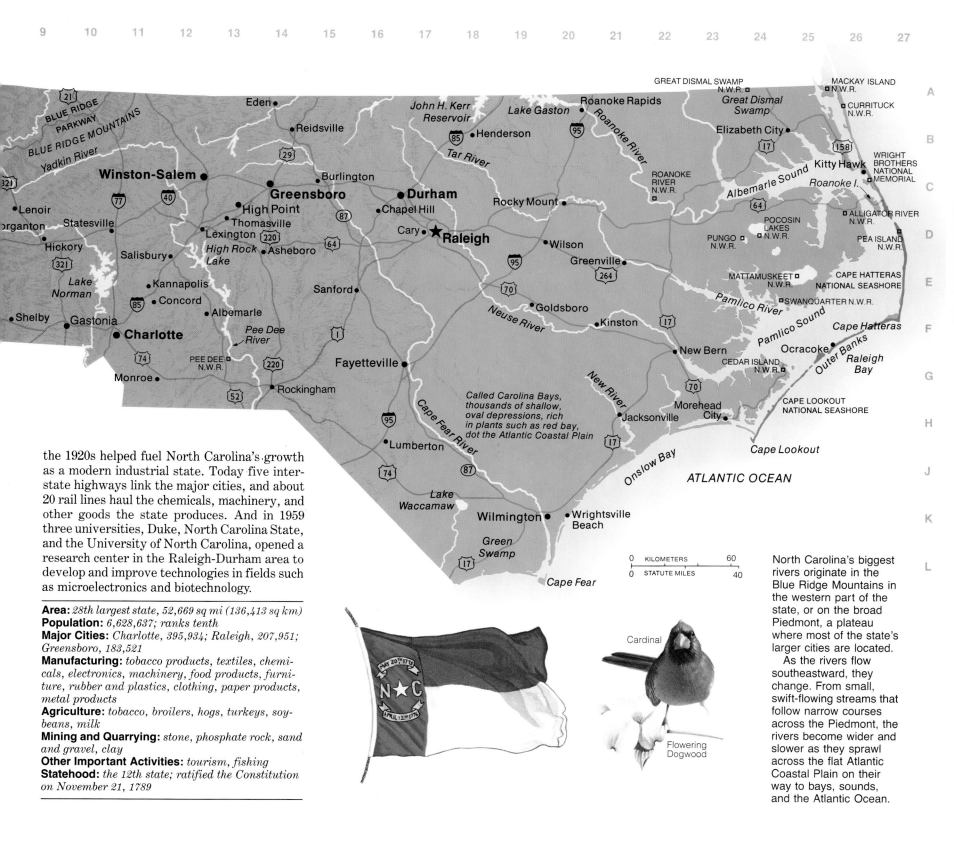

GREAT DISMAL SWAMP N.W.R.

MACKAY ISLAND N.W.R.

Great Dismal Swamp

CURRITUCK N.W.R.

Eden

Roanoke Rapids

Elizabeth City

BLUE RIDGE PARKWAY

BLUE RIDGE MOUNTAINS

Reidsville

John H. Kerr Reservoir

Lake Gaston

Roanoke River

17

WRIGHT BROTHERS NATIONAL MEMORIAL

Yadkin River

21

Henderson

95

Kitty Hawk

158

321

29

Tar River

85

Albemarle Sound

Roanoke I.

Winston-Salem

Burlington

ROANOKE RIVER N.W.R.

64

Greensboro

Durham

Rocky Mount

77 40

High Point

Chapel Hill

POCOSIN LAKES N.W.R.

ALLIGATOR RIVER N.W.R.

Lenoir

Thomasville

87

PUNGO N.W.R.

rganton

Statesville

Lexington 220

Cary ★ **Raleigh**

PEA ISLAND N.W.R.

Hickory

High Rock Lake

Asheboro

64

Wilson

Salisbury

321

Greenville

MATTAMUSKEET N.W.R.

CAPE HATTERAS NATIONAL SEASHORE

Lake Norman

Kannapolis

95

Sanford

264

SWANQUARTER N.W.R.

85

Concord

70

Pamlico River

Shelby

Gastonia

Albemarle

Goldsboro

Pamlico Sound

Cape Hatteras

Charlotte

Pee Dee River

1

Kinston

17

Ocracoke

Raleigh Bay

74

PEE DEE N.W.R.

220

Fayetteville

New Bern

CEDAR ISLAND N.W.R.

Outer Banks

Monroe

52

Rockingham

Called Carolina Bays, thousands of shallow, oval depressions, rich in plants such as red bay, dot the Atlantic Coastal Plain

New River

70

Neuse River

Morehead City

CAPE LOOKOUT NATIONAL SEASHORE

95

Jacksonville

17

Cape Lookout

Cape Fear River

87

Onslow Bay

ATLANTIC OCEAN

the 1920s helped fuel North Carolina's growth as a modern industrial state. Today five interstate highways link the major cities, and about 20 rail lines haul the chemicals, machinery, and other goods the state produces. And in 1959 three universities, Duke, North Carolina State, and the University of North Carolina, opened a research center in the Raleigh-Durham area to develop and improve technologies in fields such as microelectronics and biotechnology.

74

Lumberton

Lake Waccamaw

Wilmington

Wrightsville Beach

Green Swamp

17

Cape Fear

0 KILOMETERS 60

0 STATUTE MILES 40

Area: *28th largest state, 52,669 sq mi (136,413 sq km)*
Population: *6,628,637; ranks tenth*
Major Cities: *Charlotte, 395,934; Raleigh, 207,951; Greensboro, 183,521*
Manufacturing: *tobacco products, textiles, chemicals, electronics, machinery, food products, furniture, rubber and plastics, clothing, paper products, metal products*
Agriculture: *tobacco, broilers, hogs, turkeys, soybeans, milk*
Mining and Quarrying: *stone, phosphate rock, sand and gravel, clay*
Other Important Activities: *tourism, fishing*
Statehood: *the 12th state; ratified the Constitution on November 21, 1789*

Cardinal

Flowering Dogwood

N*C

MAY 20th 1775

APRIL 12th 1776

North Carolina's biggest rivers originate in the Blue Ridge Mountains in the western part of the state, or on the broad Piedmont, a plateau where most of the state's larger cities are located.

As the rivers flow southeastward, they change. From small, swift-flowing streams that follow narrow courses across the Piedmont, the rivers become wider and slower as they sprawl across the flat Atlantic Coastal Plain on their way to bays, sounds, and the Atlantic Ocean.

1

2

3

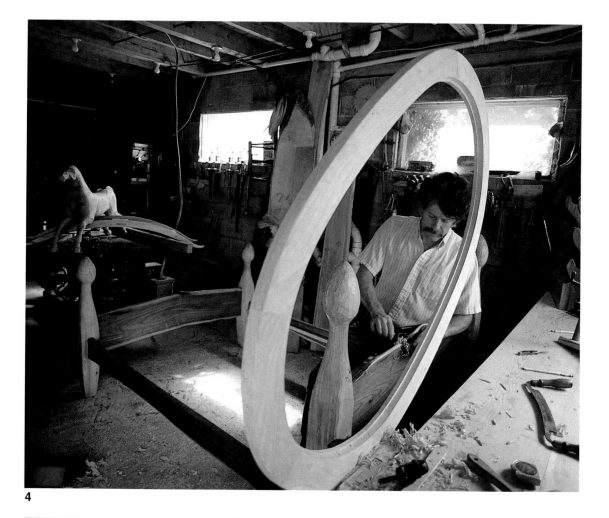

4

5

North Carolina

1 *Ringed by mountains, Asheville lies within easy reach of two national forests and Great Smoky Mountains National Park. Here its city hall stands in the shadow of the slightly taller county courthouse.*

2 *Preparing for a brain scan by a magnetic imaging machine, a technician at Duke University Hospital in Durham aligns the patient's head with help from a laser beam.*

3 *The nation's tallest lighthouse, with 257 steps to the balcony, stands guard over the shifting sands of Cape Hatteras.*

4 *Framed by a wooden oval, a craftsman near Hayesville uses a wood-shaving tool to shape a headboard. North Carolina's hardwood forests have made the state a major producer of fine furniture.*

5 *Buyers follow the distinctive singsong chant of a roving auctioneer as they bid for tobacco at a warehouse in Wilson.*

The Southeast

Most of the flat land shown in this painting was not here 600 million years ago. Its roots were attached to an ancestral continental plate known as Gondwanaland. Then, about 350 million years ago, ancestral North America, or Laurasia, and Gondwanaland began to bump together. The slow-motion collision broke or bent or melted rock and thrust up massive mountain ranges, including the Appalachians. When the two plates separated, a chunk of Gondwanaland stayed behind, stuck to North America. That chunk makes up parts of the broad, flat, low-lying Gulf and Atlantic Coastal Plains that swing through the southeastern states from the foot of the Appalachian Mountains—the Piedmont—to the Mississippi River. It also includes the flipper-shaped peninsula we know as Florida.

Part of the Coastal Plains dips beneath the waves and extends out to sea like a massive shelf bordering the continent. Called a continental shelf, the underwater part of the plains was largely dry land during the Ice Age, when sea levels were much lower because more water was frozen in glaciers. Woolly mammoths and saber-toothed cats roamed the continental shelf along Florida's west coast. Sometimes divers and fishermen bring up their bones from offshore, and geologists find their remains onshore.

Florida, a vast limestone peninsula that was once sea bottom, is part of an even larger underwater ledge that in places pops above the waves as islands in the Atlantic Ocean. Much of Florida's limestone is porous and saturated with fresh water, making the state a land of lakes.

South of the biggest lake spreads the Everglades, a vast, shallow sheet of fresh water. The water, only about six inches (15 cm) deep, moves southward so slowly that its flow is barely visible. Modern-day attempts to drain wetlands and control water supply have in some places disrupted the normal water flow, enabling salty seawater to penetrate inland and contaminate sources of fresh water.

A broad ridge of sand along the Atlantic shore, the remains of an old barrier island, provides just enough elevation to lift Miami and other seacoast cities out of the swamps.

Islands and long, thin offshore sandbars fringe much of the coast from north of Savannah to the Mississippi Delta. Yachts and fishing boats thread between the islands and the mainland, protected from storms and ocean waves. Boaters can travel this route, called the Intracoastal Waterway, much of the distance from Texas, through the Florida Keys, to Cape Cod.

Along the Gulf coast, the Mississippi River comes to an end. Sluggish and laden with silt and clay, a broth rich in sediments drained from 31 states and 2 Canadian provinces, the river slows and drops its load in a broad "bird-foot delta" that splays into three main channels as the river empties into the Gulf of Mexico.

Each year the river deposits millions of tons of mud, sand, and grit, enough to bulge Louisiana's shoreline 300 yards (270 m) seaward every year and to weigh it down so that it sinks a bit each year. New Orleans stands on land built up by the river within the last few thousand years—some of the nation's newest real estate. But today, as part of the delta reaches the outer edge of the continental shelf, the Mississippi's land-building days may dwindle as sediments sweep into the deep waters of the Gulf.

The Mississippi Valley, a floodplain varying from 25 to 125 miles (40 to 200 km) wide, merges with the Gulf Coastal Plain in a watery world of salt marshes and sluggish backwaters called bayous. Nearly a fifth of the continent's wild ducks and geese take refuge here in the winter, resting and feeding on a rich assortment of plants and insects. The valley, a downward bend in Earth's crust, is filled with fertile sediments, a gift delivered over the years by the river Indians called Missi Sipi—"father of waters."

APPALACHIAN MOUNTAINS

Atlanta

Montgomery

Savannah

St. Petersburg

Everglades

Miami

SOUTH CAROLINA
GEORGIA
ALABAMA
FLORIDA
MISSISSIPPI
LOUISIANA
ARKANSAS

Florida Keys

Arkansas

An Ozark hill woman during the 1940s makes and sells rag dolls whose faces are inspired by those of people in her community. Other Ozark dolls have heads made of dried apples or carved nuts.

The smallest state between the Mississippi River and the Pacific Ocean, Arkansas shares many characteristics of its neighboring regions. Midwestern Missouri borders the north. Solidly of the South, Louisiana, Mississippi, and Tennessee adjoin the south and east. And Texas and Oklahoma, with their southwestern flavor, border the west.

A diagonal line from the southwest to the northeast corner of Arkansas divides highlands from lowlands. West and north of the line lie the Ozark Plateau and the Ouachita Mountains. To the east and south sprawl the fertile valley of the Mississippi River and part of the wide Gulf Coastal Plain, a region that reaches into Arkansas from Texas and Louisiana and extends eastward to merge with Florida and the Atlantic Coastal Plain.

The Ozark Plateau, often called the Ozark Mountains, is an area of high tablelands eroded into rugged hills and deep valleys by swift streams. Small farmsteads nestle in isolated Ozark valleys. Settlers migrated there from the southern Appalachians in the 19th century. They and their descendants lived a hard, independent existence, farming the thin soil. But now new opportunities have come to the Ozarks. Arkansas has developed the country's largest broiler-chicken industry. Companies supply chicks and feed to farmers on credit. The farmers raise the fowl and then sell them for market.

Today, many tourists and retired people come to enjoy the natural beauty of the Ozarks. Young people often leave for the towns and cities, but Arkansas's population is still heavily rural, with almost half dwelling in the country or small towns and half in urban areas. In the Ouachita Mountains, the parallel ridges are wooded with pine and hardwood. These and other commercial forest areas provide jobs for people such as lumberjacks, pulp-mill workers, furniture makers, and workers who manufacture milk cartons and other paper products.

For thousands of years Indians bathed in the hot water of the many springs that rise in the Ouachitas. The Indians believed that the vapors were the warming breath of the Great Spirit and that their ancestors had been created in the springs. Now their sacred place has become Hot Springs National Park, the smallest and the only urban national park in the United States. At Hot Springs, water from mineral-carrying springs is piped into the town's bathhouses and fountains. Each year more than a million people visit the springs seeking relaxation or relief from arthritis and other aches and pains.

Separating the Ouachitas from the Ozark Plateau, the Arkansas River creates a broad, fertile valley, ideal for growing crops and raising cattle and poultry. Valuable deposits of coal and natural gas lie under the valley floor.

In the 18th century, French explorers from New Orleans traveled the Arkansas River. Near the middle of today's state they found a rocky outcrop on the south bank near a good crossing place. Eventually the landmark became known as *la petite roche*, the little rock. A settlement grew near the ford and took its name from the outcrop. Today Little Rock is the state capital and, with neighboring North Little Rock, a center of business and industry.

Until recently, the Arkansas carried little river traffic because it was prone to floods and to silting and snags that made navigation hazardous. Then, in 1971, with the completion of a system of locks and dams, the river opened to barge traffic that could carry goods such as sand and gravel, chemical fertilizers, or oil from the Mississippi River as far west as Tulsa, Oklahoma.

All river systems in Arkansas drain into the Mississippi. The Mississippi and its tributaries blanket the eastern third of Arkansas with alluvium, rich soil deposited by flowing water. This was cotton country in the 19th and early 20th centuries. Now fields of rice and soybeans create broad swaths of emerald green across the wide, flat valley. Arkansas grows more rice than any other state. Birds flying down the Mississippi Flyway on their fall migrations fatten on the nutritious grain during stopovers.

The western Gulf Coastal Plain possesses much of the state's mineral wealth, including natural gas and petroleum deposits. The sandy soil also supports vast pine forests and good grazing for cattle.

Attracting more industry to the state and expanding tourism will increase the prosperity of Arkansas. Nature has provided magnificent scenery and recreational opportunities, especially in the Ozarks and Ouachitas. Damming rivers for hydroelectricity and flood control has multiplied the number of lakes for fishing and boating. And, once in a while, nature unaided adds to its own bounty: A river will change course, cutting off an old, looping channel to form a new, crescent-shaped oxbow lake.

Area: *27th largest state, 53,187 sq mi (137,754 sq km)*
Population: *2,350,725; ranks 33rd*
Major Cities: *Little Rock, 175,795; Fort Smith, 72,798; North Little Rock, 61,741*
Manufacturing: *food products, electronics, paper products, metal products, machinery, lumber and wood products, chemicals*
Agriculture: *broilers, soybeans, rice, cattle, cotton, eggs, wheat, turkeys*
Mining and Quarrying: *oil and gas, sand and gravel, bromine, bauxite, stone*
Other Important Activities: *tourism*
Statehood: *the 25th state; admitted June 15, 1836*

Arkansas has no foothills. The state's highlands, the Ouachita Mountains and the Ozark Plateau, rise almost without warning from plains that are nearly flat. East of the highlands is an alluvial plain, part of a valley formed by the Mississippi River as it shifted its channel over the ages and covered bottomlands with silt.

The state has two types of highlands. The older Ozarks are an uplifted plateau carved by streams and rivers. The younger Ouachitas, by contrast, are folded sediments pushed into parallel ridges by colliding continental plates.

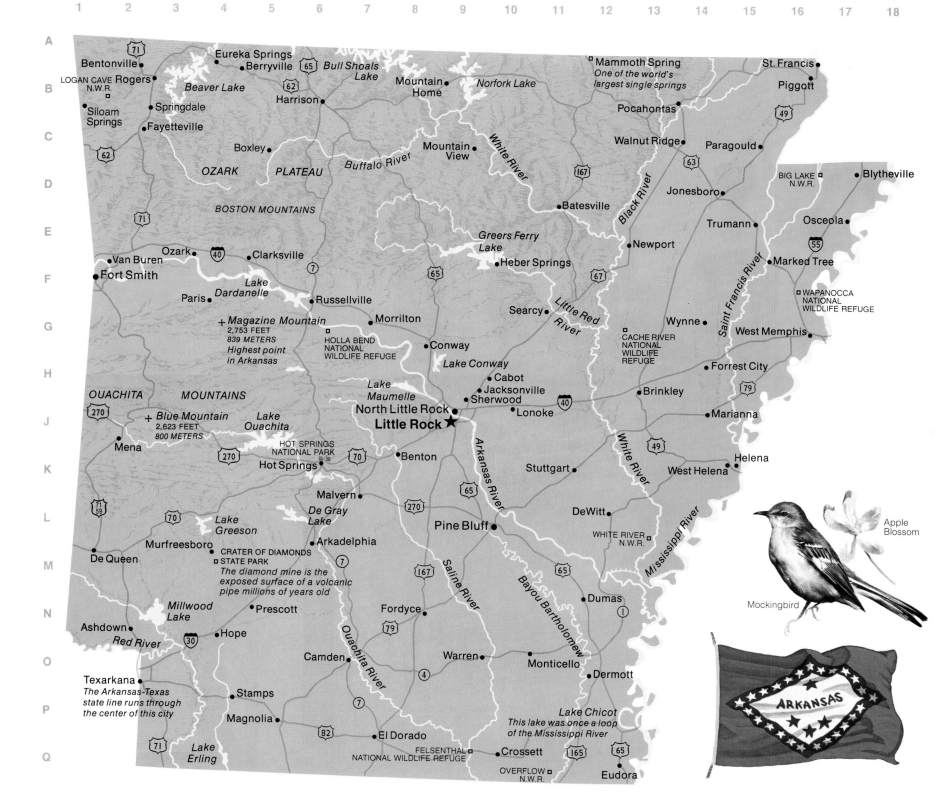

0 KILOMETERS 50
0 MILES 40

1 2 3 4 5 6 7 8 9 10 11 12 13 14 15 16 17 18

A

Bentonville
71
Eureka Springs
Berryville
65
Bull Shoals Lake
Mammoth Spring
One of the world's largest single springs
St. Francis

B
LOGAN CAVE N.W.R.
Rogers
62
Harrison
Mountain Home
Norfork Lake
Pocahontas
Piggott
49

Siloam Springs
Springdale
Beaver Lake

C
62
Fayetteville
Boxley
Buffalo River
Mountain View
White River
Walnut Ridge
Paragould
63
Blytheville

OZARK PLATEAU

D
BOSTON MOUNTAINS
Batesville
Black River
Jonesboro
BIG LAKE N.W.R.
Osceola

E
71
Ozark
40
Clarksville
Greers Ferry Lake
Newport
Trumann
55
Marked Tree

Van Buren
Fort Smith
7
65
Heber Springs
67
Saint Francis River

F
Paris
Lake Dardanelle
Russellville
Morrilton
Searcy
Little Red River
Wynne
West Memphis
WAPANOCCA NATIONAL WILDLIFE REFUGE

G
Magazine Mountain
2,753 FEET
839 METERS
Highest point in Arkansas
HOLLA BEND NATIONAL WILDLIFE REFUGE
Conway
Lake Conway
Cabot
CACHE RIVER NATIONAL WILDLIFE REFUGE
Forrest City

H
OUACHITA MOUNTAINS
Lake Maumelle
Jacksonville
Sherwood
Lonoke
40
Brinkley
79

J
270
Blue Mountain
2,623 FEET
800 METERS
Lake Ouachita
North Little Rock
Little Rock
Marianna

Mena
HOT SPRINGS NATIONAL PARK
70
Benton
Arkansas River
White River
49
Helena

K
Hot Springs
65
Stuttgart
West Helena

L
70
Lake Greeson
Malvern
De Gray Lake
270
DeWitt
Mississippi River

De Queen
Murfreesboro
Arkadelphia
Pine Bluff
WHITE RIVER N.W.R.

M
De Queen
CRATER OF DIAMONDS STATE PARK
The diamond mine is the exposed surface of a volcanic pipe millions of years old
7
167
65

N
Millwood Lake
Prescott
Fordyce
79
Saline River
Bayou Bartholomew
Dumas
1

Ashdown
Red River
30
Hope

O
Texarkana
The Arkansas-Texas state line runs through the center of this city
Camden
7
4
Warren
Monticello
Dermott

P
Stamps
Ouachita River
Lake Chicot
This lake was once a loop of the Mississippi River

Magnolia
7

Q
71
Lake Erling
82
El Dorado
FELSENTHAL NATIONAL WILDLIFE REFUGE
Crossett
165
65
Eudora
OVERFLOW N.W.R.

Apple Blossom

Mockingbird

ARKANSAS

1

Arkansas

1 *A country school and a Baptist church share a quiet corner in an Ozark valley. Such serenity appeals to a growing number of tourists and harried city folk.*

2 *Woodcarvers at the Ozark Folk Center in Mountain View preserve a centuries-old craft. People from across the U.S. come here to learn traditional handicrafts, as well as Ozark folklore and music.*

3 *An experiment at the University of Arkansas in Fayetteville envelops a superconductor in wisps of frigid nitrogen. This superconductor can suspend magnets above and below it. In the future such superconductors may be used in electric cables and in trains that speed quietly above their rails on a magnetic cushion.*

2

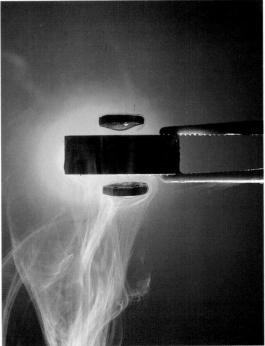

3

4

5

4 *Rice is harvested near West Memphis in the fertile Mississippi Valley. Arkansas grows one-third of all U. S. rice, some of which goes into cereal, flour, and vinegar.*

5 *Chicks gather around a water dish in a broiler house. Arkansas exports much of its dark meat to the Japanese, who prefer it to the white that most Americans buy.*

Mississippi

Choctaw Indians sit for a portrait in 1908. By 1910 only about 1,000 Mississippi Choctaw remained of the some 20,000 who lived here when Hernando de Soto and other Europeans arrived.

Before the Civil War, King Cotton ruled Mississippi. Steamboats on the rivers were heaped high with bales of the fluffy white fiber. On the plantations, young women in hoopskirts and crinolines sat under shady magnolia trees. Elegant young men galloped on horseback, small dogs yipping alongside. Papa stood on the white-columned porch, surveying his domain.

Such scenes tell only part of the story. They hark back to a time when the social world of Mississippi, as of many other parts of the country, was strictly divided. The lives of plantation owners were very different from the struggles of poor white farmers and black slaves.

The Civil War changed many things, but poor whites and poor blacks still struggled. With slavery abolished, the plantation system became one of tenant farming. Sharecroppers, both black and white, were given land to work, seeds, and tools in exchange for a hefty portion of the harvest owed to the landowner.

The rich, fertile soil that produced cotton was laid down over millennia by the Mississippi River. Each year floods sent tons of alluvium, riverborne sand and silt, over the banks. In time, soil 150 feet (45 m) deep formed on the Mississippi's alluvial plain, or the delta, as the local people call it. Topsoil, the layer from which plants get most of their nutrients, reaches a depth of 25 feet (8 m) in some places.

The alluvial plain, narrow along the state's southwestern border, widens north of Vicksburg to encompass the basin between the Mississippi and Yazoo Rivers. Levees—barriers of earth, sandbags, rock, concrete, or steel—line the banks and usually keep the rivers from overflowing. Delta farmers still raise cotton, but they also grow soybeans, rice, and wheat and have added a new, finny "crop." In purposely flooded old cotton fields, catfish fatten on grain, like livestock, until they are ready to process and ship out. Mississippi leads the country in meeting the demand for this favorite. Many delta families, for whom there often is no other work, can make some money by working in plants that process catfish and rice.

East of the delta lies the eastern Gulf Coastal Plain. Its northern part is a land of gently rolling hills and woodlands. The northeast also contains a stretch of land known as the Black Prairie, an extension of Alabama's black belt. Here corn, hay, and livestock are raised in the rich, dark soil that gives the region its name.

Three major Indian groups once lived in Mississippi: Choctaw, Chickasaw, and Natchez. Today, about 8,000 Indians remain. These are mostly Choctaw, and most of them live on or near their reservation near Philadelphia. Today's Indians are descendants of those who refused to leave their homes when the U. S. government forced the southeastern Indians westward on the march known as the Trail of Tears. One Choctaw who stayed behind gave this reason: "In those aged pines you hear the ghosts of the departed. Their ashes are here, and we have been left to protect them." Not far from Philadelphia are a cave and a mound that Choctaw revere as the birthplace of their tribe.

Jackson, the state capital, sits on the bluffs of the Pearl River and near the Natchez Trace, a wilderness road used by Indians, settlers, and traders. One in eight Mississippians lives in Jackson, and the percentage is growing as manufacturing continues to overtake farming and as people move to urban areas. Even so, Mississippi is a highly rural state, with more than half of its people living in the country or in small towns. Nearly all of Mississippi's residents were born in the United States; 35 percent are black, a higher proportion than in any other state.

About half of Mississippi is forested. Southern pine grows abundantly in the southern part of the Gulf Coastal Plain. By 1930, though, much of the state's timber had been depleted. Since then, reforestation programs and careful harvesting ensure survival of the forest industry and wildlife habitats.

A warm, sunny climate, abundant seafood, and deepwater ports have attracted settlers and vacationers to the coast along the Gulf of Mexico for nearly 300 years. Biloxi, Mississippi's oldest permanent settlement, was founded by the French in 1699 and served for a time as capital of their New World empire. Mississippian Jefferson Davis, the president of the Confederacy, spent his last years here at his estate, Beauvoir, overlooking the Gulf.

The Gulf coast's population is growing rapidly. Jobs in manufacturing, shipping, shipbuilding, and the petroleum industry draw residents from all over the state. The United States military frequently awards large contracts to the shipyards of Pascagoula. Huge catches of seafood are taken from the Gulf, including tons of its famous shrimp. Bananas, melons, coconuts, and pineapples pass through a terminal at Gulfport that is specialized to handle fruit.

Area: *32nd largest state, 47,689 sq mi (123,515 sq km)*
Population: *2,573,216; ranks 31st*
Major Cities: *Jackson, 196,637; Biloxi, 46,319; Greenville, 45,226*
Manufacturing: *food products, transportation equipment, electronics, lumber and wood products, paper products, clothing, furniture, chemicals, machinery*
Agriculture: *cotton, broilers, soybeans, cattle, aquaculture, rice, milk*
Mining and Quarrying: *oil and gas, sand and gravel, clay*
Other Important Activities: *fishing*
Statehood: *the 20th state; admitted December 10, 1817*

Mississippi's western boundary looks like a battle between bedsprings, with twists and curlicues all over the place. Some curlicues, such as Lake Mary and Moon Lake, are oxbow lakes. Both were formed when the Mississippi cut through the narrow neck of a loop and abandoned its old channel, leaving crescent-shaped lakes.

The tattered-looking western boundary results from shifting river channels. These changes, called avulsions, often leave chunks of neighboring states on the wrong side of the river but do not alter ownership of the land.

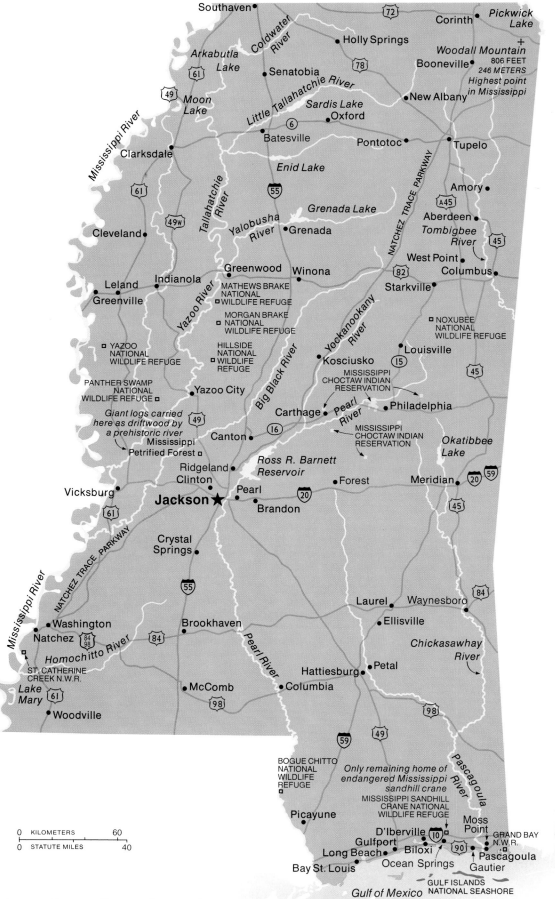

Mockingbird

Magnolia

Southaven

Holly Springs

Corinth

Pickwick Lake

Arkabutla Lake

Coldwater River

72

Woodall Mountain
806 FEET
246 METERS
Highest point in Mississippi

Senatobia

Booneville

61

49

Moon Lake

78

New Albany

Little Tallahatchie River

Sardis Lake
Oxford

6

Batesville

Pontotoc

Tupelo

Mississippi River

Clarksdale

Enid Lake

Amory

A45

61

55

Aberdeen

49W

Tallahatchie River

Grenada Lake

Tombigbee River

45

Cleveland

Yalobusha River

Grenada

West Point

Columbus

Leland

Indianola

Greenwood

Winona

82

Starkville

Greenville

MATHEWS BRAKE NATIONAL WILDLIFE REFUGE

Yockanookany River

NOXUBEE NATIONAL WILDLIFE REFUGE

Yazoo River

MORGAN BRAKE NATIONAL WILDLIFE REFUGE

YAZOO NATIONAL WILDLIFE REFUGE

HILLSIDE NATIONAL WILDLIFE REFUGE

Big Black River

Kosciusko

Louisville

15

45

PANTHER SWAMP NATIONAL WILDLIFE REFUGE

Yazoo City

MISSISSIPPI CHOCTAW INDIAN RESERVATION

Giant logs carried here as driftwood by a prehistoric river

49

Carthage

Pearl River

Philadelphia

Mississippi Petrified Forest

16

Canton

MISSISSIPPI CHOCTAW INDIAN RESERVATION

Okatibbee Lake

Ross R. Barnett Reservoir

Ridgeland
Clinton

20

Forest

Meridian

20

59

Vicksburg

Jackson ★

Pearl

Brandon

45

61

Natchez Trace Parkway

Crystal Springs

Mississippi River

84

55

Laurel

Waynesboro

Washington

Brookhaven

Ellisville

Natchez

84 98

Homochitto River

84

Chickasawhay River

ST. CATHERINE CREEK N.W.R.

Hattiesburg

Petal

Lake Mary

61

McComb

Columbia

98

Pearl River

98

59

49

Pascagoula River

BOGUE CHITTO NATIONAL WILDLIFE REFUGE

Only remaining home of endangered Mississippi sandhill crane

Picayune

MISSISSIPPI SANDHILL CRANE NATIONAL WILDLIFE REFUGE

Moss Point

GRAND BAY N.W.R.

D'Iberville

10

Gulfport

90

Long Beach

Biloxi

Pascagoula
Gautier

Bay St. Louis

Ocean Springs

GULF ISLANDS NATIONAL SEASHORE

Gulf of Mexico

0   KILOMETERS   60

0   STATUTE MILES   40

A B C D E F G H J K L M N O P Q R S T

1 2 3 4 5 6 7 8 9 10 11 12

1

Mississippi

1 *A girl tosses a ball in front of D'Evereux, her family home. Built in 1840, the columned house is one of many Greek Revival buildings surviving in the Natchez area.*

2 *Young men and women in costumes of the Old South waltz at the annual Confederate Pageant soiree in Natchez. The men are dressed as cadets from historic Jefferson College in nearby Washington.*

2

3

4

5

3 *The paddle wheeler* Delta Queen, *built in 1926, docks at Natchez-Under-the-Hill, once a rowdy section of town where rivermen and outlaws drank and gambled.*

4 *A combine harvests cotton along the Yazoo River in the rich delta region. Mechanical pickers can do the work of many people.*

5 *A rooster plays king-of-the-mountain on a henhouse plank after a flood near Vicksburg. The Mississippi sometimes overflows despite levees built to contain it.*

Alabama

In a cave in the northeastern corner of Alabama lie the remains of some of the area's earliest residents. Not only their bones but also their food, pottery, tools, and weapons give us clues to the way these prehistoric hunters and gatherers lived, camping in caves throughout the area in the fall and winter and sometimes year-round. The record of human habitation in Russell Cave is the longest. It was used for some 8,000 years, until, about a thousand years ago, the Indians became farmers and settled down in villages.

Not far from Russell Cave, the space age appears. In 1960 NASA opened the George C. Marshall Space Flight Center in Huntsville. The center's rockets sent the first American astronaut into space, and its Saturn rockets put men on the moon. Unlike other parts of the state, Huntsville draws residents from all over the country to work in its space-related industries.

The Appalachian range extends its southernmost ridges and valleys, with their mineral wealth, into northeastern Alabama. During the Civil War, the area's iron ore went into most of the shells, shot, and rifles used by the Confederacy. The Appalachians also hold coal and limestone which, together with iron, are needed to make steel. The Birmingham region filled with steel mills, creating jobs that attracted many rural Alabamians. Now cheaper iron ore from Venezuela has closed many of the iron mines, and steel has been eclipsed as an area employer by the University of Alabama's medical research center, as well as by government jobs.

Alabama's early wealth was built on enormous cotton crops grown on slave-worked plantations. Central Alabama has the richest agricultural land, a strip of rich, dark soil known as the black belt. But no matter how fertile the soil, a single crop grown season after season eventually depletes the soil's nutrients, and cotton did this. Finally it took the disastrous invasion of the cotton-destroying boll weevil in the early 1900s to convince Alabama farmers to diversify their crops. Cotton remains a major crop, but is now surpassed by peanuts. Cattle and poultry raising have also taken over many cotton fields. So grateful were the people of the town of Enterprise for the lesson taught by the boll weevil that they erected a statue to the long-snouted insect.

More than two-thirds of Alabama is forested, mostly with oak and pine. Tree farming by corporations that own 21 percent of the land replenishes the timber cut for pulp, paper, and lumber. The forest products industry is now the state's chief source of income.

For most of Alabama's history, the northwestern corner was a depressed region. People there worked hard to raise a few crops and enjoyed few amenities. The creation of the Tennessee Valley Authority by the federal government in the 1930s brought cheap and plentiful electricity to the area by damming the Tennessee River. A side benefit was a multitude of beautiful lakes offering residents and visitors choice fishing, boating, and other water sports.

In 1985 another project was completed. This one linked the Tennessee and Tombigbee river systems so that goods from the interior could reach Alabama's only port, Mobile. The building of the Tenn-Tom waterway moved more earth than the construction of the Panama Canal. It also gave Mobile access to the network of waterways in the eastern United States.

Mobile sits on the low Gulf Coastal Plain at Mobile Bay, an inlet of the Gulf of Mexico. In its architecture, gardens, and street names, Mobile bears witness to its early days of French and Spanish settlement. Today deeply dredged shipping lanes enable oceangoing vessels to berth at Mobile's docks. Cargoes leaving the port include steel, soybeans, lumber, and oil and natural gas from the state's southern region.

More than 60 percent of Alabama's population lives in cities and towns. About one-fourth of the state's residents are blacks. Some of the greatest gains of the civil rights movement of the 1950s and '60s were made in Alabama. It was here that a young Martin Luther King, Jr., led a protest against the law that jailed Rosa Parks, a black Montgomery seamstress, for not giving up her bus seat to a white man. Voting rights for blacks all over the South were won partly as the result of efforts concentrated in Alabama.

In 1902 George Washington Carver teaches at Tuskegee Institute, a black college then headed by Booker T. Washington. Carver's pioneering research helped revolutionize Southern agriculture.

Area: *29th largest state, 51,705 sq mi (133,915 sq km)*
Population: *4,040,587; ranks 22nd*
Major Cities: *Birmingham, 265,968; Mobile, 196,278; Montgomery, 187,106*
Manufacturing: *paper products, chemicals, metals, textiles, clothing, machinery, rubber and plastics, food products, transportation equipment, electronics, metal products, lumber and wood products*
Mining and Quarrying: *coal, oil and gas, stone*
Agriculture: *broilers, cattle, greenhouse and nursery products, peanuts, eggs, cotton, soybeans*
Other Important Activities: *federal government, fishing*
Statehood: *the 22nd state; admitted December 14, 1819*

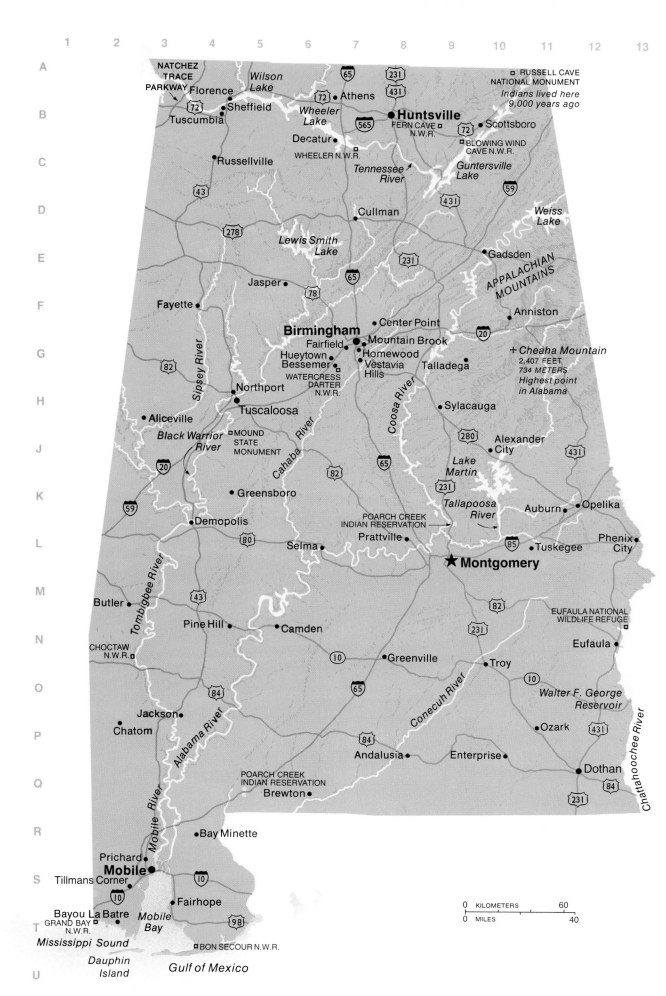

Map grid labels (top): 1 2 3 4 5 6 7 8 9 10 11 12 13

Map grid labels (side): A B C D E F G H J K L M N O P Q R S T U

NATCHEZ TRACE PARKWAY
Florence
Wilson Lake
65
231
RUSSELL CAVE NATIONAL MONUMENT
72 • Athens
431
Indians lived here 9,000 years ago
72
Sheffield
Wheeler Lake
Tuscumbia
565
•Huntsville
FERN CAVE N.W.R.
72 • Scottsboro
Decatur
BLOWING WIND CAVE N.W.R.
WHEELER N.W.R.
•Russellville
Tennessee River
Guntersville Lake
59
43
Weiss Lake
278
Cullman
431
Lewis Smith Lake
231
•Gadsden
65
APPALACHIAN MOUNTAINS
Jasper •
78
Fayette •
Anniston
20
Birmingham
• Center Point
Fairfield
Mountain Brook
+ Cheaha Mountain
2,407 FEET
734 METERS
Highest point in Alabama
82
Hueytown
Homewood
Bessemer
Vestavia Hills
Talladega
WATERCRESS DARTER N.W.R.
Northport
Sipsey River
Sylacauga
Tuscaloosa
• Aliceville
MOUND STATE MONUMENT
Black Warrior River
280
Alexander City
431
Coosa River
20
Cahaba River
82
Lake Martin
65
231
• Greensboro
Tallapoosa River
59
Auburn • Opelika
• Demopolis
POARCH CREEK INDIAN RESERVATION
Phenix City
80
Selma
Prattville •
85 • Tuskegee
Butler
43
★ Montgomery
Tombigbee River
Pine Hill •
• Camden
82
EUFAULA NATIONAL WILDLIFE REFUGE
CHOCTAW N.W.R.
231
10
• Greenville
• Eufaula
84
65
• Troy
Jackson •
Alabama River
10
Walter F. George Reservoir
Chatom •
Conecuh River
• Ozark
431
84
Andalusia •
Enterprise •
Dothan
POARCH CREEK INDIAN RESERVATION
Brewton •
84
231
• Bay Minette
Mobile River
Chattahoochee River
Prichard •
Mobile
Tillmans Corner •
10
• Fairhope
98
Bayou La Batre •
Mobile Bay
GRAND BAY N.W.R.
BON SECOUR N.W.R.
Mississippi Sound
Dauphin Island
Gulf of Mexico

0 KILOMETERS 60
0 MILES 40

In Alabama most rivers run toward Mobile Bay. That's because the land was tipped catty-corner when the Appalachian Mountains thrust up, sloping much of the area toward the bay. Today the Cahaba and Talla-poosa Rivers outline southern ramparts of the Appalachian chain.

The Tennessee River does not empty into the bay. Instead, it swoops across Alabama, forced northwestward by moun-tains to the south.

Northern Flicker

Camellia

Alabama

1 *Shrimp boats in festive bunting gather for the annual Blessing of the Fleet at Bayou La Batre. Sprinkling holy water, the archbishop on the foredeck prays for safe passage and a good catch.*

2 *The fertile fields of Alabama's black belt once lay at the ancient shoreline of the Gulf of Mexico. Ocean oozes enriched with the limy skeletons of tiny marine creatures formed the soil when the sea retreated millions of years ago.*

3 *Upraised porcelain hands at a Dothan factory will give shape to medical gloves when dipped into vats of liquid latex.*

4 *Protected by a welding hood, a student at a Bessemer technical college hones skills that will prepare her for a job in steel production or other manufacturing.*

5 *Upside-down and feeling weightless in a shuttle mock-up, a visitor at the United States Space Camp in Huntsville experiences the free-floating thrill of space flight.*

1

2

3

4

5

Georgia

An Ocmulgee River steamboat takes on cargo at Hawkinsville around 1900. Georgia riverboats carried passengers and freight such as barrels of turpentine, a product of Georgia's pine woods.

The largest state east of the Mississippi River, Georgia is also one of the most varied, physically and economically. The land slopes from the Blue Ridge Mountains in the northeast to sea level in the southeast or, as Georgians say, "from Rabun Gap to Tybee Light." Sparsely populated, the Blue Ridge region provides timber from its vast stands of pine and hardwood; its rivers supply hydroelectric power. Miners quarry the state's granite and the fine, white marble that was used for Abraham Lincoln's statue at the Lincoln Memorial in Washington, D. C.

Also in the north, farmers in the highlands raise poultry. Georgia ranks near the top in egg production—more than a million dozen a day—and in raising broiler chickens. Manufacturing, a growing industry, employs increasing numbers of people, including aircraft assemblers at the Lockheed-Georgia plant in Marietta, the state's largest private employer. There's a good chance that the carpeting in your home or your car was made in factories near Dalton. About half of the country's carpeting comes from this region, and so does much of its cloth.

At the start of the Civil War, Atlanta was a thriving town in the red clay hills of Georgia's Piedmont. Burned to the ground by the Union Army in 1864, Atlanta soon began rebuilding and has never stopped. Today it is the financial, trade, and transportation center of the South, and the world headquarters for Coca-Cola, formulated by an Atlanta druggist more than a century ago. Through the 1980s Atlanta grew rapidly, drawing residents from both inside and outside the state. Two of every five Georgians now live in the Atlanta metropolitan area; two-thirds of those in the city itself are black, as are a fourth of all Georgians. The birthplace of Martin Luther King, Jr., Atlanta became a headquarters for the civil rights movement.

Atlanta's growing population has pushed its suburbs out into an ever widening arc of housing developments, shopping centers, and office complexes, mostly to the city's north. Recently the water needs of all these people have fueled disputes with neighboring states over the resources of shared rivers.

Georgia's rivers become falls and rapids as they tumble from the Piedmont onto the Coastal Plain, the state's largest region. The most fertile farmlands are found in southern Georgia. Once cotton reigned here as the sole source of agricultural wealth. In the early 1900s, after destruction of several cotton crops by the boll weevil, Georgia farmers began to diversify. Farmers in and near the county named Peach, around Fort Valley, grow tons of that fruit. Around the town of Vidalia, farmers grow the sweet onion that can be eaten raw like an apple. Over most of southern Georgia, peanuts thrive. Peanut farmer Jimmy Carter, from Plains, be-

came the 39th President of the United States.

Forests of loblolly, slash, and shortleaf and longleaf pines cover central and southern Georgia. The timber cut in the state makes Georgia the country's leader in pulp production.

Alligators slide through Okefenokee, the country's second largest freshwater swamp. The 700-square-mile (1,820-sq-km) wetland extends into Florida, preserving an ecosystem of swamp, bog, and marsh that shelters some 12,000 gators in addition to 100 other reptile and mammal species and more than 200 bird species.

During the Civil War, when Union Gen. William Tecumseh Sherman left Atlanta smoldering and began his march to the sea, his goal was the city of Savannah. Founded by the British in 1733, Savannah soon became a major international port. Built on a bluff overlooking the Savannah River, the city preserves many beautiful homes that predate the Civil War. Unlike Atlanta and the settlements destroyed all along his march, Sherman spared Savannah, making its surrender a Christmas "gift" to President Lincoln in 1864.

Low-lying barrier islands with densely wooded interiors and sandy beaches protect Georgia's mainland and stretch up and down the coast into South Carolina and Florida. In the late 1700s, plantation owners brought in slaves to clear the islands and tend the indigo, rice, and cotton crops they planted there. Although some of the islands have been developed as resorts, descendants of the slaves remain. Isolation has helped preserve their unique language, called Gullah, rich with the sounds of 17th-century English and West African languages.

Area: *21st largest state, 58,910 sq mi (152,576 sq km)*
Population: *6,478,216; ranks 11th*
Major Cities: *Atlanta, 394,017; Columbus, 179,278; Savannah, 137,560*
Manufacturing: *transportation equipment, textiles, food products, paper products, chemicals, electronics, clothing, machinery, lumber and wood products, stone, clay, and glass products, metal products*
Agriculture: *broilers, peanuts, cattle, eggs, hogs, milk, greenhouse and nursery products*
Mining and Quarrying: *clay, stone*
Other Important Activities: *tourism, printing and publishing*
Statehood: *the fourth state; ratified the Constitution on January 2, 1788*

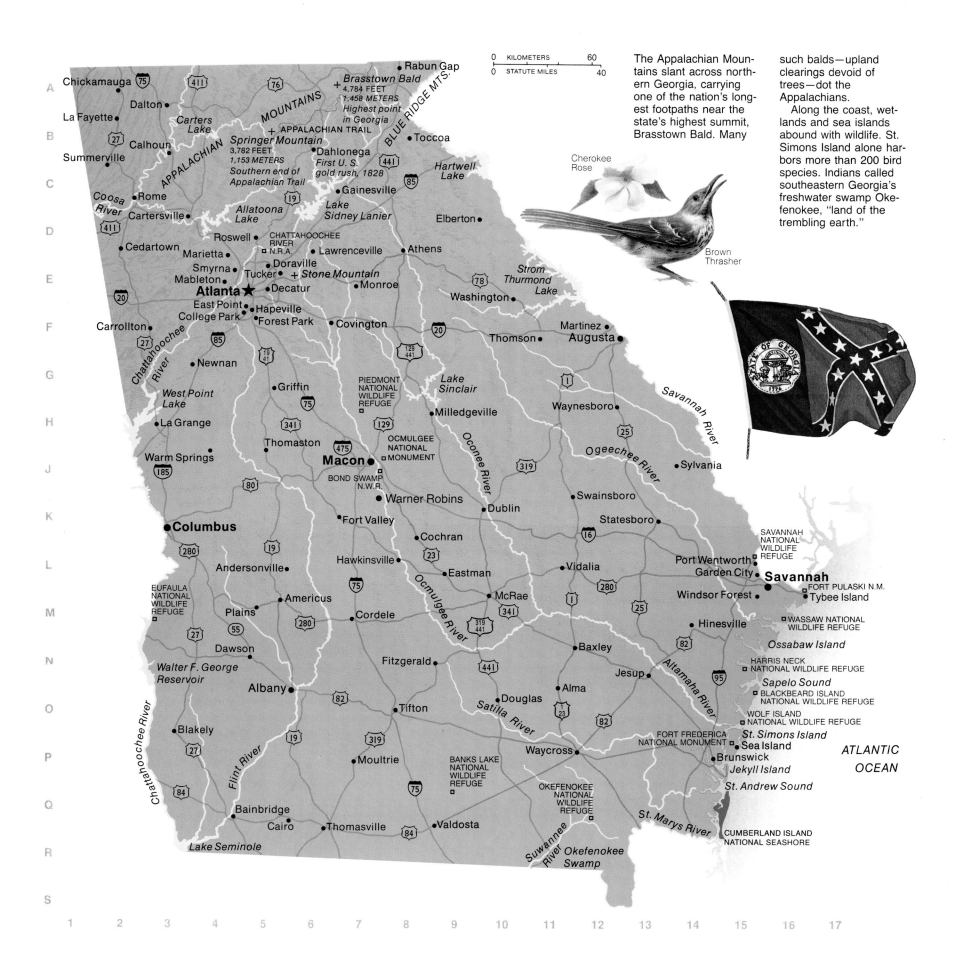

The Appalachian Mountains slant across northern Georgia, carrying one of the nation's longest footpaths near the state's highest summit, Brasstown Bald. Many such balds—upland clearings devoid of trees—dot the Appalachians.

Along the coast, wetlands and sea islands abound with wildlife. St. Simons Island alone harbors more than 200 bird species. Indians called southeastern Georgia's freshwater swamp Okefenokee, "land of the trembling earth."

Cherokee Rose

Brown Thrasher

Chickamauga

La Fayette

Dalton

Summerville

Calhoun

Rome

Cartersville

Cedartown

Carters Lake

Springer Mountain 3,782 FEET 1,153 METERS *Southern end of Appalachian Trail*

MOUNTAINS

APPALACHIAN

Brasstown Bald 4,784 FEET 1,458 METERS *Highest point in Georgia*

APPALACHIAN TRAIL

Rabun Gap

Toccoa

Dahlonega First U. S. gold rush, 1828

BLUE RIDGE MTS.

Hartwell Lake

Gainesville

Allatoona Lake

Lake Sidney Lanier

Elberton

Roswell

Marietta

Smyrna

Mableton

Tucker

Doraville

Decatur

CHATTAHOOCHEE RIVER N.R.A.

Lawrenceville

Athens

Stone Mountain

Atlanta ★

East Point

College Park

Hapeville

Forest Park

Carrollton

Monroe

Covington

Washington

Strom Thurmond Lake

Martinez

Thomson

Augusta

Coosa River

Chattahoochee River

Newnan

West Point Lake

La Grange

Warm Springs

Griffin

PIEDMONT NATIONAL WILDLIFE REFUGE

Lake Sinclair

Milledgeville

Savannah River

Waynesboro

Ogeechee River

Thomaston

Macon

OCMULGEE NATIONAL MONUMENT

Sylvania

BOND SWAMP N.W.R.

Warner Robins

Oconee River

Dublin

Swainsboro

Statesboro

Columbus

Fort Valley

Cochran

Eastman

Vidalia

SAVANNAH NATIONAL WILDLIFE REFUGE

Port Wentworth

Garden City

Savannah

Andersonville

Hawkinsville

McRae

Windsor Forest

FORT PULASKI N.M.

Tybee Island

EUFAULA NATIONAL WILDLIFE REFUGE

Plains

Americus

Cordele

Ocmulgee River

Hinesville

WASSAW NATIONAL WILDLIFE REFUGE

Ossabaw Island

Dawson

Fitzgerald

Baxley

HARRIS NECK NATIONAL WILDLIFE REFUGE

Sapelo Sound

Walter F. George Reservoir

Albany

Jesup

Altamaha River

BLACKBEARD ISLAND NATIONAL WILDLIFE REFUGE

WOLF ISLAND NATIONAL WILDLIFE REFUGE

Blakely

Tifton

Satilla River

Douglas

Alma

FORT FREDERICA NATIONAL MONUMENT

St. Simons Island

Sea Island

ATLANTIC OCEAN

Moultrie

BANKS LAKE NATIONAL WILDLIFE REFUGE

Waycross

Brunswick

Jekyll Island

St. Andrew Sound

Bainbridge

Cairo

Thomasville

Valdosta

OKEFENOKEE NATIONAL WILDLIFE REFUGE

St. Marys River

CUMBERLAND ISLAND NATIONAL SEASHORE

Lake Seminole

Flint River

Chattahoochee River

Suwannee River

Okefenokee Swamp

KILOMETERS 0 60

STATUTE MILES 0 40

A B C D E F G H J K L M N O P Q R S

1 2 3 4 5 6 7 8 9 10 11 12 13 14 15 16 17

Georgia

1 *American alligators, protected by law from poachers who sell their skins for shoes, purses, and belts, again flourish in the vegetation-stained "black water" of Okefenokee Swamp.*

2 *Delta Airlines mechanics in Atlanta check a jet engine by attaching a "bellmouth" to intensify air intake.*

3 *Enclosed skyways connect shops and hotels at Peachtree Center in downtown Atlanta.*

4 *Peanuts are Georgia's most valuable crop, and more peanuts grow here than in any other state. Sometimes peanut shells are burned for fuel at power plants.*

5 *Quarry workers near Elberton cut granite for buildings, bridges, and monuments.*

3

4

5

South Carolina

"Swamp Fox, Swamp Fox, tail on his hat. Nobody knows where the Swamp Fox's at," began the theme song of a popular 1950s television series. The show portrayed the daring exploits of Francis Marion, a South Carolina Revolutionary War leader whose ragtag band of guerrilla fighters led a Robin Hood-like existence in the state's southern swamps. Marion engaged the British in many skirmishes but never was caught. His ability to melt back into the swamps without a trace earned him the nickname Swamp Fox and his place in history and legend.

Though South Carolina has at least five distinct land regions, for centuries South Carolinians have broadly divided their state into two: the Low Country and the Up Country. Low Country is the Atlantic Coastal Plain, covering two-thirds of the state. Slow-moving rivers flow through the plain, which becomes marshy and swampy near the ocean. A winding shoreline follows bays, peninsulas, and inlets. At the northern end stretch some 60 miles (95 km) of white-sand beaches. To the south a line of lush barrier islands reaches into Georgia and Florida. Known as the Sea Islands, they are densely forested and contain both freshwater and saltwater marshes. Much Sea Islands land is protected nature reserve where wildlife abounds, including alligators and most species of poisonous snakes found in the United States.

Everything not on the Coastal Plain, South Carolinians call the Up Country. The term recognizes the land's gradual rise until it reaches the summits of the Blue Ridge Mountains in the northwestern corner, but other regions lie in between. Columbia, the capital, lies on a band of sandy hills that millions of years ago formed the ocean shoreline. West of Columbia begins the Piedmont, the foothills of the mountains.

The Low Country saw South Carolina's first European settlements. In the 1500s, both the Spanish and the French tried to colonize the coast, but failed. The English succeeded in 1670, establishing Charles Town (named for their king, Charles II) on a peninsula a few miles inland. They were soon joined by French Protestants, called Huguenots, who fled religious persecution in France, as well as by Scots, Spanish and Portuguese Jews, Irish, Germans, and Welsh. The newcomers prospered from trade

The crews of Civil War naval vessels, such as this one off Charleston, included youngsters. This "powder monkey," a boy whose job was to fetch gunpowder for cannons, was paid $8 a month.

with Indians. In time they built airy mansions along the harbor and in their leisure pursued the pleasures of music, dancing, entertaining, and fine dining. After the Revolution they changed the name of their city to Charleston.

Meanwhile, settlers of Scottish and Irish descent moved into South Carolina from highlands to the north. As Up Country farmers, they grew tobacco, corn, and cotton, a crop that was also raised in the Low Country, but with the help of thousands of slaves. Fearing the loss of their wealth if slavery were abolished, Low Country planters led the movement that, on December 20, 1860, made South Carolina the first state to secede from the Union.

The Civil War helped end South Carolina's reliance on cotton as the principal crop, as did the appearance of the destructive boll weevil in the 1920s. Today farmers throughout the state grow soybeans as well as cotton and, mainly in the east, tobacco.

In the late 1800s, South Carolina began to industrialize. The state attracted outside investment because wages were low and unions didn't exist there. Textile factories sprang up in the northwest near Greenville and Spartanburg, along the railroad. Today Interstate 85 parallels the rails through the heart of South Carolina's textile belt.

South Carolina has diversified its industry and now manufactures products ranging from furniture to chemicals for the space program. Investors are diversified as well. Factories representing more than 20 countries, including France, Germany, Japan, and the Netherlands, now operate in several areas of the state.

In September 1989, Hurricane Hugo hit South Carolina's coast. Winds reaching 135 miles an hour (217 kmph) damaged or destroyed thousands of trees lining Charleston's waterfront and tore off the roofs of many buildings and historic mansions.

The storm also ripped through some of the Sea Islands, leaving homeless many descendants of the slaves who once tended the islands' famous long-staple cotton. But even before Hugo, they had seen change come to many of their islands, including Hilton Head, developed as a resort for the rich.

In their isolation over the centuries, the Sea Islanders, who number a third of the state's black residents, developed a distinct culture and language, called Gullah. Most of them still speak this mixture of languages that has donated many words to modern English, such as goober (peanut), gumbo (okra), chigger (small flea), hoodoo (bad luck), and tote (to carry).

Area: *40th largest state, 31,113 sq mi (80,582 sq km)*
Population: *3,486,703; ranks 25th*
Major Cities: *Columbia, 98,052; Charleston, 80,414; North Charleston, 70,218*
Manufacturing: *textiles, chemicals, paper products, machinery, electronics, rubber and plastics, food products, clothing, metal products, transportation equipment*
Agriculture: *tobacco, cattle, soybeans, broilers, milk, eggs, vegetables, turkeys, peaches*
Mining and Quarrying: *stone, clay, sand and gravel*
Other Important Activities: *federal government, tourism*
Statehood: *the eighth state; ratified the Constitution on May 23, 1788*

1 2 3 4 5 6 7 8 9 10 11 12 13 14 15 16 17 18 19

A
B
C
D
E
F
G
H
J
K
L
M
N
O
P

Chattooga River

Highest point
in South Carolina
+ *Sassafras Mountain*
3,560 FEET
1,085 METERS

Wylie Lake

85 • Gaffney

Lake Jocassee
Lake Keowee

Walhalla •

Taylors •

Greer •

Spartanburg •

• York
Rock Hill •

9

• Chesterfield

9

• Cheraw

Easley •

Greenville

Catawba River

• Bennettsville

Seneca •

123

Mauldin •

CAROLINA SANDHILLS
NATIONAL WILDLIFE REFUGE

52

9

Clemson •

Simpsonville •

26

• Union

• Chester

• Lancaster

• Dillon

85

385

Broad River

77

321

1

• Hartsville

95

76

Belton •

Laurens •

• Winnsboro

Wateree Lake

Darlington •

• Mullins

76

Hartwell Lake

Anderson •

Clinton

Lake Greenwood

Newberry •

• Camden

• Bishopville

Florence •
Marion •

Little Pee Dee River

Abbeville •
Greenwood •

Saluda River

Lake Murray

20

Wateree River

Pee Dee River

52

North Myrtle Beach

25

378

• Saluda

West Columbia

★ Columbia

76
378

• Sumter

• Lake City

501

McCormick •

Cayce •

• Forest Acres

Shannontown •

378

Conway

Strom Thurmond Lake

Edgefield •

20

CONGAREE SWAMP
NATIONAL MONUMENT

• Manning

• Kingstree

Myrtle Beach

Surfside Beach

17

25

Sandhills along the
western edge of the
coastal plain are
beach remains of
an ancient sea

• St. Matthews

Lake Marion

Black River

Pawleys Island

Aiken •

North Augusta •

• Orangeburg

SANTEE
NATIONAL
WILDLIFE REFUGE

Santee River

Georgetown

78

Bamberg •

Winyah Bay

Barnwell •

Lake Moultrie

McClellanville •

Santee Point

301

Allendale •

• St. George

26

52

CAPE ROMAIN
NATIONAL
WILDLIFE REFUGE

Salkehatchie River

Edisto River

Cooper River

Summerville •
Goose Creek •

Bulls Bay

• Hampton

• Walterboro

Hanahan •
Mt. Pleasant •

North Charleston

ATLANTIC OCEAN

321

95

17

Charleston •

Isle of Palms •

FORT SUMTER
NATIONAL MONUMENT

Sullivans Island

Combahee River

ACE BASIN
N.W.R.

• Folly Beach

Kiawah Island

Savannah River

21

• Ridgeland

Yellow
Jessamine

Port Royal •

• Beaufort *St. Helena Sound*

Parris Island

PINCKNEY ISLAND
N.W.R.

St. Helena Island
Port Royal Sound

SAVANNAH
NATIONAL
WILDLIFE
REFUGE

Hilton Head Island

Carolina
Wren

TYBEE
NATIONAL
WILDLIFE
REFUGE

0 KILOMETERS 50
0 STATUTE MILES 30

With a coast 187 miles
(301 km) long, as the
crow flies, South Caroli-
na has so many bays, in-
lets, and islands south of
Georgetown that if you
pulled the shoreline
straight, it would reach
all the way across the
continent to the Pacific.

In the early 1700s, pi-
rates such as Blackbeard
loved it. They hid out in
the maze-like waterways
between raids on towns
and merchant ships.
Nowadays seaside visi-
tors prefer to loll on a
nearly unbroken line of
white-sand beaches,
including Myrtle and
Surfside, that reach
northward from George-
town into North Carolina.

South Carolina

1   *Pelicans fly over a barrier island near Charleston. Palmetto trees along the beach withstand hurricane-force winds, salt water, and shifting sands.*

2   *Fresh peaches fill market shelves all summer. South Carolina grows more peaches than any state but California.*

3   *From these mansions lining the harbor, Charlestonians watched the shelling of Fort Sumter at the start of the Civil War.*

4   *A family works together to bring in the August tobacco harvest on a farm along the Little Pee Dee River.*

5   *Jumbo shrimp pour from the scale in McClellanville, a fishing town where Gullah, an old, black language, is still spoken.*

4

5

Louisiana

Louis Armstrong began his jazz career while a teenager in New Orleans. Here, around 1920, he plays cornet with the Fate Marable Orchestra on board the paddle wheeler S.S. Capitol.

Louisiana is in many ways unique. It was founded by the French and governed by both the French and the Spanish before becoming part of the United States. It is the only state whose civil law is based on Roman law as found in French and Spanish sources, rather than on the British common law used by the other states. It is the only state where a quarter of the people speak French, and it is the only one organized into parishes instead of counties, a legacy of Roman Catholic influence during colonial days.

The French settled hot, humid New Orleans in 1718, and set out their neat, perpendicular streets on a wide bend of the Mississippi River. Though the city later spilled out of the bend, the French Quarter, or Vieux Carré ("old square"), is still its heart, attracting visitors from all over the world. They come to stroll beneath wrought-iron balconies draped with flowers and to sample the highly seasoned blend of French, Spanish, and African cuisines known as Creole. Some come to New Orleans to boat and fish on immense, brackish Lake Pontchartrain, crossed by a 24-mile (39-km) causeway, the longest over-water bridge in the world. Each winter, before the season of Lent, the population swells and the city celebrates with the round of parties, parades, and balls known as Mardi Gras.

New Orleans is Louisiana's chief port, and the metropolitan area is home to one-third of the state's population. Oceangoing vessels from Latin America, Europe, Asia, and Africa dock at New Orleans daily. Most of the cargo leaving

Louisiana is made up of corn from states upriver or the riches beneath southern Louisiana and the Gulf of Mexico, vast deposits of oil and natural gas. The banks of the Mississippi from New Orleans to Baton Rouge are lined with refineries and petrochemical plants. Lake Charles in the southwest and Shreveport in northwestern Louisiana also refine and process petroleum, while Lafayette and Morgan City in the south serve as centers for oil and gas drilling.

New Orleans still sends out cargoes of sugarcane and cotton, crops that made it rich more than 150 years ago. Alluvial soil from the Mississippi and its tributaries created fertile land throughout much of the state where other crops, such as soybeans, corn, and sweet potatoes are now also grown. After the rice harvest, farmers in the state's southern prairies often flood their fields to raise crawfish, a Louisiana delicacy, which feed on the stubble.

All along the Mississippi, people must match wits with the river's strength and capriciousness. Natural and artificial levees help keep the Mississippi in its channel. Where natural levees rise very high, from the buildup of sediment over many years, the river contained within them can flow at an elevation higher than its floodplain. In New Orleans, at five feet (1.5 m)

below sea level the lowest point in the state, the river is often higher than the land around it.

Southern Louisiana, where the river forms its delta, is a low-lying land of marshes, swamps, and cypress-studded bayous, slow-moving streams that often mark old river channels. One of the nation's most valuable wetland areas, the delta teems with wildlife, in winter sheltering up to 25 percent of North America's wild ducks and geese. Delta waters also nourish the shrimp and oysters of the seafood industry.

Generally more rural in the north, Louisiana's population is one of the most cosmopolitan in the country. Among its residents are descendants of French and Spanish settlers, former slaves, free blacks from the West Indies, German, English, and Hungarian farmers who settled the Mississippi plain, Irish, Italians, and the Cajuns. The last were French settlers from Acadia, a region of eastern Canada. The Acadians were exiled by the British in the mid-1700s, and many made their way to the bayous and prairies of southern Louisiana. There they lived by farming, fishing, hunting, and trapping. Over time the Acadians became "Cajuns." Today many still work close to the land, while others follow less traditional occupations, from law to the oil industry. Cajuns say that their cultural identity is defined by strong family bonds and a love of life.

"Laissez le bon temps rouler—Let the good times roll" characterizes the leisure time of Cajun Louisiana. On the bayou, spicy food and toe-tapping music make for good times. All it takes is a fiddle, an accordion, a guitar, and a washboard or triangle to keep Cajun feet stomping at a late night dance called a fais-dodo, literally, a "go to sleep"—probably because that's what the small children were supposed to do.

Area: *31st largest state, 47,751 sq mi (123,675 sq km)*
Population: *4,219,973; ranks 21st*
Major Cities: *New Orleans, 496,938; Baton Rouge, 219,531; Shreveport, 198,525*
Mining: *oil and gas, salt*
Manufacturing: *chemicals, food products, petroleum products, transportation equipment, paper products, electronics, lumber and wood products*
Agriculture: *soybeans, cotton, cattle, sugarcane, rice, milk*
Other Important Activities: *tourism, fishing*
Statehood: *the 18th state; admitted April 30, 1812*

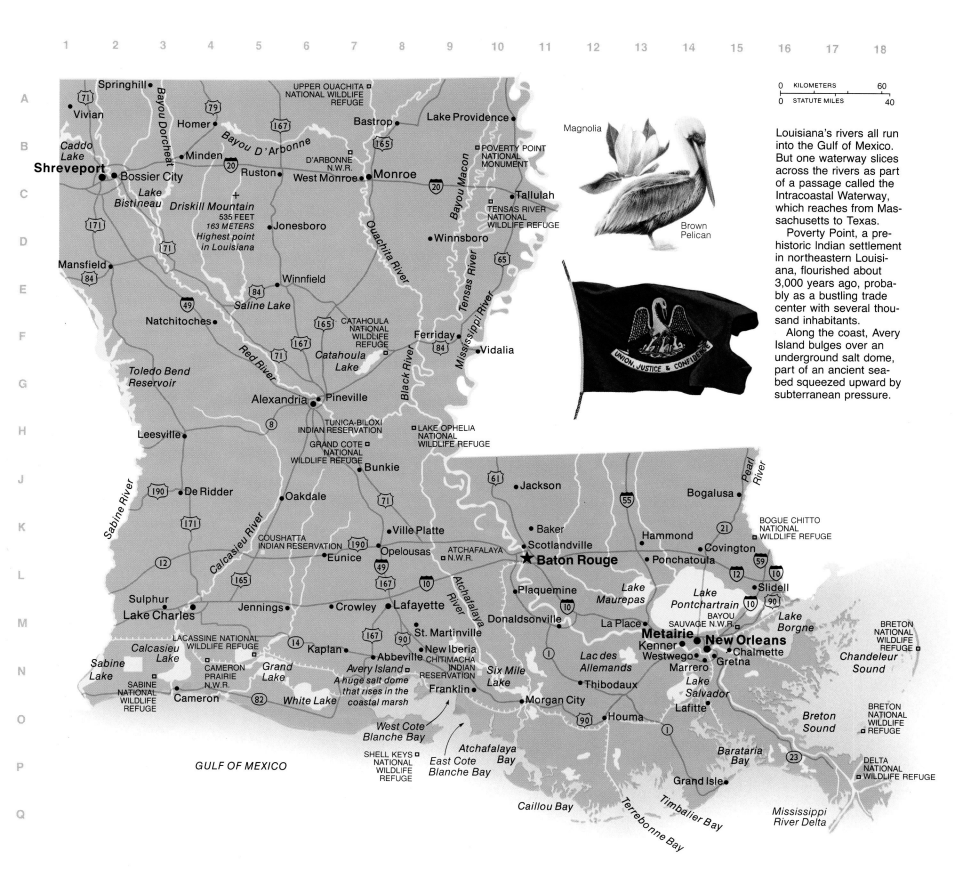

Louisiana's rivers all run into the Gulf of Mexico. But one waterway slices across the rivers as part of a passage called the Intracoastal Waterway, which reaches from Massachusetts to Texas.

Poverty Point, a prehistoric Indian settlement in northeastern Louisiana, flourished about 3,000 years ago, probably as a bustling trade center with several thousand inhabitants.

Along the coast, Avery Island bulges over an underground salt dome, part of an ancient seabed squeezed upward by subterranean pressure.

Magnolia

Brown Pelican

UNION, JUSTICE & CONFIDENCE

Springhill
Vivian
71
Homer
79
Bayou Dorcheat
167
Bayou D'Arbonne
UPPER OUACHITA NATIONAL WILDLIFE REFUGE
Bastrop
Lake Providence
165
POVERTY POINT NATIONAL MONUMENT
Caddo Lake
Minden
D'ARBONNE N.W.R.
Shreveport
Bossier City
20
Ruston
West Monroe
Monroe
Bayou Macon
Lake Bistineau
171
Driskill Mountain
535 FEET
163 METERS
Highest point in Louisiana
Jonesboro
Ouachita River
20
Tallulah
TENSAS RIVER NATIONAL WILDLIFE REFUGE
Mansfield
84
71
Winnsboro
Natchitoches
49
Winnfield
84
Saline Lake
165
167
CATAHOULA NATIONAL WILDLIFE REFUGE
Tensas River
65
Red River
71
Catahoula Lake
Black River
Ferriday
84
Vidalia
Mississippi River
Toledo Bend Reservoir
Leesville
Alexandria
Pineville
8
TUNICA-BILOXI INDIAN RESERVATION
GRAND COTE NATIONAL WILDLIFE REFUGE
LAKE OPHELIA NATIONAL WILDLIFE REFUGE
Sabine River
190
De Ridder
Oakdale
Bunkie
71
61
Jackson
55
Bogalusa
Pearl River
171
Ville Platte
Baker
Scotlandville
Hammond
21
BOGUE CHITTO NATIONAL WILDLIFE REFUGE
12
COUSHATTA INDIAN RESERVATION
190
Eunice
Opelousas
ATCHAFALAYA N.W.R.
Baton Rouge
Ponchatoula
Covington
59
12
10
Calcasieu River
12
165
167
49
10
Plaquemine
Lake Maurepas
Lake Pontchartrain
10
90
Slidell
Sulphur
Lake Charles
Jennings
Crowley
Lafayette
Atchafalaya River
Donaldsonville
La Place
BAYOU SAUVAGE N.W.R.
Lake Borgne
BRETON NATIONAL WILDLIFE REFUGE
LACASSINE NATIONAL WILDLIFE REFUGE
14
Kaplan
167
90
St. Martinville
New Iberia
CHITIMACHA INDIAN RESERVATION
Six Mile Lake
Lac des Allemands
Metairie
New Orleans
Kenner
Westwego
Chalmette
Gretna
Marrero
Chandeleur Sound
Sabine Lake
SABINE NATIONAL WILDLIFE REFUGE
CAMERON PRAIRIE N.W.R.
Grand Lake
Avery Island
A huge salt dome that rises in the coastal marsh
Franklin
Morgan City
Thibodaux
Lake Salvador
Lafitte
BRETON NATIONAL WILDLIFE REFUGE
Calcasieu Lake
Cameron
82
White Lake
West Cote Blanche Bay
SHELL KEYS NATIONAL WILDLIFE REFUGE
East Cote Blanche Bay
Atchafalaya Bay
90
Houma
1
Breton Sound
Barataria Bay
23
DELTA NATIONAL WILDLIFE REFUGE
GULF OF MEXICO
Grand Isle
Caillou Bay
Terrebonne Bay
Timbalier Bay
Mississippi River Delta

0 KILOMETERS 60
0 STATUTE MILES 40

1

2

3

Louisiana

1 *An oil rig rises from the Gulf of Mexico off Louisiana. Thousands of drilling platforms dot the offshore waters, where crews work around the clock in a region that produces some 700,000 barrels of oil a day.*

2 *The Andrew Hall Society Brass Band parades through the French Quarter. New Orleans jazz was born around 1900, when black and white musicians combined gospel music, spirituals, dance music, West African rhythms, European harmony, and the beat of brass bands.*

3 *The Mississippi River winds past New Orleans and flows its last 110 miles (177 km) southeast to the Gulf of Mexico. Cargo ships from around the world make the trip by river or artificial channel to trade millions of tons of goods a year.*

5

4 *Swamp red maple and bald cypress trees grow in a swamp along the Pearl River, home to alligators, river otters, bobcats, mink, birds, and crawfish.*

5 *On Avery Island, a worker picks hot peppers. Tabasco sauce made from these peppers has spiced Cajun and Creole dishes, such as crawfish étouffée, chicken gumbo, and shrimp jambalaya, since 1868, soon after the seeds were brought from Mexico.*

4

Florida

In 1513 Spanish explorer Juan Ponce de León landed in Florida, searching for a legendary spring that would assure him perpetual youth. He did not find the spring and died after fighting Indians on a later trip. Florida may not have the Fountain of Youth, but it does have springs, more than one-third of all the large springs in the United States and many smaller ones. Florida has water of all types, in rivers, bays, lakes, swamps, marshes, creeks, and ponds. Winds from the Atlantic Ocean on the east and the Gulf of Mexico on the west bring moist air and usually plentiful rainfall to the state.

The southernmost of all the states except Hawaii, Florida occupies a peninsula that projects 400 miles (640 km) into the sea. Including all bays, inlets, and offshore islands, Florida has a coastline that totals almost 8,500 miles (13,680 km), longer than that of any other state except Alaska. No part of Florida is more than an hour's drive from tidewater. Off the southern tip of the peninsula, the Florida Keys, a string of limestone and coral islands, trickle westward into the Gulf.

A flat, porous limestone formation underlies the Florida peninsula. Pockets in the limestone store vast quantities of groundwater. The groundwater reaches the surface in some 30,000 lakes, including 730-square-mile (1,890-sq-km) Lake Okeechobee, the largest lake in the southern United States. The groundwater also nourishes springs and streams.

This watery world has many interconnections. One is the complex system of the Everglades. For centuries, lakes in central Florida fed the Kissimmee River, which in turn fed Lake Okeechobee. This inflow and seasonal rains caused Okeechobee to spill over its southern banks, spreading as wide as 50 miles (80 km) to flow slowly 100 miles to Florida Bay. This creeping river is lifeblood to the Everglades. Often only inches deep and brimming with saw grass, it shelters alligators, crocodiles, manatees, multitudes of birds, and the rare and elusive Florida panther. It is an environment unique to Florida and to the world. At the southern tip is Everglades National Park.

From prehistoric Indians to later settlers who fished or dug clams or farmed on mounded islands called hammocks, people have lived in the Everglades for thousands of years. They made few demands on the environment, but today it is people who endanger the Everglades. The Everglades and its sources are channeled by hundreds of miles of canals and dikes to provide fresh water for the farms, cities, and developments that make southern Florida one of the fastest growing areas in the nation. The needs of humans and wildlife often conflict. Now the Everglades is in danger of dying, and this threat has led the state to pay attention to the needs of the "river of grass."

In 1565 the Spanish built the first permanent European settlement in Florida, at St. Augustine. The British and French followed, competing for control of the Gulf of Mexico. In the early 19th century, American settlers streamed in, looking for new farmland. The Seminole Indians owned some of the best land here. The U. S. government forced most of them to move to Oklahoma, all but a small band who escaped into the swamps. Their descendants live today in dis-

The 1890s brought a cycling craze to the United States and gave people a new freedom of movement. Here, cyclists and strollers congregate along the seashore at Palm Beach, a small town in 1895.

tinctive houses on stilts deep in the Everglades.

Settlers pressed southward. By the end of the 19th century, wetlands, including much of the Everglades, were drained. Fertile farmland appeared, but only for a while, since the rich muck soil of the wetlands disintegrates when exposed to air and then blows away. This did not deter developers from draining or settlers from farming. Today two-thirds of the nation's supply of oranges are grown in Florida, as well as three-fourths of its grapefruit. Farmers in southern Florida produce tomatoes, lettuce, celery, green peppers, and other vegetables.

In the late 1800s, two tycoons, both named Henry, raced to develop parts of Florida. They built railroads and many luxurious resort hotels. Henry Flagler completed his east coast railroad to Miami first. Henry Plant built his line from Jacksonville to Tampa.

Today more than four million people live on the east coast from Miami to West Palm Beach, many of them elderly retirees from northern states. St. Petersburg on Tampa Bay has large numbers of senior citizens, too. They used to come just for the winter, but air-conditioning has turned many "snowbirds" into year-round residents. Retirees give Florida the nation's oldest population; 1 in 5 residents is over 65.

No known descendants of the first Spanish colonists remain in Florida, but many newer Spanish-speaking immigrants, mostly from Cuba and other Latin American countries, live in or near Miami. With numerous trade and finance connections to the south, this port city has become a commercial partner of Latin America. Some 70 percent of U. S. trade with Latin America goes through Florida. Illegal drug traffic forms a large part of this trade, and the crime it generates is driving many older residents north along the coast. Even so, every day 800 people move into the state, and its population has grown by one-third since 1980.

Orlando's growing electronics industry has attracted many people. A large number of Floridians work for the federal government, some at military bases such as Pensacola's Naval Air Station. At Cape Canaveral, it's been more than 40 years since the first rocket took off, but launches at Kennedy Space Center still support the aerospace industry and still stop traffic.

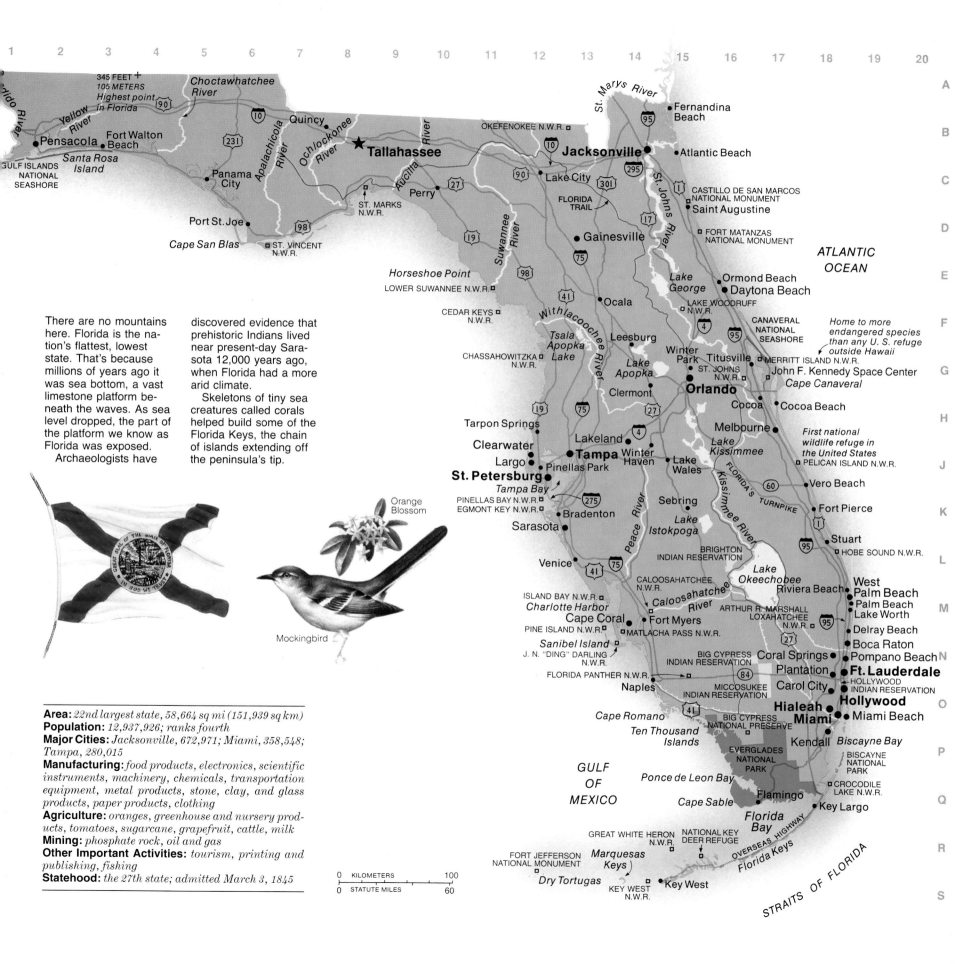

There are no mountains here. Florida is the nation's flattest, lowest state. That's because millions of years ago it was sea bottom, a vast limestone platform beneath the waves. As sea level dropped, the part of the platform we know as Florida was exposed.

Archaeologists have discovered evidence that prehistoric Indians lived near present-day Sarasota 12,000 years ago, when Florida had a more arid climate.

Skeletons of tiny sea creatures called corals helped build some of the Florida Keys, the chain of islands extending off the peninsula's tip.

Orange Blossom

Mockingbird

Area: *22nd largest state, 58,664 sq mi (151,939 sq km)*
Population: *12,937,926; ranks fourth*
Major Cities: *Jacksonville, 672,971; Miami, 358,548; Tampa, 280,015*
Manufacturing: *food products, electronics, scientific instruments, machinery, chemicals, transportation equipment, metal products, stone, clay, and glass products, paper products, clothing*
Agriculture: *oranges, greenhouse and nursery products, tomatoes, sugarcane, grapefruit, cattle, milk*
Mining: *phosphate rock, oil and gas*
Other Important Activities: *tourism, printing and publishing, fishing*
Statehood: *the 27th state; admitted March 3, 1845*

KILOMETERS 0—100
STATUTE MILES 0—60

1

2

3

4

5

Florida

1 *The gleaming hotels that line Miami Beach serve Florida's leading industry, tourism. They stand on land that, a hundred years ago, was a sandbar thick with mangroves and palmettos, and populated mostly by snakes and mosquitoes.*

2 *A picker near Clermont fills a tub with Valencia oranges, Florida's most abundant variety. Today 90 percent of Florida oranges go into making juice.*

3 *White ibises roost on mangrove roots in the Everglades, one of the United States' most threatened areas. Loss of habitat has led to a 95 percent decline in the population of Everglades wading birds. Polluted water from farms flows into the wetlands, daily destroying an area of plant and animal habitat the size of three football fields.*

4 *The space shuttle* Discovery *prepares for lift-off at Kennedy Space Center, the primary site for the launching and landing of the reusable vehicles. In 1981* Columbia *was the first shuttle to take off here.*

5 *Ranch hands round up their herd on the grassy plains near the Peace River. There have been cattle ranches in Florida since the early 1800s. Today Florida is one of the country's top five cattle-producing states.*

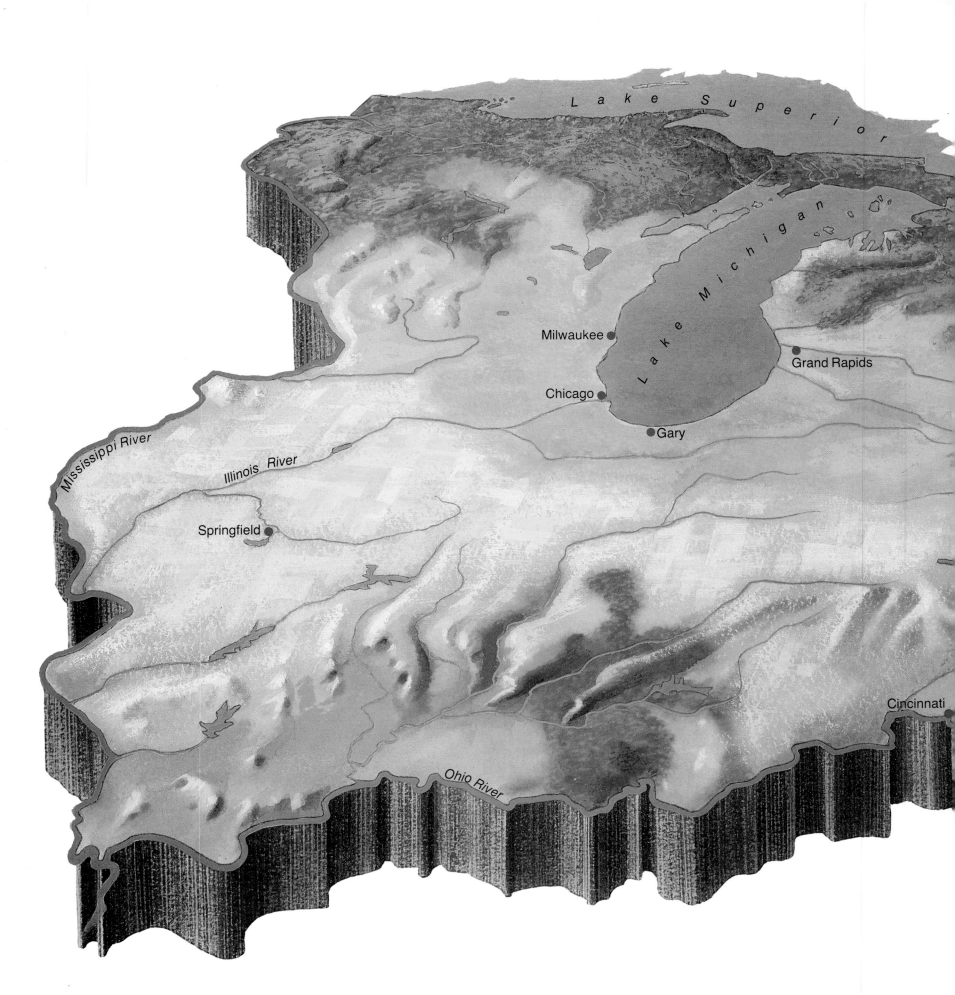

Great Lakes States

They are like oceans, these great lakes. French missionaries, gazing across a seemingly limitless horizon of water in the 17th century, thought they had found oceans—"sweetwater seas," they called them. Taken together, the Great Lakes spread some 800 miles (1,290 km) east to west across the continent's interior and hold a fifth of the planet's fresh surface water. If you emptied the lakes across the contiguous United States, their water would cover the land ten feet (3 m) deep. A raindrop falling onto the heavily forested shore of western Lake Superior would take about 215 years to wind its way east through the lakes to the St. Lawrence River outlet at the eastern tip of Lake Ontario.

Created by glaciers that withdrew about 10,000 years ago, the Great Lakes' shoreline extends 8,000 miles (12,870 km) and is sometimes called North America's fifth coast. Along the four lakes shown here cluster the nation's heaviest concentrations of industry, thanks to the region's central location and economical water transportation that brings shipments of iron and coal to lakeside mills and factories.

A quarter of the country's steel pours from furnaces in the Chicago and Gary areas of Lake Michigan. About a third of the cars roll off assembly lines in and around Detroit, and Cleveland's mills, factories, and refineries stretch 65 miles (105 km) along Lake Erie's shore. By value, about a quarter of the country's manufactured goods come from the Great Lakes region.

Beyond the cities spreads the quilt-work pattern of the corn belt, fertile farms and fields that produce about a fifth of the nation's farm income. Level terrain, hot summers, and usually plentiful rain help to produce bumper crops of corn and soybeans year after year. North of the corn belt, between lower Lake Michigan and the Mississippi River, roll the gentle hills and pastures of the nation's dairy belt. East of the lake, peach, apple, and pear orchards flourish because warm winds from the lakes help to prolong their growing season by delaying frosts.

Wisconsin

A daredevil leaps a chasm at Stand Rock around 1886 in the forested Dells region of the Wisconsin River. Over the ages the river carved a channel through sandstone, creating these formations.

"As far as a man could go to the north in a day, or a week, or a whole month, there was nothing but woods. There were no houses. There were no roads. There were no people. There were only trees and the wild animals who had their homes among them." In *Little House in the Big Woods*, Laura Ingalls Wilder describes her pioneer childhood in Wisconsin of the 1870s, a life of hunting and trapping and laying in food to last long winters snowbound in a log cabin.

Woods still cover almost half of Wisconsin, but the trees are second-growth hardwoods and evergreens. Not only big woods but also lakes big and small are part of northern Wisconsin. The state has some 14,000 lakes, a legacy of the Ice Age. The largest is Lake Winnebago. Its 215 square miles (557 sq km) teem with fish, including muskie, bass, sturgeon, and trout. Together, lakes and forests beckon thousands of vacationers to this part of Wisconsin each year.

Central highlands blocked the glaciers' path into southwestern Wisconsin and adjoining parts of Minnesota, Iowa, and Illinois. The winding ridges and steep-sloped valleys of this Driftless Area, so-called because it shows no sign of glacial debris, or drift, provide a glimpse of the region's rugged, pre-Ice Age landscape. Streams here cut down through layers of limestone and sandstone and drain into the Mississippi River, Wisconsin's western boundary. Geologists puzzle over the absence of glacial tracks in the area, because they think the ice sheets must have passed through here.

Glaciers did help carve out the Great Lakes, immense reservoirs that hold 95 percent of the fresh surface water in the United States. Two of them, Lakes Superior and Michigan, provide northwestern and eastern Wisconsin with almost 700 miles (1,130 km) of shoreline. In 1634 Jean Nicolet, a French explorer from Quebec looking for a northern passage to China, landed at Green Bay. He donned a colorful silk robe, hoping to impress the Chinese officials he was expecting to meet. Instead, he was greeted by Winnebago Indians, one of three Native American groups that inhabited Wisconsin.

The fur trade soon brought more Europeans to Wisconsin. There was a great market in Europe for gentlemen's top hats fashioned from the glossy pelts of North American beavers. Lead miners numbered among 19th-century settlers, along with farmers who found the rich glacial soil and long growing season of southern Wisconsin suitable for raising wheat.

By the late 1800s, among the green checkerboard fields of the countryside stood buildings that heralded a new era in the state's agriculture: milking barns, with their round silos full of cattle feed. The Swiss were among the Europeans who settled 19th-century Wisconsin, and they brought their cheese-making experience. By 1920, Wisconsin led the nation in dairy farming. With two million cows, it still produces more milk and cheese than any other state.

Placidly grazing cows may support a large part of Wisconsin's economy, but the pounding machines of many factories make manufacturing the state's largest industry. Germans, Poles, Italians, and British were among the Europeans who settled the industrial cities of the southeast, where one-third of Wisconsinites now live. Each group brought customs that are celebrated at festivals in cities of this industrial corner. German beer fests honor the beverage that made Milwaukee the brewing capital of the United States, a title it gained after the Chicago fire of 1871 destroyed that city's breweries.

The same night that Chicago burned, one of the country's most destructive forest fires raged in Wisconsin, laying waste a swath 40 miles (64 km) long and 10 miles (16 km) wide along the shore of Green Bay. In the town of Peshtigo and nearby villages, the fire claimed at least 1,200 lives, four times more than were lost in Chicago, but the news was not reported for days in the national newspapers because Chicago's conflagration had captured the headlines.

Wisconsinites pay high taxes, but these taxes bring them a wealth of social, educational, and community services. Many programs that improve people's lives had their start in Wisconsin. These range from the nation's first kindergarten, opened in Watertown in 1856, to minimum-wage laws, vocational schools, and the first law requiring seat belts in cars.

Wisconsin has a sizable Native American population, numbering about 40,000. Many of these people live on reservations, but by 150-year-old agreements with the federal government, they retain traditional hunting and fishing rights in territories they used to occupy outside. Disputes, both in court and out, have resulted from the exercise of these privileges, such as the right to spearfish out of season. Wisconsin's wildlife bounty now lies at the center of controversy between property owners, sport fishermen, and the area's original inhabitants, with the state striving to mediate their differences.

Area: *26th largest state, 56,153 sq mi (145,436 sq km)*
Population: *4,891,769; ranks 16th*
Major Cities: *Milwaukee, 628,088; Madison, 191,262; Green Bay, 96,466*
Manufacturing: *machinery, food products, paper products, metal products, transportation equipment, electronics, chemicals, scientific instruments, rubber and plastics, metals*
Agriculture: *milk, cattle, hogs, corn, potatoes*
Mining and Quarrying: *stone, sand and gravel*
Other Important Activities: *tourism, printing and publishing*
Statehood: *the 30th state; admitted May 29th, 1848*

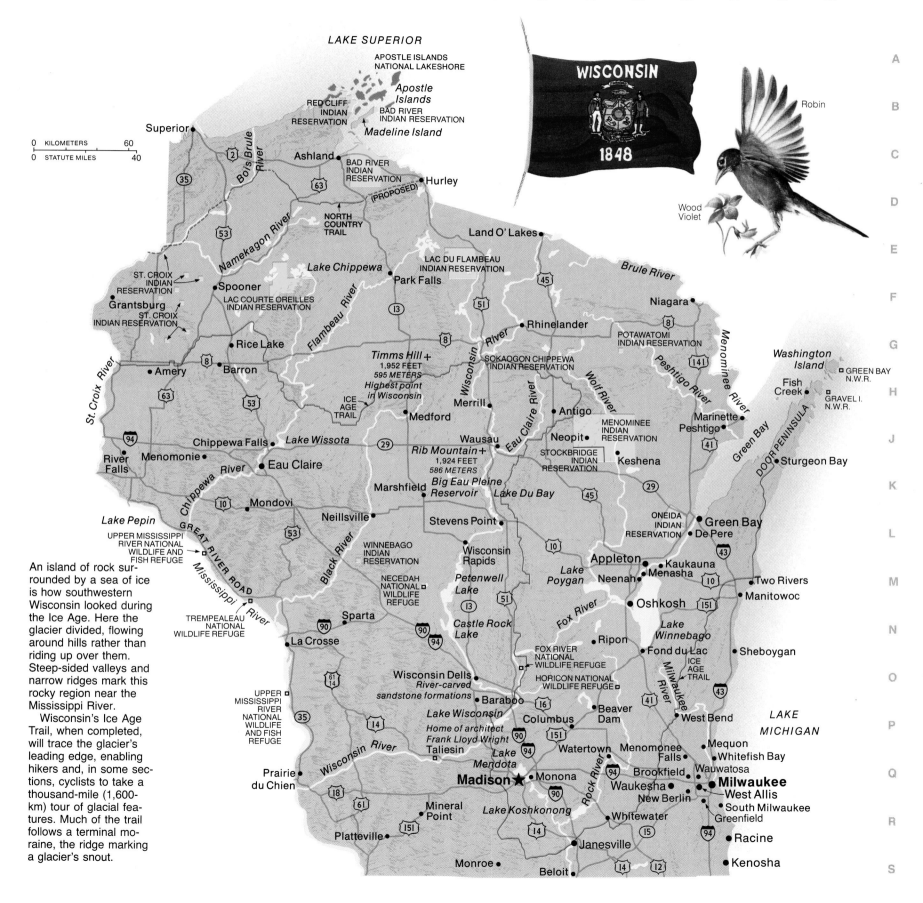

LAKE SUPERIOR

APOSTLE ISLANDS
NATIONAL LAKESHORE

*Apostle
Islands*

RED CLIFF
INDIAN
RESERVATION

BAD RIVER
INDIAN RESERVATION

Madeline Island

WISCONSIN

1848

Robin

Wood
Violet

Superior

Ashland

Hurley

(PROPOSED)

BAD RIVER
INDIAN
RESERVATION

NORTH
COUNTRY
TRAIL

Bois Brule River

0 KILOMETERS 60
0 STATUTE MILES 40

2

35

63

Namekagon River

53

Spooner

ST. CROIX
INDIAN
RESERVATION

Grantsburg

ST. CROIX
INDIAN RESERVATION

Lake Chippewa

LAC DU FLAMBEAU
INDIAN RESERVATION

Land O' Lakes

Brule River

45

Park Falls

LAC COURTE OREILLES
INDIAN RESERVATION

Rice Lake

Flambeau River

13

Rhinelander

Niagara

POTAWATOMI
INDIAN RESERVATION

8

Menominee River

Peshtigo River

141

*Washington
Island*

GREEN BAY
N.W.R.

Fish
Creek

GRAVEL I.
N.W.R.

Amery

8

Barron

63

53

Timms Hill +
1,952 FEET
595 METERS
*Highest point
in Wisconsin*

ICE
AGE
TRAIL

Merrill

Medford

Wisconsin River

SOKAOGON CHIPPEWA
INDIAN RESERVATION

Antigo

Wolf River

Neopit

MENOMINEE
INDIAN
RESERVATION

Keshena

Marinette

Peshtigo

Green Bay

DOOR PENINSULA

Sturgeon Bay

St. Croix River

94

Chippewa Falls

Lake Wissota

29

Wausau

Rib Mountain +
1,924 FEET
586 METERS

STOCKBRIDGE
INDIAN
RESERVATION

29

River
Falls

Menomonie

Chippewa River

Eau Claire

Eau Claire River

ONEIDA
INDIAN
RESERVATION

Green Bay

De Pere

43

Lake Pepin

UPPER MISSISSIPPI
RIVER NATIONAL
WILDLIFE AND
FISH REFUGE

GREAT RIVER ROAD

10

Mondovi

53

Marshfield

*Big Eau Pleine
Reservoir*

Lake Du Bay

45

Appleton

Kaukauna

Menasha

Two Rivers

Neillsville

Black River

Stevens Point

10

Neenah

10

Manitowoc

WINNEBAGO
INDIAN
RESERVATION

Wisconsin
Rapids

*Petenwell
Lake*

*Lake
Poygan*

Oshkosh

151

An island of rock surrounded by a sea of ice is how southwestern Wisconsin looked during the Ice Age. Here the glacier divided, flowing around hills rather than riding up over them. Steep-sided valleys and narrow ridges mark this rocky region near the Mississippi River.

Wisconsin's Ice Age Trail, when completed, will trace the glacier's leading edge, enabling hikers and, in some sections, cyclists to take a thousand-mile (1,600-km) tour of glacial features. Much of the trail follows a terminal moraine, the ridge marking a glacier's snout.

TREMPEALEAU
NATIONAL
WILDLIFE REFUGE

Mississippi River

Sparta

90

NECEDAH
NATIONAL
WILDLIFE
REFUGE

13

51

*Castle Rock
Lake*

Fox River

Ripon

*Lake
Winnebago*

Sheboygan

La Crosse

94

Fond du Lac

ICE
AGE
TRAIL

61
14

FOX RIVER
NATIONAL
WILDLIFE REFUGE

HORICON NATIONAL
WILDLIFE REFUGE

Milwaukee River

41

43

LAKE
MICHIGAN

UPPER
MISSISSIPPI
RIVER
NATIONAL
WILDLIFE
AND FISH
REFUGE

35

14

Wisconsin Dells
*River-carved
sandstone formations*

Baraboo

16

Lake Wisconsin

*Home of architect
Frank Lloyd Wright*
Taliesin

Columbus

Beaver
Dam

West Bend

Mequon

Whitefish Bay

90

151

Watertown

Menomonee
Falls

Wauwatosa

Prairie
du Chien

Wisconsin River

*Lake
Mendota*

94

Brookfield

Waukesha

Milwaukee

West Allis

18

Madison ★

Monona

90

Rock River

New Berlin

South Milwaukee

Greenfield

61

Mineral
Point

Lake Koshkonong

Whitewater

15

94

Racine

Platteville

151

14

Janesville

12

Kenosha

Monroe

Beloit

14

2

1

3

4

5

Wisconsin

1 *Stepping through a green carpet of duck-weed, a white-tailed buck sips from a woodland pond. In a state rich in wildlife, deer are the most numerous large mammals.*

2 *Lush pastures nourish dairy cows grazing on a southwestern farm. Nearly three-fourths of the milk that Wisconsin cows produce is destined for cheese making.*

3 *Lifting a bag of curd from a copper vat of whey, a cheese maker prepares it for molding and curing. Months later, this batch will yield a 200-pound (90-kg) wheel of Wisconsin Swiss.*

4 *At Fish Creek, on the Door Peninsula, hungry bystanders anticipate dinner at a fish boil, said to be a tradition brought by Scandinavian settlers.*

5 *A bold aerialist walks the wing of a 1940 plane at an Oshkosh International Fly-In Convention. More than a half million people and thousands of planes converge annually on Oshkosh to celebrate aviation's colorful history.*

Michigan

A dog barking at a giant mitten. That's one way to describe the shape of the two large peninsulas that make up the state of Michigan. The Straits of Mackinac (pronounced MACK-i-naw) divide the Upper Peninsula, adjoining northern Wisconsin, from the Lower Peninsula, which juts north from Indiana and Ohio.

Michigan's unusual shape goes back to a dispute with Ohio when boundaries were being drawn at the time of Michigan's admission to the Union. Both wanted a strip of territory that contained Toledo. After much squabbling, Michigan ceded it to Ohio, already a state, in exchange for the Upper Peninsula. At the time, some people considered the Upper Peninsula a useless, snowbound wilderness, but its wealth of minerals and forests proved them wrong.

Most of Michigan is surrounded by water. When the first voyageurs paddled into the area around 1620, they met Indians who masterfully plied the lakes and rivers in their birchbark canoes. As white settlers began to harvest Michigan's bountiful resources of timber, copper, and iron, they found transport easiest along the waterways. They enhanced natural routes where necessary. To move iron ore mined in Minnesota and the Upper Peninsula from Lake Superior into Lake Huron, a canal was opened in 1855. Enlarged, the Soo Canals soon ranked among the world's busiest waterways and, during World War II, the most strategic. To ensure the transport of essential raw materials, 20,000 troops protected the Soo Canals from sabotage.

But nothing can protect ships from the fearsome storms that often turn the Great Lakes into watery graveyards. In 1913 alone, Lake Superior claimed 40 ships. A song by Canadian balladeer Gordon Lightfoot about the freighter *Edmund Fitzgerald* records how, in 1975, "that good ship and true" went down with all hands "when the gales of November came early."

The Upper Peninsula (the "U.P." to Michiganders) shares a forested terrain with the northern half of the Lower Peninsula. Although it has 25 percent of the land, the U.P. contains only about 4 percent of the population. Many of its people are descendants of the early Welsh and Scottish copper miners and the Finns who came to cut white pine and then stayed on as dairy farmers when the timber was gone.

The northern half of the Lower Peninsula is sparsely populated. About 90 percent of Michiganders live south of an imaginary line between Muskegon and Bay City. Many of these people, and thousands from other states, head north to vacation among the trees, lakes, and wildlife.

People from New England and New York were the first to settle the southern Lower Peninsula, in the 1820s. Quiet towns centered around a church, a school, and a town hall reflected their Yankee origin. Fertile soils and a climate milder than up north made farming here easier, while the shore of Lake Michigan proved ideal for growing fruit.

To Michigan's Yankee character were added the customs of waves of European immigrants. The Dutch founded the city of Holland, complete with a windmill and tulip festivals. Germans, many of them shopkeepers, settled Saginaw and Ann Arbor, while Irish came to a southern part

Newly cut logs are pulled on horse-drawn skids along roads iced to make the journey smoother. This photo was taken in 1893 during a logging boom that depleted Michigan's pine forests.

of the state that reminded them of the green hills of their homeland.

A city on the narrow strait (*détroit* in French) joining Lake St. Clair and Lake Erie attracted the greatest diversity of people, many drawn by its burgeoning industries. As the logging of northern woods encouraged the building of railroads, Detroit began to produce the steel needed for railroad tracks, cars, and bridges. Into this city of promise came Germans, Poles, Hungarians, Italians, Ukrainians, and black Americans from the South. Other groups arrived later, including Mexicans and the largest population of Arab peoples in the United States.

The name "Detroit" is synonymous with the automobile. In 1896 the independent and simultaneous development of a gasoline-powered car by Henry Ford and Ransom Olds transformed Detroit, the state of Michigan, and the world.

A few huge auto companies established factories employing hundreds of thousands of people. With Detroit as its hub, the industry expanded to the suburbs and nearby cities. In recent years hard times hit. Recessions in the 1970s and '80s and consumer preference for more fuel-efficient, foreign-made cars shut down plants and cut back production, leading to 17 percent unemployment in Michigan by 1982.

Now Michigan has learned to diversify its economy. There are thousands of new jobs in small factories, in big companies that study the latest manufacturing technologies such as robotics, and in stores, restaurants, and computer firms. Even so, Michigan still produces more automobiles than any other state.

Area: *23rd largest state, 58,527 sq mi (151,586 sq km)*
Population: *9,295,297; ranks eighth*
Major Cities: *Detroit, 1,027,974; Grand Rapids, 189,126; Warren, 144,864*
Manufacturing: *transportation equipment, machinery, metal products, chemicals, food products, metals, rubber and plastics, furniture, paper products, electronics, stone, clay, and glass products, clothing*
Agriculture: *milk, vegetables, corn, cattle, soybeans, greenhouse and nursery products, fruits*
Mining and Quarrying: *oil and gas, iron ore, sand and gravel*
Other Important Activities: *tourism, printing and publishing*
Statehood: *the 26th state; admitted January 26, 1837*

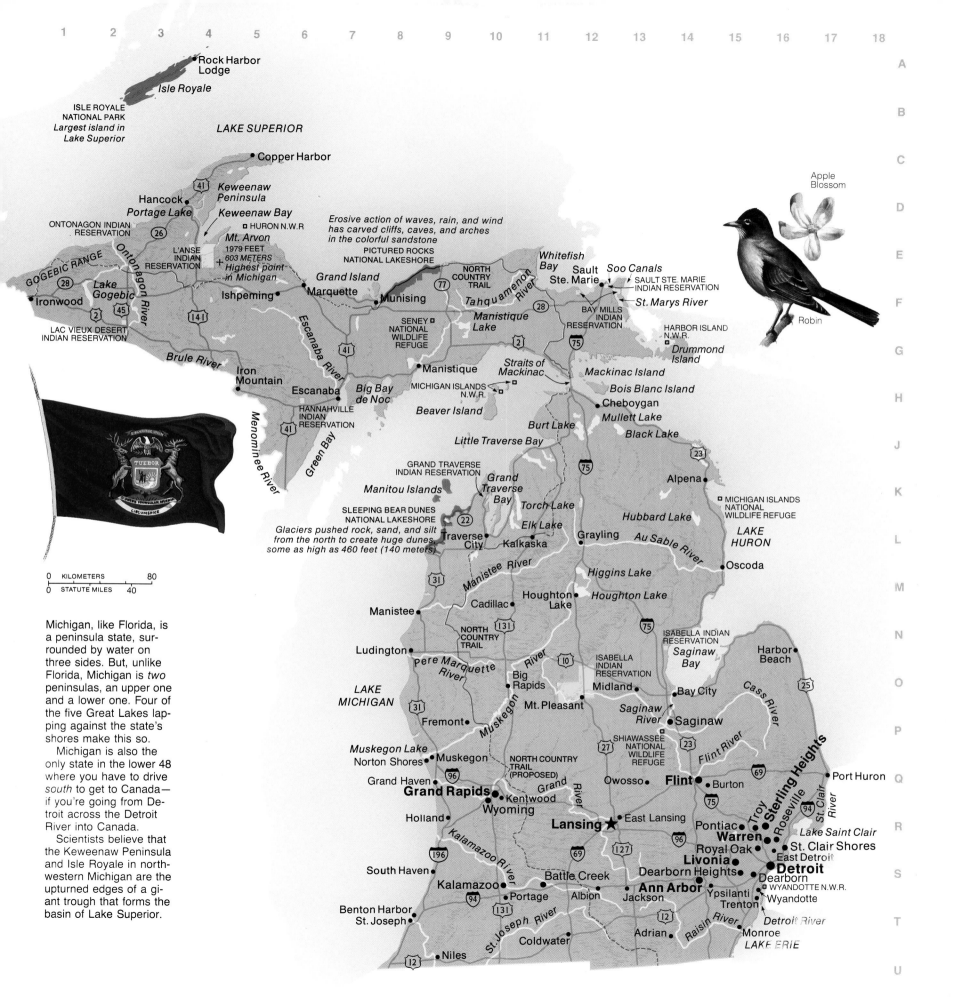

1 2 3 4 5 6 7 8 9 10 11 12 13 14 15 16 17 18

A B C D E F G H J K L M N O P Q R S T U

Rock Harbor
Lodge
Isle Royale

ISLE ROYALE
NATIONAL PARK
*Largest island in
Lake Superior*

LAKE SUPERIOR

Copper Harbor

41 Keweenaw
Peninsula
Hancock
Portage Lake Keweenaw Bay

ONTONAGON INDIAN
RESERVATION
26 HURON N.W.R
L'ANSE
INDIAN *Mt. Arvon*
RESERVATION **1979 FEET**
603 METERS
*Highest point
in Michigan*

*Erosive action of waves, rain, and wind
has carved cliffs, caves, and arches
in the colorful sandstone*
PICTURED ROCKS
NATIONAL LAKESHORE

Grand Island

GOGEBIC RANGE Ontonagon River
28 *Lake
Gogebic*
Ironwood
2
45
Ishpeming Marquette Munising
77
*Whitefish
Bay* Sault
Ste. Marie *Soo Canals*
SAULT STE. MARIE
INDIAN RESERVATION

LAC VIEUX DESERT
INDIAN RESERVATION
141
Tahquamenon River
28
BAY MILLS
INDIAN
RESERVATION
St. Marys River

Brule River Escanaba River
41
SENEY
NATIONAL
WILDLIFE
REFUGE
*Manistique
Lake*
2
75
HARBOR ISLAND
N.W.R.
*Drummond
Island*

Iron
Mountain
Escanaba
HANNAHVILLE
INDIAN
RESERVATION
41
*Big Bay
de Noc*
Manistique
MICHIGAN ISLANDS
N.W.R.
*Straits of
Mackinac*
Mackinac Island

Bois Blanc Island
Beaver Island
Cheboygan
Mullett Lake

Menominee River
Green Bay
Burt Lake
Black Lake

Little Traverse Bay
23

GRAND TRAVERSE
INDIAN RESERVATION
*Grand
Traverse
Bay*
75
Alpena

Manitou Islands
Torch Lake
Hubbard Lake
MICHIGAN ISLANDS
NATIONAL
WILDLIFE REFUGE

SLEEPING BEAR DUNES
NATIONAL LAKESHORE
*Glaciers pushed rock, sand, and silt
from the north to create huge dunes
some as high as 460 feet (140 meters)*
22
Elk Lake
Grayling
Au Sable River
**LAKE
HURON**

Traverse
City Kalkaska
Higgins Lake
Oscoda

| 0 | KILOMETERS | 80 |
| 0 | STATUTE MILES | 40 |

Manistee River
Houghton
Lake *Houghton Lake*

Manistee
31
Cadillac
75

Michigan, like Florida, is
a peninsula state, sur-
rounded by water on
three sides. But, unlike
Florida, Michigan is *two*
peninsulas, an upper one
and a lower one. Four of
the five Great Lakes lap-
ping against the state's
shores make this so.
131
NORTH
COUNTRY
TRAIL
ISABELLA INDIAN
RESERVATION

Ludington
NORTH
COUNTRY
TRAIL
*Pere Marquette
River*
River
10
ISABELLA
INDIAN
RESERVATION
*Saginaw
Bay*
Harbor
Beach

Michigan is also the
only state in the lower 48
where you have to drive
south to get to Canada—
if you're going from De-
troit across the Detroit
River into Canada.
**LAKE
MICHIGAN**
31
Big
Rapids
Midland Bay City
Cass River
25

Fremont
Mt. Pleasant
*Saginaw
River* Saginaw
27
SHIAWASSEE
NATIONAL
WILDLIFE
REFUGE

Scientists believe that
the Keweenaw Peninsula
and Isle Royale in north-
western Michigan are the
upturned edges of a gi-
ant trough that forms the
basin of Lake Superior.
Muskegon Lake
Muskegon
NORTH COUNTRY
TRAIL
(PROPOSED)
Grand
River
23
Flint River
69

Norton Shores
Muskegon
Owosso **Flint** Burton
Port Huron
75
Sterling Heights

Grand Haven
96
Kentwood
94
*St. Clair
River*

Grand Rapids
Wyoming
Lansing ★ East Lansing
96
Pontiac Troy
Roseville
Lake Saint Clair

Holland
69
127
Royal Oak
Warren
St. Clair Shores

196
Kalamazoo River
75
Livonia East Detroit†
Detroit

South Haven
69
Dearborn Heights
Dearborn
WYANDOTTE N.W.R.

Kalamazoo
Battle Creek
Ann Arbor
Ypsilanti
Wyandotte

Benton Harbor
94
Albion
Jackson
Trenton

St. Joseph
Portage
12
Raisin River
Monroe
Detroit River

131
St. Joseph River
Adrian
LAKE ERIE

Niles
12
Coldwater

TUEBOR
CIRCUMSPICE

*Apple
Blossom*

Robin

Michigan

1 *Fireworks burst over the Detroit skyline and the narrow strait that separates the city from its Canadian neighbor, Windsor, Ontario. Each year the two cities jointly celebrate their countries' independence.*

2 *Shiny cars of many makes and vintages illustrate the evolution of the automobile at the Henry Ford Museum in Dearborn.*

3 *Birch trees frame Mackinac Bridge, a five-mile-long (8-km) span connecting Michigan's Upper and Lower Peninsulas.*

4 *Modern Paul Bunyans push-pull a saw through a wooden beam in record time. Annual competitions such as this jamboree commemorate the logging history of the Upper Peninsula.*

5 *A research scientist in Midland arranges slides showing a rat's rate of absorption of a new chemical compound. Big business in Michigan, chemicals undergo testing before they are put on the market.*

1

2

3

4

5

Illinois

In 1933, six bridges raised in Chicago let barges pass into Lake Michigan. This is the end of a long gulf-to-lake trip up the Mississippi and connecting waterways from New Orleans.

From the shores of Lake Michigan, the bustling, teeming city of Chicago fans out to the Illinois prairie. By far the largest part of Illinois is prairie, pancake flat, with farms, small towns, and medium-size cities. Across the southern part of the state runs a strip of rocky, wooded hills, a bit of the Ozarks that reaches into Illinois from Missouri. The southernmost tip of the state is flat and belongs to the Gulf Coastal Plain.

Illinois marked the southern edge of glacial advance in North America. The ice sheets that descended here ground down landforms and left behind a thick blanket of dark, rich soil. Uplands appear only in the northwestern corner, a spot the glaciers skipped or touched lightly, and areas in the south and west of the Illinois River, where they never reached.

Chicago is part of Illinois only because of a proposal by territorial delegate Nathaniel Pope. At the time statehood was granted in 1818, Pope petitioned Congress to add a strip of land on the north that included some 60 miles (97 km) of Lake Michigan shoreline. Otherwise, the state's northern boundary would have ended at the tip of the lake and Chicago would be in Wisconsin.

Chicago, the country's third largest city and hub of air, rail, land, and water transportation, had its beginning in the late 1770s. Jean Baptiste Pointe du Sable, a black trapper and trader, built a cabin on marshy land along a river the Illiniwek Indians called Checagou. Chicago would undergo several transformations, including one as an army post, before a surge of growth that began in the 1860s. By then a canal had been dug that connected the city and the Great Lakes with the Mississippi River system. Chicago stood in the key spot where these important waterways linked up. A century later the completion of the St. Lawrence Seaway extended this route to the Atlantic Ocean.

From the 1860s on, Chicago offered the promise of jobs in factories, stockyards, lumberyards, and on the docks to Europeans fleeing violence or poverty at home. Southern blacks came too; today blacks make up 40 percent of Chicago's population. Migrations continue, bringing Asians, Puerto Ricans, and Mexicans as well. The city and its ever expanding suburbs are home to more than half of all Illinoisans.

Three-fifths of the factories in Illinois are in the Chicago area. The city's steel mills remain among the world's most productive. Chicago's mail-order businesses and grain exchange are the largest in the U. S., its O'Hare International Airport the world's busiest. Three of the tallest buildings in the world tower over downtown Chicago. The nation's first skyscraper rose there on a frame of steel in 1884, as part of the rebuilding after the Great Fire of 1871 destroyed the earlier wooden structures, taking 300 lives.

Some 500 rivers drain the state. The Illinois River flows 273 miles (439 km) to the Mississippi River, the western boundary. The Wabash and the Ohio form the borders on the south and southeast. The city of Cairo, where the Mississippi and the Ohio converge, was an important cotton port more than a hundred years ago. Farmers here grew cotton until the 1960s, before switching to more profitable soybeans.

This part of Illinois has a southern heritage. The first settlers here were from states to the south or southeast. Illinois pioneers included a poor farm family from Kentucky named Lincoln. They settled near Springfield, the state capital, where young Abe held a number of jobs and read law before beginning his career in politics.

After the Erie Canal was finished in 1825, providing an easy route across the Appalachians, settlers from the East and from Europe joined the southern immigrants or moved into central or northern Illinois, where they discovered the prairie, covered with tall, waving green and purplish grasses.

Prairie sod was thick and gummy, and did not yield to wooden or iron plows. But in 1837 a blacksmith named John Deere invented a self-polishing steel plow that cut through the sod with ease. Opening a factory in Moline, Deere made his fortune. The company he started still manufactures farm machinery, one of the state's largest exports.

In a state where more than 80 percent of the population lives in urban areas, a surprising 80 percent of the land is farmed. Much of the fertile glacial soil, up to 75 feet (23 m) thick in some places, supports crops of corn and soybeans. The corn in turn fattens some 4.4 million Illinois hogs that are sent to market each year.

In the ground are some of the largest coal reserves in the U. S. When burned, this mostly bituminous, or soft, coal produces more pollution than hard coal. But as cleaner methods for burning are developed, this Illinois resource could help solve the country's energy problems.

Area: *24th largest state, 56,345 sq mi (145,934 sq km)*
Population: *11,430,602; ranks sixth*
Major Cities: *Chicago, 2,783,726; Rockford, 139,426; Peoria, 113,504*
Manufacturing: *machinery, food products, chemicals, metal products, electronics, transportation equipment, metals, rubber and plastics, scientific instruments, paper products, stone, clay, and glass products, furniture, clothing*
Mining and Quarrying: *coal, oil and gas, stone, sand and gravel*
Agriculture: *soybeans, corn, hogs, cattle, milk, wheat, hay, greenhouse and nursery products*
Other Important Activities: *finance, transportation, tourism, printing and publishing*
Statehood: *the 21st state; admitted December 3, 1818*

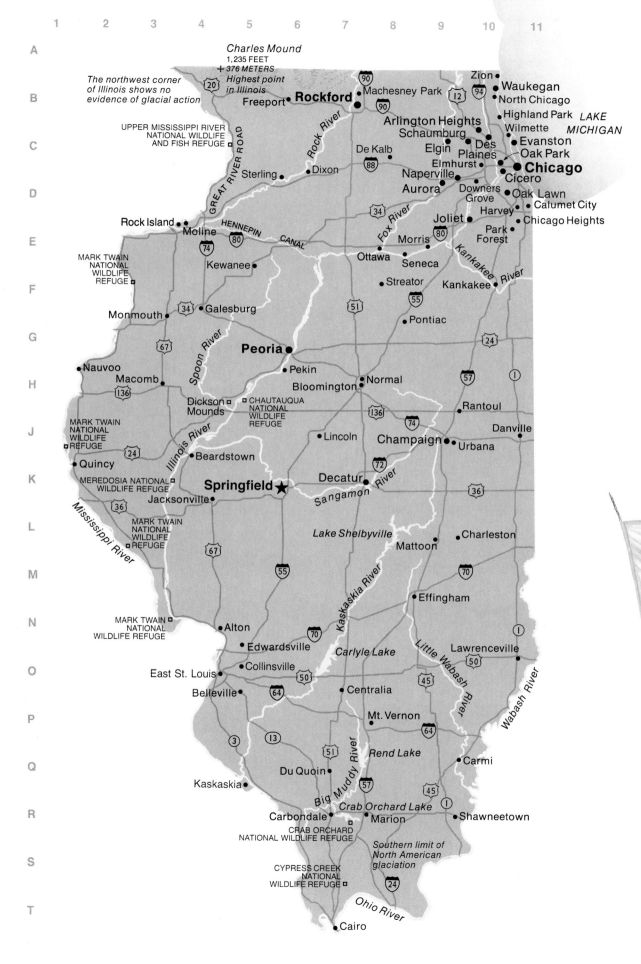

1 2 3 4 5 6 7 8 9 10 11

A

Charles Mound
1,235 FEET
+ 376 METERS
The northwest corner   Highest point
of Illinois shows no   in Illinois
evidence of glacial action

B   Freeport • **Rockford**   Machesney Park   Zion
                                              Waukegan
                                         North Chicago
                                         Highland Park   *LAKE*
                               Arlington Heights   Wilmette   *MICHIGAN*
                               Schaumburg   Evanston

C   UPPER MISSISSIPPI RIVER   De Kalb   Elgin   Des   Oak Park
    NATIONAL WILDLIFE   Plaines
    AND FISH REFUGE   Naperville   **Chicago**
    Sterling   • Dixon   Elmhurst   Cicero

D   Aurora   Downers   Oak Lawn
                                         Grove   Calumet City
    Rock Island   Harvey   Chicago Heights
E   Moline   HENNEPIN   Joliet   Park
             CANAL   Morris   Forest
    MARK TWAIN   Ottawa
    NATIONAL   Kewanee   Seneca   Kankakee
    WILDLIFE   River
    REFUGE
F   Streator   Kankakee
             Galesburg   55
    Monmouth   34   51   Pontiac
                                              24
G
             Peoria
    Nauvoo   Pekin   Normal   57
H   Macomb   Bloomington   136
    136   Dickson   CHAUTAUQUA   Rantoul
             Mounds   NATIONAL
    MARK TWAIN   WILDLIFE
    NATIONAL   REFUGE   74   Danville
J   WILDLIFE   Lincoln   Champaign
    REFUGE   24   Urbana
    Quincy   Beardstown   72
                          Decatur
K   **Springfield**★   Sangamon
    Jacksonville   River   36
    36   MARK TWAIN
L   NATIONAL   Lake Shelbyville
             WILDLIFE   Charleston
             REFUGE   67   Mattoon
M   55
    MARK TWAIN   70
N   NATIONAL   70   Alton   Effingham
    WILDLIFE REFUGE
             Edwardsville   Carlyle Lake
O   East St. Louis   Collinsville   Lawrenceville
             50   50
    Belleville   64   Centralia   45
P   Mt. Vernon
             3   13   64
Q   51   Rend Lake   Carmi
    Kaskaskia   Du Quoin   57
R   Crab Orchard Lake   45
    Carbondale   Marion   1
    CRAB ORCHARD   Shawneetown
    NATIONAL WILDLIFE REFUGE
S   CYPRESS CREEK   Southern limit of
    NATIONAL   North American
    WILDLIFE REFUGE glaciation
T   24
             Ohio River
             Cairo

The Mississippi River
forms the entire western
boundary of Illinois, or at
least it did until the flood
of 1881. In April of that
year, the raging Missis-
sippi broke through a
narrow-necked peninsula
that separated it from the
mouth of the Kaskaskia
River. Kaskaskia, a
village that had been settled by Indians and
French traders and had
served as a territorial
and state capital, found
itself a 10,000-acre
(4,050-ha) island.

Eventually the Missis-
sippi abandoned its old
channel, and Kaskaskia
became a piece of Illi-
nois on the Missouri side
of the river.

Violet

Cardinal

1

2

3

4

5

Illinois

1 *Antenna repair atop Chicago's Hancock Center requires steel nerves. Lesser high rises march along Lake Michigan's shore.*

2 *The Ohio (at right) meets the Mississippi River at Cairo. Flatlands like Egypt's Nile Delta suggested the city's name.*

3 *Steel bins store 260,000 bushels of corn on an Illinois farm. The state vies yearly with Iowa as top corn producer.*

4 *Sleeping on the job, a dummy fitted with electronic sensors tests mattress comfort at a Chicago factory.*

5 *A scientist at Fermilab, near Chicago, examines a glass-and-wire device that detects the pion, a subatomic particle. Enrico Fermi and his University of Chicago colleagues produced the world's first self-sustaining nuclear chain reaction in 1942.*

Indiana

A fertile valley of Indiana's Wabash River witnessed two attempts to form a utopia, or ideal society. The first community, named Harmonie, was founded in 1814-15 by a group of Lutheran separatists (called Harmonists) fleeing persecution in Germany. They settled in Pennsylvania before moving to Indiana. Harmonie lasted only ten years, time enough to build a village and plant fields, vineyards, and orchards; then the Harmonists returned to Pennsylvania. The second community, New Harmony, drew artists and scholars from eastern states. These pioneers came to the village in 1825 to pursue knowledge in an atmosphere of equality and independence. Their experiment lasted only two years, but the town of New Harmony remains a source of artistic creativity in modern Indiana.

The state has produced many writers whose works are regarded as American classics. Generations of schoolchildren have memorized the verses of 19th-century poet James Whitcomb Riley, including his *Little Orphan Annie*. A native of Terre Haute, Theodore Dreiser wrote the novels *An American Tragedy* and *Sister Carrie*. High school and college literature classes often read the books of Indianapolis-born Kurt Vonnegut, Jr., author of *Slaughterhouse Five* and *Cat's Cradle*.

Indiana bears the marks of glaciers over five-sixths of its terrain. In the north, glaciers left behind moraines, deposits of rocks and debris, and depressions that filled with water to form kettle hole lakes. Along part of the Lake Michigan shore, winds have piled immense hills of sand called the Indiana Dunes. The largest dune, Mount Baldy, is bare of vegetation, and is called a "live" dune because prevailing winds move it slowly away from the lakeshore. Older dunes, stabilized by a covering of soil, grasses, and trees, lie farther inland.

On the western end of the Lake Michigan shore stands a group of industrial cities, midway between sources of materials needed by the steel industry: the iron ranges of Minnesota and the coalfields of southern Indiana and Illinois.

In the early 20th century one of the world's largest steel mills was built in Gary. Like Chicago, and unlike the rest of Indiana, the area drew large numbers of Poles, Hungarians, Czechs, Italians, and other European immigrants, as

By the early 1900s, roads like this had been improved to ease the farmer's trip from farm to market. Smooth roads did nothing to improve the behavior of these wayward hogs.

well as blacks from southern states. Even after suffering severe economic problems, northern Indiana remains the country's largest steel producer. But the people pay a price. Smokestacks spew out pollutants that, despite attempts to control them, can darken the sky at noon.

Central Indiana is covered by till plains that create a gently rolling landscape. Till, or glacial debris, is a mixture of rocks, clay, sand, and other sediment deposited by glaciers. The deep, rich soil of the till plains provides the state's best farmland. Pioneers of the early 19th century flocked to this part of Indiana to buy farms from the federal government at low rates.

The glaciers stopped short of south-central Indiana, leaving there a more rugged terrain of steep hills interspersed with lowlands. Large deposits of coal and petroleum underlie the area. So does a valuable outcrop of limestone that "cutters," generations of quarry workers from Bloomington and nearby towns, have carved up to build landmarks such as the Empire State

Building and Rockefeller Center in New York City, the Pentagon in northern Virginia, and the U. S. Treasury in Washington, D. C.

A road map of Indiana shows at its center a ring around the state capital, Indianapolis. Of the 91,395 miles (147,055 km) of roads in the state, many converge on Indianapolis. Among them are U. S. 40, once called the National Road, a wide, bumpy track that took pioneers to the western frontier.

The state was an early center of the automobile industry, producing some 200 makes of cars before being eclipsed by Michigan's carmakers. Today, Indiana-made Stutzes, Duesenbergs, and Maxwells rank among the antique autos most prized by collectors. Each year, on Memorial Day weekend, Indianapolis resumes its place as automotive capital with the running of the Indianapolis 500. Drivers in state-of-the-art cars circle the Indy track 200 times, hoping to win the prize of more than three million dollars that is awarded for the fastest time.

As a transportation hub, Indianapolis became a center for the processing and distribution of farm products. The manufacturing of medicines, cars, aircraft parts, and electrical goods also made the city an industrial center. When hard times hit the auto industry in the 1970s and '80s and other factories began to close, the leaders of Indianapolis looked for new ways to help the city prosper. Sports was one solution, suggested by the popularity of the Indy 500. The city built the 61,000-seat Hoosier Dome. Newly constructed facilities for swimming, bicycle racing, tennis, and track-and-field have turned Indianapolis into a world-recognized center for amateur and professional sports.

Area: *38th largest state, 36,185 sq mi (93,720 sq km)*
Population: *5,554,159; ranks 14th*
Major Cities: *Indianapolis, 731,327; Ft. Wayne, 173,072; Evansville, 126,272*
Manufacturing: *metals, chemicals, transportation equipment, electronics, machinery, food products, metal products, rubber and plastics, scientific instruments, furniture, lumber and wood products*
Mining and Quarrying: *coal, limestone, sand and gravel, oil and gas*
Agriculture: *soybeans, corn, hogs, cattle, milk, eggs*
Other Important Activities: *printing and publishing*
Statehood: *19th state; admitted December 11, 1816*

Indiana is mostly flat. As the drainage pattern of the rivers shows, it also slopes to the southwest. Most of the rivers flow toward the Wabash River, which marks the southwestern border.

Some southern parts, untouched by glaciers during the Ice Age, are hilly and wooded. Here, towns with names such as Stoney Lonesome and Beanblossom attract artists and artisans.

Quarries south of Indianapolis produce some of the nation's finest limestone, formed from the skeletons of tiny sea creatures that lived here when ancient oceans covered the area.

Cardinal

Peony

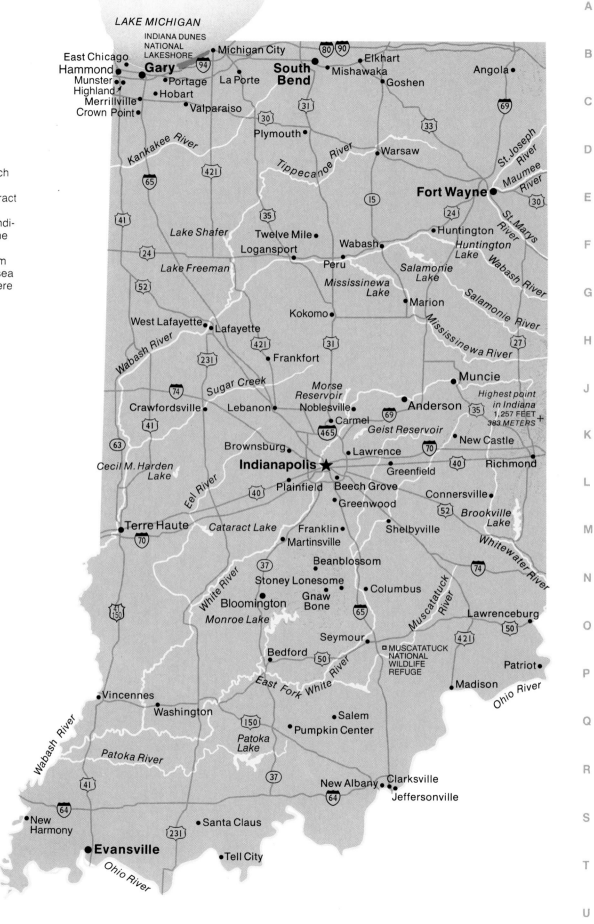

LAKE MICHIGAN

INDIANA DUNES NATIONAL LAKESHORE

Michigan City

East Chicago
Hammond
Munster
Highland
Merrillville
Crown Point
Gary
Portage
Hobart
Valparaiso

La Porte

South Bend
Mishawaka

Elkhart
Goshen

Angola

Kankakee River

Plymouth

Warsaw

St. Joseph River
Maumee River

Fort Wayne

St. Marys River

Tippecanoe River

Lake Shafer

Twelve Mile

Logansport
Peru

Wabash
Huntington
Huntington Lake

Wabash River

Lake Freeman

Mississinewa Lake

Salamonie Lake

Salamonie River

West Lafayette
Lafayette

Wabash River

Kokomo

Marion

Mississinewa River

Frankfort

Sugar Creek

Muncie

Morse Reservoir

Highest point in Indiana
1,257 FEET
383 METERS

Crawfordsville
Lebanon
Noblesville
Anderson
New Castle

Carmel

Geist Reservoir

Brownsburg
Lawrence

Indianapolis

Greenfield
Richmond

Cecil M. Harden Lake

Eel River

Plainfield
Beech Grove
Greenwood

Connersville
Brookville Lake

Terre Haute

Cataract Lake

Franklin
Martinsville

Shelbyville

Whitewater River

Beanblossom

White River

Stoney Lonesome
Gnaw Bone

Columbus

Muscatatuck River

Lawrenceburg

Bloomington

Monroe Lake

Seymour

MUSCATATUCK NATIONAL WILDLIFE REFUGE

Patriot

Bedford

East Fork White River

Madison

Ohio River

Vincennes

Washington

Salem
Pumpkin Center

Patoka Lake

New Albany
Clarksville
Jeffersonville

Wabash River

Patoka River

New Harmony

Santa Claus

Evansville

Tell City

Ohio River

0 KILOMETERS 60
0 STATUTE MILES 40

Indiana

1 *A craftsman polishes a saxophone at a factory in Elkhart. The city is one of the world's chief producers of band instruments.*

2 *Sitting on some of the lowest land in Indiana, the town of New Harmony overlooks the Wabash River as it flows southward to its confluence with the Ohio.*

3 *Skilled nurses attend a patient at a children's hospital in Indianapolis. The capital has become a regional center for advanced medical care.*

4 *Home to pro football's Colts, the Hoosier Dome symbolizes Indianapolis's commitment to sports. In 1984 the city used the 61,000-seat stadium to entice the team to leave Baltimore, Maryland.*

5 *Polluting smoke billows from a steel mill in northwestern Indiana. Foreign competition, automation, and other kinds of new technology mean fewer jobs for residents of this industrial region.*

1

2

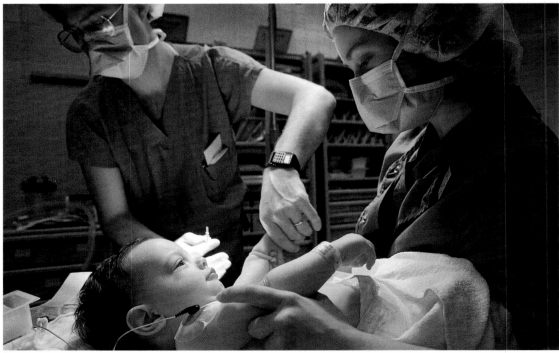

3

5

4

Ohio

In Harriet Beecher Stowe's 1852 antislavery novel, *Uncle Tom's Cabin*, the slave Eliza and her baby made a daring winter escape across the Ohio River from Kentucky, leaping from one floating raft of ice to another, "till dimly, as in a dream, she saw the Ohio side, and a man helping her up the bank."

During the mid-1800s, Ohio abolitionists, with antislavery workers in other states, provided sanctuaries called stations along the Underground Railroad, a network of escape routes for slaves from the South. The fugitives usually moved at night on foot, often alone, but sometimes sheltering in the homes of sympathizers across the state, until they could board boats and cross Lake Erie to freedom in Canada.

About 2,000 years ago, Indians hunted, fished, and farmed in the river valleys of central and southern Ohio and traded for raw materials from the Rocky Mountains to the Gulf of Mexico. They left evidence of remarkable engineering ability: thousands of hand-built earthen mounds, many of them immense and often made in geometric or animal shapes. These Mound Builders were gone, and other Indian cultures had taken their place, when the first white explorers arrived in the 17th century.

At the end of the Revolutionary War, parcels of land in Ohio were awarded or sold to war veterans and others who wanted to start new lives on the frontier. In 1788 a group from Massachusetts and Connecticut sailed down the Ohio to its confluence with the Muskingum River. Their community, Marietta, opened Ohio to permanent white settlement and became the first of many prosperous ports along the river.

The most famous is Cincinnati, which sits on a graceful bend of the Ohio in a low basin backed by seven hills. In the early 1800s, the port moved the grain, produce, and livestock of central Ohio farmers, first on flatboats and then on steamboats. Early settlers from New Jersey, Virginia, and New England were soon joined by Germans, who worked in the slaughterhouses and sausage factories. Today many people help manufacture soap products and machine tools—machines that shape metal for making parts for automobiles, refrigerators, and other products. Residents of Ohio, Indiana, and Kentucky head to cosmopolitan Cincinnati, shopping lists in

Around 1895 an elementary school teacher maintained authority with a pointer and a stern manner. Fractions on the blackboard signify a typical, fact-oriented education based on the three R's.

hand. The Ohio River still moves the state's resources, often in lines of 20 barges, each loaded with thousands of pounds of coal, oil, iron ore, chemicals, metals, salt, sand, or gravel.

In 1796 New Englanders arrived on the shores of Lake Erie, shallowest of the Great Lakes. By the mid-1800s, Cleveland was one of the fastest growing cities in the third most populous state in the country. Cleveland became home to the largest assortment of ethnic groups in Ohio. Germans, Irish, Poles, Italians, Czechs, Russians, southern blacks, and Greeks number among the dozens of different groups who came, especially after the Civil War. They worked in the iron and steel mills, oil refineries, and other factories that line Lake Erie and the Cuyahoga River. By the early 1900s, Ohio was an industrial state, three-fourths of whose people would eventually live in urban areas. Throughout most of the state, large cities and towns punctuate vast spreads of corn, wheat, and cattle pasture.

Other factory towns face Lake Erie. Toledo makes glass and automobile parts, and serves as a regional coal distribution center. Lorain makes steel, as well as cars, trucks, and buses.

Akron used to make more bias-ply rubber tires than any city in the world. But foreign competition, the popularity of longer wearing radial tires, and the moving of factories south and west forced Akron's rubber plants to close. Thousands of people lost their jobs. Now city leaders look for ways to restore prosperity. One hope is the Thomas Edison Program, a state project that brings together Ohio companies, up-to-date technologies, and the financing that makes industrial development possible.

Columbus, Ohio's capital and largest city, has mostly light industry. But what it has more of than any other U. S. city except Washington, D. C., is data base information. Enormous quantities of data are stored at Ohio State University and at labs, research institutes, scientific information services, and computer libraries.

The landscape of southeastern Ohio is steep, rugged, and heavily wooded, part of the Appalachian Plateau that also extends into Pennsylvania and West Virginia. Rich natural resources including coal, clay, oil, salt, and natural gas provide mining jobs for the area's residents.

For more than a century, Ohio's industries grew unchecked. Factories belched out smoke and sent chemical waste into rivers and lakes. In the 1960s, Lake Erie was declared "dead" from pollution, and recreational uses of the lake were banned. Since then, laws passed to clean up the lake by limiting industrial waste have paid off, although toxic sediments still cause concern. Swimming beaches are now open, and walleye by the million again await fishermen's lures.

Area: *35th largest state, 41,330 sq mi (107,044 sq km)*
Population: *10,847,115; ranks seventh*
Major Cities: *Columbus, 632,910; Cleveland, 505,616; Cincinnati, 364,040*
Manufacturing: *transportation equipment, machinery, metal products, chemicals, metals, food products, electronics, rubber and plastics, stone, clay, and glass products, paper products, scientific instruments*
Mining: *coal, oil and gas*
Agriculture: *soybeans, milk, corn, cattle, hogs*
Other Important Activities: *printing and publishing*
Statehood: *the 17th state; admitted March 1, 1803*

Prehistoric Indians lived along waterways such as the Ohio River, which today forms much of the state's eastern and southern borders. Some of the mounds they built still exist, linked by a national scenic trail.

Dashed red lines on the map show unfinished parts of the North Country Trail, planned as the nation's longest marked footpath. When completed, the trail will extend 3,200 miles (5,150 km) from North Dakota to New York. Ohio's section will link archaeological sites along the Little Miami River to Great Serpent Mound and Mound City near Chillicothe.

KILOMETERS 60
0
STATUTE MILES 30
0

1 2 3 4 5 6 7 8 9 10 11 12 13 14 15

A
B
C
D
E
F
G
H
J
K
L
M
N
O
P
Q
R

Ashtabula

LAKE ERIE

CEDAR POINT NATIONAL WILDLIFE REFUGE
WEST SISTER ISLAND NATIONAL WILDLIFE REFUGE
Kelleys Island

Toledo
Oregon
Maumee
OTTAWA NATIONAL WILDLIFE REFUGE

Painesville
Willoughby
Euclid Mentor
East Cleveland Wickliffe
Cleveland South Euclid
Lakewood Cleveland Heights
Lorain Shaker Heights
North Olmsted Garfield Heights
Elyria Parma
Strongsville CUYAHOGA VALLEY NATIONAL RECREATION AREA
Brunswick
Cuyahoga River
Cuyahoga Falls Kent
Mosquito Creek Lake
Warren
Niles
Austintown
Youngstown
Struthers
Boardman

Bryan

Defiance
Maumee River

Bowling Green

Fremont
Sandusky

Norwalk

Findlay

Blanchard River

Van Wert

Lima
Ottawa River

Celina
Grand Lake

Wapakoneta
Indian Lake

Bellefontaine
Campbell Hill 1,550 FEET +472 METERS Highest point in Ohio

Sidney
Great Miami River

Piqua

Greenville
Troy

Huber Heights
Springfield

Dayton
Kettering
Fairborn
Beavercreek
Xenia

Middletown

Hamilton
Fairfield
North College Hill
Cheviot
Sharonville
Reading
Norwood
Cincinnati

Fostoria

Tiffin
Sandusky River

Shelby
Ashland

Kenton
Scioto River
Marion

Marysville

Mansfield

Olentangy River

Delaware Lake
Mt. Vernon
Delaware

Alum Creek Lake
Hoover Reservoir

Upper Arlington
Worthington
Whitehall
Columbus
Reynoldsburg

Newark

Wooster
Massillon
Barberton
Akron

Tuscarawas River
North Canton
Canton

East Liverpool

New Philadelphia
Atwood Lake
Leesville Lake

Mohican River

Coshocton

Steubenville

Cambridge
New Concord
Zanesville
Senecaville Lake (PROPOSED)
NORTH COUNTRY TRAIL

Dillon Lake

Martins Ferry

Ohio River

Buckeye Lake

Lancaster

Washington Court House

Wilmington

Paint Creek

Circleville
Ancient Indians shaped mounds from the earth to cover their dead
MOUND CITY GROUP NATIONAL MONUMENT
Chillicothe

Rocky Fork Lake

GREAT SERPENT MOUND

Scioto River

Jackson

Athens
Belpre

Hocking River

Marietta

NORTH COUNTRY TRAIL

Muskingum River

Portsmouth

Gallipolis

Ironton

Ohio River

NORTH COUNTRY TRAIL
(PROPOSED)

Cardinal

Scarlet Carnation

1

2

Ohio

1 *Lighted buildings old and new illuminate downtown Cleveland. In the background flows the Cuyahoga River.*

2 *Native Americans built this earthen coiled serpent more than 1,500 years ago. The Great Lakes region has thousands of these mounds, used for rituals or burials.*

3 *Pitching straw is all in a day's work at a county fair. Rural traditions remain strong in largely industrial Ohio.*

3

4 *In a lab near Cincinnati, researchers sample the breath of people testing the effectiveness of toothpaste and mouthwash.*

5 *Young racers in engineless cars burn up the track at the All-American Soap Box Derby, held each August in Akron. Children from around the world bring home-made cars to compete in the downhill race.*

The Heartland

When pioneering settlers rolled westward across the heart of the continent, they found themselves adrift on a sea of grass that seemed to stretch onward endlessly. It could be unnerving, especially for those who had lived all their lives in the comforting shade of eastern forests. For now they were venturing into a new land, a place of endless open sky and sun and wind, a realm of rolling prairies with only widely scattered hills and highlands. What trees grew here stood mainly along rivers and in upland areas such as the Black Hills, the Ozark Plateau, and along Lake Superior.

In the eastern part of the prairie rainfall was usually plentiful. Here the Indian grass and big bluestem grew up to eight feet (2 m) tall. The land was fertile, but so thickly and tightly matted with grass roots that it took as many as 20 draft animals to drag a wooden or cast-iron plow through the sod. It wasn't until John Deere's Prairie Queen plow of self-polishing steel came into widespread use in the 1850s that a farmer working alone could break through the sod and turn the fertile glacial soil beneath.

Farther west, pioneer families found that the land gradually grew drier and the grasses grew shorter. On the Great Plains—the western part of the prairie—they encountered what was at first thought to be the Great American Desert, a semiarid expanse of short, bunched grasses best suited to raising cattle. But the plains, though dry, were fertile. What they needed was water. Under large areas of the land lay a layer of sand and gravel so vast that it could hold enough water to fill Lake Huron. Windmills that drew water out of the ground made parts of the high plains ideal for growing wheat—spring wheat in the colder north, and winter wheat in the milder south.

This heartland region, with less than 15 percent of the land in the United States, raises more corn than all of Europe, more wheat than South America, and more cattle than Australia. Cities from Minneapolis and St. Paul to Wichita and St. Louis rose to prominence as transportation and processing centers to serve farmers and cattlemen. Although they have since branched into other businesses, they still thrive as centers of agribusiness, the modern farming industry that finds its roots deep in heartland soil.

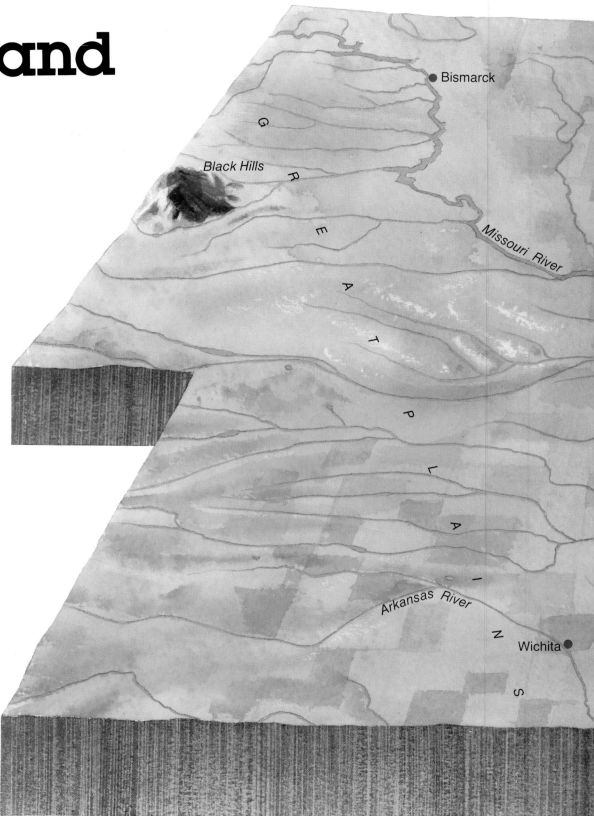

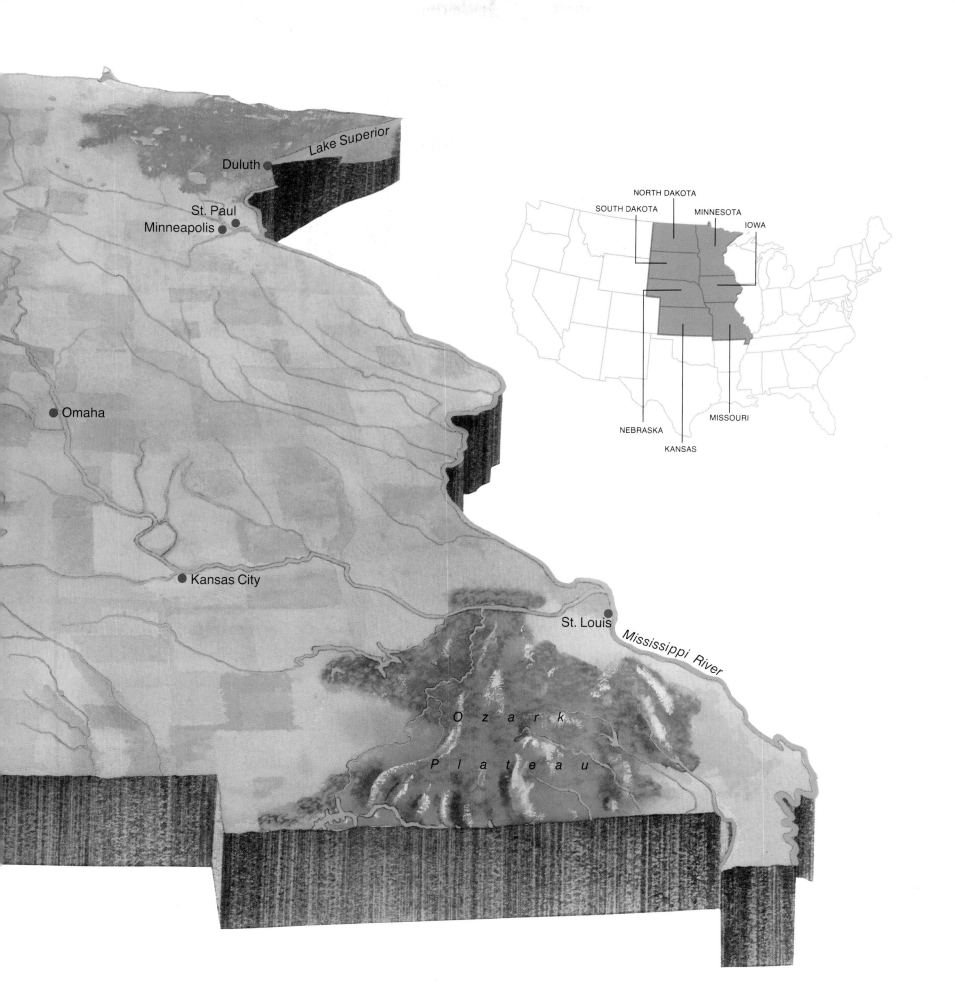

Lake Superior

Duluth

St. Paul
Minneapolis

Omaha

Kansas City

St. Louis

Mississippi River

O z a r k

P l a t e a u

NORTH DAKOTA

SOUTH DAKOTA

MINNESOTA

IOWA

NEBRASKA

MISSOURI

KANSAS

North Dakota

Geographically, North Dakota is right in the middle of it all. A stone monument near the town of Rugby marks the dead center of the continent. From there it is about 1,500 miles (2,400 km) to the Atlantic Ocean, Pacific Ocean, Arctic Ocean, and the Gulf of Mexico.

North Dakota has endless prairie horizons and few people. Only half of North Dakotans are urban dwellers and about 15 percent live on farms or ranches. In the 1980s North Dakota faced a population drain. Near the Montana line a billboard pleaded, "Stay in North Dakota—Custer was healthy when he left." Now there are predictions that the state's oil reserves may need new workers and that the population may rise a little.

North Dakota's wild and woolly weather contributes to its loneliness. Dust storms, raging blizzards, and some of the hottest and coldest temperatures ever recorded on the continent help "keep the riffraff out," as one hard-bitten Dakotan explained. North Dakota lies far from the moderating influences of oceans and large lakes. It has no mountains and few trees to blunt the winds that race across its open expanses.

For those who tough it out, there are compensations. The valley of the Red River of the North has some of the world's best cropland, black soil rich in humus, decomposed plant and animal matter. These bottomlands are the bed of a glacial lake that drained away when the ice retreated about 10,000 years ago. The fertile topsoil, combined with long summer days and adequate rainfall, produces bumper crops. Huge farms, typical of today's agribusiness, are not new to North Dakota. In the 1870s, speculators bought hundreds of thousands of acres of cheap land and created what were called "bonanza farms" to grow wheat and attract settlers as workers.

West of the Red River Valley, at a steeply pitched slope called an escarpment, the gently rolling Drift Prairie steps upward. The prairie gets its name from drift, rock debris carried here by glaciers. Over thousands of years, with weathering and the addition of organic matter, drift becomes soil.

The Drift Prairie is dimpled by thousands of kettle hole lakes and ponds that occupy depressions formed by the melting of large chunks of buried glacial ice. Today the kettle hole regions are a haven for millions of migrating ducks and geese, as well as for resident pheasants, grouse, partridges, and meadowlarks.

Farmers here grow wheat, a lot of it. No other state grows more spring durum wheat, used to make spaghetti and other pasta. Nor does any other state grow more barley, or flaxseed, used to make linseed oil for paint, or sunflowers, whose seeds are pressed for high-protein vegetable oil.

Near the northern part of the Drift Prairie,

On a day in 1905 the citizens of Mott turn out to await the arrival of the stagecoach and the mail. This settlement on the Great Plains was established as a trading center on the Cannonball River.

along the border with Canada, rises a cluster of low, lake-studded hills called the Turtle Mountains. This is one of the state's few forested areas. It is also the site of a summer camp for artists and musicians, and a spectacular international garden that commemorates the years of peace between Canada and the United States.

The Great Plains rise west of the Drift Prairie. North Dakotans call this region the Missouri Plateau, for the river that curves across the western part of the state. On the east bank of the Missouri the state capital, Bismarck, serves the surrounding region with agriculture-related industries such as food processing, the manufacture of farm machinery, and shipping. A two-mile-wide (3-km) dam across the river, the nation's largest earthen dam, creates Lake Sakakawea, named for the Indian woman who accompanied explorers Meriwether Lewis and William Clark on their trek across the continent in the early 1800s. The plateau is hilly, stony country wrinkled by gorges and ravines. Rain is sparse here, and cattle graze the shortgrasses.

Here, too, are found oil and lignite, a soft, brownish coal that fuels local power plants. The lignite lies close to the surface. Huge shovels and draglines gouge it out of the earth, often scarring the countryside.

The Indians who lived in the western Dakotas knew a section of the Missouri Plateau as Mako Sica—"land bad." We know this jumbled maze of hills and pinnacles carved by the Little Missouri River as the Badlands. It was here that Theodore Roosevelt ranched during the 1880s, before he became President of the United States. Today his Elkhorn Ranch makes up part of North Dakota's only national park, a place where bison roam and coyotes prowl.

Area: *17th largest state, 70,703 sq mi (183,121 sq km)*
Population: *638,800; ranks 47th*
Major Cities: *Fargo, 74,111; Grand Forks, 49,425; Bismarck, 49,256*
Agriculture: *wheat, cattle, barley, sunflowers, sugar beets, milk*
Mining: *oil and gas, coal*
Manufacturing: *food products, machinery, transportation equipment, stone, clay, and glass products, chemicals, metal products*
Other Important Activities: *tourism, printing and publishing*
Statehood: *39th state; admitted November 2, 1889*

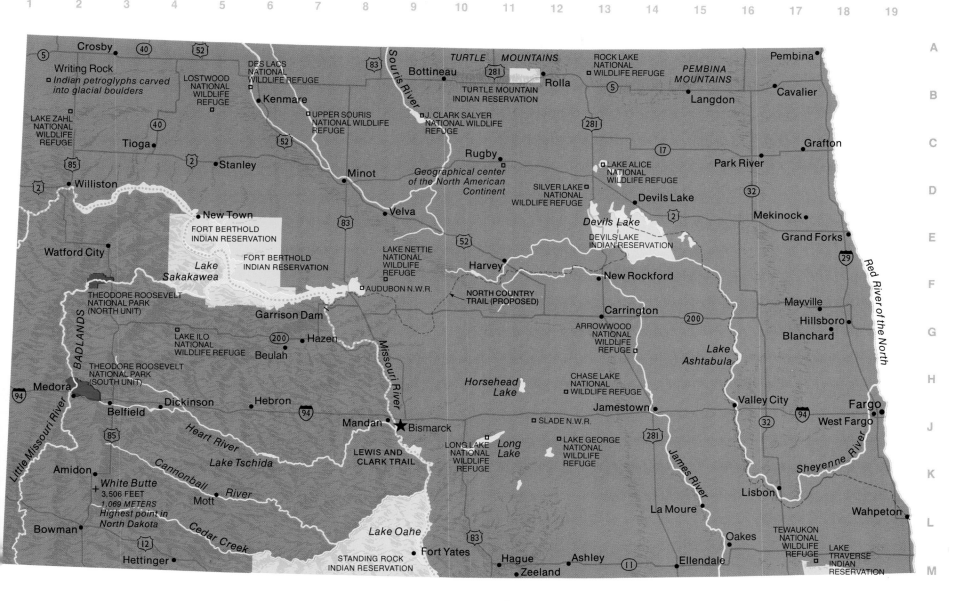

1　2　3　4　5　6　7　8　9　10　11　12　13　14　15　16　17　18　19

A

Crosby ● ⑳

Writing Rock ☐52

□ *Indian petroglyphs carved into glacial boulders*

⑤

DES LACS NATIONAL WILDLIFE REFUGE

LOSTWOOD NATIONAL WILDLIFE REFUGE

TURTLE MOUNTAINS

ROCK LAKE NATIONAL WILDLIFE REFUGE

PEMBINA MOUNTAINS

Pembina ●

A

Souris River

Bottineau ●

②⑧① Rolla ●

TURTLE MOUNTAIN INDIAN RESERVATION

□ LAKE ALICE NATIONAL WILDLIFE REFUGE

Langdon ●

Cavalier ●

B

LAKE ZAHL NATIONAL WILDLIFE REFUGE

Kenmare ●

⑳

②⑧①

UPPER SOURIS NATIONAL WILDLIFE REFUGE

J. CLARK SALYER NATIONAL WILDLIFE REFUGE

Rugby ●

⑤

⑰

Grafton ●

C

Tioga ●

⑤②

Stanley ●

②

Minot ●

Geographical center of the North American Continent

SILVER LAKE NATIONAL WILDLIFE REFUGE □

Park River ●

㉜

D

⑧⑤

Williston ●

②

Velva ●

⑧③

Devils Lake ●

②

Mekinock ●

Grand Forks ●

Watford City ●

New Town ●

FORT BERTHOLD INDIAN RESERVATION

Lake Sakakawea

FORT BERTHOLD INDIAN RESERVATION

⑤②

LAKE NETTIE NATIONAL WILDLIFE REFUGE □

Harvey ●

Devils Lake

DEVILS LAKE INDIAN RESERVATION

㉙

Red River of the North

E

□ AUDUBON N.W.R.

NORTH COUNTRY TRAIL (PROPOSED)

New Rockford ●

Mayville ●

Hillsboro ●

F

BADLANDS

THEODORE ROOSEVELT NATIONAL PARK (NORTH UNIT)

Garrison Dam

LAKE ILO NATIONAL WILDLIFE REFUGE □

②⑳

Hazen ●

Carrington ●

②⑳

ARROWWOOD NATIONAL WILDLIFE REFUGE

Lake Ashtabula

Blanchard ●

G

THEODORE ROOSEVELT NATIONAL PARK (SOUTH UNIT)

Beulah ●

Missouri River

Horsehead Lake

CHASE LAKE NATIONAL WILDLIFE REFUGE □

Medora ●

⑨④

Dickinson ●

Hebron ●

①④

Jamestown ●

Valley City ●

Fargo ●

H

Little Missouri River

Belfield ●

Heart River

Mandan ●

★ Bismarck

SLADE N.W.R. □

West Fargo ●

⑨④

J

⑧⑤

Cannonball ●

River

Lake Tschida

LEWIS AND CLARK TRAIL

LONG LAKE NATIONAL WILDLIFE REFUGE

Long Lake

LAKE GEORGE NATIONAL WILDLIFE REFUGE

②⑧①

James River

㉜

Sheyenne River

Amidon ●

+ White Butte 3,506 FEET 1,069 METERS *Highest point in North Dakota*

Mott ●

Lisbon ●

K

Bowman ●

Cedar Creek

Lake Oahe

La Moure ●

Wahpeton ●

L

⑫

Hettinger ●

STANDING ROCK INDIAN RESERVATION

Fort Yates ●

⑧③

Hague ●

● Zeeland

Ashley ●

⑪

Ellendale ●

Oakes ●

TEWAUKON NATIONAL WILDLIFE REFUGE

LAKE TRAVERSE INDIAN RESERVATION

M

0 KILOMETERS 80
0 STATUTE MILES 40

Glaciers helped shape much of North Dakota. Moving sheets of ice reached almost to the present-day Missouri River. Ice blocked pre-glacial rivers from their old channels and forced them to cut new southerly courses. Several combined to form the Missouri.

South and west of the river, the land is rough and hilly, slashed and carved by erosion. No glacier smoothed the land here. East of the river the land is mostly flat to gently rolling, and twice drops down toward the north-flowing Red River of the North, the state's eastern boundary.

Wild Prairie Rose

Western Meadowlark

North Dakota

1 *A young brave takes part in the Grass Dance at a powwow held each July near Lake Sakakawea. "It is a time," according to one participant, "to teach children to share in our culture." The dance recalls past hunts and memorable deeds.*

2 *A country churchyard greens checkerboard farmland in the Red River Valley. Land now lush with wheat fields reaching to the horizon once lay at the bottom of ancient glacial Lake Agassiz.*

3 *Beneath a brooding sky, six-foot-tall (2-m) sunflowers face the sun near an old grain elevator in the Red River Valley. Heads containing up to a thousand protein-rich seeds produce high-quality oils for cooking and making margarine.*

4 *Technicians check a Minuteman missile, one of 300 buried in steel silos beneath the state's prairies. This one, at Grand Forks Air Force Base, is used for training.*

5 *A baby pelican begs a meal from its parent. These white pelicans, and half the wild ducks in the lower 48 states, are among the 353 bird species found in North Dakota.*

1

2

3

4

5

Minnesota

Minnesota has some 22,000 lakes, wetlands, and ponds, more than any other state except Texas and Alaska, thanks mostly to glaciers that left behind hollowed-out places that filled with water. One of them, Lake Itasca, is the source of the Mississippi River. Minnesota's rivers and streams extend 92,000 miles (148,000 km) and flow in three directions. The Mississippi drains southward into the Gulf of Mexico, while rivers in the northern part of the state flow north into Hudson Bay or east into Lake Superior.

Water has helped make Minnesota a transportation and commercial center for the upper Midwest. Duluth, with its neighbor, Superior, Wisconsin, is the world's busiest freshwater port. From the western end of Lake Superior, Duluth has access to the Atlantic Ocean through the Great Lakes and the St. Lawrence Seaway. Ships from Duluth carry grain and iron ore overseas or to factories near the Great Lakes.

Frontiersmen and trappers could travel up the Mississippi as far as the Falls of St. Anthony without stopping to portage their goods. Indians camped near the falls, fur traders set up posts, and in the 1820s the U. S. Army built an outpost there. Settlers arrived, and the twin cities of Minneapolis and St. Paul grew up on either side of the river. Minnesota's capital, St. Paul, was briefly known in its earliest days as Pig's Eye, after a voyageur who lived there. It became St. Paul when a Roman Catholic priest built a chapel near the river, dedicating it to the saint. The Falls of St. Anthony provided power for milling grain and cutting wood, activities that in time became giant industries. Today electronics and other high-tech industries are also economically important to both cities.

About half of all Minnesotans live in and around the Twin Cities, an area that includes 1,650 parks and 650 lakes. In summer, people swim and sail. They canoe from lake to lake. Winter finds them skating, ice fishing, and even playing softball on ice.

Minneapolis has rebuilt much of its downtown. An elevated network of glass-enclosed, climate-controlled walkways, called skyways, links buildings in a large area of downtown Minneapolis. The skyways shelter pedestrians from cold, snowy winters and summer heat.

In the early days Minnesota's great forests of white and red pine supplied much of the lumber used to build towns and cities across the Great Plains. The northern third of the state still is wild and woodsy, a haven for deer, moose, bears, and birds. Waterfowl find food and shelter in bogs and marshes. Along the border with Canada spreads the Boundary Waters Canoe Area Wilderness, a thousand lakes in a million acres. Through this watery maze paddled Indians, explorers, and voyageurs. Today it is the country's only national canoe area, a haven that

In costumes white as snow and sparkly as ice, Minneapolis children present a winter pageant in 1925. Minnesota residents traditionally enliven winter with festivals and seasonal sports.

shuts out most intrusions of the modern world.

Minnesota's rich glacial soils, covering the western part of the state, attracted throngs of farmers from eastern states and from Germany, Scandinavia, and other parts of Europe. Sprinkled with lakes and streams, the rolling farmlands of the region are home to the dairy cattle that make Minnesota a leading producer of milk, butter, and cheese.

In 1865 a geologist discovered rich deposits of iron ore in the northeastern wedge of the state known as Arrowhead Country. Soon other rich deposits turned up in the Mesabi Range. Glaciers had nearly exposed these deposits, leaving only a thin layer of drift soil to cover them. They were easily mined by stripping away the topsoil and digging giant pits to get the ore out of the ground. By the beginning of the 20th century more than 100 open-pit mines dotted the Mesabi Range. Mining camps such as Hibbing, Virginia, and Gilbert grew into prosperous towns.

Minnesota provides about 80 percent of the nation's iron ore, but most of the richest deposits have been depleted. The chief ore mined now comes from a hard rock called taconite. The taconite is processed to extract the ore, which is made into pellets and shipped to steel mills around the Great Lakes.

The processing of taconite produces tailings, or waste materials, that carry cancer-causing asbestos. Controversy began to flare in the 1960s over the dumping of these tailings into Lake Superior by a plant near Duluth. Some of the fibers were entering the city's water supply. In 1976, after years of arguments, a federal judge ordered the dumping halted. Now the tailings are deposited in a huge, specially built basin on land where they no longer pose a threat.

Area: *12th largest state, 84,402 sq mi (218,601 sq km)*
Population: *4,375,099; ranks 20th*
Major Cities: *Minneapolis, 368,383; St. Paul, 272,235; Bloomington, 86,335*
Manufacturing: *machinery, food products, metal products, scientific instruments, electronics, paper products, transportation equipment*
Agriculture: *milk, soybeans, cattle, corn, hogs, turkeys, wheat*
Mining and Quarrying: *iron ore, sand and gravel*
Other Important Activities: *shipping, tourism, printing and publishing*
Statehood: *the 32nd state; admitted May 11, 1858*

NORTHWEST ANGLE
Area of Minnesota resulting from inaccurate maps used for Treaty of Paris at close of American Revolution

RED LAKE INDIAN RESERVATION

Lake of the Woods

A

B

Warroad

Hallock

11

Rainy River

Baudette

11

International Falls

89

VOYAGEURS NATIONAL PARK

C

59

72

AGASSIZ NATIONAL WILDLIFE REFUGE

BOIS FORTE INDIAN RESERVATION

GRAND PORTAGE INDIAN RESERVATION

D

75

1

Thief River Falls

Upper Red Lake

71

Vermilion Lake

Ely

BOUNDARY WATERS CANOE AREA

Eagle Mountain+
2,301 FEET
701 METERS
Highest point in Minnesota

GRAND PORTAGE NATIONAL MONUMENT

E

East Grand Forks

RED LAKE INDIAN RESERVATION

Lower Red Lake

1

VERMILLION LAKE INDIAN RESERVATION

Grand Marais

Crookston

DEER CREEK INDIAN RESERVATION

F

Red River of the North

2

Cass Lake

Lake Winnibigoshish

Chisholm

MESABI RANGE

Virginia

Lake Superior

Bemidji

Gilbert

G

WHITE EARTH INDIAN RESERVATION

LEECH LAKE INDIAN RESERVATION

Hibbing

169

Largest open-pit iron ore mine in U.S.

61

Lake Itasca

Leech Lake

Grand Rapids

2

SANDY LAKE INDIAN RESERVATION

53

Two Harbors

H

HAMDEN SLOUGH N.W.R.

NORTH COUNTRY TRAIL

St. Louis River

Moorhead

TAMARAC NATIONAL WILDLIFE REFUGE

Mississippi River

FOND DU LAC INDIAN RESERVATION

Duluth

J

Detroit Lakes

(PROPOSED)

210

RICE LAKE NATIONAL WILDLIFE REFUGE

35

Cloquet

94

Crow Wing River

K

10

Wadena

Brainerd

MILLE LACS NATIONAL WILDLIFE REFUGE

SANDSTONE NATIONAL WILDLIFE REFUGE

Fergus Falls

Mille Lacs Lake

MILLE LACS INDIAN RESERVATION

MILLE LACS INDIAN RESERVATION

L

10

Little Falls

St. Croix River

M

Lake Traverse

Wheaton

Alexandria

169

N

Morris

Sauk Rapids

95

SHERBURNE N.W.R.

Rum River

35

Big Stone Lake

St. Cloud

GREAT RIVER ROAD

O

BIG STONE NATIONAL WILDLIFE REFUGE

71

Litchfield

Blaine

Willmar

12

Brooklyn Park

Brooklyn Center

94

Lake Minnetonka

Minneapolis

★**St. Paul**

P

Montevideo

Hutchinson

St. Louis Park

Bloomington

Richfield

UPPER SIOUX INDIAN RESERVATION

212

MINNESOTA VALLEY NATIONAL WILDLIFE REFUGE

Burnsville

PRAIRIE ISLAND INDIAN RESERVATION

Minnesota River

75

SHAKOPEE INDIAN RESERVATION

Q

Redwood Falls

LOWER SIOUX INDIAN RESERVATION

169

Red Wing

Lake Pepin

UPPER MISSISSIPPI RIVER NATIONAL WILDLIFE AND FISH REFUGE

Marshall

Northfield

R

59

New Ulm

St. Peter

Faribault

52

GREAT RIVER ROAD

Mississippi River

14

Mankato

PIPESTONE NATIONAL MONUMENT

Waseca

Owatonna

Rochester

S

Winona

35

T

Worthington

Fairmont

90

Albert Lea

Austin

52

1   2   3   4   5   6   7   8   9   10   11   12   13   14   15   16   17

Showy Lady's Slipper

Common Loon

Part of Minnesota jogs into Canada, cut off from the rest of the state by the waters of Lake of the Woods. That's because after the American Revolution, when diplomats drew up the new nation's boundaries, they tried to include the headwaters of the Mississippi River. But it wasn't until nearly 150 years later that the river's real source, Lake Itasca, was identified. Thus the Northwest Angle is an enclave, a piece of American territory surrounded by a foreign country.

0   KILOMETERS   80
0   STATUTE MILES   40

1

Minnesota

1 *A trader fills orders at the Minneapolis Grain Exchange, the nation's largest cash grain market. Tins hold grain samples ranging from barley to soybeans. Minneapolis, settled by European immigrants in the 1800s, ranks among the world's leading grain and flour centers.*

2 *Contour plowing protects a field near Rochester. Rows of corn and alfalfa weave across slopes, rather than up and down, to help keep the soil from washing away when it rains.*

2

3

4

5

3 *Blanket tossers loft a girl into the air as part of St. Paul's Winter Carnival, a two-and-a-half-week-long midwinter celebration that dates back to 1886. One of the carnival's oldest features, blanket bouncing is a traditional northland sport.*

4 *Dusted with snow, a gray wolf roams the forests of northern Minnesota. Deep woods, although heavily logged in the past, still cover about a third of the state and shelter some 1,400 wolves.*

5 *Split Rock Lighthouse, a beacon for sailors since 1910, crowns a cliff along the shore of Lake Superior near Two Harbors. For more than half a century the landmark light warned ore ships and other vessels away from submerged reefs and ledges.*

South Dakota

In about the middle of South Dakota, the Missouri River divides the state into two very different parts. The river marks the leading edge of glacial ice that had retreated by 10,000 years ago. The river and the rich, loamy soils and gently swelling hills of eastern South Dakota are its legacy. To the west of the river spread the grasslands of the Great Plains and rugged land carved into hills and canyons by wind and water.

Glaciers also created thousands of kettle hole lakes and ponds across eastern South Dakota. Once farmers drained the wetlands in their fields because they were a nuisance to plow around and they took up space that could be used for crops. But draining led to a declining duck population; the soil began to dry out as water tables dropped; and without the ponds to hold excess water, floods sometimes occurred.

Today water holes are being preserved or restored, many with money raised from the sale of state and federal duck stamps to hunters and collectors. Some farmers stock the ponds with fish. Others rent them in season to duck hunters. During dry spells, grasses sprout for animal pasture. "Early settlers found wetlands dotting the landscape," observes one soil expert, "and valued them for their water, hay, and fire protection." Now they are valued again.

West of the Missouri River, ranchers graze sheep and cattle. Not many trees grow in western South Dakota except on the weathered granite pinnacles and ridges of the Black Hills. Their name comes from thick stands of pondero-

Each fall in the 1890s, Indian children were transported to boarding schools where they were required to dress and act like whites, to study in English, and to take an English name.

sa pine, aspen, and spruce that make the hills appear darker than the surrounding land.

East of the Missouri, rainfall is usually adequate, and farmers grow crops and operate feedlots to fatten cattle shipped from western parts of the state. With 91 percent of its land devoted to agriculture, South Dakota earns about 12 percent of its income from farming and ranching, a higher percentage than any other state.

The eastern half is the most heavily populated. Nearly two-thirds of all South Dakotans live here, most on farms or in small rural communities. Sioux Falls is a center for meat-packing and other agriculture-related businesses. Computer industries have come to the city, and banks and insurance companies process information there.

Native Americans make up more than 7 percent of South Dakota's population, a greater proportion than in any other state except Alaska, Oklahoma, and New Mexico. Most live on huge reservations where poor land makes farming and ranching difficult. But the Pine Ridge Reservation has begun to experiment with farming methods such as drip irrigation and wind fences to protect crops. The reservation has a radio station that broadcasts in the Lakota Sioux language. Young leaders are

working to build new pride in a people who have suffered a hard life.

The Sioux regarded the Black Hills as sacred, the center of their spiritual world, "the heart of everything that is." In the Black Hills they found bountiful hunting grounds filled with streams and lush meadows grazed by deer, elk, pronghorns, and bison. When gold was discovered there in 1874, miners and settlers swarmed into the hills, onto land that the government had given to the Indians and eventually took back. The invasion touched off a series of skirmishes that led to Lt. Col. George A. Custer's defeat in nearby Montana Territory.

Gold still comes from the Black Hills. Near the town of Lead (pronounced Leed, from the miners' term for the ore deposit) is the Homestake Mine. The country's oldest gold mine in continuous operation, Homestake produces about 160 million dollars' worth of gold a year and ranks in production second only to Nevada's Carlin Mines. The Indians still battle for the return of their sacred hills, but now the struggle takes place in courts and in Congress. In 1985 Sioux leaders won the right to set up a community in the Black Hills near Rapid City, where they practice and teach religious traditions.

Tourism is an important source of income for South Dakota, ranking right behind agriculture. Each year, from spring to fall, more than two million visitors come to the Black Hills to see the immense faces of Presidents Washington, Jefferson, Lincoln, and Theodore Roosevelt carved out of Mount Rushmore. But when winter comes, snow whitens the granite heads and, except for the sweep of cold wind, quiet descends on the Black Hills.

Area: *16th largest state, 77,116 sq mi (199,730 sq km)*
Population: *696,004; ranks 45th*
Major Cities: *Sioux Falls, 100,814; Rapid City, 54,523; Aberdeen, 24,927*
Agriculture: *cattle, hogs, soybeans, corn, milk, wheat*
Manufacturing: *food products, machinery, electronics, lumber and wood products, metal products, stone, clay, and glass products, transportation equipment, jewelry*
Mining: *gold*
Other Important Activities: *tourism*
Statehood: *the 40th state; admitted November 2, 1889*

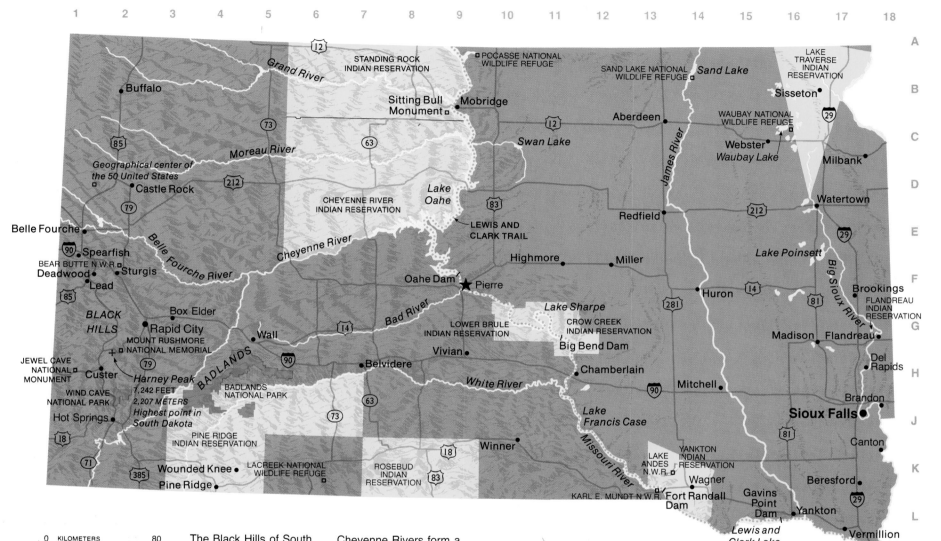

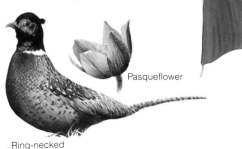

| | 1 | 2 | 3 | 4 | 5 | 6 | 7 | 8 | 9 | 10 | 11 | 12 | 13 | 14 | 15 | 16 | 17 | 18 | |

A

B
Buffalo

STANDING ROCK INDIAN RESERVATION

POCASSE NATIONAL WILDLIFE REFUGE

SAND LAKE NATIONAL WILDLIFE REFUGE   Sand Lake

LAKE TRAVERSE INDIAN RESERVATION

Grand River

Sitting Bull Monument   Mobridge

Sisseton

C
Moreau River

Aberdeen

Swan Lake

WAUBAY NATIONAL WILDLIFE REFUGE

Webster
Waubay Lake

Milbank

James River

Geographical center of the 50 United States

D
Castle Rock

CHEYENNE RIVER INDIAN RESERVATION

Lake Oahe

LEWIS AND CLARK TRAIL

Redfield

Watertown

E
Belle Fourche

Spearfish

Cheyenne River

Highmore   Miller

Lake Poinsett

BEAR BUTTE N.W.R.   Sturgis
Deadwood
Lead

Belle Fourche River

F
Oahe Dam   Pierre

Huron

Brookings

G
BLACK HILLS

Box Elder

Rapid City
MOUNT RUSHMORE NATIONAL MEMORIAL

Bad River

LOWER BRULE INDIAN RESERVATION

Lake Sharpe

CROW CREEK INDIAN RESERVATION

Big Bend Dam

FLANDREAU INDIAN RESERVATION

Madison   Flandreau

H
JEWEL CAVE NATIONAL MONUMENT   Custer

Harney Peak
7,242 FEET
2,207 METERS
Highest point in South Dakota

Wall

BADLANDS

BADLANDS NATIONAL PARK

Vivian

White River

Chamberlain

Mitchell

Del Rapids

WIND CAVE NATIONAL PARK

Belvidere

J
Hot Springs

PINE RIDGE INDIAN RESERVATION

Lake Francis Case

Brandon

Sioux Falls

K
Winner

Wounded Knee   LACREEK NATIONAL WILDLIFE REFUGE

ROSEBUD INDIAN RESERVATION

YANKTON INDIAN RESERVATION

LAKE ANDES N.W.R.   Wagner

Beresford

Canton

Pine Ridge

Missouri River

L
KARL E. MUNDT N.W.R.   Fort Randall Dam

Gavins Point Dam

Yankton

Lewis and Clark Lake

Vermillion

M

The Black Hills of South Dakota are not hills. They are the stubs of mountains much older than the Rocky Mountains, the remnants of a molten dome called a batholith that blistered up beneath the Earth's crust about 55 million years ago. Untouched by the glaciers that smoothed much of the state east of the Missouri River, the Black Hills survive as the highest mountains east of the Rockies.

The Belle Fourche and Cheyenne Rivers form a necklace around the hills before they join the Missouri River. Dams have widened parts of the river into long lakes.

Pasqueflower

Ring-necked Pheasant

1

2

3

4

5

South Dakota

1 *The bones of a rhinoceros-like titanothere rise at a museum in Rapid City. The now parched Badlands, rich in fossils, were lush and green when titanotheres lived here some 25 million years ago. Indians, who first found the huge skulls, called the fearsome beast Thunderhorse.*

2 *A high-school band performs in the Black Hills beneath the stony gaze of Presidents Washington, Jefferson, Theodore Roosevelt, and Lincoln. Carved from the granite flanks of Mount Rushmore, each head is as tall as a six-story building.*

3 *Beneath grassy plateaus, the ridges and canyons of the Badlands reveal layers of time. The whitish band near the top was formed by ash from volcanoes to the west or southwest, ejected some 25 million years ago. Streams gradually gnawed away at the plateaus, exposing layers of pinkish siltstone, clay, sand, and the lowest and oldest—65-million-year-old black shale that formed the bottom of an ancient sea.*

4 *A bearskin, the heads of elk and a bighorn sheep, and other Wild West memorabilia adorn the walls and rafters of an old-style saloon in Deadwood.*

5 *A black-tailed prairie dog in Wind Cave National Park near Custer throws its head back to shrill an "all clear" signal. Some 350 bison and 18 prairie dog villages share this remnant patch of America's once vast interior grasslands.*

Nebraska

Some people thought Nebraska was a desert. Its hills and grasslands rolled on as far as the eye could see. What trees there were grew only in draws and along riverbanks. How could crops grow here? "Almost wholly unfit for cultivation," reported Maj. Stephen Long, who led an expedition along the Platte River in 1820.

Major Long was mistaken. He was traveling in a year of drought more severe than the Dust Bowl years of the 1930s. Almost from the day it became a state, in 1867, Nebraska has ranked as a leading farm state. Beef, corn, and dairy products are important income producers, and the state vies with Indiana as the top grower of the hard-kerneled corn used for popcorn.

Farms and ranches take up about 96 percent of Nebraska's land, a greater percentage than in any other state. In eastern Nebraska, where rainfall is usually sufficient, corn and soybeans are the big crops. Oats grow there, too, and wheat, alfalfa, and a feed grain called sorghum. Farmers also raise corn-fed hogs and poultry.

Most of the rest of the state lies in the Great Plains, rolling terrain that slopes gradually upward toward the west. Rainfall here is usually sparse, but by irrigating their fields farmers can grow bountiful crops. Only Texas raises more beef cattle than Nebraska. A writer once described this part of the state as a land of "broad fields, deep skies, wind, and sunlight; clouds racing over prairie swells; herds of cattle grazing on the sandhills; red barns and white farmhouses surrounded by fields of tasseling corn and ripening wheat."

The Missouri River runs along Nebraska's eastern boundary. The Platte River, "a mile wide and an inch deep" in pioneer days, cuts across the state from west to east and joins the Missouri near Omaha. Nebraska's central location and the route along the Platte Valley made Nebraska a funnel for transcontinental travelers. Steamboats traveled the Missouri, and the lush Platte floodplains provided water and fodder for wagon trains, stagecoaches, and the Pony Express. During the 1840s and 1850s hundreds of thousands of pioneers bound for Utah, Oregon, or California rumbled through the state in their covered wagons. In places their wheels wore ruts that can be seen to this day.

In time the Platte became the route followed

On trial in 1879 for leaving his reservation without government permission, Ponca chief Standing Bear, shown here with his friend Julius Meyer, won acquittal and recognition that an Indian "is a person" in the eyes of the law.

by the nation's first transcontinental railroad, as well as by Interstate 80, the most heavily traveled east-west highway. Today the Platte, much less than a mile wide and far more than an inch deep, is regulated, its water released from reservoirs to meet the needs of irrigation, recreation, flood control, and power generation.

Nebraska's two biggest cities, Omaha and Lincoln, the capital, are near the Missouri River. Omaha, once known mainly for meat-packing and food processing, is now a center for finance, insurance, telecommunications, and the transportation and distribution of goods. Offutt Air Force Base, a few miles south of the city, serves as headquarters for the Air Force's Strategic Air Command and provides thousands of jobs.

Omaha is one of the country's largest processors of meats and meat products. Hogs, for example, supply not only pork and bacon for the table but also heart valves for human use, insulin for diabetics, and skin to help treat burn victims. Other towns, such as Fremont and Lincoln, also have large meat-packing plants. Mills in central and western Nebraska produce large quantities of food for livestock.

Nebraska's Sand Hills cover about 20,000 square miles (51,800 sq km) of the plains in the north-central part of the state. These low, undulating hills are dunes covered with grass, the largest dune area in North America. The sand, blown here from dry river bottoms within the last few thousand years, acts like a sponge, absorbing and holding much of the rain that falls here. Some scientists believe that the grass that now holds the dunes in place began to grow here only a few hundred years ago.

Hundreds of small lakes and ponds glitter among the Sand Hills and provide food, shelter, and nesting sites for trumpeter swans, geese, and ducks. But the lakes are not the only source of water. The Sand Hills lie on top of one of the nation's largest underground water supplies, the Ogallala Aquifer. Water seeping from this 2,000-square-mile (5,180-sq-km) underground reserve keeps the Loup and Elkhorn Rivers flowing year-round. The aquifer also supplies abundant fresh water for cattle and crops. Farmers have tapped the aquifer with some 73,000 wells to irrigate more than 8 million acres (3 million ha), more land than in any other state except California. Now some people worry that the water may someday run out.

To help save water, many plains farmers practice dry farming. They leave some of their land unplanted for a season or so, enabling it to conserve moisture from melting snow. At planting time they till the soil in shallow grooves, rather than plowing it deeply. This helps reduce evaporation by exposing less soil to the air.

Many farmers also leave dead stalks and stubble in the fields after harvesting a crop. The stalks catch and hold snow in the winter, and in the spring they help shield the moist soil from drying sun and wind. Contour plowing, across a slope rather than up and down, is another dry farming technique used by many Nebraska farmers; so is planting hardy, frost-resistant crops such as barley and wheat that can be harvested ahead of the blazing heat of summer.

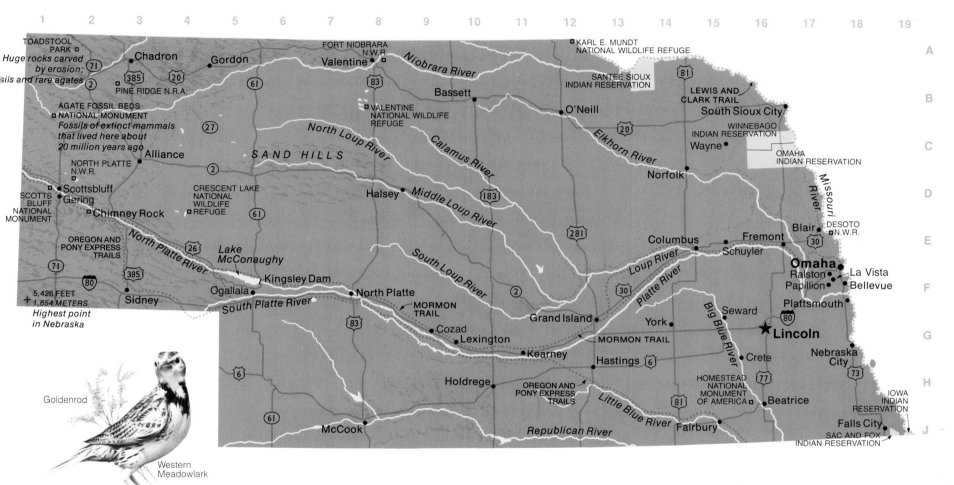

SAND HILLS

Niobrara River
North Loup River
Calamus River
Middle Loup River
South Loup River
Loup River
Platte River
North Platte River
South Platte River
Elkhorn River
Big Blue River
Little Blue River
Republican River
Missouri River

Toadstool Park — Huge rocks carved by erosion; fossils and rare agates

Agate Fossil Beds National Monument — Fossils of extinct mammals that lived here about 20 million years ago

+ 5,426 FEET 1,654 METERS Highest point in Nebraska

Chadron · Gordon · Valentine · Fort Niobrara N.W.R. · Karl E. Mundt National Wildlife Refuge · Bassett · O'Neill · Santee Sioux Indian Reservation · Lewis and Clark Trail · South Sioux City · Winnebago Indian Reservation · Wayne · Omaha Indian Reservation · Norfolk · Pine Ridge N.R.A. · Alliance · North Platte N.W.R. · Scottsbluff · Gering · Scotts Bluff National Monument · Chimney Rock · Crescent Lake National Wildlife Refuge · Halsey · Columbus · Fremont · Blair · Desoto N.W.R. · Schuyler · Oregon and Pony Express Trails · Lake McConaughy · Kingsley Dam · Ogallala · Sidney · North Platte · Mormon Trail · Grand Island · York · Seward · Lincoln · Omaha · Ralston · La Vista · Papillion · Bellevue · Plattsmouth · Cozad · Lexington · Kearney · Hastings · Mormon Trail · Crete · Nebraska City · Holdrege · Oregon and Pony Express Trails · Homestead National Monument of America · Beatrice · Iowa Indian Reservation · McCook · Fairbury · Falls City · Sac and Fox Indian Reservation

Goldenrod

Western Meadowlark

0 KILOMETERS 80
0 STATUTE MILES 60

Area: *15th largest state, 77,355 sq mi (200,350 sq km)*
Population: *1,578,385; ranks 36th*
Major Cities: *Omaha, 335,795; Lincoln, 191,972; Grand Island, 39,386*
Manufacturing: *food products, electronics, machinery, chemicals, transportation equipment, metal products, rubber and plastics, metals*
Agriculture: *cattle, corn, hogs, soybeans, wheat, sorghum, milk*
Mining and Quarrying: *oil and gas, sand and gravel, stone*
Other Important Activities: *printing and publishing*
Statehood: *the 37th state; admitted March 1, 1867*

Dinohyus, the "Terrible Pig," was a ferocious, heavily tusked animal that at the shoulder stood taller than a man. About 20 million years ago it roamed the wilds of what is now western Nebraska. So did other long-gone creatures— Menoceras, a small rhinoceros; Moropus, a clawed early relative of the horse; and alligators and other animals that lived here even earlier, when much of the region was a tropical swamp.

Today rainfall is scarce in western Nebraska. But over the years what moisture does fall has carved the land into hills and gullies, exposing a wealth of fossils. Many such treasures can be seen at Agate Fossil Beds National Monument and at Toadstool Park, where erosion has also carved hills and rocks into wonderful shapes.

1

2

3

Nebraska

1 *This western Nebraska farm family keeps track of costs and prices on a computer. Today many farmers are university educated and use the latest technology.*

2 *Checking the gears of a windmill, a cattle rancher near Alliance draws water from the Ogallala Aquifer, an underground layer of sand and gravel that provides fresh water to parts of seven states.*

3 *Ripening wheat spreads a golden blanket on this Great Plains farm near Scottsbluff.*

4 *Chimney Rock, 325 feet (99 m) high and visible for 30 miles (48 km), became a beacon for westward-bound pioneers as they followed the Oregon and Mormon Trails.*

5 *Heralds of spring, sandhill cranes pause to rest and feed along the shallow Platte River on their northward journey from Mexico to Arctic nesting grounds.*

Iowa

If you set out to invent a farming state, you couldn't do much better than to come up with Iowa. For one thing, the state lies between two great rivers, the Mississippi, which forms its eastern border, and the Missouri, which defines most of Iowa's western boundary. In the days before roads and railways, these rivers served as ready-made highways for canoes, flatboats, and paddle-wheel steamboats carrying citizens and products of a young nation. Today tugs churn along these rivers, hauling barges of grain, coal, and other goods, a relatively inexpensive way to move bulky cargoes.

For another thing, glaciers overran the land, smoothing off hilltops and filling in valleys with glacial drift, a mixture of clay, sand, gravel, and boulders that weathers over millions of years to become soil. In some places Iowa soil is as deep as 600 feet (183 m) and contains a rich mixture of humus. Then, after the glaciers receded, winds blowing across the open plains laid down layers of powdery soil called loess. Farmers like loess because it has no rocks or boulders in it to break a plow.

Fertile soil is Iowa's greatest treasure. Farms cover about 92 percent of the state and supply the entire United States with about 7 percent of its food, even though only 4 percent of all Iowa workers are farmers. Iowa's farmers grow great quantities of corn, soybeans, oats, and hay, and raise about a third of the nation's hogs, more than any other state.

Before white settlers arrived, western Iowa's gently rolling prairie lands grew grass as tall as a rider on horseback, a sea of grass that reached to the horizon in all directions. Most of the grass is gone now, although patches of it survive on old floodplains, along streams and railroad rights-of-way, and in forgotten corners of pioneer graveyards. Today, great rectangular fields glow with ripening grain. Distant towns signal their presence with sheltering trees, church steeples, and tall grain elevators.

Its growing season with many long, sunny summer days helps to make Iowa a leading farm state. Although there can be times of drought, deep winter snows and up to 36 inches (91 cm) of rain during the growing season usually result in bumper crops year after year.

Sometimes crops are too plentiful. When that

Ready to race, with boots, goggles, and number patch on his back, a Cedar Rapids motorcyclist of the early 1900s shows that early motorcycles were little more than bikes with engines attached.

happens, prices drop. Also, land values and interest rates rise and fall. A farmer who goes heavily into debt to buy expensive land and equipment can have a hard time paying off his loans. Then, if the bank takes over the property, the farm may be lost, and the family may move away to find work in town or in another state.

Over the years hard times have hit Iowa and other farming states several times, most recently in the 1980s. Between 1980 and 1989, some 208,000 Iowans, many of them young people, moved to other states. As small farmers have sold out to richer neighbors and agricultural corporations, farm sizes have increased even as the number of farms has dropped. And bigger, more efficient farms mean bigger, costlier machines, with fewer jobs for individual farmhands.

When farms fail, the small towns that depend on farmers' business find themselves in trouble, too. Car dealers, small banks, and sellers of farm implements often find that they can't keep going. Grocery stores and coffee shops lose customers. Small schools close and students must transfer to larger ones nearby. Townspeople who want to stay often commute to city jobs. Bad times threaten traditional small-town life.

In trying to hold on to its people and prevent the wide swings between good times and bad, Iowa has sought to attract nonfarm industries.

Des Moines, home to more than 50 insurance firms, ranks as one of the nation's leading insurance centers. In recent years Cedar Rapids and other towns have expanded into computers, fiber optics, and other high-tech businesses.

The number of such industries is growing, but most of Iowa's businesses still are related to agriculture. Waterloo has a large meat-packing industry and manufactures farm equipment. Cedar Rapids and Keokuk have cereal mills. Sioux City has the world's largest popcorn factory, and several cities produce large quantities of corn oil, cornstarch, and dairy products. Cedar Rapids has attracted a facility that will develop and produce enzymes, or proteins, for human and animal nutrition.

Many people think of Iowa as flat, but it is mostly hilly; there is rugged terrain in the northeast corner, which was ice covered only in an early period of glaciation, more than half a million years ago. Here the exposed bedrock has been cut by streams into deep valleys with steep bluffs. On the other side of the state rise the loess hills of the Missouri River Valley. Wind has piled up these thick deposits, which water has eroded into sharp-ridged hills, crests, and ravines, making a rumpled landscape.

Mound Builders lived in Iowa as long ago as 1000 B.C. In the northeastern part of the state these prehistoric Indians made their homes along bluffs overlooking the Mississippi River. About 2,500 years ago they built many earthen mounds, some in the shape of birds and other animals. Animal-shaped mounds are called effigy mounds. One group consists of the figures of ten marching bears. Some mounds held the bones of people buried with jewelry or weapons or the teeth of bears.

Area: *25th largest state, 56,275 sq mi (145,753 sq km)*
Population: *2,776,755; ranks 30th*
Major Cities: *Des Moines, 193,187; Cedar Rapids, 108,751; Davenport, 95,333*
Manufacturing: *food products, machinery, electronics, chemicals, metal products, rubber and plastics, transportation equipment*
Agriculture: *hogs, soybeans, cattle, corn, milk*
Mining and Quarrying: *stone, sand and gravel*
Other Important Activities: *insurance, printing and publishing*
Statehood: *the 29th state; admitted December 28, 1846*

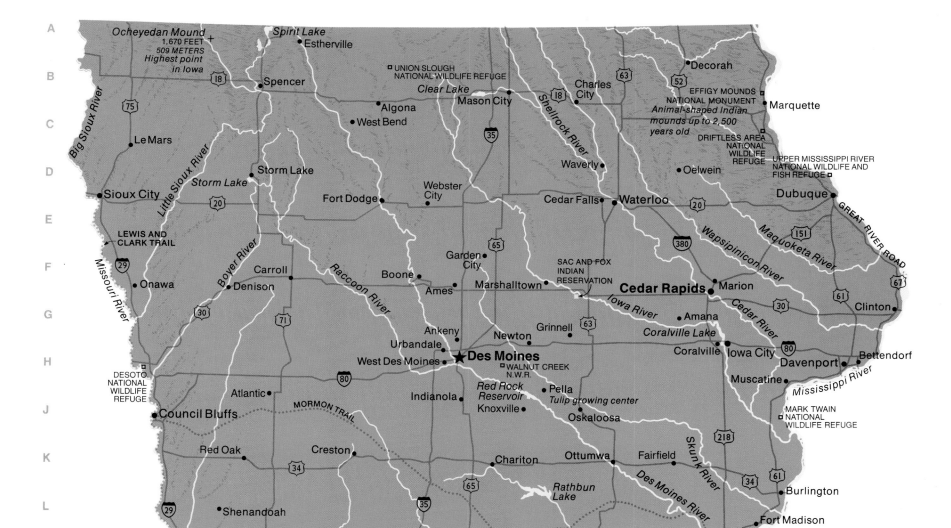

Several great glaciers shaped Iowa over the past two million years, smoothing the land by covering the bedrock with varying thicknesses of glacial drift. In the northeastern corner, around Decorah, erosion wore away the drift, exposing the bedrock, which has since been cut by streams into ridges and valleys. Caves and caverns developed where groundwater dissolved parts of the limestone bedrock.

Swamps and lakes dot the state's north-central region. They serve as headwaters for several rivers, including the Raccoon, Skunk, and Iowa, and provide habitat for ducks and geese.

Wild Rose

American Goldfinch

1

2

3

4

Iowa

1 *Its dome gleaming like Iowa's golden corn, the state capitol, at Des Moines, has served as the seat of government since 1884.*

2 *A barn peeps between corn tassels. Hybrid corn, pioneered in the state, has helped double and redouble yields since the 1930s.*

3 *Bicyclists take a refreshing watermelon break in West Bend, partway through the annual back-road jaunt across the state sponsored by the* Des Moines Register.

4 *Garden City, a town near Ames, springs like a prize crop from soil that is a glacial legacy, enriched by the prairie grasses that once grew here.*

5 *"Berry Patch Kids," the grandchildren of dairy farmers, coax a hesitant calf at the state fair in Des Moines. Iowa families have enjoyed the August fair since 1854.*

5

Kansas

"No matter where you deliver an airplane from Wichita, you're already halfway there." So said Walter Beech, founder of the Beech Aircraft Corporation. Behind Beech's joke is the fact that Kansas lies exactly in the middle of the lower 48 states. A limestone column in a pasture near Lebanon marks the spot.

Kansas's central location and its extensive transportation network haven't gone unnoticed by businesses. Some 4,000 manufacturing and processing plants are located throughout the state, among them many meat-packing and flour-milling plants. Since 1952, industry has surpassed agriculture as a source of income. In Wichita alone, four large aircraft manufacturers turn out nearly two-thirds of the world's private and commercial airplanes and give jobs to more than 36,000 skilled workers.

Other Kansas enterprises include the manufacture of camping equipment and greeting cards. At Hutchinson, one company stores everything from Hollywood films to government documents in parts of a salt mine deep beneath the town, where constant temperature and low humidity make a good place to keep valuable objects. The salt was left behind by shallow seas that washed over the middle of the continent millions of years ago, then evaporated. The salt was covered by sediment. Thick salt deposits underlie parts of central and western Kansas.

Kansas also produces a lot of oil, gas, and coal. It is one of the few sources for helium, the gas used to lift balloons. Some 60,000 wells pump oil and gas from beneath the state's prairies. In southeastern Kansas, one of the world's largest electric coal shovels, a 16-story-high monster known as Big Brutus, for many years dug dirt and rocks to expose surface coal seams for strip miners. Big Brutus was retired in 1974.

Kansas is a leading agricultural state, too. Most of the land has fine loess soil. Kansas produces some 17 percent of the nation's wheat, usually more than any other state. In most years, the harvest would fill a train reaching from western Kansas to the Atlantic Ocean. Much of this wheat is hard red winter wheat, a hardy grain planted in the fall and harvested the following spring. It was developed from Turkey Red, a type of wheat introduced into Kansas in the 1870s by Mennonite settlers who had fled religious persecution in Russia. Kansas farmers also grow bumper crops of corn, milo, soybeans, and other feed crops eaten by the more than six million beef cattle that go to market each year.

In the drier regions of western Kansas, farm-

Separating grain from straw, a 1930s steam threshing machine pours out smoke from its coal fire. To bring in the wheat harvest, neighbors worked together in crews of 12 or more.

ers irrigate their fields with water from a vast underground supply, the Ogallala Aquifer, a thick layer of waterlogged sand and gravel. But farmers have been using the water faster than rainfall can replenish it, and some geologists now warn that parts of the aquifer could run dry.

In the days before white settlers came, head-high bluestem grass blanketed the prairies, providing forage for enormous herds of bison. Maj. Richard Dodge in 1871 reported riding 25 miles through a single herd of bellowing bison, which he said took "about five days passing a given point." When railroads reached Kansas after the Civil War, cowboys herded cattle from Texas to railroad towns such as Abilene, Wichita, and Dodge City. Here the cattle were fed and loaded aboard trains to be shipped east. These were rough-and-tumble times that gave rise to legendary lawmen and gunslingers such as Wyatt Earp, Bat Masterson, and Doc Holliday.

Cattle still come to these and other Kansas towns, but now they stay in large, scientifically run feedlots where computers measure out fattening diets of grains and vitamins.

Many people think of Kansas as a flat, featureless place where a girl named Dorothy tangled with a tornado that swept her off to a storybook land named Oz. Actually, Kansas is not particularly flat. Low hills wrinkle much of the state, and eastward-draining rivers cross the sloping plains and prairies. East of Wichita the Flint Hills, mostly too stony to plow, preserve a 50-mile-wide (80-km) swath of the tallgrass prairie that extends from northern Kansas to Oklahoma. Here bluestem and Indian grasses, sprinkled with wildflowers in the spring, carpet the land as far as the eye can see.

In southern Kansas the flat-topped mesas and buttes of the Red Hills get their name from reddish rock and soil that contains iron oxide, or rust. The Smoky Hills stand in the north-central part of the state. Largely limestone and sandstone deposits laid down by ancient seas, they contain fossil seashells and sharks' teeth, as well as castle-like formations carved by rivers and streams. Trees here are few and far between. Wood was so scarce for the early settlers that they quarried and cut limestone for fence posts. Examples of their handiwork, a hundred years old, still stand, marking off old fields.

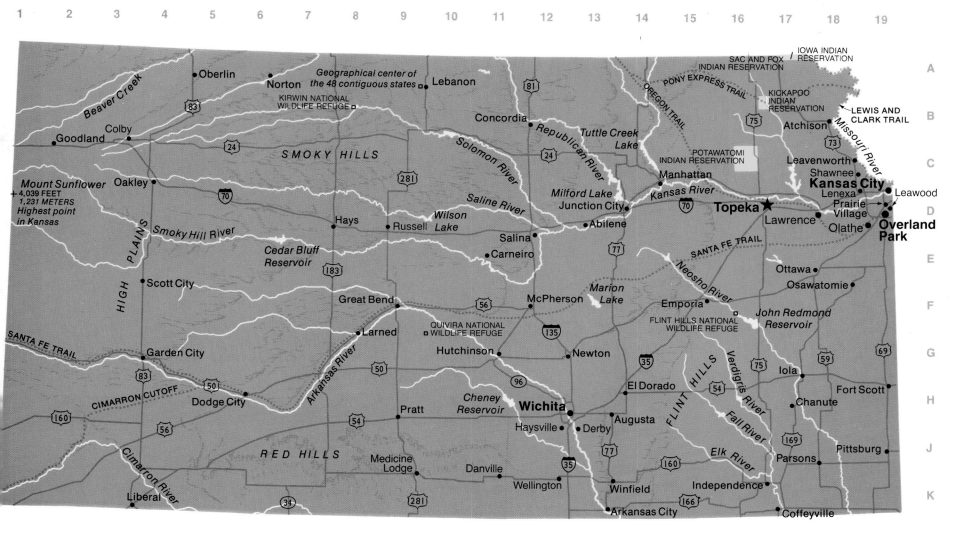

1 2 3 4 5 6 7 8 9 10 11 12 13 14 15 16 17 18 19

A B C D E F G H J K

IOWA INDIAN RESERVATION
SAC AND FOX INDIAN RESERVATION
KICKAPOO INDIAN RESERVATION
LEWIS AND CLARK TRAIL
PONY EXPRESS TRAIL
OREGON TRAIL
POTAWATOMI INDIAN RESERVATION

Oberlin
Norton
Geographical center of the 48 contiguous states
Lebanon
81
Beaver Creek
KIRWIN NATIONAL WILDLIFE REFUGE
Concordia
Tuttle Creek Lake
Atchison
75
73
Missouri River
Goodland
Colby
83
24
SMOKY HILLS
Solomon River
Republican River
24
Leavenworth
Shawnee
Kansas City
Manhattan
Mount Sunflower
4,039 FEET
1,231 METERS
Highest point in Kansas
Oakley
70
281
Saline River
Milford Lake
Junction City
Kansas River
70
Topeka
Lenexa
Prairie Village
Leawood
Overland Park
HIGH PLAINS
Smoky Hill River
Hays
Russell
Wilson Lake
Abilene
Lawrence
Olathe
Cedar Bluff Reservoir
183
Salina
Carneiro
77
SANTA FE TRAIL
Neosho River
Ottawa
Osawatomie
Scott City
Marion Lake
McPherson
Emporia
FLINT HILLS NATIONAL WILDLIFE REFUGE
John Redmond Reservoir
Great Bend
56
SANTA FE TRAIL
Larned
QUIVIRA NATIONAL WILDLIFE REFUGE
135
FLINT HILLS
Verdigris River
Garden City
83
CIMARRON CUTOFF
50
Hutchinson
Newton
35
75
Iola
59
69
Dodge City
50
96
El Dorado
54
Fort Scott
Chanute
160
56
Cheney Reservoir
Wichita
Augusta
Fall River
169
Pratt
54
Haysville
Derby
Elk River
Parsons
Pittsburg
RED HILLS
Medicine Lodge
Danville
77
160
Independence
Cimarron River
34
Wellington
Winfield
166
Liberal
281
Arkansas City
Coffeyville
Arkansas River

Area: *14th largest state, 82,277 sq mi (213,098 sq km)*
Population: *2,477,574; ranks 32nd*
Major Cities: *Wichita, 304,011; Kansas City, 149,767; Topeka, 119,883*
Manufacturing: *transportation equipment, food products, chemicals, machinery, electronics, paper products, petroleum and coal products, stone, clay, and glass products, metal products*
Mining: *oil and gas*
Agriculture: *cattle, wheat, sorghum, soybeans, corn, hogs, milk*
Other Important Activities: *printing and publishing*
Statehood: *the 34th state; admitted January 29, 1861*

There used to be sharks in Kansas . . . and flying reptiles with wingspans close to 20 feet (6 m). But that was millions of years ago, when much of the continent lay at the bottom of a great shallow sea. When these animals died, marine oozes covered them and later hardened into layers of sedimentary rocks. Today their fossil skeletons turn up in chalk beds in the Smoky Hills.

East of the Flint Hills lie coal deposits formed millions of years ago, when rotting vegetation was buried and compressed beneath layers of sediments laid down by encroaching seas.

KILOMETERS 0 — 80
STATUTE MILES 0 — 40

Western Meadowlark

Sunflower

KANSAS

1

2

3

4

Kansas

1 *Grain elevators and a church stand side by side in Danville, a small town whose population soars on Sundays and at harvesttime.*

2 *High-school football teams in sparsely populated western Kansas play with squads of eight, rather than the regulation eleven. And on a frosty October evening, fans are also scarce.*

3 *Kansas City, long a low-rise industrial town, displays a new skyline of office buildings along the Missouri River.*

4 *Where's the beef? Right here in a western Kansas packing plant, speeding along a line to become steaks and hamburger.*

5 *Merry maidens perform a 16th-century English country dance at a Renaissance festival near Kansas City.*

5

Missouri

"Meet me in St. Louie, Louie," at the 1904 World's Fair in St. Louis, where ice-cream cones were first sold. They were invented, the story goes, by a salesman packing ice cream into rolled-up waffles.

If all the people of the United States, standing exactly where they live, were balanced on a giant seesaw shaped like a map of the country, the seesaw would center in Missouri. The national census, ever since the first in 1790, has shown that, as our country expanded, the geographical center of the population moved steadily westward and a little southward. It now lies at a point southwest of St. Louis.

Missouri is central in other ways, too. In the heart of the country, it has geographical features like those of many areas around it, north, south, east, and west. Within Missouri's borders you can find low forested mountains, fertile farmlands built by glaciers, cotton-growing bottomlands like those of the Deep South, and the Big Sky plains and prairies of the West.

Also, two of the continent's mightiest rivers, the Mississippi and the Missouri, have their confluence near St. Louis. This has helped to make the state a key transportation center since the earliest days. Fur trappers, traders, gold seekers, and tens of thousands of settlers arriving by riverboat at St. Louis and other river ports outfitted themselves for the long westward trek along the Oregon and Santa Fe Trails. Near St. Louis, explorers Meriwether Lewis and William Clark began their epic journey to the Pacific Ocean. On the Missouri River, Pony Express riders headed west from St. Joseph on a ten-day gallop to California. Mark Twain, who spent his boyhood in Hannibal, apprenticed at the age of 22 to learn the trade of a steamboat pilot. His adventures appear in his autobiographical *Life on the Mississippi.*

Some 20 rail lines, 300 airports, and 109,000 miles (175,000 km) of highways have turned the state into a leading trucking and shipping center. Boats and barges on the Mississippi and Missouri make St. Louis and Kansas City two of the nation's busiest inland ports.

Today the Gateway Arch, a gleaming curve of stainless steel, rises above St. Louis to honor the city's position as a portal between East and West. Designed by architect Eero Saarinen and completed in 1965, the 630-foot (192-m) arch can be seen from miles away and is judged to be a marvel of modern engineering. It arcs across a stretch of riverfront where the early travelers came ashore to do business. The arch itself tapers to an observation room at the top and is designed to withstand winds of up to 150 miles an hour (240 kmph). Its curve, called an inverted catenary, like the upside-down curve of a loose-hanging chain, thrusts its weight downward onto feet anchored to bedrock.

Because of their strategic riverside locations, St. Louis and Kansas City have become important manufacturing centers. More than half the state's 8,700 factories are located in and around the two cities. Missouri factories employ about a quarter of the state's workers, many of whom turn out transportation equipment: autos, barges, bus and truck bodies, railroad cars, airplanes, and aerospace equipment.

The state's varied geography contributes to a wide variety of crops, from corn and soybeans, grown in the glacial soils north of the Missouri River, to fruits and vegetables in the Ozark region and cotton along the Mississippi River.

Forests once covered nearly two-thirds of Missouri, but long ago fell to loggers' axes. Now most of the state's forests blanket the rugged hills and valleys of the Ozark Plateau. Today their oak, hickory, and pine make the state a leading producer of charcoal and barrel staves.

Ages ago, the Ozarks were a region of volcanic peaks. As volcanism subsided, the land sank and was flooded by shallow seas into which sediments washed from surrounding highlands. The sediments slowly became bedrock, and eventually the sea bottom was pushed upward to become dry land. Soon, swift-flowing streams and rivers went to work, carving valleys into the uplifted tableland, so that Ozark people say that their mountains may not be very high but their valleys sure are deep. Underground water hollowed out more than 5,000 caves in the limestone bedrock and created thousands of springs, including some of the world's largest. Big Spring in the eastern Ozarks each day discharges enough water into the Current River to fill 12 million swimming pools. The Ozarks also contain the world's most productive lead mines.

In the southeastern corner of the state, along the Mississippi, lies the "boot heel" region. A low-lying floodplain that was once swampy and heavily forested, the boot heel was drained and cleared to make fertile fields for growing cotton, soybeans, and rice. Meandering streams were straightened to improve drainage; levees were built to hold back floodwaters.

Over the years most of Missouri's wetlands were converted to farmlands. The great, soggy forests that once grew along river floodplains have become croplands. Birds and animals that depended on these wetlands are threatened or endangered. But now conservation groups are working to restore Missouri's river wetlands.

Area: *19th largest state, 69,697 sq mi (180,516 sq km)*
Population: *5,117,073; ranks 15th*
Major Cities: *Kansas City, 435,146; St. Louis, 396,685; Springfield, 140,494*
Manufacturing: *transportation equipment, chemicals, food products, metal products, electronics, machinery, paper products, rubber and plastics, stone, clay, and glass products, metals, scientific instruments, clothing*
Agriculture: *soybeans, cattle, hogs, milk, corn, wheat, turkeys*
Mining and Quarrying: *stone, lead*
Other Important Activities: *tourism, printing and publishing*
Statehood: *the 24th state; admitted August 10, 1821*

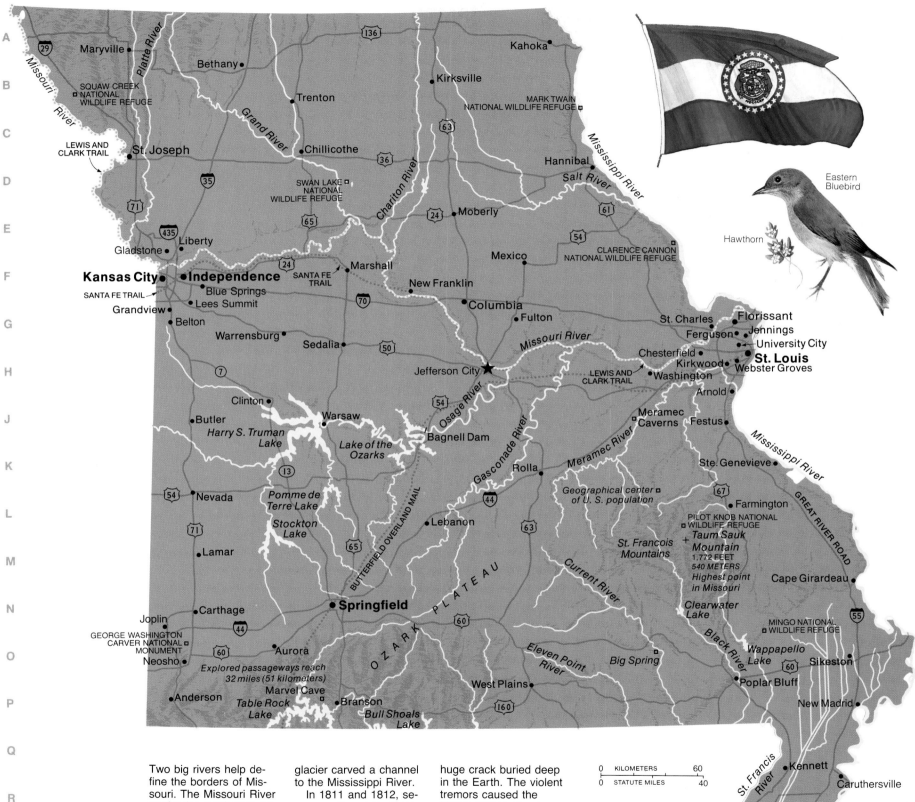

Two big rivers help define the borders of Missouri. The Missouri River marks the southernmost reach of the great glaciers. Meltwater running along the edge of the glacier carved a channel to the Mississippi River.

In 1811 and 1812, severe earthquakes shook the area around New Madrid, where the Mississippi flows above a huge crack buried deep in the Earth. The violent tremors caused the Mississippi to change course, and sinking land formed a new lake in neighboring Tennessee.

1

2

3

4

5

Missouri

1 *Canoeists wind past wooded Ozark bluffs in southern Missouri, exploring part of the mid-continent's only extensive highlands.*

2 *Soaring above riverboats on the Mississippi, St. Louis's Gateway Arch celebrates the city's early days as a key transportation link between East and West.*

3 *Quilters work in a Ste. Genevieve backyard, preserving skills that hark back to the town's founding by French traders and planters in the mid-1700s.*

4 *A St. Louis baseball fan keeps a vendor busy at a game in Busch Stadium. Service jobs in wholesale and retail trade employ more Missourians than any other work.*

5 *Patchwork fields form a tapestry of plenty along the fertile bottomlands of the Missouri River near the town of Washington.*

Colorado River

Grand Canyon

Colorado Plateau

Phoenix

Albuquerque

ROCKY MOUNTAINS

Carlsbad Caverns

Amarillo

Pecos River

ARIZONA

NEW MEXICO

TEXAS

OKLAHOMA

The Southwest

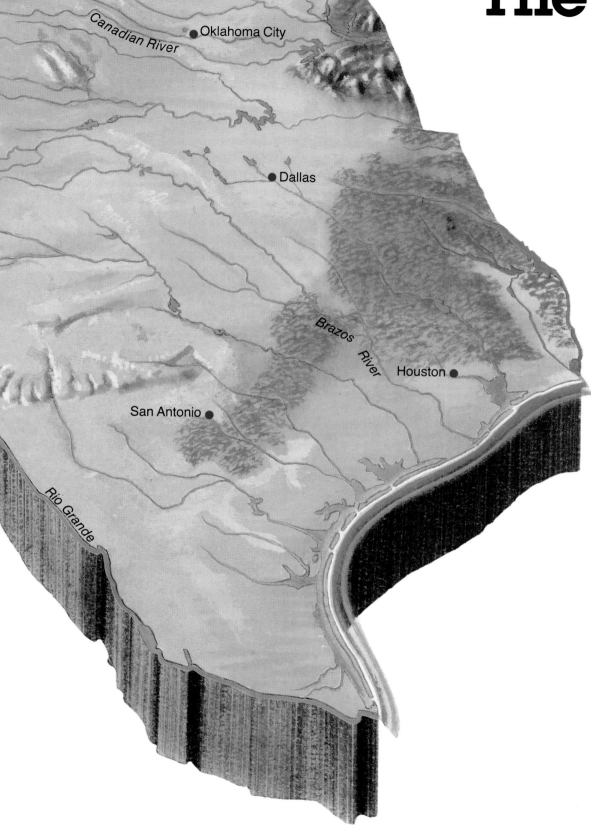

Canadian River

Oklahoma City

Dallas

Brazos River

Houston

San Antonio

Rio Grande

Variety is the spice of life in the Southwest. This region sprawls across almost every kind of terrain imaginable. In the west, awesome chasms and canyons slice downward through multicolored layers of sedimentary and volcanic rock that form the uplifted tablelands of the Colorado Plateau. Here the Colorado River, fed by snowmelt from the mountains, slowly grinds its way through layers of shale, sandstone, and limestone to bedrock nearly two billion years old.

Here, too, bone-dry deserts dotted with flat-topped mesas and buttes, giant stone arches, and other spectacular rock formations spread across the land toward the western slopes of the Rocky Mountains and southern spurs, or branches, of the range. From time to time through geologic history much of the Southwest lay beneath shallow seas. Gradually, as continental plates nudged one another, the ancient seabeds got squeezed and bent and broken and lifted. Volcanoes helped shape the region, too, spewing immense layers of ash and lava across the countryside as part of the mountain-building process that gave rise to the Rockies.

In the Rocky Mountains, the Rio Grande—Spanish for "big river"—begins a journey that trails southeastward to form part of the boundary between the United States and Mexico. Winding through deep canyons and flat lowlands, the river provided life-giving water to Indian farmers who grew corn, beans, and squash here for hundreds of years before Spanish explorers arrived in the 16th century.

Broad and broken grasslands slope from the eastern foothills of the Rockies. In places the plains are so flat and featureless that early travelers drove stakes into the ground to help guide the way back home again. Along the Gulf coast, barrier islands shield small boats from the open water and offer shelter and food to millions of migrating ducks, geese, egrets, and to the rare and endangered whooping crane.

East of Oklahoma City, along the northeastern edge of this region, spread the Ozark hardwood forests. Farther south, piney woods blanket much of the coastal lowlands nearly all the way to an escarpment north of San Antonio. The escarpment, formed when Earth's crust broke and slipped, marks the boundary between the humid coastal lowlands and the drier plains.

Arizona

In 1858 a surveyor, Lt. Joseph Ives, visited Arizona and reported back to the U. S. Congress that the area was "altogether valueless." His opinion was not shared by the generations of Hopi Indians who have lived at Oraibi since the 12th century, making it perhaps the oldest continuously inhabited settlement in the country. And it's unlikely to be shared by the almost one million people who have moved to Arizona in the last ten years, making it, after Nevada, the fastest growing state in the United States.

Few people who have ever visited the Grand Canyon would agree with Lieutenant Ives. During a 1903 visit, the well-traveled President Theodore Roosevelt declared the Grand Canyon "the most impressive piece of scenery I have ever looked at." The Colorado River has been carving the Grand Canyon for some six million years, cutting into the layers of rock that form the Colorado Plateau. The river exposed rock almost two billion years old, some of the oldest on Earth. In places the canyon is a mile (1.6 km) deep and up to 18 miles (29 km) wide, and the action of wind and water continues to enlarge it.

The Grand Canyon is one of many ravines carved by rivers and streams in the tablelands of northern Arizona. Canyon de Chelly was fashioned by the Chinle Wash and its tributaries. Today the Chinle Wash is an intermittent stream. Ancient Native American groups settled among the area's red-rock canyons, caves, and mesas some 2,000 years ago. Later, the Anasazi, ancestors of the modern Hopi, built dwellings in thousand-foot (300-m) cliffs.

Canyon de Chelly is now part of the reservation that is the headquarters of the Navajo nation. The Navajo, along with the Apache, are relative newcomers to Arizona, having arrived just before the Spanish explored the region in the 1500s. The Navajo learned sheepherding from the Spanish and even today move their flocks from pasture to pasture. They have had a long and difficult relationship with the settled Hopi farmers who shared land where there were disputes over ownership and land use. In the 1980s, to help end the conflicts, the U. S. government divided the jointly used area.

Arizona's plateau region ends south of Flagstaff in a 200-mile-long (320-km) line of cliffs about 2,000 feet (610 m) high. To the south is the

The Cisco Kid, *filmed in 1913, used an adobe house in Tucson as a studio. The town and nearby mountains were a popular backdrop for silent movies and, later, talkies.*

Basin and Range region. Here a series of thickly forested mountain ranges runs northwest to southeast, providing vast stands of ponderosa pine for the state's lumber industry. Farther south and west are lower ranges that separate broad desert basins, such as the Sonoran Desert, a land of cactus and scrub where July temperatures average 103°F (39°C).

Though dry, this land can be very fertile, a fact discovered by the Hohokam, a people who built dams and ditches to irrigate their crops in the valleys of the Salt and Gila Rivers more than 1,500 years ago. They grew corn, beans, squash, and cotton, a crop that European settlers later reintroduced. Cotton, along with copper mining and cattle raising, was the basis of Arizona's economy until the mid-20th century.

When Spanish, Mexican, and Anglo settlers came to Arizona, beginning in the late 1700s, they found it hard to displace the Native Americans from their lands. Indian resistance continued until 1886, when Geronimo and his Apache raiders finally surrendered to the U.S. Army.

Early settlement concentrated in Tombstone, Bisbee, and other silver-mining and copper-mining towns. Tucson, in the mountains, retains much of the flavor of its early days as a walled Spanish city with strong ties to Mexico.

Like the Hohokam, farmers in Arizona today

rely on irrigation. Billions of dollars have been spent to bring river water to thirsty crops. The Colorado has been dammed to provide water for farming and hydroelectricity. Agriculture around Phoenix, the capital, expanded rapidly after completion of the Theodore Roosevelt Dam and Lake on the Salt River in 1911. Arizonans also draw on underground water, at a rate faster than it can be replenished. As a result, the water table drops, land subsides, and deep cracks develop in the ground.

If dams and reservoirs met the need for water, air-conditioning conquered the extreme heat of southern Arizona. By the mid-20th century, the desert stood ready to receive hundreds of thousands of new inhabitants. Sunshine and clean air brought retirees and people with respiratory problems. Its wide-open spaces and clear blue skies made Arizona ideal for the location of air bases and other military sites. Manufacturers of computers, weapons, aircraft, and other high-tech products located their factories in Arizona. Today three-fourths of the population lives around Phoenix and Tuscon. Demand for homesites has developers bulldozing and negotiating for the federal lands (about 60 percent of the state) that sometimes come up for sale.

To meet the water needs of a growing population, the Central Arizona Project is being built. This 336-mile (540-km) series of pipes and canals will bring water from Lake Havasu on the Colorado River to Phoenix and Tucson. Scheduled to be completed in 1992, the project will draw Arizona's maximum allotment from the Colorado, a situation that worries Californians, who have long been using some of Arizona's share.

Area: *the sixth largest state, 114,000 sq mi (295,260 sq km)*
Population: *3,665,228; ranks 24th*
Major Cities: *Phoenix, 983,403; Tucson, 405,390; Mesa, 288,091*
Manufacturing: *transportation equipment, electronics, machinery, scientific instruments, food products, metals, stone, clay, and glass products, chemicals, metal products*
Mining and Quarrying: *copper, coal, sand and gravel, stone*
Agriculture: *cattle, cotton, lettuce, milk, hay*
Other Important Activities: *federal government, tourism, printing and publishing*
Statehood: *48th state; admitted February 14, 1912*

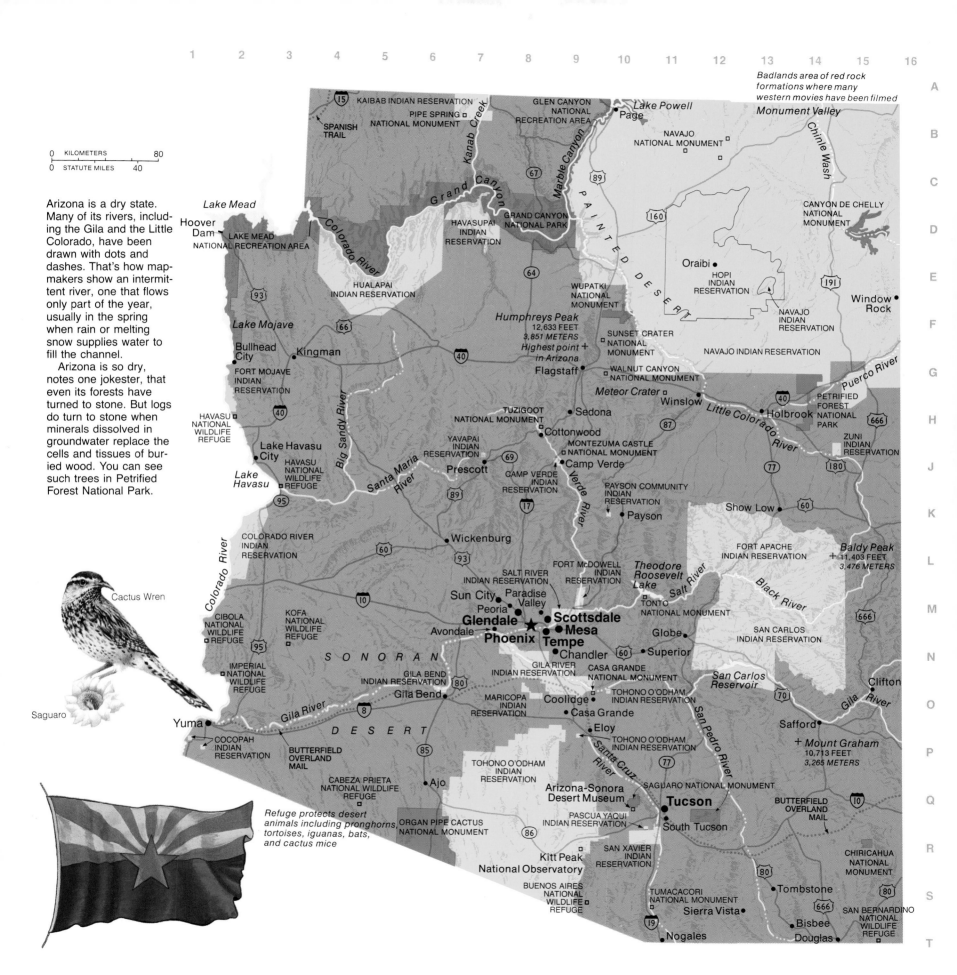

Arizona is a dry state. Many of its rivers, including the Gila and the Little Colorado, have been drawn with dots and dashes. That's how mapmakers show an intermittent river, one that flows only part of the year, usually in the spring when rain or melting snow supplies water to fill the channel.

Arizona is so dry, notes one jokester, that even its forests have turned to stone. But logs do turn to stone when minerals dissolved in groundwater replace the cells and tissues of buried wood. You can see such trees in Petrified Forest National Park.

KILOMETERS 80
STATUTE MILES 40

Cactus Wren

Saguaro

Badlands area of red rock formations where many western movies have been filmed

Refuge protects desert animals including pronghorns, tortoises, iguanas, bats, and cactus mice

1 2 3 4 5 6 7 8 9 10 11 12 13 14 15 16
A B C D E F G H J K L M N O P Q R S T

Lake Mead
Hoover Dam
LAKE MEAD NATIONAL RECREATION AREA

KAIBAB INDIAN RESERVATION
PIPE SPRING NATIONAL MONUMENT
SPANISH TRAIL

GLEN CANYON NATIONAL RECREATION AREA
Lake Powell
Page
Monument Valley

NAVAJO NATIONAL MONUMENT
Chinle Wash

GRAND CANYON NATIONAL PARK
HAVASUPAI INDIAN RESERVATION

CANYON DE CHELLY NATIONAL MONUMENT

HUALAPAI INDIAN RESERVATION

Colorado River

Lake Mojave
Bullhead City
Kingman

FORT MOJAVE INDIAN RESERVATION

HAVASU NATIONAL WILDLIFE REFUGE
Lake Havasu City
HAVASU NATIONAL WILDLIFE REFUGE
Lake Havasu

Big Sandy River

Santa Maria River

COLORADO RIVER INDIAN RESERVATION

Colorado River

CIBOLA NATIONAL WILDLIFE REFUGE

KOFA NATIONAL WILDLIFE REFUGE

IMPERIAL NATIONAL WILDLIFE REFUGE

Yuma
COCOPAH INDIAN RESERVATION
BUTTERFIELD OVERLAND MAIL

CABEZA PRIETA NATIONAL WILDLIFE REFUGE
Ajo

ORGAN PIPE CACTUS NATIONAL MONUMENT

BUENOS AIRES NATIONAL WILDLIFE REFUGE

Oraibi
HOPI INDIAN RESERVATION
NAVAJO INDIAN RESERVATION

Window Rock

PAINTED DESERT

Humphreys Peak 12,633 FEET 3,851 METERS Highest point in Arizona
SUNSET CRATER NATIONAL MONUMENT
Flagstaff
WALNUT CANYON NATIONAL MONUMENT

WUPATKI NATIONAL MONUMENT

Meteor Crater
Winslow
Little Colorado River
Holbrook

PETRIFIED FOREST NATIONAL PARK

ZUNI INDIAN RESERVATION

Puerco River

TUZIGOOT NATIONAL MONUMENT
Sedona
Cottonwood

YAVAPAI INDIAN RESERVATION

MONTEZUMA CASTLE NATIONAL MONUMENT
Camp Verde

Prescott

CAMP VERDE INDIAN RESERVATION

PAYSON COMMUNITY INDIAN RESERVATION

Show Low

Verde River

Wickenburg

Payson

FORT APACHE INDIAN RESERVATION

Baldy Peak 11,403 FEET 3,476 METERS

SALT RIVER INDIAN RESERVATION
FORT McDOWELL INDIAN RESERVATION

Theodore Roosevelt Lake
Salt River
TONTO NATIONAL MONUMENT

Black River

Sun City
Paradise Valley
Peoria
Glendale
Scottsdale
Avondale
Phoenix
Mesa
Tempe
Chandler

Globe
Superior

SAN CARLOS INDIAN RESERVATION

San Carlos Reservoir

Clifton

Gila River

SONORAN

GILA BEND INDIAN RESERVATION
Gila Bend
Gila River

GILA RIVER INDIAN RESERVATION
CASA GRANDE NATIONAL MONUMENT
MARICOPA INDIAN RESERVATION
Coolidge
Casa Grande
Eloy

TOHONO O'ODHAM INDIAN RESERVATION

TOHONO O'ODHAM INDIAN RESERVATION

San Pedro River

Safford
Mount Graham 10,713 FEET 3,265 METERS

DESERT

TOHONO O'ODHAM INDIAN RESERVATION

Santa Cruz River

SAGUARO NATIONAL MONUMENT

Arizona-Sonora Desert Museum
Tucson
PASCUA YAQUI INDIAN RESERVATION
South Tucson

SAN XAVIER INDIAN RESERVATION
Kitt Peak National Observatory

TUMACACORI NATIONAL MONUMENT
Sierra Vista

Nogales

BUTTERFIELD OVERLAND MAIL

CHIRICAHUA NATIONAL MONUMENT

Tombstone

SAN BERNARDINO NATIONAL WILDLIFE REFUGE

Bisbee
Douglas

1

Arizona

1 *Sprinkled with sacred cattail pollen, an Apache girl celebrates her coming-of-age among tribe members.*

2 *Sunset burnishes eroded slopes and towering buttes of the Grand Canyon. Rock revealed here is 1.7 billion years old.*

2

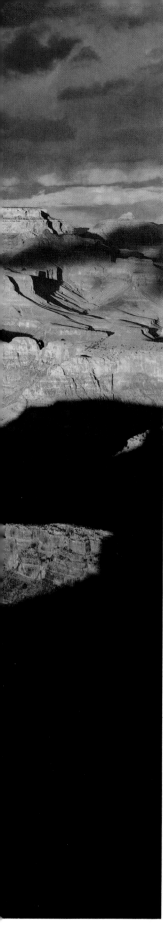

3

4

5

3 *Founded by the Spanish in 1700 to Christianize the Indians, San Xavier del Bac, near Tucson, is the Southwest's best preserved mission.*

4 *At dawn, the huge steel eyelids of the optical telescopes at Kitt Peak National Observatory shut tight for the day.*

5 *Giant saguaros dwarf bird-watchers at Saguaro National Monument. The armed cactuses are unique to this region.*

New Mexico

An elderly woman sat on the ground, coiling red clay with gnarled hands. Slowly and steadily the years of experience in her fingertips transformed the clay into a perfectly proportioned pot. Then she painted geometric designs on it and scratched her name on the bottom. She fired the pot in an open fire. There its color changed to black, the dull finish of the painted designs a subtle contrast to the pot's satiny smoothness.

The woman was Maria Martinez, a Native American who lived in the San Ildefonso Pueblo, north of Santa Fe. She died in 1980, but her pottery has become the trademark of her pueblo and is prized by museums and collectors. Maria Martinez's work is part of an artistic legacy that goes back some 2,000 years to the Anasazi, the ancestors of today's Pueblo Indians.

The landscape of New Mexico is varied and, in many places, rugged. The Great Plains extend into the eastern third of New Mexico. In the late 19th century, Texans began to settle there. Today, cattle ranches, oil fields, small towns and cities, and military bases give the region an appearance similar to its next-door neighbor, earning it the nickname Little Texas.

The southernmost spurs of the Rocky Mountains reach into central New Mexico, rising abruptly from the plains to the east. The Rio Grande, from its source in the Colorado Rockies, cuts down through the ranges of New Mexico. Snowmelt from mountain streams brings water to the fertile Rio Grande Valley. The river has also been dammed and diverted to irrigate crops and produce hydroelectricity.

The Spanish settled north-central New Mexico beginning in the late 16th century. They set up ranches, some on vast tracts of land granted by the king of Spain. Many intermarried with Indians. Far from the Spanish government in Mexico City, they existed in isolation. Until early in the 20th century, the language spoken in some villages was closer to that of 16th-century Spain than it was to that of neighboring Mexico, whose people have also come to settle, legally or illegally, in New Mexico. Mexicans and descendants of the original Spanish settlers give the state a population that is 37 percent Hispanic, the highest proportion in the country.

Santa Fe has been the seat of government in New Mexico since 1610. For some two centuries

New Mexico's first railroad line, the Atchison, Topeka, and Santa Fe, opened in 1878, connecting Albuquerque to small, isolated towns and permanently changing the lives of their inhabitants.

the Spanish discouraged outsiders from entering. Spanish soldiers, friars, colonists, and traders traveled between Mexico City and Santa Fe and Taos on El Camino Real, "the royal road." When Mexico gained independence from Spain in 1821 and New Mexico became a Mexican province, Santa Fe soon was bursting at the seams with merchants eager to do business there. They came in long wagon trains along the Santa Fe Trail until the Atchison, Topeka, and Santa Fe Railway neared Santa Fe in 1879.

For a hundred years, Taos and Santa Fe have drawn artists and writers from eastern states and from Europe. The clear blue sky, it is said, renders details more clearly. Multihued landscapes of rock and the changing tints of the desert also help explain the state's long tradition of creative inspiration. The writer John Gunther described a New Mexico night of "purple desert flowing endlessly under lonely stars."

In the 1940s, a group of men arrived in New Mexico. They were quickly spirited away to the site of a boarding school on a ranch near Santa Fe. Here, at Los Alamos, the federal government set up a laboratory to develop atomic bombs. The scientists brought here for this purpose worked feverishly and in utmost secrecy to produce the bombs dropped on Hiroshima and Nagasaki to hasten the end of World War II. Los Alamos and Albuquerque are two of several centers in the state for research and development for weaponry, the space program, nuclear energy, and electronics. These industries receive a large part of their support from the federal government and attract a young and highly educated work force, often from outside the state. This helps make Albuquerque one of the fastest growing cities in the United States.

The Rio Grande courses south into the Basin and Range region, where rugged ranges separate low-lying desert basins. One basin, Jornada del Muerto ("journey of the dead man"), was the bane of the Spanish who had to flee across its burning sands and lava rock after a 1680 Indian revolt. The Jornada del Muerto also witnessed the ultimate challenge to human survival when the atomic bomb, developed at Los Alamos, was tested in 1945. So intense was the heat from the blast that it fused the basin's desert sand into glass. The area has remained a testing ground for rockets and missiles.

The northwestern corner of New Mexico is part of the Colorado Plateau, an immense upland cut into cliffs, canyons, valleys, and mesas. About a thousand years ago the Anasazi built large, complex settlements all over the area. Many Navajo now live there on a reservation that extends into Arizona and Utah. The Navajo, together with the Apache, fought Spanish and Anglo settlers in New Mexico until almost the end of the 19th century.

Area: *the fifth largest state, 121,593 sq mi (314,925 sq km)*
Population: *1,515,069; ranks 37th*
Major Cities: *Albuquerque, 384,736; Las Cruces, 62,126; Santa Fe, 55,859*
Mining: *oil and gas, coal, copper, uranium, potash, lead*
Manufacturing: *electronics, food products, stone, clay, and glass products, petroleum products, lumber and wood products*
Agriculture: *cattle, milk, hay, greenhouse and nursery products, chili peppers*
Other Important Activities: *federal government, tourism, printing and publishing*
Statehood: *the 47th state; admitted January 6, 1912*

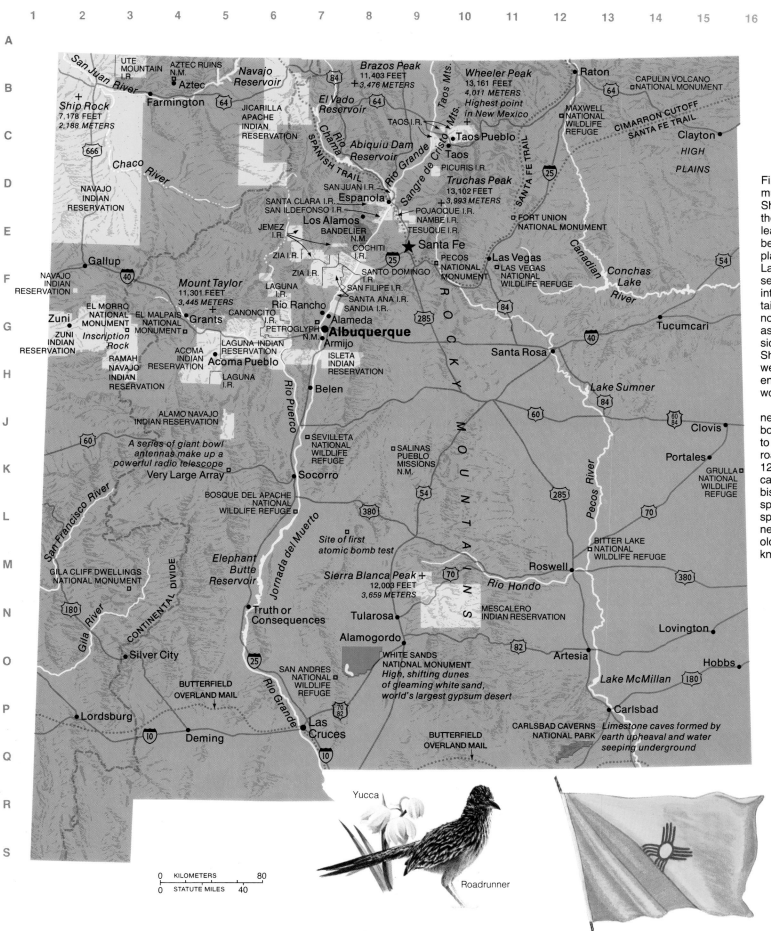

Fire and water formed much of New Mexico. Shallow oceans covered the region several times, leaving sediments that became the parched plains in the southeast. Later, as the ancient seabeds folded and lifted into the Rocky Mountains, enormous volcanoes spewed lava and ash across the countryside for millions of years. Ship Rock, in the northwest corner, is the hardened lava throat of a worn-down volcano.

The town of Clovis, near the state's eastern boundary, gave its name to Ice Age hunters who roamed the West about 12,000 years ago, killing camels, mammoths, and bison with stone-tipped spears. The grooved spearheads, discovered near the town by archaeologists in the 1930s, are known as Clovis points.

Yucca

Roadrunner

0 KILOMETERS 80
0 STATUTE MILES 40

1

2

3

New Mexico

1 *Electrical charges from a Particle Beam Fusion Accelerator at Albuquerque's Sandia National Laboratories hint at the hundred trillion watts of electricity the device can produce. Sandia is one of many New Mexico facilities that specialize in nuclear energy research.*

2 *Limestone-bearing drops of water create fantastic formations at Carlsbad Caverns, in southeastern New Mexico. Humorist Will Rogers called the vast cave system the "Grand Canyon with a roof on it."*

3 *Below peaks of the Taos Mountains sacred to Indians, winter snow covers desert vegetation of sagebrush, piñon, and juniper.*

4 *Mexican Americans harvest chili peppers on a farm north of Las Cruces. One in three New Mexico residents is Hispanic.*

5 *Young dancers enter the low door of a ceremonial room, or kiva, during the celebration of the corn harvest at their pueblo near Santa Fe. Although Indians were converted to Christianity under Spanish influence, today's Native Americans strive to preserve their ancient religious traditions.*

4

5

Oklahoma

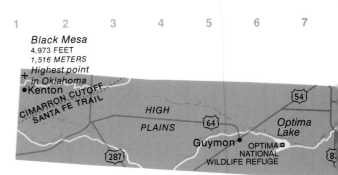

Black Mesa
4,973 FEET
1,516 METERS
Highest point
in Oklahoma

Each summer, people of the town of Tahlequah in eastern Oklahoma reenact one of the most significant events in the state's history and one of the most tragic. Tahlequah is headquarters of the Cherokee nation. The Cherokee, along with the Choctaw, Chickasaw, Creek, and Seminole, lived originally in the southeastern states. There they had adopted many of the customs of the white settlers, who called them the Five Civilized Tribes. When white settlers demanded more farmland, these Indians were forcibly removed from their lands. Beginning in the 1820s, they were marched under guard of federal troops to the territory now known as Oklahoma. On one such march, in the winter of 1838-39, thousands of Indians died along the way. The journey to Oklahoma became known as the Trail of Tears, its memory kept alive by the yearly reenactment at Tahlequah.

In Oklahoma, the Five Civilized Tribes joined local Indians such as the Caddo, Wichita, Pawnee, and Osage, as well as Plains tribes such as the Comanche, Apache, and Cheyenne. For a time, most of Oklahoma became Indian territory. Today some 252,000 members of 67 different tribes give Oklahoma the country's largest Native American population.

The Five Civilized Tribes took the lead in the territory by establishing their own forms of government, courts, newspapers, and the first schools in Oklahoma. But the press for land by white settlers squeezed Oklahoma Indians into smaller areas. The federal government surveyed the land, marking precisely measured parcels of 160 acres (65 ha). On April 22, 1889, the first of several runs on Oklahoma land began. At the signal of gunshots, homesteaders rushed across the borders to stake their claims. Oklahoma City, just a spot on the plains, became a city of 10,000 tent-dwelling inhabitants in a matter of hours. By evening, Guthrie had a population of 15,000. Homesteaders came from all over the country, from Canada, Mexico, and Europe, and from as far away as China and Japan.

Oklahoma encompasses many different landforms. Highlands cover its eastern third, including part of the Ozark Plateau shared with Arkansas and Missouri. This area of steep bluffs and swiftly running streams contains deposits of lead, zinc, and coal. Miners from Europe came

here in the 1870s; their descendants still live among the descendants of the southeastern tribes. Many lakes, some created for flood control, irrigation, or hydroelectricity, make the plateau a major recreation area. To the south the sandstone ridges of the Ouachita Mountains form Oklahoma's roughest terrain. Forests make lumbering the area's chief industry.

West of the highlands stretch large areas of plains that alternate with bands of hills, all the way to the panhandle. In these areas farmers raise wheat and also cattle, which provide most of the state's agricultural income. Down along the southern border, in the humid valley of the Red River, farmers grow cotton, peanuts, and vegetables. This area has much in common with

A 1936 dust storm in Oklahoma's Panhandle sends a farmer and his sons running for cover. Severe droughts and wind erosion in the 1930s turned the plains into a wasteland called the Dust Bowl.

the southern states from which most of its settlers came in the 19th century.

Although oil and natural gas are found in nearly every county, the area around Tulsa saw the first oil strike in 1901 and remains the state's oil headquarters. Like the land rushes of the 1800s, oil created boom times in Oklahoma. Oil leases for Osage lands in the 1920s temporarily made tribe members the richest people in the state. Eighteen wells once pumped on the

grounds of the state capitol in Oklahoma City.

Today, about two-thirds of all Oklahomans live in urban areas, half of them in or around Tulsa and Oklahoma City. The two cities are major manufacturing centers. Tulsa also has large aircraft and aerospace industries. The city's data-processing centers handle the largest number of credit card slips in the world.

In the 1930s, another "Trail of Tears" carried hundreds of thousands of mostly white Oklahomans westward. Many were farmers hit by the Great Depression and years of drought that turned western Oklahoma into a Dust Bowl. "People sat in Oklahoma City . . . holding dust masks over their faces . . . while the farms blew by," wrote American journalist John Gunther.

Improved farming methods and tree planting have brought productive farmland back to the former Dust Bowl counties.

Area: 18th largest state, 69,956 sq mi (181,186 sq km)
Population: 3,145,585; ranks 28th
Major Cities: Oklahoma City, 444,719; Tulsa, 367,302; Lawton, 80,561
Mining: oil and gas
Manufacturing: transportation equipment, machinery, electronics, rubber and plastics, food products, metal products, stone, clay, and glass products, chemicals, scientific instruments, paper products
Agriculture: cattle, wheat, greenhouse and nursery products, broilers, milk
Other Important Activities: printing and publishing
Statehood: the 46th state; admitted November 16, 1907

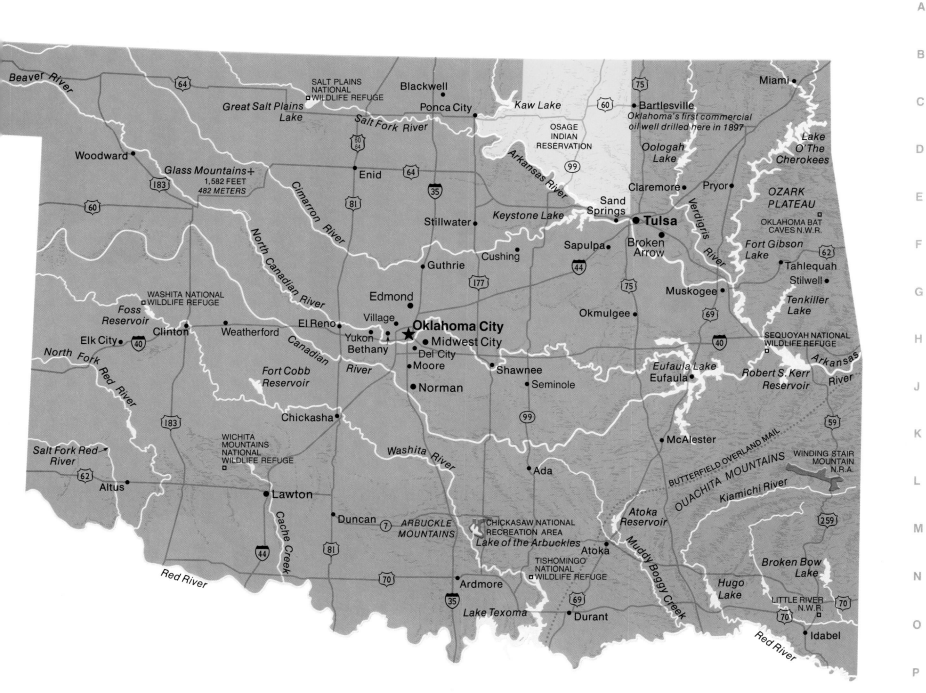

Shaped like a meat cleaver with a ragged-edged blade formed by the Red River, Oklahoma is an easy state to recognize. Its western panhandle, part of the Great Plains, helps give the state its distinctive outline. To this day the panhandle bears the wheel ruts made by wagon trains rolling along the Cimarron Cutoff section of the old Santa Fe Trail.

Although landlocked, Oklahoma has access to the Gulf of Mexico via the Verdigris, Arkansas, and Mississippi Rivers. Channel dredging and lock building completed in 1971 make Tulsa and Muskogee inland ports.

Mistletoe

Scissor-tailed Flycatcher

1

2

Oklahoma

1 *The tanks of a Tulsa oil refinery sprawl along the bank of the Arkansas River.*

2 *Four generations of an Oklahoma Panhandle farm family stand in a field of milo, a kind of sorghum. This family survived the Dust Bowl years of the 1930s that drove a half million farmers out of Oklahoma and nearby states.*

3 *Oil wealth brought art to Tulsa, including these spirited bronzes by sculptor-painter Frederic Remington. They are displayed at the Thomas Gilcrease Institute of American History and Art.*

3

4

5

4 *An Oklahoma scientist uses computers to monitor the exchange of gases in a blade of grass. This research is part of a project to develop drought-resistant plants that could help avoid future Dust Bowl conditions.*

5 *Computing cowhand, a young Cherokee logs on at his school near Stilwell. Cherokee Indians opened Oklahoma's first schools in the mid-1800s, after completing a forced march that tore them from their homelands in the Southeast.*

Texas

The year 1901 saw North America's first gusher at Spindletop oil field near Beaumont. Within two years, hundreds of derricks owned by some 50,000 potential millionaires crowded the field.

For almost a decade during the mid-19th century, Texas was a country apart from the United States. From 1836 to 1845, after it fought off Mexican rule, the Republic of Texas existed as a sovereign nation that was recognized by Great Britain, France, the Netherlands, and the United States. It had its own army and navy, its own currency, and its own postal service. In 1839 Austin became its capital.

Spanish missionaries from Mexico were the first Europeans to successfully settle Texas, beginning in the 1690s. They established fortified missions, including one at San Antonio de Bexar, now San Antonio.

It was in the mission church, the Alamo, that some 188 Texans held off the army of the Mexican general Santa Anna for almost two weeks before losing in a bloody battle in 1836. All the Texans inside the Alamo died, including legendary heroes Davy Crockett and Jim Bowie. But only six weeks later, with "Remember the Alamo!" as their war cry, the army of Texas under Sam Houston defeated Santa Anna and his men. This victory freed the territory from Mexican rule and eventually confirmed the independence of Texas.

Huge debts from its war with Mexico and the continued threat of Mexican invasion and Indian attacks led Texas to join the United States in 1845. The largest of the 48 contiguous states, Texas has the greatest amount of farmland and the largest reserves of oil and natural gas in the country, as well as a fast-growing population. One-third of its residents have arrived in the state since 1970.

Many early Texas settlers were southern farmers, drawn by the immense plots of land they could obtain. Europeans came too, including Belgians, French, English, Irish, Czechs, and large numbers of Germans escaping political turmoil in their homeland. The Germans created the communities of Fredericksburg and New Braunfels and also settled in San Antonio.

From Waco southward there is an escarpment, an east-facing rim of land, that curves southwestward to Del Rio. It separates the moist, green lowlands of the east from the higher, drier, and largely treeless plains of the west.

East of the escarpment the Gulf Coastal Plain contains the state's most fertile farmland, with cotton and rice as the major crops. In the valleys of the lower Rio Grande and the Nueces River, an 11-month growing season yields winter vegetables and citrus fruits. The Rio Grande has long witnessed Mexican immigration, both legal and illegal. Many border cities, such as El Paso, Laredo, and Brownsville, have economies that are closely tied to nearby cities in Mexico. One in five Texans today has Hispanic origins.

Along the Gulf coast are a number of major ports, including Corpus Christi, Port Arthur, and Brownsville. Houston, fueled by the oil industry and close to the rich East Texas fields, is the state's largest port. Although Houston is 50 miles (80 km) inland, a large ship channel, opened in 1914, connects it with Galveston Bay. Houston also leads the Texas space industry. Its Johnson Space Center guides the flights of all manned spacecraft, including the space shuttle. Fluctuation in oil prices has hit Houston hard, but like other Texas cities, it seeks economic security through diversity of its industries.

Dallas and Fort Worth have expanded toward each other over the years. They now form a single large metropolitan area and share a huge international airport. Dallas, once a market center for cotton, has become a center for banking, insurance, rail freight, and, most recently, the computer and defense industries. The old cow town of Forth Worth shares Dallas's growth in high-tech and defense companies, especially in aviation.

West of the escarpment begin the upland plains, starting with rolling prairies where cattle raising is the major occupation. Among Texas cattle breeds are the original longhorns, brought in from Mexico and now making a comeback because of their leaner meat, and the Santa Gertrudis, a breed resistant to heat and insects and the first one developed in the United States.

Cattle ranches spill onto the high plains of the Texas Panhandle, where farmers also grow wheat, cotton, sugar beets, and other crops in irrigated fields. The 1920s strike in the oil fields of the southern panhandle made oil and finance centers of the cities of Midland and Odessa.

West Texas is a hot, dry, rugged land. With the help of underground water, wheat and feed crops grow in huge, target-shaped fields watered by pivoting sprinklers. There are huge ranches here and a frontier atmosphere. College students can take courses in rodeo riding, and bulldogging, saddle bronc riding, and calf roping are intercollegiate sports.

Area: *the second largest state, 266,807 sq mi (691,030 sq km)*
Population: *16,986,510; ranks third*
Major Cities: *Houston, 1,630,553; Dallas, 1,006,877; San Antonio, 935,933*
Manufacturing: *chemicals, food products, transportation equipment, electronics, petroleum products, machinery, scientific instruments, metal products, stone, clay, and glass products, rubber and plastics*
Mining: *oil and gas, coal*
Agriculture: *cattle, cotton, milk, greenhouse and nursery products, broilers, vegetables, corn, sorghum*
Other Important Activities: *finance and insurance, tourism, printing and publishing, shrimp fishing*
Statehood: *the 28th state; admitted December 29, 1845*

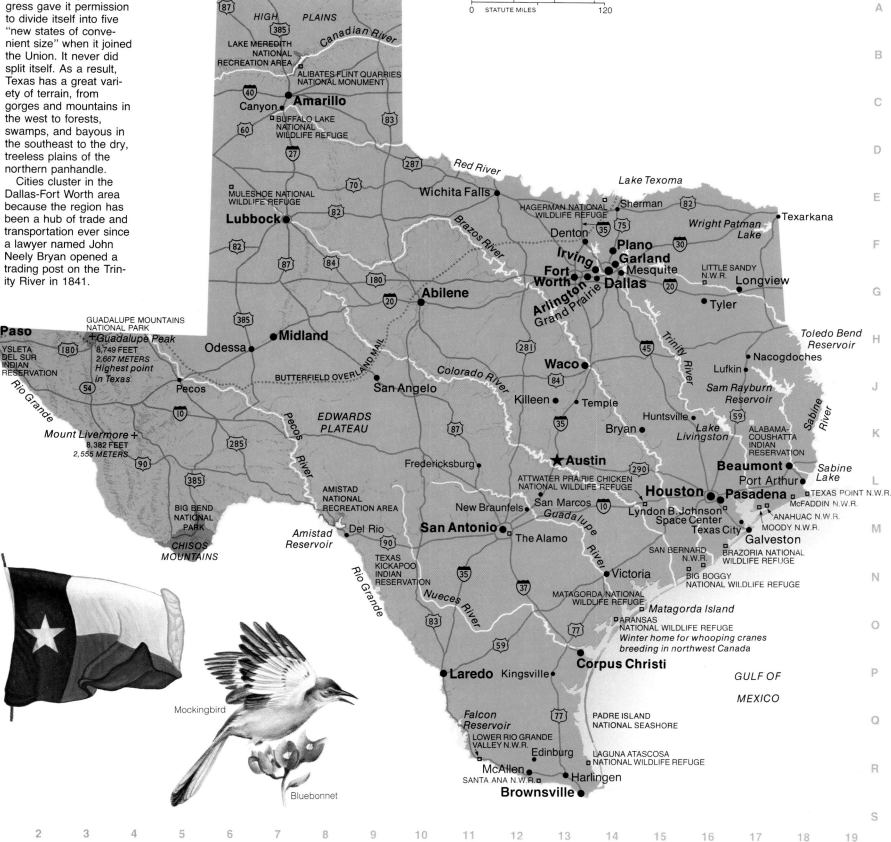

Texas is so big that Congress gave it permission to divide itself into five "new states of convenient size" when it joined the Union. It never did split itself. As a result, Texas has a great variety of terrain, from gorges and mountains in the west to forests, swamps, and bayous in the southeast to the dry, treeless plains of the northern panhandle.

Cities cluster in the Dallas-Fort Worth area because the region has been a hub of trade and transportation ever since a lawyer named John Neely Bryan opened a trading post on the Trinity River in 1841.

KILOMETERS 180
STATUTE MILES 120

HIGH PLAINS
Canadian River
LAKE MEREDITH NATIONAL RECREATION AREA
ALIBATES FLINT QUARRIES NATIONAL MONUMENT
Canyon
Amarillo
BUFFALO LAKE NATIONAL WILDLIFE REFUGE
Red River
Lake Texoma
MULESHOE NATIONAL WILDLIFE REFUGE
Wichita Falls
Sherman
HAGERMAN NATIONAL WILDLIFE REFUGE
Wright Patman Lake
Texarkana
Lubbock
Brazos River
Denton
Plano
Garland
Irving
Mesquite
LITTLE SANDY N.W.R.
Longview
Fort Worth
Dallas
Abilene
Arlington
Grand Prairie
Tyler
GUADALUPE MOUNTAINS NATIONAL PARK
El Paso
Guadalupe Peak 8,749 FEET 2,667 METERS Highest point in Texas
Midland
Odessa
Colorado River
Waco
Toledo Bend Reservoir
YSLETA DEL SUR INDIAN RESERVATION
BUTTERFIELD OVERLAND MAIL
Nacogdoches
Lufkin
Sam Rayburn Reservoir
Mount Livermore + 8,382 FEET 2,555 METERS
Pecos
San Angelo
Killeen
Temple
Huntsville
Sabine River
Rio Grande
Pecos River
EDWARDS PLATEAU
Bryan
Lake Livingston
ALABAMA-COUSHATTA INDIAN RESERVATION
Fredericksburg
Austin
Beaumont
AMISTAD NATIONAL RECREATION AREA
ATTWATER PRAIRIE CHICKEN NATIONAL WILDLIFE REFUGE
Port Arthur
Sabine Lake
BIG BEND NATIONAL PARK
Amistad Reservoir
New Braunfels
San Marcos
Houston
Pasadena
TEXAS POINT N.W.R.
CHISOS MOUNTAINS
Del Rio
San Antonio
Lyndon B. Johnson Space Center
McFADDIN N.W.R.
ANAHUAC N.W.R.
MOODY N.W.R.
The Alamo
Guadalupe River
Texas City
Galveston
SAN BERNARD N.W.R.
BRAZORIA NATIONAL WILDLIFE REFUGE
TEXAS KICKAPOO INDIAN RESERVATION
Victoria
BIG BOGGY NATIONAL WILDLIFE REFUGE
Rio Grande
Nueces River
MATAGORDA NATIONAL WILDLIFE REFUGE
Matagorda Island
ARANSAS NATIONAL WILDLIFE REFUGE
Winter home for whooping cranes breeding in northwest Canada
Corpus Christi
GULF OF
MEXICO
Laredo
Kingsville
Falcon Reservoir
PADRE ISLAND NATIONAL SEASHORE
LOWER RIO GRANDE VALLEY N.W.R.
Edinburg
LAGUNA ATASCOSA NATIONAL WILDLIFE REFUGE
McAllen
Harlingen
SANTA ANA N.W.R.
Brownsville

Mockingbird

Bluebonnet

A B C D E F G H J K L M N O P Q R S
1 2 3 4 5 6 7 8 9 10 11 12 13 14 15 16 17 18 19

1

2

3

Texas

1 *Harvest of beauty: Giant claws gently vacuum coreopsis seeds for gardeners at a wildflower farm near Houston.*

2 *An agave symbolizes the desert that meets the Chisos Mountains as the Rio Grande makes its curve in Big Bend country.*

3 *Modern cowboys whoop it up in a town southwest of Pecos, proving that the spirit of the frontier lives on in West Texas.*

4 *Stone-still, a Texas horned lizard waits for insects. The species is threatened by loss of habitat and by collectors who prize its movie-monster looks.*

5 *Highways and high rises sprout from the northern plains in Dallas, the state's second largest city. Four of five Texans now reside in urban areas.*

5

4

Mountain States

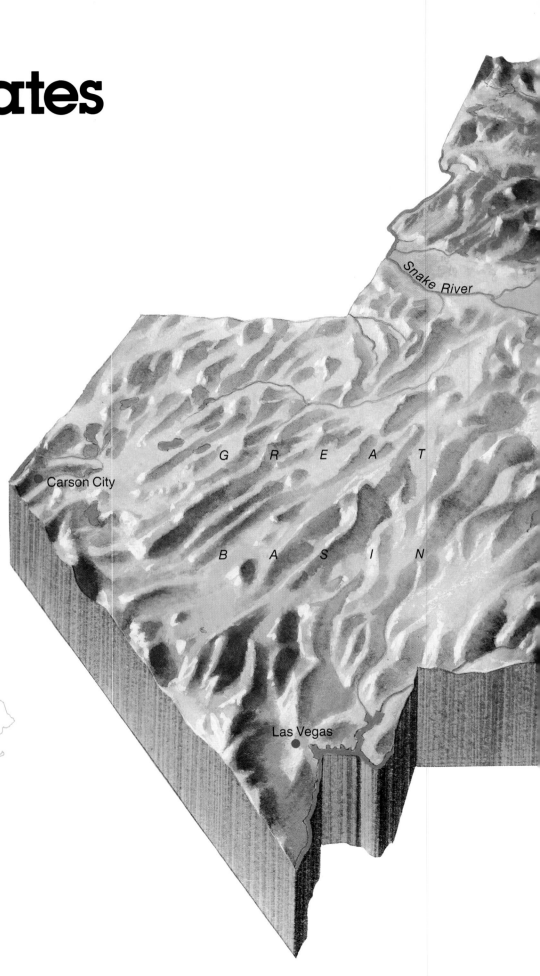

High, wide, and rumpled describes these western states. Some parts are downright dry and desolate. The Rocky Mountains form the backbone of this region that makes up about a fifth of the land area of the 48 contiguous states. If you crossed the widest part, as some pioneers and gold seekers did, you would cover about a third of the distance between the Atlantic Ocean and the Pacific Ocean.

There's plenty of room here to get lonely, too. Fewer than 4 of every 100 Americans live in this region, mostly in the few big cities located on either side of the Rockies. The climate is dry, especially in the Great Basin area. That's because high mountains farther west wring out much of the moisture carried by winds from the Pacific Ocean. As the winds rise to clear these ridges, they cool. Their moisture condenses and falls as rain or snow. Only about 12 inches (30 cm) of precipitation dampens these mountain states most years, while the Great Basin receives much less. The Rockies themselves prevent moisture from reaching the plains farther east.

The Rockies are young mountains; only about 65 million years ago colliding continental plates thrust them thousands of feet above sea level. The Great Basin began forming 40 million years ago, cracking the crust into faults and folds. But here the pressure relaxed and some slices of crust slipped downward, forming parallel valleys and ridges.

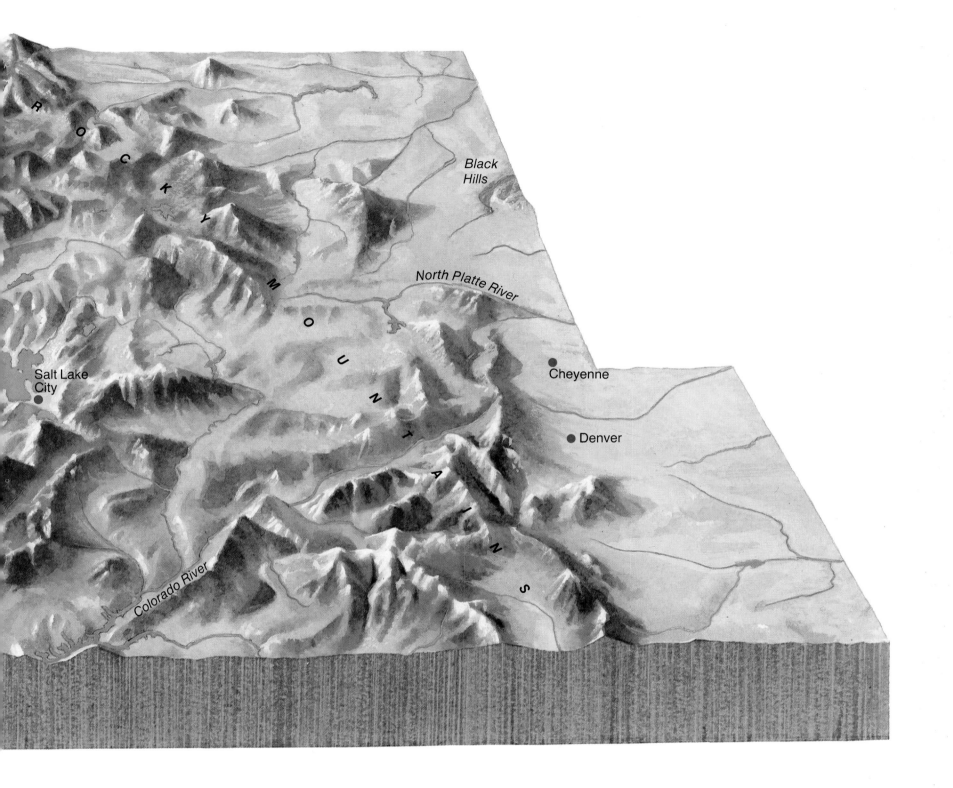

ROCKY

Black
Hills

North Platte River

Salt Lake
City

Cheyenne

Denver

Colorado River

Idaho

A Chinese immigrant peddles homegrown vegetables. The first Chinese came to Idaho in 1865 to work in gold mines, but many who followed opened shops, restaurants, and laundries.

Idaho leads the country in potato growing. Each year farmers harvest billions of pounds, mainly from the irrigated, fertile plain of the Snake River Valley. History credits a Presbyterian missionary with starting Idaho's potato industry. In the 1830s Henry Harmon Spalding showed Nez Perce Indians at his mission how to plant potatoes to supplement their diet when hunting was poor.

A generation ago most of Idaho's prized Russet Burbank spuds left the state whole. Today most potatoes exit after processing that includes transformation into potato chips and one-fourth of all the French fries served in fast-food restaurants. Not surprisingly, Idaho guards its precious tuber fiercely. It has sued those who use the name "Idaho" to market potatoes grown outside the state.

But many Idahoans feel that the Snake River Plain and its main cash crop get too much atten-

tion. Some argue that Idaho is really three states in one, three distinct regions that had little to do with one another until the development of modern communications and transportation. In fact, each year the people of the panhandle, the Snake River Plain, and the arid southeastern area flock to their own separate state fairs. Most other states have only one fair where people gather to celebrate their state's identity.

Made from leftover territory of some of its neighbors after they became states, Idaho lacks the rectangular regularity of nearby states. Its unusual shape and varied terrain create the three divisions. The panhandle region, which merges into the state's central wilderness, is made up of the Bitterroot, Clearwater, and other ranges of the Rocky Mountains. It contains large, deep lakes. The panhandle's dense forests of fir, pine, and spruce provide lumber and other wood products. Deposits of valuable minerals spurred a mining heyday there in the 19th century. Although many deposits played out, mining remains a major industry.

People of the panhandle have to be independent and self-reliant. They live in some of the most rugged and remote territory in the United States. Early travelers called the middle part of the Salmon the River of No Return because they could not navigate its volatile currents.

Rising in Yellowstone National Park, in Wyoming, the Snake River winds 500 miles (800 km) through southern Idaho. As the river turns north to form the border with Oregon, it carves deep down through the mountains, where it has helped create Hells Canyon.

But for most of its course the Snake River flows through a broad plain. Lava that erupted repeatedly from cracks in Earth's crust thousands of years ago contributes to the plain's rich soil. The lava also fashioned desolate landscapes where few plants can grow. The cinder buttes, spatter cones, and twisted lava flows of Craters of the Moon National Monument so resemble the moon's surface that Apollo astronauts traveled there in the 1960s.

Unlike many other parts of the West, Idaho does not often face a shortage of water. The state has many rivers and underground water sources. Waters of the Snake River, distributed by irrigation channels, nourish the plain's potato

crop and also sugar beets, wheat, alfalfa, and hops. Despite dams upstream, the Snake plunges 212 feet (65 m) at Shoshone Falls, higher than the Niagara's by about 30 feet (9 m).

Most Idahoans have settled on the Snake River Plain. Boise is one of the fastest growing cities in the West, strong in electronics, lumber, agribusiness, and other industries.

At the Basque Center in Boise, the haunting strains of a *txistu*, or flute, echo the homeland for Boise's 10,000 Basques. Work as sheepherders drew these natives of the French and Spanish Pyrenees to Idaho and nearby states. The life was a lonely one. For months at a time the herder, with his flock, would roam the high pastures. On visits to town he would seek out the company of other Basques to speak the ancient, unique Basque language. Though sheepherding is on the decline, and Basques have entered the ranks of ranchers, lawyers, and politicians, Basque culture proudly lives on in Boise.

Southeastern Idaho is part of the arid Great Basin region that extends into Nevada and other western states. Mountains interspersed with grass-covered valleys and plateaus support cattle and sheep and irrigated farming. Most people here are Mormons and have strong ties to Salt Lake City, Utah, the headquarters of the Mormon Church.

Some people think that Idaho's split personality makes a section of it ripe for secession. Proponents in the panhandle note the area's ties with nearby parts of Washington and Montana. One name proposed for this potential 51st state is Washtanaho—with a license plate that reads "No Small Potatoes."

Area: *the 13th largest state, 83,564 sq mi (216,432 sq km)*

Population: *1,066,749; ranks 42nd*

Major Cities: *Boise, 125,738; Pocatello, 46,080; Idaho Falls, 43,929*

Manufacturing: *food products, lumber and wood products, machinery, chemicals, electronics, rubber and plastics, metal products*

Agriculture: *cattle, potatoes, milk, wheat, sugar beets, barley, hay*

Mining and Quarrying: *silver, phosphate rock, lead, copper*

Other Important Activities: *tourism, printing and publishing*

Statehood: *the 43rd state; admitted July 3, 1890*

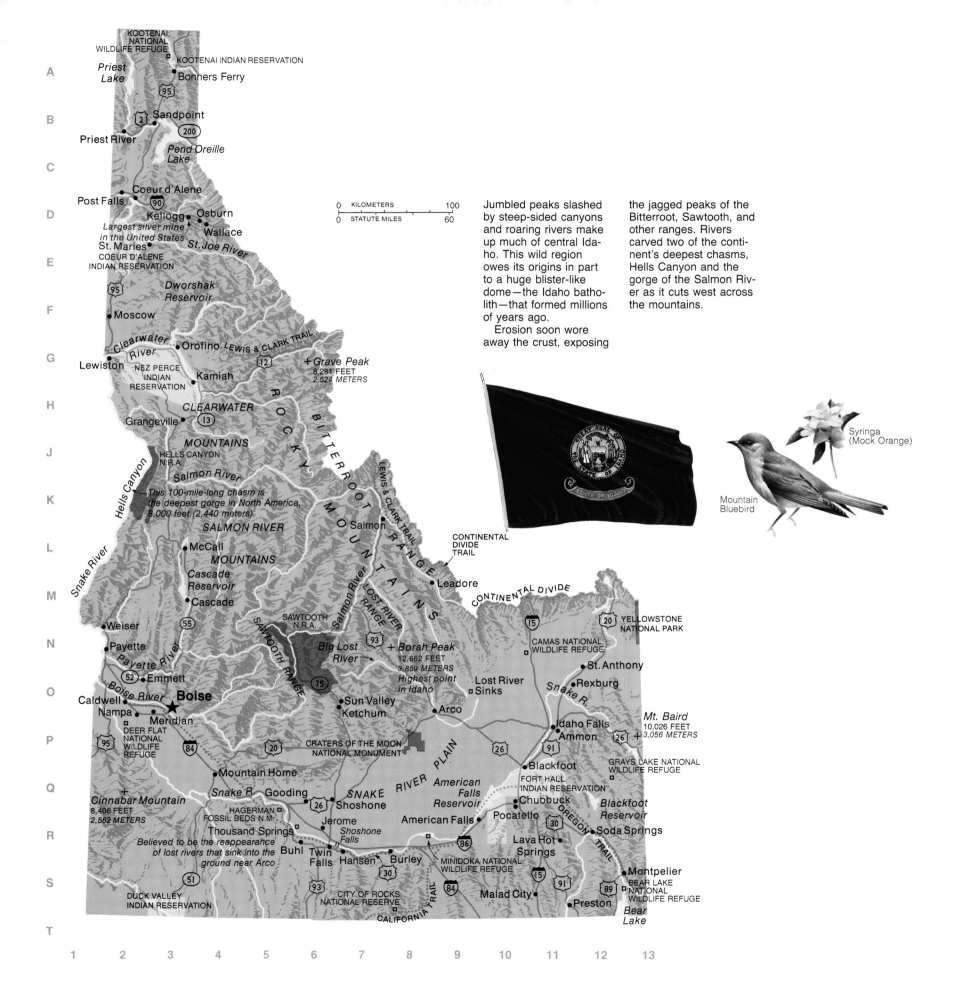

A KOOTENAI NATIONAL WILDLIFE REFUGE
KOOTENAI INDIAN RESERVATION
Priest Lake
Bonners Ferry
95

B 2 Sandpoint
200
Priest River

C *Pend Oreille Lake*

D Coeur d'Alene
90
Post Falls
Kellogg • Osburn
Largest silver mine in the United States
Wallace
St. Maries •
COEUR D'ALENE INDIAN RESERVATION
St. Joe River

E 95

F *Dworshak Reservoir*
• Moscow

G *Clearwater River*
Orofino • LEWIS & CLARK TRAIL
Lewiston
NEZ PERCE INDIAN RESERVATION
Kamiah
+ *Grave Peak*
8,281 FEET
2,524 METERS
12

H CLEARWATER
Grangeville • 13
MOUNTAINS
ROCKY

J HELLS CANYON N.R.A.
BITTERROOT

K Hells Canyon
Salmon River
This 100-mile-long chasm is the deepest gorge in North America, 8,000 feet (2,440 meters)
LEWIS & CLARK TRAIL
CONTINENTAL DIVIDE TRAIL
Salmon

L SALMON RIVER
• McCall
MOUNTAINS
Salmon River
LOST RIVER RANGE
• Leadore

M *Cascade Reservoir*
• Cascade
MOUNTAINS
CONTINENTAL DIVIDE

N • Weiser
55
SAWTOOTH N.R.A.
Big Lost River
93
+ *Borah Peak*
12,662 FEET
3,859 METERS
Highest point in Idaho
CAMAS NATIONAL WILDLIFE REFUGE
15
20 YELLOWSTONE NATIONAL PARK
• St. Anthony

O • Payette
Payette River
52 • Emmett
Boise River
Caldwell •
★ **Boise**
SAWTOOTH RANGE
75
Sun Valley
Ketchum
Lost River Sinks
• Arco
Snake R.
• Rexburg
Idaho Falls
Ammon
Mt. Baird
10,026 FEET
3,056 METERS
26

P Nampa
Meridian
DEER FLAT NATIONAL WILDLIFE REFUGE
95
84
20
CRATERS OF THE MOON NATIONAL MONUMENT
SNAKE RIVER PLAIN
26
91
26
• Blackfoot
GRAYS LAKE NATIONAL WILDLIFE REFUGE

Q + *Cinnabar Mountain*
8,406 FEET
2,562 METERS
Mountain Home
Snake R. Gooding
26 • Shoshone
SNAKE RIVER PLAIN
American Falls Reservoir
FORT HALL INDIAN RESERVATION
• Chubbuck
OREGON TRAIL
Blackfoot Reservoir

R HAGERMAN FOSSIL BEDS N.M.
Jerome
Shoshone Falls
Pocatello
30
• Soda Springs
Thousand Springs
American Falls
86
Lava Hot Springs
Believed to be the reappearance of lost rivers that sink into the ground near Arco
Buhl
Twin Falls
Hansen • Burley
MINIDOKA NATIONAL WILDLIFE REFUGE

S 51
DUCK VALLEY INDIAN RESERVATION
93
CITY OF ROCKS NATIONAL RESERVE
30
84
CALIFORNIA TRAIL
Malad City
15
91
89
• Montpelier
BEAR LAKE NATIONAL WILDLIFE REFUGE
Preston •
Bear Lake

T

KILOMETERS 0 — 100
STATUTE MILES 0 — 60

Jumbled peaks slashed by steep-sided canyons and roaring rivers make up much of central Idaho. This wild region owes its origins in part to a huge blister-like dome—the Idaho batholith—that formed millions of years ago.

Erosion soon wore away the crust, exposing the jagged peaks of the Bitterroot, Sawtooth, and other ranges. Rivers carved two of the continent's deepest chasms, Hells Canyon and the gorge of the Salmon River as it cuts west across the mountains.

Syringa (Mock Orange)

Mountain Bluebird

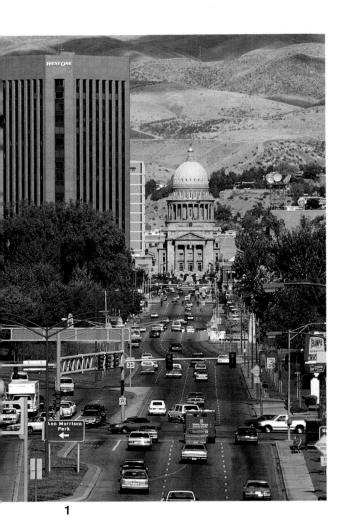

1

2

Idaho

1 *Boise, Idaho's capital, lies in a valley protected from winter's worst storms by mountains to the north of the city.*

2 *Powder snow flies around a skier above the Sun Valley resort, in the Sawtooth Range of the Rocky Mountains.*

3 *A Basque sheepherder pursues his lonely work in the hills of southwestern Idaho.*

4 *French fries for your Big Mac undergo inspection for proper size and texture. Most are made from Idaho's long, oval Russet Burbank, a potato variety that finds ideal growing conditions along the Snake River.*

5 *A sprinkler rig brings water from the Snake River to irrigate crops.*

3

4

5

Montana

As a young boy in the 1940s, writer Ivan Doig lived on a small sheep ranch in a valley of Montana's Rocky Mountain foothills. The world he knew was one of mountains sliced by slanting rivers and covered with timber and high pastures. Ivan was a teenager before he glimpsed the state's other, larger landscape, "a land of steady expanse, of crisp-margined distances set long and straight on the earth."

Montana is two-fifths mountains and three-fifths rolling, shortgrass prairie. Range after range of the Rockies rises in western Montana. The Continental Divide rides the crests of these ranges. It also gives Montana two climates. West of the divide, the climate is moderate and relatively humid year-round. East of it, extremes are the norm: very cold winters and very hot summers with less rainfall than the west. Sometimes, though, winter's grip on the eastern plains will be broken by chinooks. These warm winds blow down the eastern slopes of the Rockies, raising temperatures and melting snow so that pasture for livestock is exposed.

Eighty million years of mountain building put broad streaks of gold, silver, and copper into many Montana ranges. Water, wind, and glaciers carried minerals to rivers and streams, forming deposits called placers. Beginning in 1862, Montana's gold rush made places like Butte and Virginia City wild and wealthy towns. As the gold rush waned, miners sought silver and the copper that long drove the economy. Mining interests held great power. Until the mid-1960s the Anaconda Copper Mining Company owned many Montana newspapers and controlled many of the politicians.

Anaconda closed its main smelter in 1980. Today metal mining continues on a smaller scale, and Montana leads the country in the extraction of talc and vermiculite, used chiefly in insulation. Butte supplements its reduced mining income with light industry and livestock sales.

Miners have long shared Montana's mountains with loggers. The fir, pine, cedar, and spruce they cut are turned into lumber and other wood products before leaving the state. How much lumbering is in Montana's future has rekindled a dispute between conservationists who worry about Montana's federal forestlands and loggers and sawmill workers who worry about jobs. For one section a landmark compromise was reached in 1990 that would set aside almost equal areas of wilderness and land for logging, mining, and other development.

Montana's eastern prairie supports most of the state's agriculture. Only Texas has more acreage devoted to farming. Furrowed stripes

In 1887 immigrants from Europe and Asia built the Great Northern Railroad across 640 miles of plains and mountains in Montana and North Dakota in just one season.

of wheat cover much of the plains, along with barley, hay, and other crops. Where cattle once ranged freely, grazing on prairie grasses under the watch of cowboys, fences now mark the boundaries of Montana's vast ranches.

Today both ranchers and environmentalists eye with apprehension the further development of eastern Montana's energy resources. Oil brings in about half of Montana's mineral income. Worldwide concern about oil puts a premium on the state's enormous reserves as well as its reserves of coal.

Lewis and Clark were the first white Americans to view the Great Falls of the Missouri River, which drains most of the state and is its principal waterway. "The grandest sight I ever beheld," wrote Meriwether Lewis in his 1805 journal. But would he recognize the Missouri today? At Fort Peck, one of the world's largest earthen dams impounds the river's water, creating a lake bigger than the city of Chicago.

And what would the explorers say about the Blackfeet, Flathead, Crow, Sioux, Cheyenne, and other tribes that in their time commanded the mountain passes and the plains teeming with bison? About 6 percent of Montanans today are Native Americans whose reservation councils often face controversy over whether or not to exploit their land's natural resources, particularly coal and oil. More than a century ago, their ancestors gave an answer to the federal troops moving onto their lands. On a lonely hill near the Little Bighorn River, on a June Sunday in 1876, Lt. Col. George A. Custer and 215 men of his Seventh Cavalry fell at the hands of some 2,000 Indian warriors.

Area: *the fourth largest state, 147,046 sq mi (380,848 sq km)*
Population: *799,065; ranks 44th*
Major Cities: *Billings, 81,151; Great Falls, 55,097; Missoula, 42,918*
Manufacturing: *lumber and wood products, food products, petroleum products*
Mining and Quarrying: *oil and gas, coal, gold, silver, sand and gravel*
Agriculture: *cattle, wheat, barley, hay, sugar beets, milk*
Other Important Activities: *tourism, printing and publishing*
Statehood: *the 41st state; admitted November 8, 1889*

1 2 3 4 5 6 7 8 9 10 11 12 13 14 15 16 17 18 19

A
B
C
D
E
F
G
H
J
K
L

Eureka
Kootenai River
Libby
Flathead River
Kalispell
GLACIER NATIONAL PARK
CONTINENTAL DIVIDE TRAIL
BLACKFEET INDIAN RESERVATION
Browning
Cut Bank
Shelby
CREEDMAN COULEE NATIONAL WILDLIFE REFUGE
LAKE THIBADEAU N.W.R.
BLACK COULEE N.W.R.
HEWITT LAKE N.W.R.
Havre
BOWDOIN N.W.R.
Malta
FORT PECK INDIAN RESERVATION
Plentywood
MEDICINE LAKE N.W.R.
Thompson Falls
Flathead Lake
Hungry Horse Reservoir
SWAN RIVER N.W.R.
Lake Elwell
ROCKY BOYS INDIAN RESERVATION
FORT BELKNAP INDIAN RESERVATION
Glasgow
Fort Peck Dam
Fort Peck Lake
Poplar
Sidney
Polson
PABLO N.W.R.
FLATHEAD INDIAN RESERVATION
NINE-PIPE N.W.R.
NATIONAL BISON RANGE N.W.R.
Choteau
Teton River
Fort Benton
BENTON LAKE N.W.R.
Sun River
Missouri River
LEWIS AND CLARK TRAIL
CHARLES M. RUSSELL NATIONAL WILDLIFE REFUGE
U L BEND N.W.R.
Clark Fork
ROCKY MOUNTAINS
CONTINENTAL DIVIDE
Great Falls
Missouri River
Circle
Glendive
Wibaux
RATTLESNAKE N.R.A.
Blackfoot River
Missoula
Helena
Canyon Ferry Lake
White Sulphur Springs
WAR HORSE N.W.R.
Lewistown
Jordan
LAMESTEER N.W.R.
LEE METCALF N.W.R.
Hamilton
LAKE MASON N.W.R.
Roundup
Musselshell River
Miles City
Baker
BITTERROOT RANGE
Bitterroot River
Anaconda
Butte
Jefferson River
Townsend
HAILSTONE N.W.R.
HALFBREED LAKE N.W.R.
Forsyth
Powder River
Tongue River
Baldy Mountain +
10,568 FEET
3,221 METERS
Virginia City
Dillon
Gallatin River
Madison River
Livingston
Bozeman
Columbus
Billings
Hardin
Little Bighorn River
CUSTER BATTLEFIELD N.M.
NORTHERN CHEYENNE INDIAN RESERVATION
Broadus
LEWIS & CLARK TRAIL
Red Lodge
Granite Peak
12,799 FEET
3,901 METERS
Highest point in Montana
Clarks Fork
Bighorn River
Bighorn Lake
CROW INDIAN RESERVATION
BIGHORN CANYON NATIONAL RECREATION AREA
CONTINENTAL DIVIDE TRAIL
Hebgen Lake
YELLOWSTONE NATIONAL PARK
RED ROCK LAKES NATIONAL WILDLIFE REFUGE

0 KILOMETERS 125
0 STATUTE MILES 75

Angling westward from Yellowstone National Park, the Continental Divide follows Rocky Mountain ridges, forming part of the border with Idaho before turning eastward. A hiking trail traces the watershed through Montana to Glacier National Park.

Journeying to the Pacific Ocean, Meriwether Lewis and William Clark followed the Missouri River in 1804 and returned along the Yellowstone in 1806.

Many other trails also led west (map at right), including those traveled by pioneer families during the great migrations of the 1840s and 1850s.

LEWIS AND CLARK ROUTE
OREGON TRAIL
MORMON TRAIL
CALIFORNIA TRAIL
Sacramento
PONY EXPRESS
Salt Lake City
Nauvoo
San Francisco
SPANISH TRAIL
Independence
St. Joseph
St. Louis
Santa Fe
SANTA FE TRAIL
BUTTERFIELD OVERLAND MAIL

Bitterroot
Western Meadowlark

MONTANA

1

2

3

4

Montana

1 *In the mountains of south-central Montana, cowboys herd their cattle on a fall drive from high summer pastures to a lower, warmer winter range.*

2 *A bighorn sheep, safe in the mountain meadows of Glacier National Park, nibbles on favorite blossoms.*

3 *On the Continental Divide, a gigantic limestone wall is honeycombed with fossils of creatures that lived here 500 million years ago, when shallow seas covered the land.*

4 *Harvested wheat, Montana's most valuable crop, pours from a combine as the farmer levels his load.*

5 *A mile-wide (1.6-km) pit, once mined for copper, edges Butte. Now the pit is being filled with groundwater drained from nearby underground metal mines.*

5

Wyoming

Endless lines of covered wagons, creaking and groaning under the weight of precious possessions. Zealous Latter-day Saints, or Mormons, searching for a peaceful promised land. Hopeful prospectors rushing to stake their claims in California's goldfields. Wiry youths spurring on their lightning-fast mounts to the next relay point. All of these pioneers, forty-niners, and Pony Express riders passed through Wyoming on essentially the same trail: a route that followed the North Platte and Sweetwater Rivers, up a gradual slope and across the Continental Divide at South Pass, the best natural gap in the Rocky Mountains. So well chosen was this route that rail and road traffic still follow it today.

In the 19th century, hundreds of thousands of people passed through Wyoming, but few stayed. Most early settlements rose around army forts and along the route of the Union Pacific Railroad in southern Wyoming. Mining, cattle ranching, and the discovery of oil near Casper in 1888 added other settlements. Some places, like Cheyenne, bear the names of Indian groups driven off their land by the newcomers.

In Wyoming, the Great Plains meet the Rocky Mountains. From the Absaroka Range and Bighorn Mountains in the north to the Wind River Range to the Laramie Mountains in the southeast, most Wyoming ranges stretch north to south. Between them lie high, dry, cold basins covered with the sagebrush and short-grasses that are natural forage for the widespread herds of pronghorns. In places, flat-topped towers of weathered rock called buttes punctuate the desolate basins. Most of Wyoming is high; its average elevation of 6,100 feet (1,860 m) is second only to Colorado's.

Driving the high roads of the mountain West, writer and California native Gretl Ehrlich can always sense when she approaches her adopted state. "When the wind starts blowing, I know I'm near Wyoming," she wrote. Wyoming is so windy that winter often brings "ground blizzards." Though no snow is falling and the day may be sunny and bright, westerly winds whip up dry snow from the ground into blinding swirls, easy to get lost in.

The railroad spread across southern Wyoming in the late 1860s. As it did, cattlemen came from Texas, eager to graze their longhorns on the nutritious grasses before moving them to market by rail. As ranchers they would take the 160 acres (65 ha) that the federal government allotted to homesteaders and then graze their animals on the open range. To combat cattle rustlers, the ranchers banded together in a Stock Growers' Association that registered the brands used by each ranch. Other homesteaders, who were farmers, resented the ranchers' grazing practices and began to fence in their spreads to protect their crops. Sheep ranchers

A rancher shows off Buster, a fine-wooled Rambouillet sheep, in 1945. Buster's thick coat provides good protection in subfreezing winters. His ancestors came to the U. S. from Spain and Germany.

competed for pasture with the cattle ranchers. All these rivalries developed into a series of ferocious range wars among sheepherders, cattlemen, and farmers.

Essential to each ranch's operations was the cowboy. Willing to perform ceaseless chores and endure long, lonesome hours in the saddle, braving the wind and weather, cowboys have kept Wyoming's vast cattle ranches running. Today cowboying in Wyoming has taken on an international flavor. While some Americans still want the job, some ranches have *vaqueros* from Mexico, Chile, and Peru, and one Wyoming sheep rancher has looked even farther—all the way to Mongolia—for herders to look after his flocks.

Wyoming's people live mostly in small towns. Although the state has the smallest population in the nation, what it lacks in year-round residents it makes up for in visitors. Each year some five million tourists flock to the natural wonders of Yellowstone National Park, to the wildlife and scenery of the Teton Range, to vacation ranches, and to the rodeos and other celebrations of Wyoming's frontier heritage. The money they spend every year rivals the income earned from agriculture and creates many jobs for Wyoming citizens.

Most of Wyoming's economic resources lie with the mineral riches under the land. The area around Green River contains the world's largest source of trona, the ore that yields soda ash, a chemical used in making glass, detergent, and baking soda. Wyoming also holds the second largest reserve of uranium in the country (after New Mexico), most of it in the state's central basins. Enormous deposits of oil, natural gas, and coal have been mined in fits and starts, depending on the nation's energy needs—thus producing ups and downs in Wyoming's economy. Knowing that its future most likely lies with increased mining, Wyoming is acting to prevent permanent damage to the environment. At all strip-mining projects in eastern Wyoming, earthmovers continually backfill the cut as the excavation proceeds, and the fill is then replanted under the supervision of ecologists.

Area: *the ninth largest state, 97,809 sq mi (253,326 sq km)*
Population: *453,588; ranks 50th*
Major Cities: *Cheyenne, 50,008; Casper, 46,742; Laramie, 26,687*
Mining: *oil and gas, coal, trona, clay*
Manufacturing: *chemicals, petroleum products, food products, lumber and wood products*
Agriculture: *cattle, hay, sugar beets, sheep and wool, wheat, barley*
Other Important Activities: *tourism, printing and publishing*
Statehood: *the 44th state; admitted July 10, 1890*

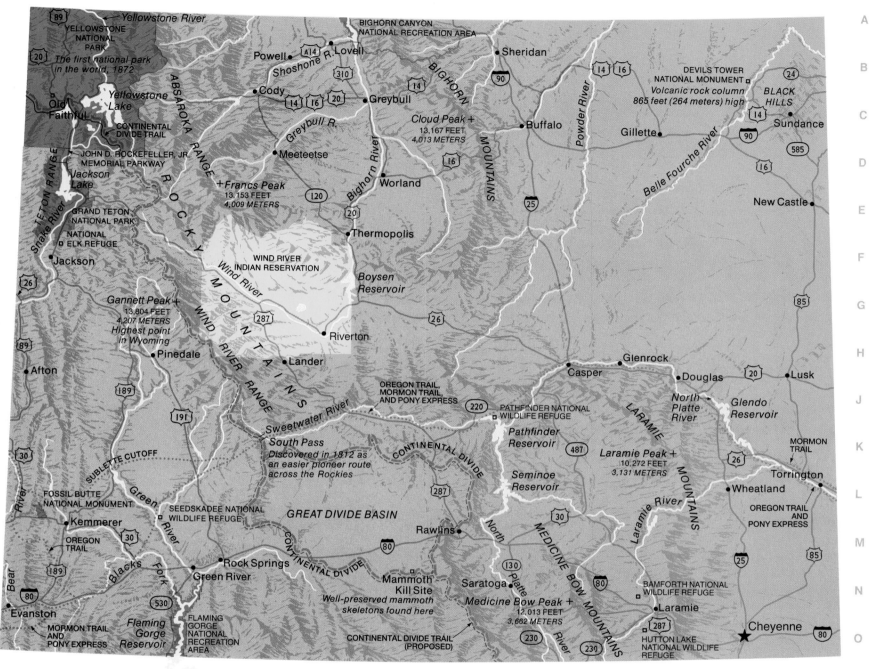

89
YELLOWSTONE
NATIONAL
PARK
*The first national park
in the world, 1872*
20

Yellowstone River

BIGHORN CANYON
NATIONAL RECREATION AREA

Powell
A14
R. Lovell
Shoshone
310
Sheridan
90
14 16
DEVILS TOWER
NATIONAL MONUMENT
*Volcanic rock column
865 feet (264 meters) high*
24

Cody
14 16
20
Greybull
14
BLACK
HILLS

Yellowstone
Lake
Old
Faithful
CONTINENTAL
DIVIDE TRAIL

ABSAROKA RANGE

BIGHORN

Cloud Peak +
13,167 FEET
4,013 METERS

Buffalo

Gillette

Sundance
14
90
585

JOHN D. ROCKEFELLER, JR.
MEMORIAL PARKWAY
Jackson
Lake
Snake River

Meeteetse
Greybull R.

MOUNTAINS

Powder River

Belle Fourche River
16

GRAND TETON
NATIONAL PARK
NATIONAL
ELK REFUGE

+ Francs Peak
13,153 FEET
4,009 METERS
120
Worland
16
25

New Castle

TETON RANGE

Jackson
26

ROCKY

20
Thermopolis

WIND RIVER
INDIAN RESERVATION

Boysen
Reservoir
85

Gannett Peak +
13,804 FEET
4,207 METERS
*Highest point
in Wyoming*
MOUNTAINS
Wind River
287

26

89

Pinedale
WIND RIVER RANGE
Riverton

Glenrock
Casper
Douglas
20
Lusk

Afton
Lander
OREGON TRAIL,
MORMON TRAIL,
AND PONY EXPRESS
220
PATHFINDER NATIONAL
WILDLIFE REFUGE

North
Platte
River
Glendo
Reservoir

189
Sweetwater River
Pathfinder
Reservoir
487
LARAMIE
MORMON
TRAIL

191
*South Pass
Discovered in 1812 as
an easier pioneer route
across the Rockies*
CONTINENTAL DIVIDE

Laramie Peak +
10,272 FEET
3,131 METERS
26

SUBLETTE CUTOFF
287
Seminoe
Reservoir
MOUNTAINS
Torrington

30
FOSSIL BUTTE
NATIONAL MONUMENT
SEEDSKADEE NATIONAL
WILDLIFE REFUGE
GREAT DIVIDE BASIN
Rawlins
30
Laramie River
Wheatland
OREGON TRAIL
AND
PONY EXPRESS

Green River
CONTINENTAL DIVIDE
80
25
85

Kemmerer
OREGON
TRAIL
30
Blacks
Rock Springs
Mammoth
Kill Site
*Well-preserved mammoth
skeletons found here*
130
Saratoga
North
MEDICINE BOW MOUNTAINS
BAMFORTH NATIONAL
WILDLIFE REFUGE
80

189
Green River
Fork
Medicine Bow Peak +
12,013 FEET
3,662 METERS
Platte
Laramie

Bear River
530
FLAMING
GORGE
NATIONAL
RECREATION
AREA
CONTINENTAL DIVIDE TRAIL
(PROPOSED)
230
River
230
287
HUTTON LAKE
NATIONAL WILDLIFE
REFUGE
Cheyenne
80

Evanston
80
Flaming
Gorge
Reservoir
MORMON TRAIL
AND
PONY EXPRESS

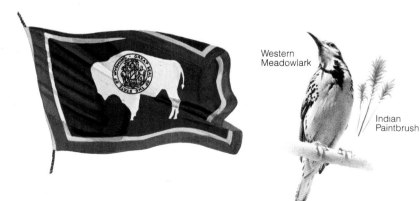

Western
Meadowlark

Indian
Paintbrush

Just south of Wyoming's
Wind River Range the
Continental Divide splits
in two and circles the rim
of Great Divide Basin. In
an otherwise forbidding
wall of mountains, South
Pass provided such an
easy route that many
travelers never realized
they had crested the
Rocky Mountains.

In the northwest, the
Teton Range began to
rise about ten million
years ago, making these
mountains the youngest
in the Rockies. And still
they grow, about a foot
(0.3 m) every 400 years.

0   KILOMETERS   75
0   STATUTE MILES   50

1

Wyoming

1 *A froth of white water drenches a kayaker riding the rapids of the Snake River.*

2 *A herd winters at the National Elk Refuge below the Teton Range. To supplement grazing, the refuge distributes hay pellets to the animals. The elk help pay the food bill when Boy Scouts gather antlers shed by the bulls and auction the antlers to contribute to the costs.*

2

3

4

5

3 *Old Faithful, Yellowstone National Park's most reliable geyser, blasts off about every 50 to 100 minutes. Molten rock beneath Earth's crust heats groundwater, which turns into steam that forces water above it to explode from the hot spring.*

4 *In southwestern Wyoming a helicopter and a cowboy round up wild mustangs. Every year, under the federal government's Adopt-a-Horse program, several thousand find new homes all across the country.*

5 *A ranch foreman and his young apprentice take a break at their cabin on the ranch's summer range near Meeteetse. With their two dogs, they herd 2,500 head of cattle.*

Nevada

In 1864 Mark Twain, working in Virginia City, wrote of Nevada: "The country looks something like a singed cat, owing to the scarcity of shrubbery, and also resembles that animal in the respect that it has more merits than its personal appearance would seem to indicate."

More than 125 years later Twain's description still fits pretty well. Most of the state is windy and barren, and most of it lies within the Great Basin, which is not one basin but at least 90. These valleys are separated by some 160 mountain ranges that on a map, said a geographer, look like an army of caterpillars crawling toward Mexico. In the west the Sierra Nevada range blocks moisture borne on westerly winds from the Pacific Ocean, making Nevada the driest state in the country. It receives, on average, only nine inches (23 cm) of precipitation a year, resulting in scant desert vegetation of shrubby shad scale and sagebrush and, higher up, scattered piñon and juniper trees.

The Great Basin sends no rivers to the sea. The rivers dead-end into lakes or into wide, shallow depressions called sinks. These sinks dry up in the summer, leaving cracked, salty or alkaline mud flats. Most of Nevada's rivers appear only seasonally and dry up in the long, hot summers. Even permanent rivers such as the snow-fed Humboldt are not large.

In contrast to Nevada's wide, parched basins are its forest-rimmed mountain lakes. One of the merits of the state that Mark Twain praised was beautiful, deep, crystal-clear Lake Tahoe, on the California border. Human hands, not natural forces, created Lake Mead, Nevada's largest lake, the reservoir of one of the world's largest dams. Built of enough concrete to make a two-lane highway from New York City to San Francisco, Hoover Dam holds back the water of the Colorado River for hydroelectricity and irrigation. Lake Mead, with Lake Mohave, forms one of the nation's largest recreation areas.

For millennia, bands of Northern and Southern Paiute, Shoshone, and Washoe Indians and their ancestors roamed Nevada, living by hunting and gathering. A staple food was the nutritious nut of the piñon pine.

In the 1770s, Spanish monks blazed parts of a trail from New Mexico to California to promote communication between Spanish settlements

In 1905 Las Vegas, less than a year old, had grown from a temporary settlement for railroad workers into a thriving town with stores, hotels, restaurants, tent homes, and this men's clothing store.

and to find Indians to convert to Christianity. The Spanish Trail, as it became known, was used later by traders and pioneers. It passed through a mountain-ringed valley that the Spanish called Las Vegas, "the meadows." In the 1850s, Mormons settled at Las Vegas and other Nevada sites, where they raised livestock and, by irrigation, coaxed crops out of the arid land. The discovery of the multimillion-dollar Comstock Lode of silver and gold ore in 1859 brought hordes of miners to western Nevada to settle Virginia City and other mining camps. One of them was Carson City, which became the capital in 1861, while Nevada was still a territory.

Early in the 20th century, Nevada found its mining fortunes waning and its population greatly outnumbered by sheep and cattle. In 1931 the state legislature decided to legalize gambling. Reno and Las Vegas became the centers of the gaming industry. Hotels patterned after Roman palaces or medieval castles provide nonstop opportunities for 30 million people a year to gamble, eat, and be entertained.

Gambling, along with the hotels, restaurants, and other services that support it, employs about 57 percent of Nevada's population and brings in more revenue than agriculture, mining, and manufacturing combined. Slot machines and other gambling equipment are important manufactured goods.

Between 1980 and 1990, Nevada's population increased by almost 50 percent, making it the fastest growing state in the country. Nearly all newcomers settle in existing urban areas. In

Las Vegas, houses rise at an astonishing rate of a thousand a month, straining water and power supplies. The reach of gambling and population has spread even to Lake Tahoe, where casinos and condominiums crowd the shores and pollute the once pristine waters.

Nevadans often refer to the parts of the state beyond Las Vegas and Reno as the "cow counties." Raising cattle and sheep and growing alfalfa for hay are the main agricultural activities. Many of Nevada's sheepherders and cowboys are Basques from the French and Spanish Pyrenees. The Basques migrated to the mountain West because their tradition ties them to mountain villages and farms where they followed this often lonely kind of work.

Mining is also important in several of the cow counties. Nevada leads the nation in the production of gold and silver. Copper, sand, and gravel are used by the construction industry that houses Nevada's booming population.

More than 85 percent of Nevada's land is federally owned. Many Nevadans want control over it to avoid hazards such as the nuclear weapons testing that went on in the 1950s, '60s, and '70s. More than 20,000 years must pass before radiation will disappear from the test site in the Nevada desert.

Much of the land of Nevada resembles an old-fashioned washboard. Most of the mountains run parallel to one another and are separated by broad, flat valleys.

Geologists explain that, beginning some 150 million years ago, Nevada was squeezed together and then, 17 million years ago, stretched apart like a giant accordion as the continent's crust shifted. These movements created long, parallel cracks, or faults, in the crust. As the crust continued to move, some strips slipped downward, forming valleys. The upthrust strips became fault-block mountains.

Area: *the seventh largest state, 110,561 sq mi (286,352 sq km)*
Population: *1,201,833; ranks 39th*
Major Cities: *Las Vegas, 258,295; Reno, 133,850; Henderson, 64,942*
Manufacturing: *food products, machinery, stone, clay, and glass products, chemicals, metal products, electronics, metals, rubber and plastics, scientific instruments*
Mining: *gold, diatomite, oil and gas, silver*
Agriculture: *cattle, hay, milk, potatoes, barley*
Other Important Activities: *legalized gambling, tourism, entertainment, printing and publishing*
Statehood: *the 36th state; admitted October 31, 1864*

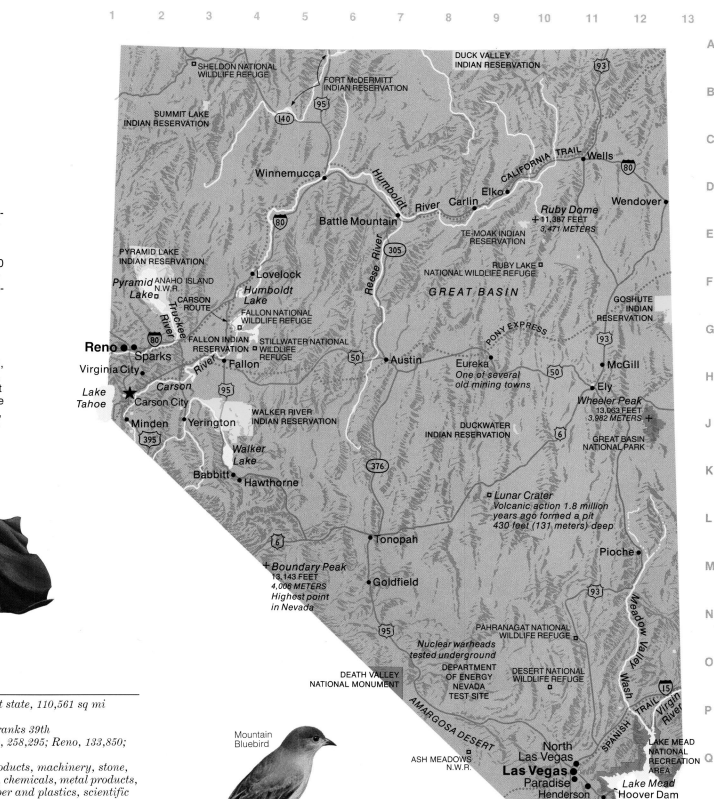

0 KILOMETERS 100
0 STATUTE MILES 60

SHELDON NATIONAL WILDLIFE REFUGE

DUCK VALLEY INDIAN RESERVATION

93

FORT McDERMITT INDIAN RESERVATION

95

SUMMIT LAKE INDIAN RESERVATION

140

CALIFORNIA TRAIL

Wells

80

Winnemucca

Humboldt

Elko

Carlin

River

Wendover

Battle Mountain

Ruby Dome
+11,387 FEET
3,471 METERS

80

TE-MOAK INDIAN RESERVATION

PYRAMID LAKE INDIAN RESERVATION

305

Reese River

RUBY LAKE NATIONAL WILDLIFE REFUGE

GREAT BASIN

Lovelock

Pyramid Lake

ANAHO ISLAND N.W.R.

Humboldt Lake

GOSHUTE INDIAN RESERVATION

CARSON ROUTE

FALLON NATIONAL WILDLIFE REFUGE

PONY EXPRESS

93

Truckee River

Reno

Sparks

80

FALLON INDIAN RESERVATION

STILLWATER NATIONAL WILDLIFE REFUGE

50

Austin

Eureka
One of several old mining towns

50

McGill

Virginia City

Fallon

Carson River

Ely

Lake Tahoe

95

Carson

Wheeler Peak
13,063 FEET
3,982 METERS +

★ Carson City

WALKER RIVER INDIAN RESERVATION

DUCKWATER INDIAN RESERVATION

6

Minden

Yerington

GREAT BASIN NATIONAL PARK

395

Walker Lake

376

Babbitt

Hawthorne

Lunar Crater
Volcanic action 1.8 million years ago formed a pit 430 feet (131 meters) deep

6

Tonopah

Pioche

+Boundary Peak
13,143 FEET
4,006 METERS
Highest point in Nevada

Goldfield

93

95

PAHRANAGAT NATIONAL WILDLIFE REFUGE

Meadow Valley Wash

Nuclear warheads tested underground

DEATH VALLEY NATIONAL MONUMENT

DEPARTMENT OF ENERGY NEVADA TEST SITE

DESERT NATIONAL WILDLIFE REFUGE

15

SPANISH TRAIL

Virgin River

AMARGOSA DESERT

LAKE MEAD NATIONAL RECREATION AREA

Mountain Bluebird

ASH MEADOWS N.W.R.

North Las Vegas

Las Vegas

Paradise

Henderson

Lake Mead

Hoover Dam

Boulder City

15

95

Lake Mohave

Colorado River

Sagebrush

A B C D E F G H J K L M N O P Q R S T

1 2 3 4 5 6 7 8 9 10 11 12 13

1

2

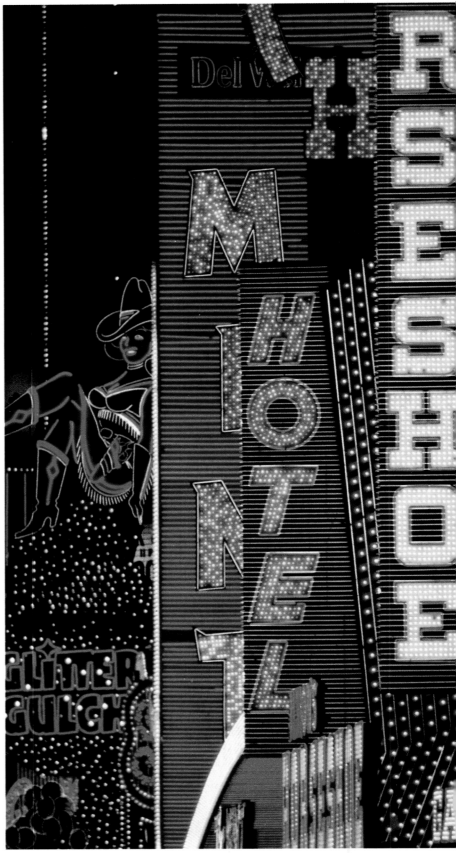

3

Nevada

1 *Defying centuries of harsh weather, a bristlecone pine clings to a peak in Great Basin National Park. Some bristlecones are 4,600 years old, and stood on western mountains when pharaohs ruled Egypt.*

2 *A three-minute haircut at the hands of a skilled shearer crops a year's growth of wool from sheep on their way to spring lambing grounds in eastern Nevada.*

3 *Neon glitter spells out the attractions of Las Vegas, where nightclubs and gambling casinos yearly lure millions of tourists.*

4

5

4 *Virginia City, a boomtown in the 1860s and 1870s, stands over the remains of the Comstock Lode, one of the richest veins of gold and silver ever discovered.*

5 *Paiute Indians pull trout from a spawning channel at Pyramid Lake. Sometimes nomadic, Paiute fished and hunted in this region centuries ago.*

Utah

The weary party had reached journey's end but did not yet know it. Their 1,350-mile (2,172-km) trek across the Great Plains and through the Rocky Mountains would take many lives from among the 1,900 refugees who would follow them, seeking freedom from religious persecution in the East. Now, in July 1847, a small advance band stood on the western slope of the Wasatch Range, gazing out over the Great Salt Lake and the valley below. Their ailing leader, Brigham Young, peered from his wagon to share the view. "This is the right place," he announced, and so the immigrants made their way to the valley floor.

Brigham Young and his followers are known as Mormons, or members of the Church of Jesus Christ of Latter-day Saints. Mormon doctrine contains many precepts for everyday life. It forbids the consumption of alcohol, tobacco, coffee, and tea. Marriages in a Mormon temple can last beyond death, since families may be united for all eternity. Also, young Mormon men, and sometimes young women and retired couples, work for a time without pay as missionaries.

But above all, it was the Mormon values of discipline, hard work, and of putting the community before the needs of the individual that enabled them to quickly settle their land. Within a month of their arrival, the Mormons had plowed, irrigated, and planted more than a hundred acres (40 ha). Within a year, they laid out a plan for Salt Lake City that included a site for their temple. They soon established hundreds of other settlements in places far less hospitable than the Salt Lake Valley.

The eastern edge of the Salt Lake Valley is green and lush because of irrigation. It lies at the foot of the Wasatch Range, part of the Rockies. Sediments wash down from the mountains to create a narrow strip of productive soil. Most of Utah's population today clusters along this front: 80 percent in the 80-mile (129-km) stretch from Ogden to Provo.

Forming an "L" with the Wasatch, the Uinta Mountains are the only range of the Rockies with an east-west orientation. While numerous ski resorts cover the slopes of the Wasatch, the Uinta's heavily forested slopes provide a primitive recreation area.

The Great Salt Lake grows and shrinks with

The Saltair resort and amusement palace was an attraction for visitors, invited to "try to sink" in the Great Salt Lake in the early 1900s. This area now lies beneath the lake's surface.

changes in inflow and evaporation. In recent years, heavy rains and strong spring snowmelt sent it over its beaches to high levels. Giving its name to the fertile valley, the Great Salt Lake actually lies in an arid area of small mountain ranges separated by broad basins. Minerals in the runoff from rivers to the east give it a high salt content. The lake is the remnant of an ancient inland freshwater sea called Lake Bonneville. During the Ice Age, Bonneville covered an area almost the size of Lake Michigan. Lake Bonneville has also left its legacy on the slopes of the Wasatch: wide shorelines, or terraces, with the caves of hunter-gatherers who inhabited the area 12,000 years ago.

The Colorado Plateau forms the largest part of Utah. This is an area of rugged uplands cut by deep canyons and valleys. National monuments, state parks, and national parks, including Bryce Canyon, Zion, and Canyonlands, preserve the fantastic landforms shaped by the action of wind, water, snow, and ice on the plateau's multihued layers of rock. The parks, together with

the large recreational Lake Powell created on the Colorado River by the Glen Canyon Dam, bring millions of tourists to southern Utah each year—one of the largest sources of revenue.

Today seven of every ten Utahns are Mormons. The mining of copper and other minerals and the opening of the railroad in the late 1800s brought in large numbers of gentiles, as non-Mormons are called. But the Mormon Church continues to extend its influence to many aspects of life in Utah. The church holds tracts of land throughout the state. It also owns a newspaper, a radio station, a television station, an insurance company, and half-interest in a department store. The Mormon preference for large families keeps Utah's birthrate at about twice the national average. A high regard for learning places the population among the nation's best educated.

The federal government is another major influence in Utah. Owning almost two-thirds of the land, the government is also the state's largest employer. Since World War II, federally sponsored manufacturing of rocket engines and weapons parts by private companies has played a large role in the economy. Food processing and, more recently, the electronics and computer industries also employ many residents.

The growth of urban areas brings the usual problems of traffic, pollution, and industrial waste to the Salt Lake Valley. Potential growth and development threaten the southern plateau region. The nation's energy demands are likely to press the exploration of this area's large reserves of coal, natural gas, oil shale, and uranium, much to the dismay of those who seek to preserve the fragile and unique terrain.

Area: *the 11th largest state, 84,899 sq mi (219,889 sq km)*
Population: *1,722,850; ranks 35th*
Major Cities: *Salt Lake City, 159,936; West Valley City, 86,976; Provo, 86,835*
Manufacturing: *transportation equipment, food products, scientific instruments, machinery, metal products, electronics, metals, stone, clay, and glass products, chemicals, clothing*
Mining: *oil and gas, coal, copper, gold*
Agriculture: *cattle, milk, hay, turkeys, wheat*
Other Important Activities: *tourism, federal government, printing and publishing*
Statehood: *the 45th state; admitted January 4, 1896*

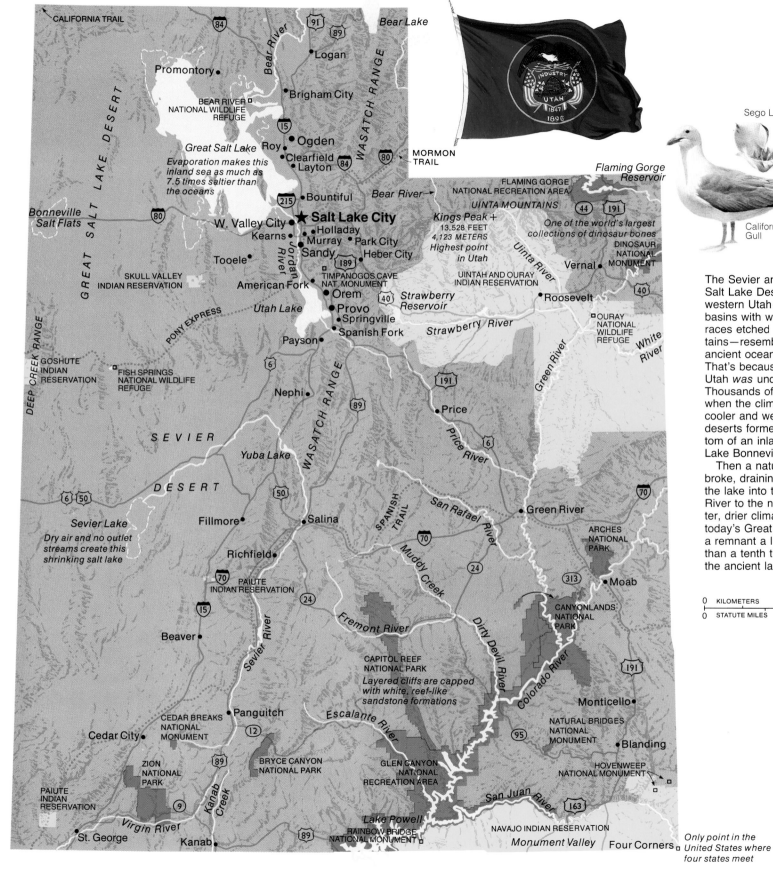

A — CALIFORNIA TRAIL

84 — 91 — 89 — *Bear Lake*

Bear River

WASATCH RANGE

• Logan

Promontory •

• Brigham City

BEAR RIVER
NATIONAL WILDLIFE
REFUGE

15

Great Salt Lake — Roy • — • Ogden
Evaporation makes this
inland sea as much as — • Clearfield
7.5 times saltier than — • Layton
the oceans

GREAT SALT LAKE DESERT

84 — 80 — MORMON TRAIL

FLAMING GORGE
NATIONAL RECREATION AREA

Flaming Gorge
Reservoir

UINTA MOUNTAINS

Bear River →

215 — • Bountiful

Bonneville
Salt Flats

80

★ **Salt Lake City**

W. Valley City •

Holladay •

Kings Peak +
13,528 FEET
4,123 METERS
Highest point
in Utah

One of the world's largest
collections of dinosaur bones

DINOSAUR
NATIONAL
MONUMENT

Kearns • — Murray • — • Park City
Sandy • — • Heber City

189

Uinta River

• Vernal

40

Tooele •

SKULL VALLEY
INDIAN RESERVATION

Jordan River

TIMPANOGOS CAVE
NAT. MONUMENT

American Fork •
• Orem
40 — *Strawberry*
Reservoir

UINTAH AND OURAY
INDIAN RESERVATION

• Roosevelt

OURAY
NATIONAL
WILDLIFE
REFUGE

White River

DEEP CREEK RANGE

GOSHUTE
INDIAN
RESERVATION

FISH SPRINGS
NATIONAL WILDLIFE
REFUGE

PONY EXPRESS

Utah Lake

• Provo
• Springville
• Spanish Fork

Payson •

Strawberry River

6

WASATCH RANGE

• Nephi

89

191

Green River

• Price

SEVIER

Yuba Lake

50

Price River

6

DESERT

Fillmore •

Salina •

SPANISH TRAIL

San Rafael River

• Green River

ARCHES
NATIONAL
PARK

Sevier Lake
Dry air and no outlet
streams create this
shrinking salt lake

Richfield •

70

Muddy Creek

24

313

• Moab

15

PAIUTE
INDIAN RESERVATION

70

24

Sevier River

Fremont River

Dirty Devil River

CANYONLANDS
NATIONAL
PARK

Beaver •

CAPITOL REEF
NATIONAL PARK
Layered cliffs are capped
with white, reef-like
sandstone formations

191

Colorado River

• Monticello

NATURAL BRIDGES
NATIONAL
MONUMENT

Cedar City •

CEDAR BREAKS
NATIONAL
MONUMENT

• Panguitch

12

Escalante River

95

• Blanding

ZION
NATIONAL
PARK

89

BRYCE CANYON
NATIONAL PARK

GLEN CANYON
NATIONAL
RECREATION AREA

HOVENWEEP
NATIONAL MONUMENT

San Juan River

163

PAIUTE
INDIAN
RESERVATION

9

Virgin River

Kanab Creek

Lake Powell

RAINBOW BRIDGE
NATIONAL MONUMENT

NAVAJO INDIAN RESERVATION

St. George •

Kanab •

89

Monument Valley

Four Corners

Only point in the
United States where
four states meet

0 KILOMETERS 75
0 STATUTE MILES 50

MORMON TRAIL

Sego Lily

California
Gull

The Sevier and Great
Salt Lake Deserts of
western Utah—vast, flat
basins with wave-cut ter-
races etched into moun-
tains—resemble an
ancient ocean floor.
That's because much of
Utah *was* underwater.
Thousands of years ago,
when the climate was
cooler and wetter, these
deserts formed the bot-
tom of an inland sea,
Lake Bonneville.

Then a natural dam
broke, draining much of
the lake into the Snake
River to the north. A hot-
ter, drier climate left only
today's Great Salt Lake,
a remnant a little more
than a tenth the size of
the ancient lake.

1

2

3

5

Utah

1 *Before their 11,000-pipe organ, the Mormon Tabernacle Choir raise their voices.*

2 *On the Bonneville Salt Flats, drivers have tried to set land speed records since 1914.*

3 *Now a metropolis, Salt Lake City gleams below the Wasatch Range, where, in 1847, Brigham Young and his followers saw the valley of the Great Salt Lake.*

4 *Weathered red sandstone "windows" in Arches National Park tower over the tiny silhouette of a visitor.*

5 *On the wall of a remote canyon in southeastern Utah, ancient Indians, using red earth for pigment, painted figures of humans and animals.*

4

Colorado

The state of Colorado is named for the Colorado River but, in a way, it is also named for the land itself. Spanish explorers called the river *colorado*, meaning "ruddy," for the reddish silt it carried, eroded from red-rock canyon walls. The river originates in a lake in the Rocky Mountains. Some people think that if you wanted to choose a natural feature to name the state, the Rockies would be a better choice.

Colorado's share of the Rocky Mountain system is certainly the loftiest. Of the Rockies' 80 or so "fourteeners," peaks over 14,000 feet (4,270 m) above sea level, Colorado boasts more than 50 of them. And with an average elevation of 6,800 feet (2,100 m), Colorado stands head and shoulders above all other states. Even the

West of the Rockies lies the Colorado Plateau, a region of hills, valleys, plateaus, and flat-topped hills called mesas, from the Spanish for "tables." Farmers plant crops in the valleys and graze sheep and cattle on the high pastures.

In Colorado's southwestern corner lived ancient Indian farmers known as the Anasazi. They planted corn, beans, and squash, and carved elaborate buildings in the sandstone cliffs of the Colorado Plateau. The Anasazi lived in settlements such as Mesa Verde for a few generations, then they departed. Much mystery surrounds the lives of these Indians, but archaeologists have recently come to believe that they followed a pattern of repeated settling, then moved on to create new communities.

on surrounding grasslands before making their journey to eastern markets.

Denver became first the territorial, then the state capital. Today it is the trade, transportation, and financial center for the mountain West and the focus of an ever broadening string of cities along the eastern front of the Rocky Mountains. Eighty percent of Colorado's people live here, many of them drawn to the area in the 1970s and early '80s by the boom in Colorado's energy resources such as coal, petroleum, natural gas, and oil shale, a type of rock that can yield oil with expensive processing.

Denver has one of the two working federal mints that produce circulating coins. Defense-related employers—ranging from the Air Force Academy at Colorado Springs, to manufacturers of rockets and nuclear weapons, to the North American Aerospace Defense Command Center, an underground fortress near Colorado Springs—bring millions of dollars to the state.

There was a time when victims of lung diseases made trips to Colorado to breathe the pure air. Those days are clearly over, for Denver at least. The change can be blamed mostly on automobile pollution. Cars burn fuel inefficiently at the high altitude, and brown smog sits over the city in its bowl-shaped location. In winter the smog shows up on the ground, quickly turning new-fallen snow to brown slush.

Fortunately, fresh, white snow is abundant elsewhere. People come from all over the world to ski the famous dry powder at places such as Aspen, Vail, and Telluride. Skiers and other tourists spend billions of dollars a year.

state's plains start high and get higher. Forming two-fifths of the state, the sunny, semiarid plains slope gradually upward from the eastern border to the foothills of the mountains.

Along the high peaks of Colorado's Rockies runs the natural watershed of the Continental Divide. The Rockies also divide Colorado's water resources. The western slopes receive two-thirds of the runoff from rain and snow, while the eastern slopes, with two-thirds of the land, receive only one-third. To compensate, dams and tunnels carry water from the west through the mountains to the east for homes and industry and irrigation of crops on the plains.

Deep snow halts a steam locomotive in the 1920s along a high stretch of the old Santa Fe Trail. Trains that were unable to plow through the drifts often needed a team of shovelers to help out.

The source of Denver's population is no mystery. Soon after an 1858 gold strike was made in the region, people flocked there. Successful "fifty-niners" poured money into the town. Many failed prospectors stayed on, too, finding work or opening up businesses. By 1870, railroads linked Denver to the rest of the country. More people came, and more cattle left, fattened

Area: *the eighth largest state, 104,091 sq mi (269,596 sq km)*
Population: *3,294,394; ranks 26th*
Major Cities: *Denver, 467,610; Colorado Springs, 281,140; Aurora, 222,103*
Manufacturing: *scientific instruments, food products, machinery, electronics, transportation equipment, metal products, stone, clay, and glass products, rubber and plastics, chemicals, metals*
Mining and Quarrying: *oil and gas, coal, gold, sand and gravel, stone*
Agriculture: *cattle, wheat, corn, vegetables, milk, hay, poultry, eggs*
Other Important Activities: *tourism, finance, printing and publishing*
Statehood: *the 38th state; admitted August 1, 1876*

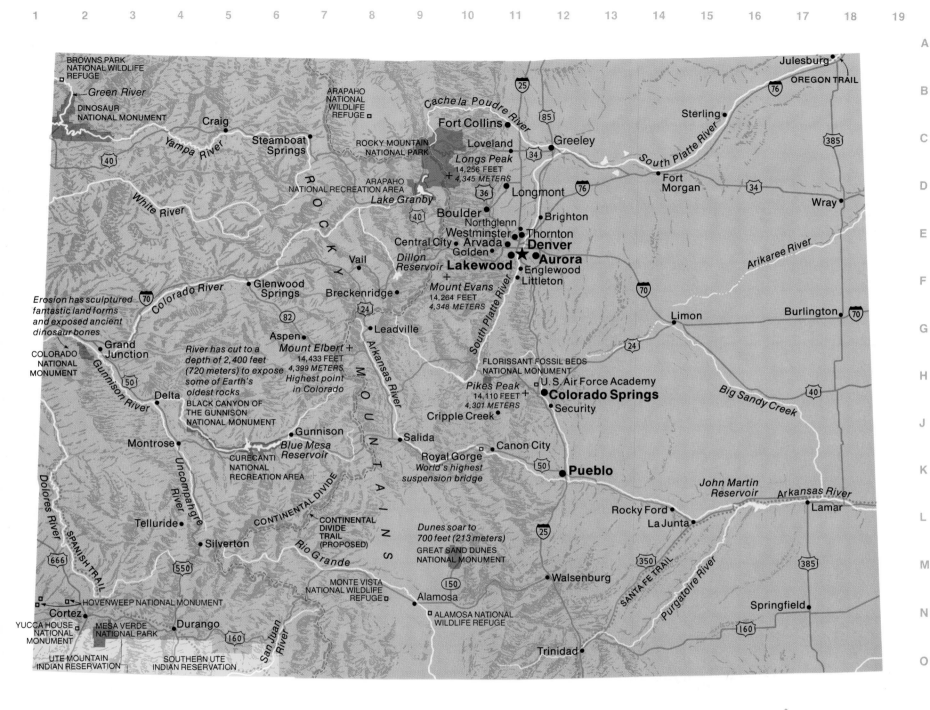

BROWNS PARK
NATIONAL WILDLIFE
REFUGE

Green River

DINOSAUR
NATIONAL MONUMENT

Craig

Steamboat
Springs

Yampa River

40

ARAPAHO
NATIONAL
WILDLIFE
REFUGE

ROCKY MOUNTAIN
NATIONAL PARK

Cache la Poudre River

25

Fort Collins

Loveland

85

Greeley

Sterling

OREGON TRAIL

76

South Platte River

Julesburg

385

34

Longs Peak
14,256 FEET
4,345 METERS

ARAPAHO
NATIONAL RECREATION AREA

Lake Granby

36

Longmont

76

Fort
Morgan

34

Wray

White River

Boulder

Northglenn

Westminster

40

Thornton

Brighton

E

Colorado River

70

Glenwood
Springs

Vail

Central City

*Dillon
Reservoir*

Golden

Arvada

Denver

Aurora

Englewood

Arikaree River

*Erosion has sculptured
fantastic land forms
and exposed ancient
dinosaur bones*

COLORADO
NATIONAL
MONUMENT

Grand
Junction

82

Breckenridge

Lakewood

Littleton

24

Mount Evans
14,264 FEET
4,348 METERS

South Platte River

Limon

Burlington

70

Gunnison River

50

Aspen

*River has cut to a
depth of 2,400 feet
(720 meters) to expose
some of Earth's
oldest rocks*

Mount Elbert +
14,433 FEET
4,399 METERS
*Highest point
in Colorado*

Arkansas River

Leadville

FLORISSANT FOSSIL BEDS
NATIONAL MONUMENT

U.S. Air Force Academy

24

40

Delta

BLACK CANYON OF
THE GUNNISON
NATIONAL MONUMENT

Pikes Peak
14,110 FEET +
4,301 METERS

Colorado Springs

Security

Big Sandy Creek

Montrose

Uncompahgre River

Gunnison

*Blue Mesa
Reservoir*

CURECANTI
NATIONAL
RECREATION AREA

Salida

Cripple Creek

Royal Gorge
*World's highest
suspension bridge*

Canon City

50

Pueblo

*John Martin
Reservoir*

Rocky Ford

La Junta

Arkansas River

Lamar

Dolores River

SPANISH TRAIL

666

Telluride

CONTINENTAL DIVIDE

CONTINENTAL
DIVIDE
TRAIL
(PROPOSED)

*Dunes soar to
700 feet (213 meters)*

GREAT SAND DUNES
NATIONAL MONUMENT

25

Walsenburg

350

SANTA FE TRAIL

Purgatoire River

385

Silverton

550

Rio Grande

MONTE VISTA
NATIONAL WILDLIFE
REFUGE

150

Alamosa

Springfield

HOVENWEEP NATIONAL MONUMENT

Cortez

YUCCA HOUSE
NATIONAL
MONUMENT

MESA VERDE
NATIONAL PARK

Durango

160

San Juan River

ALAMOSA NATIONAL
WILDLIFE REFUGE

Trinidad

160

UTE MOUNTAIN
INDIAN RESERVATION

SOUTHERN UTE
INDIAN RESERVATION

ROCKY MOUNTAINS

---

0   KILOMETERS   75

0   STATUTE MILES   50

Four out of five Colora-
dans live on the high
plains near the foot of
the Rocky Mountains.
That's where the biggest
cities are, in a strip
reaching from Fort Col-
lins to Pueblo.

To the east stretch the
plains, high, dry, and
populated mostly where
streams provide water.

To the west rise a thou-
sand or so peaks reach-
ing almost two miles (3
km) or more above sea
level—beautiful country,
but, again, not heavily
populated.

Job opportunities,
scenery, and water have
helped make the foot of
the mountains an attrac-
tive place to live.

Columbine

Lark
Bunting

1

2

3

4

5

Colorado

1 *The U. S. Space Command in Colorado Springs monitors the paths of orbiting satellites and Soviet space vehicles.*

2 *At the U. S. Air Force Academy in Colorado Springs a female cadet challenges classmates at push-ups.*

3 *Quaking aspens, named for their trembling leaves that shimmer in sunlight, stand in a Colorado autumn woodland.*

4 *In the early 13th century, Anasazi Indians built multistoried dwellings in the cliffs at Mesa Verde.*

5 *Looking to the eastern slopes of the Rocky Mountains, Denver stands a mile (1.6 km) above sea level.*

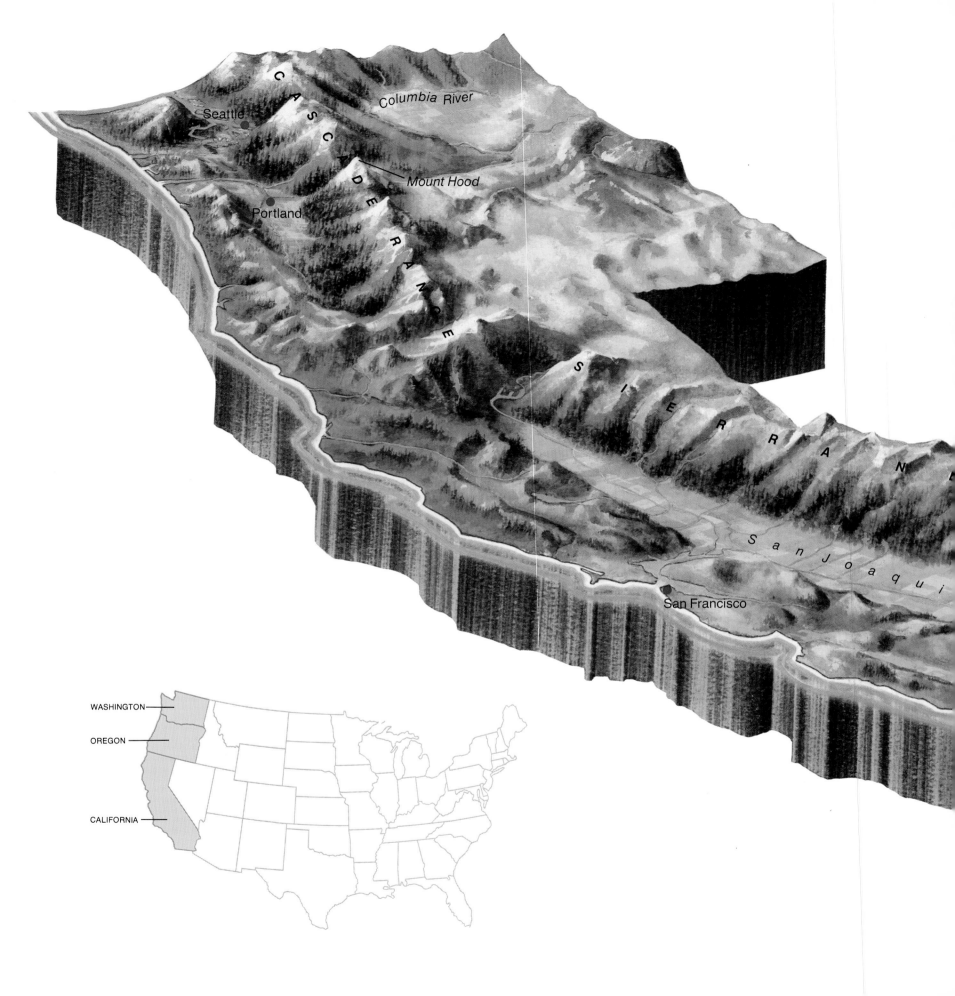

Seattle

Columbia River

C A S C A D E

Mount Hood

Portland

R A N G E

S I E R R A

N

San Joaqui

San Francisco

WASHINGTON

OREGON

CALIFORNIA

Pacific Coast States

Plate tectonics has created plenty of spectacular scenery along this span of states edged by the Pacific Ocean. Rugged, snowcapped mountains, some of them volcanoes, thrust into the sky. Great evergreen forests cloak the lower slopes—soggy, mossy forests along the Cascade Range; drier ones along the Sierra Nevada. Streams fed by rain or melting snow spill from the heights, channeling water to thirsty crops and cities in the fertile valleys below.

Beyond the Cascades and the Sierra Nevada, the forests give way to arid highlands and to hot deserts. Mountains between the deserts and the ocean block rain clouds drifting inland, depriv-ing the deserts of nearly all airborne moisture.

Along the coast rise lesser mountains known as the Coast Ranges. Like others, they are the result of a geological process called plate tecton-ics. "Tectonic" comes from a Greek word mean-ing "builder." In part it describes what happens when large, seemingly rigid slabs of Earth's crust, called plates, slowly drift and bump to-gether. As the plates collide, they crumple and fold, thrusting up mountain ranges where one plate remains on top and creating deep valleys, called trenches, when one plate slides under-neath. When a continental plate encounters an oceanic plate, the heavier ocean floor slides be-neath the more buoyant rocks of the continent.

Eventually the oceanic plate melts far be-neath the continent, and parts of it rise toward the surface as molten rock, blistering the land with volcanoes and lava flows. This is what hap-pened in the Cascades region. The volcanic mountains here formed within the last million years or so. They may seem quiet now, but they aren't always. The most recent eruption was in 1980, when Mount St. Helens, near Portland, suddenly blew up, killing 57 people. East of the Cascades, enormous cracks in the Earth's crust opened up some 20 million years ago. What was then a deep basin filled with molten rock, creat-ing the highlands south of the Columbia River.

In contrast, the Sierras are fault-block moun-tains, enormous chunks of crust that crunched together and tilted as the North American plate rode up over the Pacific plate. Even today the two plates continue to grind slowly past each other, cracking along fracture zones, called faults. From time to time, as tension builds be-tween the plates, they snap apart, touching off a round of earthquakes and aftershocks.

Some of the Channel Islands are mountain peaks that emerge from the ocean. Today they are a refuge for seals, whales, dolphins, and sea-birds. About a million years ago, when sea levels were lower, the Channel Islands were the home of pygmy elephants. Scientists think that the elephants swam there from the mainland.

Washington

On Sunday morning, May 18, 1980, Mount St. Helens erupted. A towering cloud of burning gases, pulverized rock, and gray ash spread destruction that toppled 230 square miles (600 sq km) of forest. Tons of melted snow and ice created floods and mud slides. Dozens of people died. The eruption, the first in the contiguous 48 states since California's Lassen Peak exploded in 1915 and 1921, was a violent reminder that Mount St. Helens is part of a chain of volcanoes, the snowcapped Cascade Range.

The Cascades divide the state of Washington into two very different worlds: the soggy, rainy west and the much drier east. The mountains themselves are largely responsible for these different climates. As moist ocean winds sweep eastward, they drop their moisture on the windward slopes. Leeward slopes, on the opposite side, get very little rain or snow. A journey of only a few miles, from one side of a mountain to the other, can spell the difference between forest and semidesert.

On the Olympic Peninsula in Washington's northwest corner, more than 200 inches (500 cm) of precipitation a year nourishes a lush rain forest shadowed by towering pines and hemlocks and thickly carpeted with ferns and mosses. A Quileute Indian myth tells of Thunderbird, a huge winged creature that lived in a cave in the Olympic Mountains and dined on whales he snatched from the sea. Thunderbird had "feathers as long as a canoe paddle." The flapping of his wings created wind and thunder, and lightning flashed from his eyes. Today much of Thunderbird's domain has been preserved as wilderness in Olympic National Park.

Generous rainfall also sustains vast forests on the western slopes of the Cascades. Here Douglas fir and other conifers provide raw materials for Washington's lumber, plywood, and paper industry. As much as 20 percent of the harvested timber is trucked as logs to dockside terminals in Tacoma and shipped to ports in Japan, China, and South Korea.

Puget Sound, a flooded valley carved by glaciers, is the site of several islands and many good harbors as it curves inland near the foot of Mount Olympus. The state capital, Olympia, rises at the head of the sound. The San Juan Islands dot the waters north of the sound. Island

The Tacoma Narrows Bridge collapsed in 1940 under winds of 42 miles an hour (68 kmph). Nicknamed Galloping Gertie, the suspension bridge rippled and bounced with every breeze.

dwellers rely on ferries to commute to work in Seattle and other mainland cities. Sometimes the boats are also used for picnic cruises, weddings, and school outings.

Seattle, which grew up as a center for the logging industry, was named for Chief Sealth, a Duwamish Indian who befriended the settlers. On a clear day, Seattle residents can see the snowy summits of Mount Rainier to the southeast, Mount Baker to the north, and the Olympic Mountains to the west.

More than half of Washington's people live within 50 miles (80 km) of Seattle. The city and neighboring communities are headquarters for a host of companies that make products ranging from giant airliners to computer software programs. One reason so many firms locate here is that the region offers a variety of outdoor recreational activities. On weekends, area residents can sail and swim in Puget Sound or the Pacific

Ocean, or go hiking, fishing, mountain climbing, hunting, or skiing.

Although about two-thirds of the state of Washington lies east of the Cascade Range, only about one-third of the people live there. Spokane, the region's only large city, rises along the Spokane River. Two waterfalls add sparkle to the downtown business district, and provide hydroelectric power as well. Factories in Spokane produce aluminum, computer hardware, and communications equipment.

North of the city, the Columbia River flows into Franklin Delano Roosevelt Lake, formed by Grand Coulee Dam, the largest concrete dam in the United States. Many tributaries feed into the Columbia and irrigate fields that produce apples, asparagus, cherries, and red raspberries. Grapes ripen in vineyards of the Columbia River basin, where warm summer days, cool nights, and sandy loam soil create growing conditions much like those found in the great vineyards of France.

Curving westward through the mountains, the Columbia forms much of the boundary between Washington and Oregon. Several dams along this stretch of the river make Washington the number one state in the country for hydroelectric power production. Major customers for this electricity are the aluminum smelting plants at Tacoma, Vancouver, and Longview.

Another producer of electricity is the Hanford nuclear power plant. Once a secret facility that produced plutonium for atomic weapons, Hanford today faces an urgent need to safely clean up its stock of dangerous radioactive wastes.

Area: *20th largest state, 68,138 sq mi (176,477 sq km)*
Population: *4,866,692; ranks 18th*
Major Cities: *Seattle, 516,259; Spokane, 177,196; Tacoma, 176,664*
Manufacturing: *food products, lumber and wood products, paper products, chemicals, machinery, scientific instruments, metals, metal products, petroleum and coal products*
Agriculture: *cattle, milk, apples, wheat, potatoes, greenhouse and nursery products, hay, pears, barley, cherries, eggs*
Mining and Quarrying: *gold, stone, sand and gravel, coal*
Other Important Activities: *federal government, tourism, printing and publishing, salmon fishing*
Statehood: *42nd state; admitted November 11, 1889*

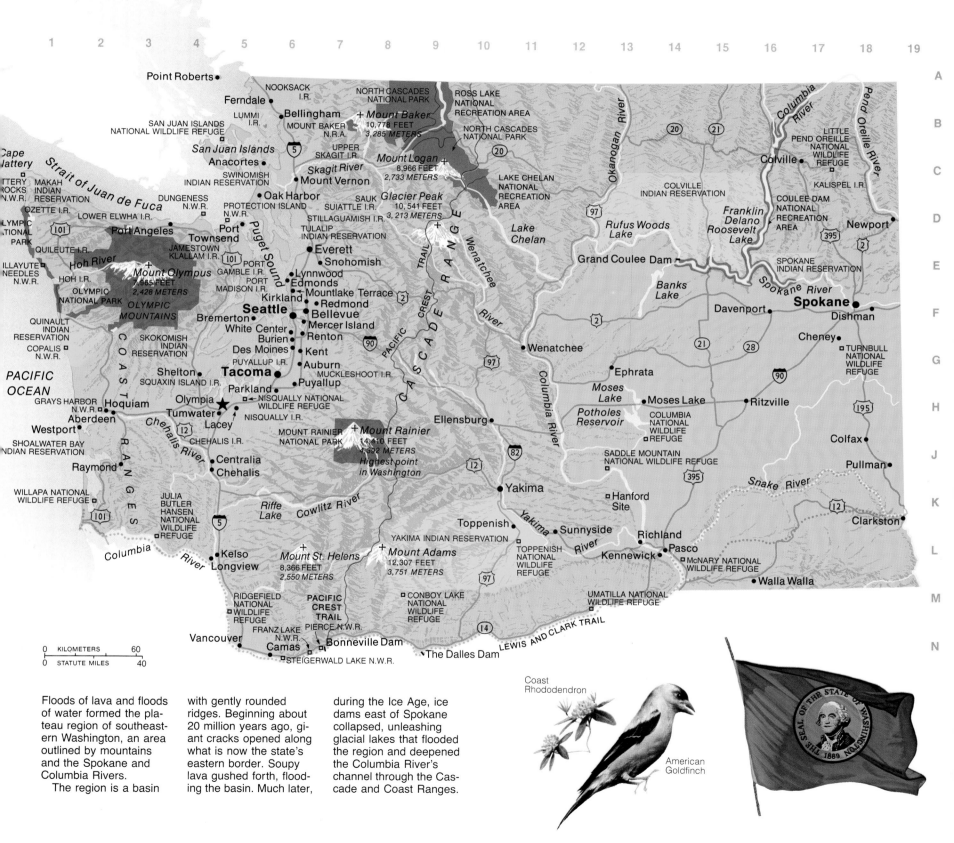

1 2 3 4 5 6 7 8 9 10 11 12 13 14 15 16 17 18 19

A
B
C
D
E
F
G
H
J
K
L
M
N

Point Roberts

NOOKSACK
I.R.

Ferndale

LUMMI
I.R.

Bellingham

SAN JUAN ISLANDS
NATIONAL WILDLIFE REFUGE

MOUNT BAKER
N.R.A.

NORTH CASCADES
NATIONAL PARK

+ Mount Baker
10,778 FEET
3,285 METERS

ROSS LAKE
NATIONAL
RECREATION AREA

NORTH CASCADES
NATIONAL PARK

Columbia
River

Pend Oreille River

Cape
Flattery

San Juan Islands

Anacortes

UPPER
SKAGIT I.R.

Skagit River

Mount Logan
8,966 FEET
2,733 METERS

20

LITTLE
PEND OREILLE
NATIONAL
WILDLIFE
REFUGE

TTERY
ROCKS
N.W.R.

MAKAH
INDIAN
RESERVATION

SWINOMISH
INDIAN RESERVATION

Mount Vernon

Glacier Peak
10,541 FEET
3,213 METERS

Colville

KALISPEL I.R.

Strait of Juan de Fuca

DUNGENESS
N.W.R.

Oak Harbor

SAUK
SUIATTLE I.R.

LAKE CHELAN
NATIONAL
RECREATION
AREA

97

COLVILLE
INDIAN RESERVATION

COULEE DAM
NATIONAL
RECREATION
AREA

OZETTE I.R.

LOWER ELWHA I.R.

PROTECTION ISLAND
N.W.R.

STILLAGUAMISH I.R.

Rufus Woods
Lake

Franklin
Delano
Roosevelt
Lake

Newport

OLYMPIC
NATIONAL
PARK

Port Angeles

Port
Townsend

TULALIP
INDIAN RESERVATION

Lake
Chelan

Grand Coulee Dam

SPOKANE
INDIAN RESERVATION

395

QUILEUTE I.R.

JAMESTOWN
KLALLAM I.R.

PORT
GAMBLE I.R.

Everett

Wenatchee

2

ILLAYUTE
NEEDLES
N.W.R.

Hoh River

HOH I.R.

+ Mount Olympus
7,965 FEET
2,428 METERS

PORT
MADISON I.R.

Lynnwood
Edmonds

Snohomish

Banks
Lake

Spokane River

Spokane

Mountlake Terrace

Davenport

Dishman

OLYMPIC NATIONAL PARK

OLYMPIC
MOUNTAINS

Kirkland

Seattle

Redmond

Bellevue

2

21

28

Cheney

QUINAULT
INDIAN
RESERVATION

SKOKOMISH
INDIAN
RESERVATION

Bremerton

White Center

Mercer Island

Wenatchee

Ephrata

TURNBULL
NATIONAL
WILDLIFE
REFUGE

COPALIS
N.W.R.

Burien

Renton

90

97

Moses
Lake

Moses Lake

Ritzville

PACIFIC
OCEAN

Des Moines

Kent

Columbia River

Potholes
Reservoir

COLUMBIA
NATIONAL
WILDLIFE
REFUGE

195

GRAYS HARBOR
N.W.R.

Shelton

Tacoma

Auburn

MUCKLESHOOT I.R.

Ellensburg

SADDLE MOUNTAIN
NATIONAL WILDLIFE REFUGE

Colfax

Hoquiam

SQUAXIN ISLAND I.R.

Parkland

Puyallup

82

Aberdeen

Olympia

PUYALLUP I.R.

NISQUALLY NATIONAL
WILDLIFE REFUGE

12

Pullman

Westport

Tumwater

NISQUALLY I.R.

395

Snake River

SHOALWATER BAY
INDIAN RESERVATION

Lacey

CHEHALIS I.R.

MOUNT RAINIER
NATIONAL PARK

+ Mount Rainier
14,410 FEET
4,392 METERS
Highest point
in Washington

Yakima

Hanford
Site

Clarkston

Raymond

Chehalis River

Centralia
Chehalis

12

WILLAPA NATIONAL
WILDLIFE REFUGE

101

Riffe
Lake

Cowlitz River

Yakima River

Toppenish

Sunnyside

Richland

JULIA
BUTLER
HANSEN
NATIONAL
WILDLIFE
REFUGE

5

YAKIMA INDIAN RESERVATION

TOPPENISH
NATIONAL
WILDLIFE
REFUGE

Kennewick

Pasco

McNARY NATIONAL
WILDLIFE REFUGE

Columbia

River

Kelso

Longview

+ Mount St. Helens
8,366 FEET
2,550 METERS

+ Mount Adams
12,307 FEET
3,751 METERS

97

Walla Walla

RIDGEFIELD
NATIONAL
WILDLIFE
REFUGE

PACIFIC
CREST
TRAIL

CONBOY LAKE
NATIONAL
WILDLIFE
REFUGE

UMATILLA NATIONAL
WILDLIFE REFUGE

Vancouver

FRANZ LAKE
N.W.R.

PIERCE N.W.R.

14

Camas

Bonneville Dam

LEWIS AND CLARK TRAIL

STEIGERWALD LAKE N.W.R.

The Dalles Dam

0 KILOMETERS 60

0 STATUTE MILES 40

Floods of lava and floods of water formed the plateau region of southeastern Washington, an area outlined by mountains and the Spokane and Columbia Rivers.

The region is a basin with gently rounded ridges. Beginning about 20 million years ago, giant cracks opened along what is now the state's eastern border. Soupy lava gushed forth, flooding the basin. Much later,

during the Ice Age, ice dams east of Spokane collapsed, unleashing glacial lakes that flooded the region and deepened the Columbia River's channel through the Cascade and Coast Ranges.

Coast
Rhododendron

American
Goldfinch

1

2

3

5

Washington

1 *Slickers keep field hands dry on this tulip farm near Mount Vernon. Abundant rain nurtures the area's prizewinning flowers.*

2 *Wielding a traditional dip net, a Yakima Indian snags his prey near the Columbia River, where his tribe has fishing rights.*

3 *A logger shoulders the chain saw that took 15 minutes to topple this 600-year-old Douglas fir in Olympic National Forest.*

4 *Seattle's landmark Space Needle holds a revolving restaurant that offers vistas of Puget Sound and the Cascade Range.*

5 *Aircraft workers assemble Boeing 747s in an Everett plant that encloses more indoor space than any other building in the world.*

4

Oregon

Oregon is a tangle of topography, a land of wild and rugged coasts, snowcapped mountains, high deserts, awesome chasms, and fertile valleys. Along much of the Pacific coast, great cliffs rise sheer from the sea, creating a massive wall of indented bays and jutting promontories known as headlands. In places, rocky pinnacles called sea stacks stand like ponderous sentinels in the surf. Wind and waves eroded these megaliths, leaving only the hardest rock, basalt, as a reminder of a long-vanished headland.

A few towns and fishing villages and many state parks line the coast. Mostly this is the foggy, forested realm of shorebirds, sea lions, and occasional flotillas of humpback whales. When the wild gales of winter lash the headlands and beaches, dedicated "storm watchers" hurry to seaside parks or cozy, cliff-top inns to witness the ocean slamming against the continent in a howling symphony of wind and spray.

Parallel to the shore rise the Coast Ranges, low mountains clad mostly with misty, rain-drenched forests of Douglas firs, hemlocks, and spruce. This part of the region was created 200 to 50 million years ago, when the Pacific plate collided with the North American plate and thrust up enormous sandstone and basalt blocks. At least one mystery still shrouds the mountains of the Pacific Northwest. Here, according to local lore, roams Sasquatch, the shadowy, ape-like monster also known as Bigfoot. Most people doubt the reality of Sasquatch. But scores of people claim to have seen the creature, just as people have believed in the existence of monsters throughout human history.

Between the Coast Ranges and the Cascade Range lies the Willamette Valley. By the 1840s, word of the valley's fertility had spread back East. It became the destination for most pioneer families following the Oregon Trail. Willamette Valley farmers boasted that you could poke a broomstick into the ground and it would grow. Settlers cleared forests and built the covered bridges and trim, white-clapboard houses that reflected their New England origins. Many of these houses and bridges still stand. Salem, the state capital, was founded by a New Englander as a missionary settlement. Its name comes from *shalom*, a Hebrew word meaning "peace."

Today the mineral-rich soil supports abundant crops of vegetables and fruits, including peas, onions, snap beans, berries, and plums, as well as nearly all the nation's hazelnuts.

Portland, a major port, ranks as the state's leading commercial and industrial center. Here dockworkers unload most of the Japanese cars sold in the United States. Views of snowcapped Mount Hood to the east and the Coast Ranges to the west, and more than 160 parks and gardens help make the city a pleasant place to live.

Men and women of the Mazama mountaineering club, founded on the summit of Mount Hood, participate in a 1913 expedition up the mountain. Mazama means "mountain goat."

Eugene, a riverside city threaded by hiking paths and bike trails, is also a processing hub for the valley's agricultural products.

Traditionally, Oregon's most important product has been the logs and lumber hauled from forests that cover half the state, mostly in the mountains of the west and northeast. Oregon's evergreen forests supply more than a fourth of the nation's softwood boards, more than half of its plywood, and much of its particleboard, paper, and pulp. The lumber industry got its start in 1883, when the Northern Pacific Railroad reached Oregon. By 1939 it was the state's leading industry, a position it still holds.

But today controversy swirls over the cutting down of old-growth forests, moss-grown stands of giant firs, cedars, spruce, and hemlocks untouched by saw or ax. Some of these trees grew here when Columbus reached the New World. Modern clear-cutting techniques strip away trees from entire mountainsides, scarring the land, choking streams with mud and debris, and destroying the habitats of scores of forest creatures, including the endangered northern spotted owl that nests in old-growth forests. Loggers prefer the old-growth forests because their giant trees yield great quantities of straight-grain, knot-free lumber. But once downed, such a forest may take a thousand years to renew itself, if it can be replaced at all.

East of the Cascade Range, the Harney Basin is wide open and semiarid. Here cowboys ride the range, and wheat and hay grow under irrigation. To the north rise the Blue Mountains, uplifted fragments of ancient continental plates eroded into peaks and valleys. The Snake River traces part of the state boundary here. Nearby, vast marshes serve as winter homes for migrant ducks and Canada geese.

In 1805, nearing the end of their long westward journey, the explorers Meriwether Lewis and William Clark followed the Snake River to the Columbia. At the mouth of the Columbia, they climbed a high cape above the shoreline of the Pacific Ocean. Clark recorded in his journal their joyous astonishment at "the high waves dashing against the rocks & this emence Ocian."

Area: *10th largest state, 97,073 sq mi (251,419 sq km)*
Population: *2,842,321; ranks 29th*
Major Cities: *Portland, 437,319; Eugene, 112,669; Salem, 107,786*
Manufacturing: *lumber and wood products, food products, paper products, machinery, scientific instruments, electronics, metals, metal products, transportation equipment*
Agriculture: *cattle, greenhouse and nursery products, milk, wheat, onions, ryegrass, potatoes, fescue, pears, mint*
Mining and Quarrying: *stone, sand and gravel*
Other Important Activities: *tourism, printing and publishing, crab and salmon fishing*
Statehood: *33rd state; admitted February 14, 1859*

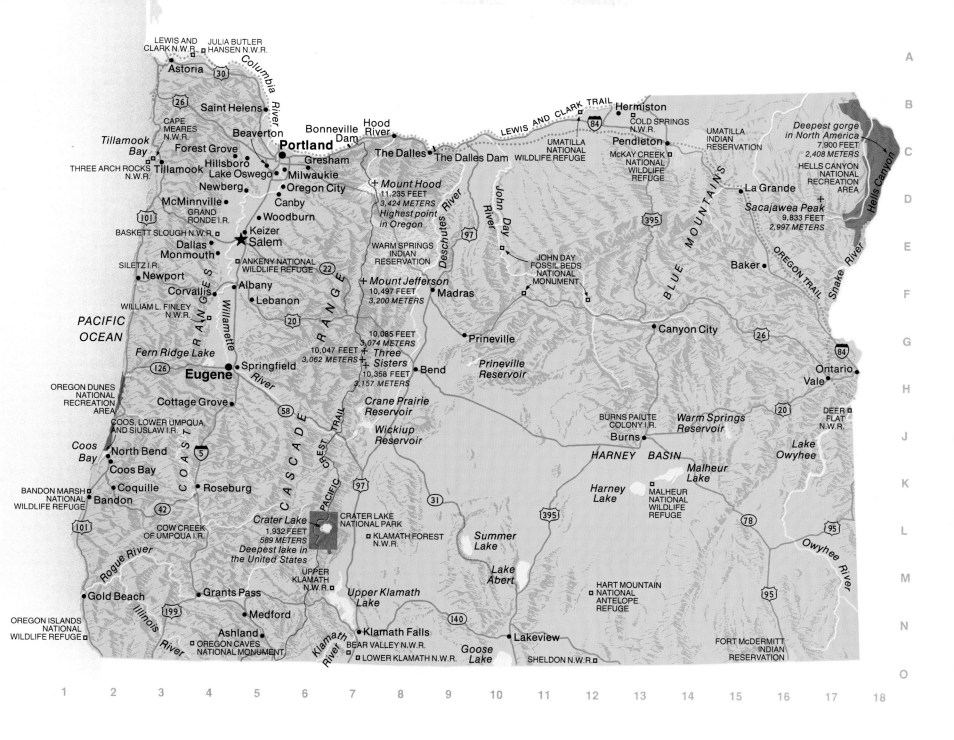

LEWIS AND
CLARK N.W.R.
JULIA BUTLER
HANSEN N.W.R.

Astoria

Saint Helens

Cape
Meares
N.W.R.

*Tillamook
Bay*

THREE ARCH ROCKS
N.W.R.

Tillamook

Forest Grove

Beaverton

Hillsboro

Lake Oswego

McMinnville

GRAND
RONDE I.R.

BASKETT SLOUGH N.W.R.

Newberg

Woodburn

Keizer

Salem

Dallas

Monmouth

SILETZ I.R.

Newport

Corvallis

WILLIAM L. FINLEY
N.W.R.

Albany

Lebanon

Portland

Gresham

Milwaukie

Oregon City

Canby

ANKENY NATIONAL
WILDLIFE REFUGE

Columbia River

Bonneville
Dam

Hood
River

The Dalles

The Dalles Dam

LEWIS AND CLARK TRAIL

Hermiston

COLD SPRINGS
N.W.R.

UMATILLA
NATIONAL
WILDLIFE REFUGE

McKAY CREEK
NATIONAL
WILDLIFE
REFUGE

Pendleton

UMATILLA
INDIAN
RESERVATION

*Deepest gorge
in North America*
7,900 FEET
2,408 METERS

HELLS CANYON
NATIONAL
RECREATION
AREA

La Grande

+ Mount Hood
11,235 FEET
3,424 METERS
*Highest point
in Oregon*

WARM SPRINGS
INDIAN
RESERVATION

Deschutes River

John Day River

JOHN DAY
FOSSIL BEDS
NATIONAL
MONUMENT

Sacajawea Peak
9,833 FEET
2,997 METERS

Baker

+ Mount Jefferson
10,497 FEET
3,200 METERS

Madras

10,085 FEET
3,074 METERS

10,047 FEET + *Three*
3,062 METERS + *Sisters*
10,358 FEET
3,157 METERS

Bend

Prineville

Canyon City

BLUE MOUNTAINS

OREGON TRAIL

Snake River

Hells Canyon

*PACIFIC
OCEAN*

Fern Ridge Lake

Eugene

Springfield

Willamette River

*Crane Prairie
Reservoir*

*Wickiup
Reservoir*

*Prineville
Reservoir*

Ontario

Vale

OREGON DUNES
NATIONAL
RECREATION
AREA

Cottage Grove

*Coos
Bay*

North Bend

Coos Bay

BANDON MARSH
NATIONAL
WILDLIFE REFUGE

Bandon

Coquille

Roseburg

COW CREEK
OF UMPQUA I.R.

COOS, LOWER UMPQUA,
AND SIUSLAW I.R.

COAST RANGE

CASCADE RANGE

PACIFIC CREST TRAIL

BURNS PAIUTE
COLONY I.R.

Burns

*Warm Springs
Reservoir*

HARNEY BASIN

*Harney
Lake*

MALHEUR
NATIONAL
WILDLIFE
REFUGE

*Malheur
Lake*

*Lake
Owyhee*

DEER
FLAT
N.W.R.

Crater Lake
1,932 FEET
589 METERS
*Deepest lake in
the United States*

CRATER LAKE
NATIONAL PARK

KLAMATH FOREST
N.W.R.

UPPER
KLAMATH
N.W.R.

*Upper Klamath
Lake*

*Summer
Lake*

*Lake
Abert*

HART MOUNTAIN
NATIONAL
ANTELOPE
REFUGE

Owyhee River

Gold Beach

OREGON ISLANDS
NATIONAL
WILDLIFE REFUGE

Grants Pass

Medford

Ashland

OREGON CAVES
NATIONAL MONUMENT

Rogue River

*Illinois
River*

Klamath River

Klamath Falls

BEAR VALLEY N.W.R.

LOWER KLAMATH N.W.R.

*Goose
Lake*

Lakeview

SHELDON N.W.R.

FORT McDERMITT
INDIAN
RESERVATION

A B C D E F G H J K L M N O

1 2 3 4 5 6 7 8 9 10 11 12 13 14 15 16 17 18

0 KILOMETERS 80
0 STATUTE MILES 40

Like a pot of gold at the end of the Oregon Trail, the fertile soils of the Willamette River Valley attracted thousands of settlers in the 1800s. Today more than half the people in the state live along the 60-mile-wide (97-km) valley.

The Oregon Trail joins the Lewis and Clark Trail, then crosses a modern-day footpath, the ridge-running Pacific Crest Trail that winds between Canada and Mexico. This trail skirts Crater Lake, born when a volcano known as Mount Mazama blew its top some 7,000 years ago. A volcanic cone forms an island in the lake.

Western
Meadowlark

Oregon
Grape

STATE OF OREGON

1859

1

2

Oregon

1 *A lariat loops toward a calf at a roundup in southeast Oregon's Great Basin country.*

2 *A waterfall tumbles into a jumble of boulders near the Three Sisters peaks in the Cascades. Mist and rain nourish a lush carpet of mosses.*

3 *Beyond the twilight sparkle of Portland, alpenglow rouges Mount Hood's snowy cone. The city stands near the confluence of the Willamette and Columbia Rivers.*

4 *At a Willamette Valley vineyard near the foot of the Coast Ranges, workers harvest Chardonnay grapes for white wine.*

5 *A seabird roosts on a sea stack, a remnant of a coastal headland crumbling under the pounding of Pacific Ocean waves.*

3

4

5

California

California is almost a country unto itself. The value of goods and services the state produces would, if California were a separate country, rank it sixth among the world's richest nations.

No other state turns out more manufactured goods, whether airplanes, computers, or missiles. No other state ships as many canned or frozen or dried fruits and vegetables to all parts of the United States. Or wine. Or television and movie films. California's fields and orchards grow more than 200 kinds of fruits, nuts, and vegetables. California's fields also produce great amounts of illegal marijuana.

Mountains, valleys, and deserts mark California's geography. In the northwest, the Klamath Mountains are high and steep. In the northeast stands an active volcano, Lassen Peak. The Sierra Nevada form a great wall of rock with many high peaks. Naturalist John Muir said that here, in Yosemite Valley, "Nature had gathered her choicest treasures." Some of the mountains in the Coast Ranges rise abruptly from the sea. In southern California, deserts such as the Mohave are part of the Basin and Range region that extends into Nevada and other states. Near Los Angeles are mountains that, unlike the others, trend east-west.

The chief agricultural region is the great Central Valley, between the Coast Ranges and the Sierra Nevada. Two major rivers bring water to the valley, the south-flowing Sacramento and the north-flowing San Joaquin. Both meet about halfway through the valley and turn west, flowing out to sea at San Francisco Bay. The valley's mild climate gives it a long growing season, and so its produce can be shipped to market while farmlands elsewhere lie covered in snow.

California has almost every kind of climate you can think of—damp and cool, with more than a hundred inches (254 cm) of rain along parts of the northern coast; sunny and mild most of the year in the south. Inland, snow drapes the Sierra Nevada, while Death Valley, in July 1913, had a temperature of 134°F (57°C), the highest ever recorded in the United States.

California also has the biggest, the oldest, and some of the tallest trees in the world. The biggest trees, the giant sequoias of the southern Sierra Nevada, can reach a girth of 80 feet (24 m). The oldest trees, bristlecone pines high in the

A family dines outdoors the day after the 1906 San Francisco earthquake. Unstable buildings and widespread fires made cooking, eating, and sleeping indoors unsafe.

eastern Sierra, were seedlings when Stonehenge and the Egyptian Pyramids were being built 4,600 years ago. The redwoods that grow along the northern coast reach higher than 300 feet (90 m). No other state has a bigger, rarer, or more endangered bird—the California condor, with a wingspan of nine feet (2.7 m) or more. Ancestors of this bird soared widely over Ice Age North America. Its last stronghold was the rugged mountains of southern California, but by 1987 there were none left in the wild. Breeding programs with captive birds have been successful enough that officials now hope that the release of a pair of young condors into a bird sanctuary will begin the recovery of the species.

California's people are almost as diverse as the land. Spanish explorers first entered the territory in the mid-1500s. Priests set up missions in the 1770s, using Indian converts as laborers. Spanish and Mexican settlers, called Californios, soon followed, carving out huge ranches worked by Indian slaves. Today California has nearly 250,000 Native Americans, more than any other state except Oklahoma.

The 1848 discovery of gold near Sacramento brought a stampede of gold prospectors from all over the world, the forty-niners. In 12 years

California's population soared from about 26,000 to 380,000. Thousands of Chinese arrived during this period to take part in the Gold Rush and to build the transcontinental railroads.

World War II brought in thousands of military personnel and defense workers, including blacks from the rural South. Many stayed. More recent arrivals have included large numbers of Asians and Hispanics.

Most of California's growth has taken place along the coast south of San Francisco. But much of the region is arid. To bring in water, the state and federal governments have built canals and aqueducts, some from as far away as the Colorado River and northern California. As more and more people move to southern California, they need more and more water. Northern Californians have begun to protest, and some southern Californians must ration water.

Within California are more than a dozen major faults, fractures in Earth's crust. The best known of these is the San Andreas Fault, which reaches from near the Mexican border through San Francisco to the coast and into the sea near Clear Lake. Severe earthquakes have taken place along the San Andreas, such as those that hit San Francisco in 1906 and 1989. Others will come. Many Californians appreciate the need to prepare for the next big one. Laws require the strengthening of old buildings. Engineers develop earthquake-resistant construction for new ones. Youngsters are encouraged to help in "hazard hunts" at home, finding and securing heavy shelves and other objects that could cause injury if shaken loose during an earthquake.

Area: *the third largest state, 158,706 sq mi (411,049 sq km)*

Population: *29,760,021; ranks first*

Major Cities: *Los Angeles, 3,485,398; San Diego, 1,110,549; San Jose, 782,248*

Manufacturing: *transportation equipment, electronics, machinery, food products, scientific instruments, metal products, chemicals, rubber and plastics, clothing*

Agriculture: *milk, cattle, greenhouse and nursery products, grapes, cotton, tomatoes, lettuce, almonds, hay, strawberries*

Mining: *oil and gas*

Other Important Activities: *tourism, printing and publishing, tuna and crab fishing*

Statehood: *31st state; admitted September 9, 1850*

A B C D E F G H I J K L M N O P Q R S T U

1 2 3 4 5 6 7 8 9 10 11 12 13 14 15 16 17

LOWER KLAMATH NATIONAL WILDLIFE REFUGE
TULE LAKE NATIONAL WILDLIFE REFUGE
Goose Lake
FORT BIDWELL INDIAN RESERVATION

101
Klamath River
LAVA BEDS NATIONAL MONUMENT
CLEAR LAKE NATIONAL WILDLIFE REFUGE

REDWOOD NATIONAL PARK
KLAMATH MOUNTAINS
5
+ *Mount Shasta* 14,162 FEET 4,317 METERS
MODOC NATIONAL WILDLIFE REFUGE

YUROK INDIAN RESERVATION
HOOPA VALLEY INDIAN RESERVATION
395

Eureka
299
WHISKEYTOWN-SHASTA-TRINITY NATIONAL RECREATION AREA
Shasta Lake

Eel River
44
Redding
LASSEN VOLCANIC NATIONAL PARK
Lassen Peak + 10,457 FEET 3,187 METERS

ROUND VALLEY INDIAN RESERVATION
Sacramento River

SAN ANDREAS FAULT
SACRAMENTO NATIONAL WILDLIFE REFUGE
Feather River
PACIFIC CREST TRAIL
S I E R R A

101
DELEVAN NATIONAL WILDLIFE REFUGE
CALIFORNIA TRAIL
Donner Pass

Clear Lake
Folsom Lake
Lake Tahoe
PONY EXPRESS

Santa Rosa
Sacramento ★
50
395
Sonoma Napa
80
99
POINT REYES NATIONAL SEASHORE
MUIR WOODS NATIONAL MONUMENT
SAN PABLO BAY N.W.R.
YOSEMITE NATIONAL PARK
Mono Lake
N E V A D A

GOLDEN GATE N.R.A.
Berkeley Stockton
Tuolumne River

San Francisco Oakland
DEVILS POSTPILE NATIONAL MONUMENT

Palo Alto Fremont Modesto
140
Owens R.

Sunnyvale
Merced

San Jose
San Joaquin River
KESTERSON N.W.R.
KINGS CANYON NATIONAL PARK

Monterey Bay
SAN LUIS NATIONAL WILDLIFE REFUGE
S A N

Salinas
180
Fresno
SEQUOIA NATIONAL PARK
Kern River
Death Valley
Lowest point in the Western Hemisphere −282 FEET − 86 METERS

Monterey
PINNACLES NATIONAL MONUMENT
Kings River
+ *Mount Whitney* 14,494 FEET 4,418 METERS *Highest point in the 48 contiguous states*
190

Big Sur
J O A Q U I N
Visalia
DEATH VALLEY NATIONAL MONUMENT

101
Salinas River
PIXLEY NATIONAL WILDLIFE REFUGE
TULE RIVER INDIAN RESERVATION

PACIFIC OCEAN
5
KERN NATIONAL WILDLIFE REFUGE
V A L L E Y
99
LOS ANGELES AQUEDUCT
SPANISH TRAIL
127
15

CALIFORNIA AQUEDUCT
Bakersfield

San Luis Obispo
BUTTERFIELD OVERLAND MAIL
M O J A V E   D E S E R T

Santa Maria
58
Barstow
FORT MOJAVE INDIAN RESERVATION

BITTER CREEK N.W.R.
SAN ANDREAS FAULT
14
395
40
Needles

Lompoc
5
HAVASU NATIONAL WILDLIFE REFUGE
CHEMEHUEVI INDIAN RESERVATION

Santa Barbara
Simi Valley
Glendale Pasadena
San Bernardino
MORONGO INDIAN RESERVATION
COLORADO RIVER AQUEDUCT

Ventura
Hollywood
JOSHUA TREE NATIONAL MONUMENT
COLORADO RIVER INDIAN RESERVATION

SANTA MONICA MOUNTAINS NATIONAL RECREATION AREA
Oxnard
Los Angeles
Riverside
Palm Springs

Long Beach Anaheim
10
Blythe

CHANNEL ISLANDS NATIONAL PARK
Garden Grove Santa Ana
AGUA CALIENTE INDIAN RESERVATION
Colorado River

Newport Beach
15
Salton Sea

CHANNEL ISLANDS
Palomar Mountain 6,140 FEET 1,871 METERS +
SALTON SEA N.W.R.
IMPERIAL NATIONAL WILDLIFE REFUGE

Gulf of Santa Catalina
BUTTERFIELD OVERLAND MAIL
Imperial Valley

8
5
El Cajon
FORT YUMA INDIAN RESERVATION

San Diego Chula Vista
El Centro
ALL AMERICAN CANAL
CABRILLO NATIONAL MONUMENT

Golden Poppy

California Quail

Shoved, pulled, bent, lifted, fractured. All this and more has happened to California. A glance at the map shows the results: inland, a rugged landscape of mountains traced by the Pacific Crest Trail; along the coast, range upon range of accordion-pleated mountains where continental plates slowly crunch past one another.

West of the San Andreas Fault, the Pacific plate creeps northwestward past the rest of the state at a rate of about two inches (5.5 cm) a year. The result: earthquakes, as tension between the two plates suddenly snaps.

CALIFORNIA REPUBLIC

0 KILOMETERS 125
0 STATUTE MILES 75

1

California

1 *The double-deck, earthquake-resistant Bay Bridge crosses San Francisco Bay to link San Francisco (background) with Oakland and Berkeley.*

2 *A young Newport Beach fisherman shows off a rockfish from his morning catch. For a hundred years, fishermen of his fleet have set out from Newport Beach, each man working alone in his flat-bottomed, sharp-bowed dory.*

2

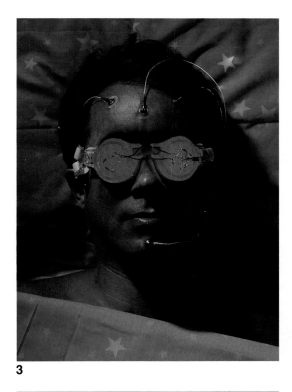

3

5

4

3 *In a Stanford University sleep laboratory at Palo Alto, pulsing red lights glow as sensors detect the eye movements that accompany vivid dreams.*

4 *Lettuce ready for harvest greens an irrigated field in the valley of the Salinas River. Other vegetables grown here include artichokes, broccoli, and cauliflower.*

5 *Shadows of storm clouds over Death Valley darken dunes and a silhouetted figure.*

Alaska, Hawaii, and Distant Shores

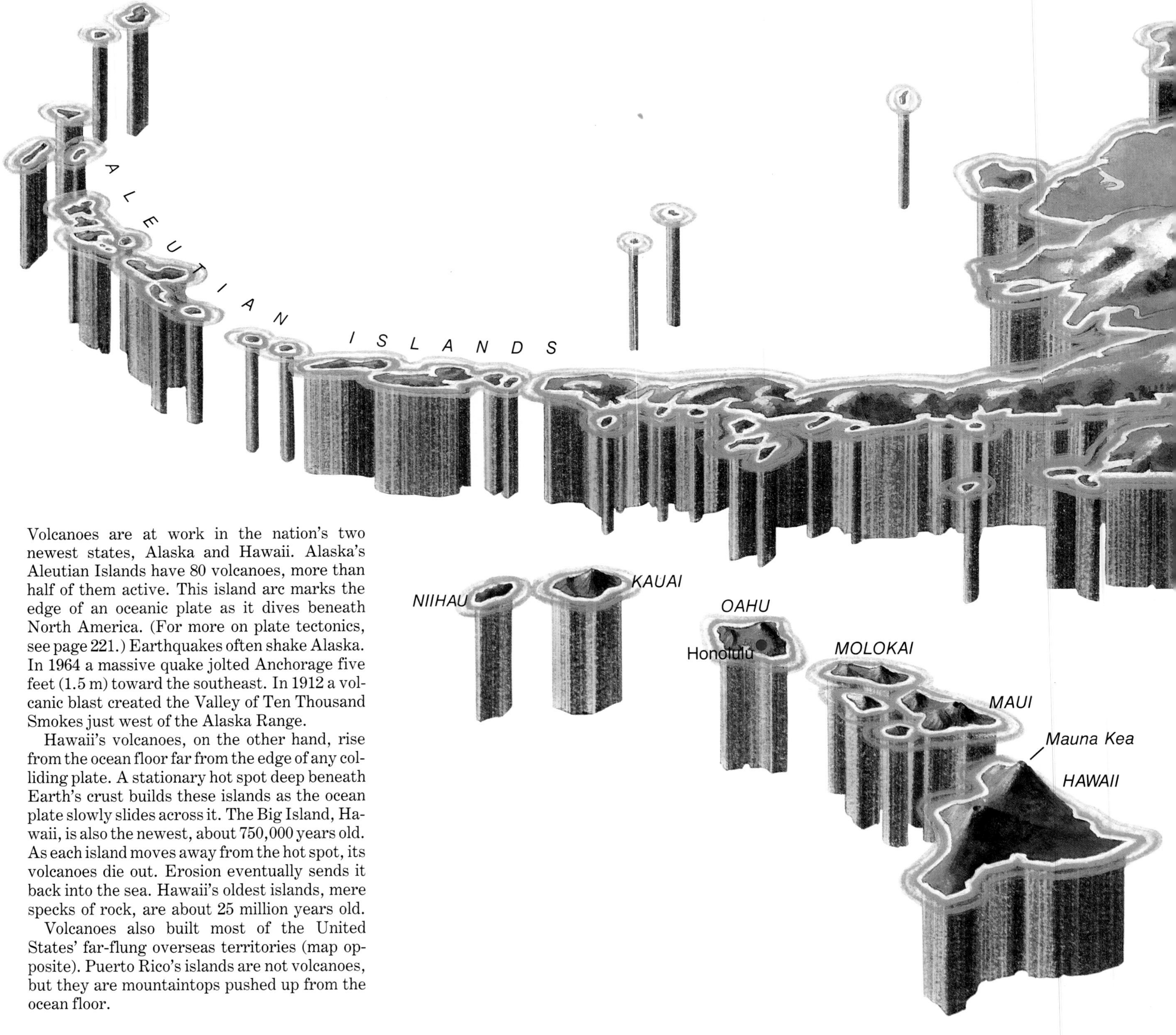

ALEUTIAN ISLANDS

NIIHAU

KAUAI

OAHU

Honolulu

MOLOKAI

MAUI

Mauna Kea

HAWAII

Volcanoes are at work in the nation's two newest states, Alaska and Hawaii. Alaska's Aleutian Islands have 80 volcanoes, more than half of them active. This island arc marks the edge of an oceanic plate as it dives beneath North America. (For more on plate tectonics, see page 221.) Earthquakes often shake Alaska. In 1964 a massive quake jolted Anchorage five feet (1.5 m) toward the southeast. In 1912 a volcanic blast created the Valley of Ten Thousand Smokes just west of the Alaska Range.

Hawaii's volcanoes, on the other hand, rise from the ocean floor far from the edge of any colliding plate. A stationary hot spot deep beneath Earth's crust builds these islands as the ocean plate slowly slides across it. The Big Island, Hawaii, is also the newest, about 750,000 years old. As each island moves away from the hot spot, its volcanoes die out. Erosion eventually sends it back into the sea. Hawaii's oldest islands, mere specks of rock, are about 25 million years old.

Volcanoes also built most of the United States' far-flung overseas territories (map opposite). Puerto Rico's islands are not volcanoes, but they are mountaintops pushed up from the ocean floor.

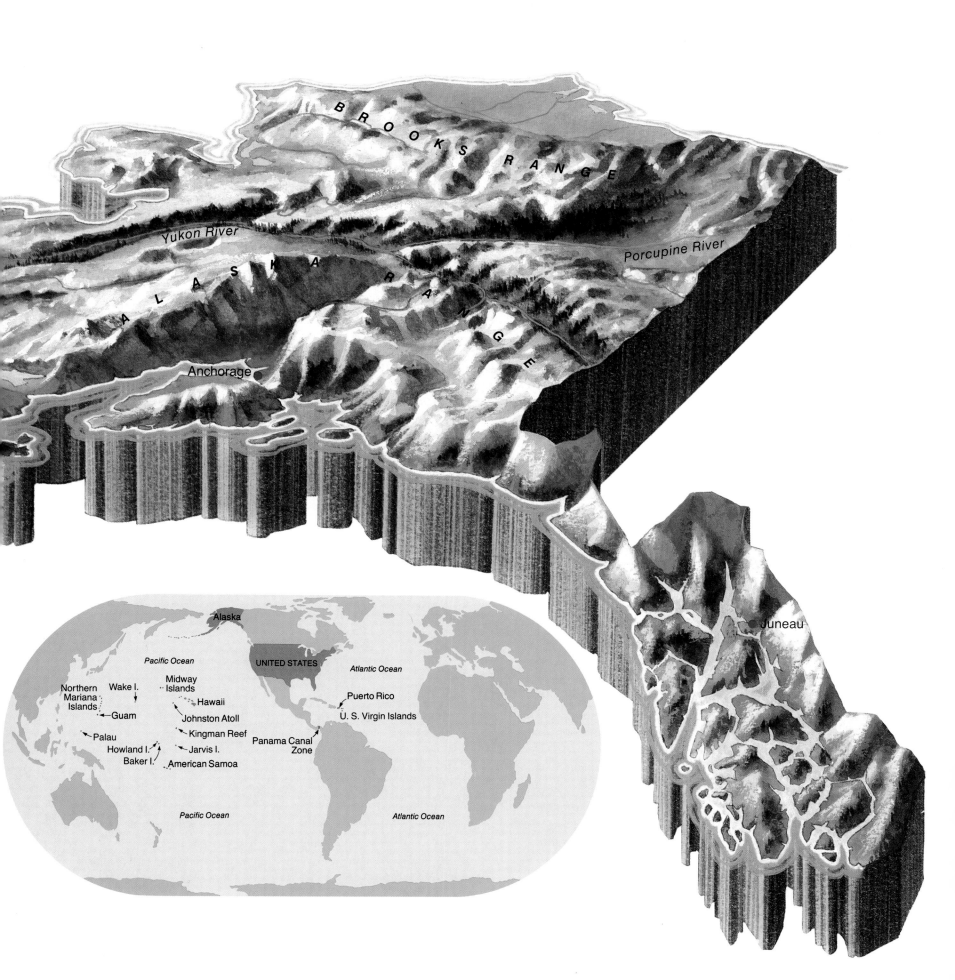

BROOKS RANGE

ALASKA RANGE

Yukon River

Porcupine River

Anchorage

Juneau

Alaska

Pacific Ocean

UNITED STATES

Atlantic Ocean

Northern
Mariana
Islands

Wake I.

Midway
Islands

Guam

Hawaii

Johnston Atoll

Puerto Rico

U. S. Virgin Islands

Palau

Kingman Reef

Panama Canal
Zone

Howland I.

Jarvis I.

Baker I.

American Samoa

Pacific Ocean

Atlantic Ocean

Alaska

In 1867 two cents bought an acre of the Russian territory known as Alaska. The whole region cost 7.2 million dollars. What did Americans get for their money? A land so big that if placed on top of the contiguous 48 states it would stretch from Florida to Los Angeles and reach north to Lake Superior. A land where the grizzly bear roams free and caribou in the tens of thousands migrate across the tundra.

Alaska is an immense peninsula. The name Alaska is a Russian word, adapted from a native Aleut term that means "great land." Smaller peninsulas extend from the mainland. The 200-island Aleutian chain reaches far into the Pacific Ocean and Bering Sea. With the Arctic Ocean, these waters wash a coastline that is more than 6,000 miles (9,700 km) long.

Mountain systems arc through the state. Among the southernmost are the Saint Elias and the actively volcanic Wrangell Ranges. The

Aleutian Range is a caldron of volcanic activity. In the interior, Mount McKinley rises out of the Alaska Range; the Brooks Range is the northernmost reach of the Rocky Mountains.

The native groups of Alaska today form almost 15 percent of the population. Traditionally, Eskimos lived mainly in the north and west along the coasts, hunting whales and other marine mammals. The Aleuts inhabited the rugged, fogbound islands named for them. Of the Indian groups, the Tlingit, Haida, and Tsimshian lived in the coastal areas of southeastern Alaska, sharing a culture based on fishing and the carving of tall cedar totem poles depicting animals and supernatural spirits. Central Alaska was the domain of Athapaskans. Old customs persist in some places, but the years have brought changes in ways of life and work.

When the United States acquired Alaska, many resources spurred settlement. Salmon fishing prompted the building of canneries and turned many towns into commercial fishing ports. The discovery of gold in the Canadian Yukon in 1896 brought people through southeastern Alaska and later to the goldfields of Nome and Fairbanks. Logging brought settlers and led to the construction of pulp and plywood mills near Juneau. During the Depression, farmers from Dust Bowl states came to the Matanuska River Valley, Alaska's main farming region. The 1968 discovery of immense fields of oil and gas at Prudhoe Bay on the North Slope started an oil boom. Thousands of people came from the lower 48 states to work on a pipeline that would carry the oil from the Arctic Ocean to the ice-free port of Valdez on Prince William Sound, where a disastrous oil spill occurred in 1989.

In the summer, Matanuska Valley farmers benefit from Alaska's far northern location. Then the North Pole tilts toward the rays of the sun, giving the valley mild weather and sunny, 19-hour days. The farther north you go, the longer summer days become. At Point Barrow the midsummer sun never sets. In the winter, parts of northern Alaska seldom see the sun. Even in the south, winter sunlight is scarce, and children attend school in the dark.

Alaska's climate challenges and limits human activity. Mountains, ice fields, and other barriers make travel difficult. The state has fewer

miles of road than Vermont, although it is 60 times larger. Military needs during World War II pushed the building of the Alaska Highway.

While ferries ply coastal and inland waterways, many villages and towns can be reached only by air. Alaska has the country's highest proportion of pilots; about one in 50 Alaskans is licensed to fly. Planes bring food, supplies, and medical care to isolated residents.

A 1971 law gave Alaskan Native Americans 44 million acres (18 million ha) and 962 million dollars to be managed by native corporations. Profits from oil, gas, and timber have brought some groups wealth, but others want to sell land back to the government. The proposed exploitation of natural resources that lie on both native lands and federal lands pits conservationists against developers in a controversy likely to rage for decades.

Area: *largest state, 591,004 sq mi (1,530,700 sq km)*
Population: *550,043; ranks 49th*
Major Cities: *Anchorage, 226,338; Fairbanks, 30,843; Juneau, 26,751*
Mining and Quarrying: *oil and gas, gold, sand and gravel, stone*
Manufacturing: *food products, petroleum products, lumber and wood products*
Other Important Activities: *federal government, salmon and crab fishing, printing and publishing, greenhouse and nursery products, milk, fur*
Statehood: *the 49th state; admitted January 3, 1959*

Warmly dressed young Alaskans in a Yukon fishing camp study a mail-order catalog to keep up on 1929 fashions from the United States. The book also helped them practice reading English.

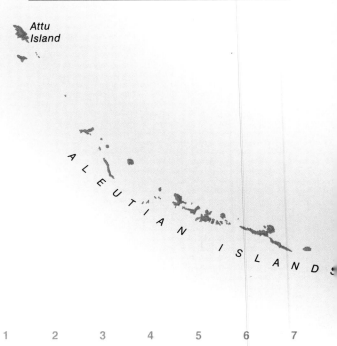

Attu Island

ALEUTIAN ISLANDS

1   2   3   4   5   6   7

Alaska, twice as big as the next largest state, Texas, is 488 times bigger than the smallest state, Rhode Island.

In the southern panhandle, fingers of the Pacific Ocean reach far inland, making a watery maze of fjords. The Inside Passage provides a sheltered water route between Skagway and Seattle, Washington.

White patches rimming the Gulf of Alaska show ice fields and glaciers. The mountains here capture as much moisture as a tropical forest, while farther north the air is desert dry. Hence, northern mountains have only a few small glaciers.

KILOMETERS 0 — 300
STATUTE MILES 0 — 200

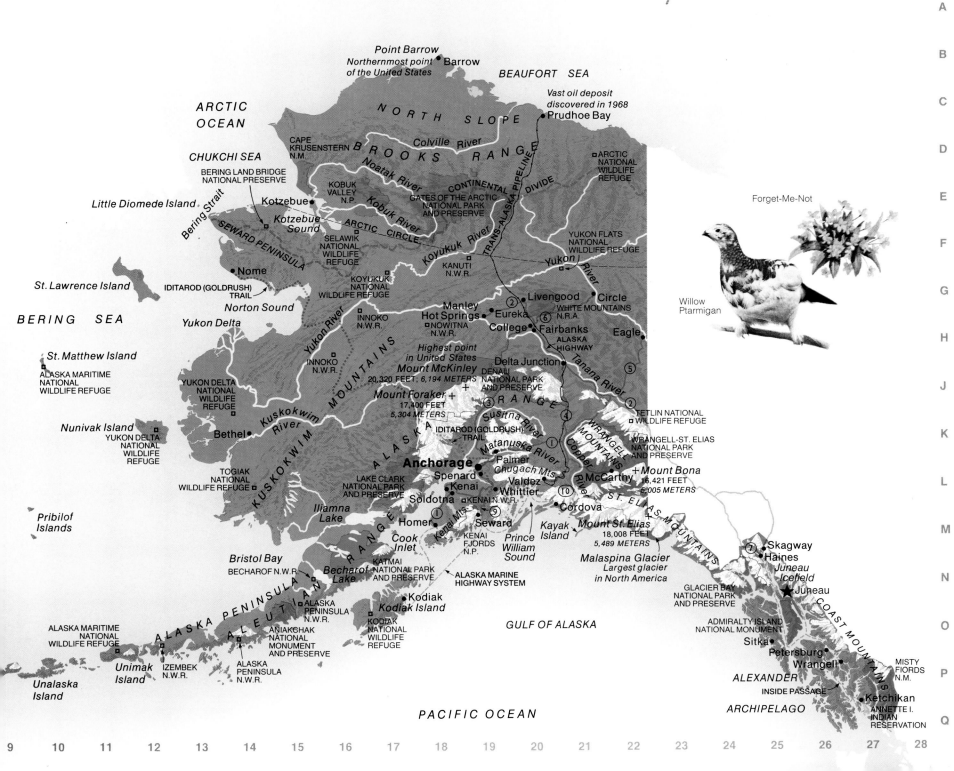

A
B
C
D
E
F
G
H
J
K
L
M
N
O
P
Q

Forget-Me-Not

Willow
Ptarmigan

ARCTIC OCEAN

CHUKCHI SEA

Point Barrow
Northernmost point of the United States • Barrow

BEAUFORT SEA

Vast oil deposit
discovered in 1968
• Prudhoe Bay

NORTH SLOPE

CAPE KRUSENSTERN N.M.

Colville River

BROOKS RANGE

ARCTIC NATIONAL WILDLIFE REFUGE

BERING LAND BRIDGE NATIONAL PRESERVE

Noatak River

CONTINENTAL DIVIDE

TRANS-ALASKA PIPELINE

Little Diomede Island

• Kotzebue

KOBUK VALLEY N.P.

Kobuk River

GATES OF THE ARCTIC NATIONAL PARK AND PRESERVE

Kotzebue Sound

ARCTIC CIRCLE

Koyukuk River

YUKON FLATS NATIONAL WILDLIFE REFUGE

Bering Strait

SEWARD PENINSULA

SELAWIK NATIONAL WILDLIFE REFUGE

Yukon River

• Nome

KOYUKUK NATIONAL WILDLIFE REFUGE

KANUTI N.W.R.

Livengood • • Circle

St. Lawrence Island

IDITAROD (GOLDRUSH) TRAIL

Norton Sound

INNOKO N.W.R.

Manley Hot Springs • • Eureka

WHITE MOUNTAINS N.R.A.

BERING SEA

Yukon Delta

NOWITNA N.W.R.

College • • Fairbanks

Eagle •

St. Matthew Island

Yukon River

INNOKO N.W.R.

Highest point in United States
Mount McKinley
20,320 FEET; 6,194 METERS

ALASKA HIGHWAY

ALASKA MARITIME NATIONAL WILDLIFE REFUGE

YUKON DELTA NATIONAL WILDLIFE REFUGE

KUSKOKWIM Mountains

DENALI NATIONAL PARK AND PRESERVE

Delta Junction •

Tanana River

Nunivak Island

YUKON DELTA NATIONAL WILDLIFE REFUGE

Mount Foraker +
17,400 FEET
5,304 METERS

RANGE

TETLIN NATIONAL WILDLIFE REFUGE

Kuskokwim River

• Bethel

ALASKA

Susitna River

WRANGELL-ST. ELIAS NATIONAL PARK AND PRESERVE

Pribilof Islands

TOGIAK NATIONAL WILDLIFE REFUGE

IDITAROD (GOLDRUSH) TRAIL

Matanuska River

WRANGELL MOUNTAINS

Cooper River

+ Mount Bona
16,421 FEET
5,005 METERS

RANGE

Anchorage
Spenard •

Palmer •
Chugach Mts

McCarthy •

ST. ELIAS MOUNTAINS

Iliamna Lake

LAKE CLARK NATIONAL PARK AND PRESERVE

• Kenai

Valdez •
Whittier •

Skagway •
Haines •

Soldotna •

KENAI N.W.R.

• Cordova

Juneau Icefield

KENAI Mts

Mount St. Elias
18,008 FEET
5,489 METERS

GLACIER BAY NATIONAL PARK AND PRESERVE

Homer •

Kayak Island

★ Juneau

Bristol Bay

BECHAROF N.W.R.

Becharof Lake

KATMAI NATIONAL PARK AND PRESERVE

• Seward

KENAI FJORDS N.P.

Prince William Sound

Cook Inlet

Malaspina Glacier
Largest glacier in North America

ADMIRALTY ISLAND NATIONAL MONUMENT

COAST MOUNTAINS

ALASKA MARINE HIGHWAY SYSTEM

Sitka •

ALASKA PENINSULA

ALEUTIAN RANGE

ALASKA PENINSULA N.W.R.

• Kodiak

Petersburg • •
Wrangell •

ALASKA MARITIME NATIONAL WILDLIFE REFUGE

IZEMBEK N.W.R.

ANIAKCHAK NATIONAL MONUMENT AND PRESERVE

Kodiak Island

KODIAK NATIONAL WILDLIFE REFUGE

GULF OF ALASKA

ALEXANDER ARCHIPELAGO

INSIDE PASSAGE

MISTY FIORDS N.M.

Unimak Island

ALASKA PENINSULA N.W.R.

• Ketchikan

Unalaska Island

ANNETTE I. INDIAN RESERVATION

PACIFIC OCEAN

9 10 11 12 13 14 15 16 17 18 19 20 21 22 23 24 25 26 27 28

1

2

Alaska

1 *A brown bear snags a chum salmon meal in southern Alaska. The coastal brown bear and its interior kin, the grizzly, feed at rivers during the salmon's spawning voyage, which begins in late summer.*

2 *Buried where possible, the 800-mile (1,290-km) trans-Alaska pipeline rises on supports in areas where its heat would thaw underground permafrost. Its height provides clearance for migrating caribou.*

3 *Sorting quickly, fishermen look for "keepers" in a haul of Alaska king crab. Females and small males go back into the water. Per pound, king crab is the state's most valuable shellfish.*

4 *An Eskimo youth displays skill in the traditional sport of the high kick at a school gym in Kotzebue.*

5 *Glaciers from the Juneau Icefield merge in the mountains north of Alaska's capital. The long dark stripes are moraines formed by debris shed at the glaciers' edges.*

3

4

Hawaii

Hawaii is a young landform. The islands that make up the state grew as volcanic mountains from the seafloor of the Pacific Ocean. The tops of these volcanoes are now the mostly lush, tropical islands of Hawaii.

The chain's northern islands are the oldest. The island of Hawaii, called the Big Island, is the youngest, and there is another island on the way. About 20 miles (32 km) southeast of the Big Island, the underwater Loihi Seamount must grow about half a mile (0.8 km) more before it reaches daylight. This could take from 2,000 to 20,000 years, depending on volcanic activity.

As Hawaii's volcanic slopes began to erode into soil, settlement by plant and animal life began. The early seeds of Hawaii's native vegetation arrived on the waves or the wind, or were carried by birds. Insects, too, rode the wind or pieces of driftwood. Only two mammals made the trip to land on their own, the monk seal and the hoary bat. Brought by people in canoes and on ships, introduced mammals such as rats, pigs, and goats now flourish on the islands.

The first settlers were Polynesians from islands 2,400 miles (3,860 km) to the southeast. About 1,500 years ago they sailed to Hawaii in double-hulled canoes with only the stars and migratory birds to guide them. Some 500 years later other Polynesian people arrived from Tahiti. The Polynesians settled the larger islands, living in tribal groups ruled by chiefs.

Capt. James Cook was the first known European to land here, in 1778, changing Hawaiian life forever. Diseases unknown in Hawaii, carried on Cook's and later ships, included cholera and measles. Such diseases eventually brought death to almost 250,000 vulnerable islanders.

In 1795 a Hawaiian chief unified the islands, naming himself King Kamehameha I. When missionaries landed in 1820, Kamehameha II and the islanders were interested in the new beliefs and most converted to Christianity.

European and American planters established sugarcane and pineapple plantations on the islands, importing workers from Japan, Korea, China, and the Philippines. The newcomers and the Polynesians, joined by settlers from Europe and the United States, endowed Hawaii with its unique ethnic diversity. People descended from the original Polynesian settlers now form

Japanese women work in a sugarcane field on Maui. By the early 1900s, people had come to Hawaii from Europe, Asia, and other Pacific islands to work on sugar and pineapple plantations.

less than one percent of the population.

Hawaii's major islands have mountainous interiors that slope shoreward. Hawaiians distinguish two main directions: *mauka*, toward the mountains, and *makai*, toward the sea. Most islands also have a windy, wet windward side and a calmer, drier leeward side. The difference can be great. On Kauai, winds bring 55 *feet* (17 m) of rain each year to the heights of Waialeale, while sheltered parts of some islands receive less than 20 inches (51 cm). The islands see many typhoons and tsunamis, destructive ocean waves

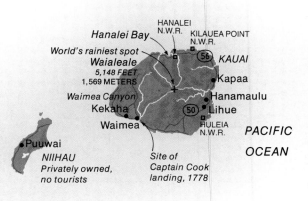

caused by earthquakes and volcanic eruptions.

Of the eight major islands, one, Kahoolawe, is uninhabited. Barren and windy, it has served as a target for military bombing practice. The island of Niihau is owned by a family that discourages visitors. Niihau is home to the state's only group of pure-blooded Hawaiians, who raise sheep and cattle and keep their language alive.

Visitors to Hawaii are greeted with flower leis and a warm aloha, meaning both "hello" and "good-bye" as well as "love." Tourists come to Hawaii at a rate of five million a year, and the money they spend is now the state's major source of income. Four of every five Hawaiians live on Oahu. U. S. military personnel and their families form about 12 percent of the state's population. The Japanese bombing of the strategic military base at Pearl Harbor near Honolulu brought the United States into World War II.

The island of Molokai, to which victims of leprosy once were banished, has a large ethnic Hawaiian population. Residents ranch and farm and tend to visitors. Lanai has the largest pineapple plantation in the world. Tourism may take hold there, too, if the island's owner follows through with plans to end pineapple cultivation. Maui's beaches attract droves of tourists. The slopes of Haleakala, a dormant volcano, are home to honeycreepers, possibly descendants of the first land birds to reach Hawaii.

The Big Island comprises 60 percent of the

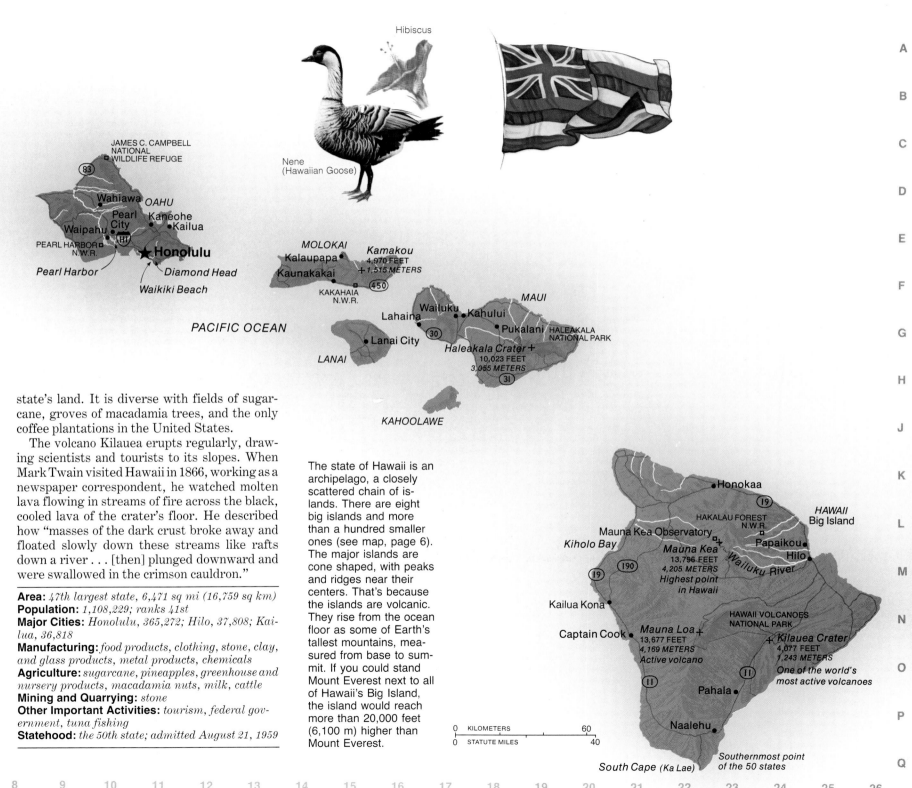

Hibiscus

Nene
(Hawaiian Goose)

JAMES C. CAMPBELL
NATIONAL
WILDLIFE REFUGE

83

Wahiawa *OAHU*

Pearl
City
Kaneohe
Waipahu
•Kailua

PEARL HARBOR
N.W.R.
HI

★ **Honolulu**

Pearl Harbor
Diamond Head

Waikiki Beach

MOLOKAI
Kalaupapa•
Kamakou
4,970 FEET
+1,515 METERS
Kaunakakai•

KAKAHAIA
N.W.R.
450

PACIFIC OCEAN

Wailuku
Lahaina
•Kahului
MAUI

Pukalani
HALEAKALA
NATIONAL PARK

Lanai City
30

LANAI
Haleakala Crater +
10,023 FEET
3,055 METERS

31

KAHOOLAWE

state's land. It is diverse with fields of sugarcane, groves of macadamia trees, and the only
coffee plantations in the United States.

The volcano Kilauea erupts regularly, drawing scientists and tourists to its slopes. When
Mark Twain visited Hawaii in 1866, working as a
newspaper correspondent, he watched molten
lava flowing in streams of fire across the black,
cooled lava of the crater's floor. He described
how "masses of the dark crust broke away and
floated slowly down these streams like rafts
down a river . . . [then] plunged downward and
were swallowed in the crimson cauldron."

Area: *47th largest state, 6,471 sq mi (16,759 sq km)*
Population: *1,108,229; ranks 41st*
Major Cities: *Honolulu, 365,272; Hilo, 37,808; Kai-*
lua, 36,818
Manufacturing: *food products, clothing, stone, clay,*
and glass products, metal products, chemicals
Agriculture: *sugarcane, pineapples, greenhouse and*
nursery products, macadamia nuts, milk, cattle
Mining and Quarrying: *stone*
Other Important Activities: *tourism, federal gov-*
ernment, tuna fishing
Statehood: *the 50th state; admitted August 21, 1959*

The state of Hawaii is an
archipelago, a closely
scattered chain of is-
lands. There are eight
big islands and more
than a hundred smaller
ones (see map, page 6).
The major islands are
cone shaped, with peaks
and ridges near their
centers. That's because
the islands are volcanic.
They rise from the ocean
floor as some of Earth's
tallest mountains, mea-
sured from base to sum-
mit. If you could stand
Mount Everest next to all
of Hawaii's Big Island,
the island would reach
more than 20,000 feet
(6,100 m) higher than
Mount Everest.

•Honokaa
19
HAWAII
Big Island

HAKALAU FOREST
N.W.R.
Mauna Kea Observatory

Kiholo Bay
Mauna Kea
13,796 FEET
4,205 METERS
Highest point
in Hawaii

Papaikou•
•Hilo

Wailuku River

19
190

Kailua Kona•

HAWAII VOLCANOES
NATIONAL PARK

Captain Cook•
Mauna Loa +
13,677 FEET
4,169 METERS
Active volcano

+ *Kilauea Crater*
4,077 FEET
1,243 METERS
One of the world's
most active volcanoes

11
11

Pahala•

0 KILOMETERS 60
0 STATUTE MILES 40

Naalehu•

South Cape (Ka Lae)

Southernmost point
of the 50 states

Hawaii

1 *A fountain of lava spews from Kilauea on Hawaii's Big Island. Among the world's most active volcanoes, Kilauea's eruptions create lava flows that may damage property but rarely cause loss of life.*

2 *Where fields of taro once stood, high rises crowd Honolulu's reef-protected Waikiki Beach. Diamond Head, an extinct volcano (background), got its name from glittery crystals that 19th-century sailors mistook for diamonds.*

3 *In traditional costume, chanting hula dancers interpret island stories with their hands and faces.*

4 *Colored-sand beaches are a legacy of Hawaii's volcanoes. Pounding surf breaks up obsidian, or volcanic glass, creating this black sand on the Big Island's southeastern coast. Green sand occurs, too, from pulverized olivine, a volcanic mineral.*

5 *A conveyor belt moves pineapples harvested on Lanai. Laborers wear protective clothing to guard against the prickly fruit.*

1

2

3

4

5

Distant Shores

At a 1950s festival on St. Thomas, a Mockoo Jumby balances on stilts. Dressed in women's clothing for the starring carnival role, he dances the bamboula, *brought from Africa by slaves.*

A number of island territories scattered throughout the Pacific Ocean and the Caribbean Sea are associated with the United States under different kinds of relationships. These include commonwealth status, with U. S. citizenship and other rights and obligations, and self-government with special help from the U. S.

Most of these islands grew from volcanic activity. In some places erosion wore away a central volcanic island, leaving behind only a fringe of built-up coral reefs called an atoll. Some of the islands have mountainous interiors, while many rise only a few feet above surrounding seas.

Altogether there are more than 2,300 islands and islets under U. S. jurisdiction. Together they form less land area than Connecticut. The Commonwealth of Puerto Rico alone accounts for half of that area and also for 90 percent of the total population. Jarvis, Baker, and Howland Islands in the central Pacific (see map, page 235) are uninhabited and are wildlife refuges.

Except for the Midway Islands, all the U. S. territories lie in the tropics. Ocean breezes keep temperatures from climbing too high, and varying amounts of rainfall produce lush vegetation in some places, near-desert conditions in others. Hurricanes in the Atlantic and typhoons in the Pacific often buffet the islands. Another threat in the Pacific comes from tsunamis, powerful waves that are caused by earthquakes and volcanic eruptions. Tsunamis can wipe out settlements and cause great loss of life.

Puerto Rico lies 1,000 miles (1,600 km) southeast of Florida in a group of islands that separates the Caribbean waters from the rest of the Atlantic Ocean. Puerto Rico was claimed for Spain by Christopher Columbus and named "rich port" by Ponce de León. Arawak Indians were the original inhabitants, but Spanish contact brought death, disease, and intermarriage, and the Arawak no longer exist as a separate group. Many residents of the coastal lowlands descend from Africans brought in to work on sugarcane plantations in the 16th century, but most Puerto Ricans today are largely of Spanish descent. Puerto Ricans are mainly urban dwellers, with one in eight living in San Juan.

Sugar, coffee, and tobacco long formed the basis of Puerto Rico's economy. They remain important, but manufacturing is the largest source of income. The chief industries include chemicals, especially medicines, electronics, and food processing. In addition, the tourists who flock to Puerto Rico's beaches and historic districts spend about a billion dollars a year.

Puerto Rico may soon be asked to decide officially whether it wants to remain a commonwealth, become an independent country, or become the 51st state. Although statehood and independence have some support among Puerto Ricans, many favor remaining a commonwealth because their U. S. citizenship gives them freedom to emigrate to the mainland but does not require them to pay federal income tax.

In 1917 the Danish sold to the United States a group of islands and islets in the Caribbean east of Puerto Rico. The main islands, St. Thomas, St. Croix, and St. John, held sugarcane plantations that were abandoned when slavery was abolished there in 1848. Today vacationers arrive by plane or cruise ship to swim and snorkel in sparkling blue waters and to absorb the Danish atmosphere of the island towns. Tourism brings in 70 percent of the Virgin Islands' income and employs 70 percent of the people. Other islanders work in the large oil refinery on St. Croix or raise fruits, vegetables, and cattle.

In 1988 the country's newest national park was established in American Samoa, a territory made up of five volcanic islands and two uninhabited atolls in the Pacific. The park preserves a unique rain forest that includes five different forest zones: lowland, mountainous, coastal, ridge, and cloud forest. The Samoan rain forest is the only one of its kind on U. S. soil and is similar to forests in Africa and Asia.

Populated by descendants of ancient Polynesians, American Samoa is perhaps the least changed of the territories in the Pacific. Islanders still live in remote village settlements in family groups headed by chiefs and raise subsistence crops. Most Samoans have converted to Christianity, and their large churches of coral cement blend into the traditional rural landscape. Pago Pago, the capital and chief port on Tutuila, has a more modern flavor, with shopping malls and tourist hotels. Tuna canning has long been the islands' chief industry.

Some volcanoes on the Northern Mariana Islands are likely to erupt at any time. This arc of 14 islands in the western Pacific Ocean is a commonwealth. Most of the people live on Saipan, Tinian, and Rota at the southern end of the chain. The original inhabitants came from Indonesia and the Philippines. Spanish rule from the 17th through the 19th century produced a people of mixed ancestry called Chamorros. Culturally they are Spanish but speak the Chamorro language, related to Indonesian. Islanders raise crops for their own use and also work for the government or in the growing tourist trade.

The U. S. military owns about one-third of the land on Guam. The people, most of Chamorro ancestry, are a varied ethnic mix with cultures from Europe, Asia, and Pacific islands. Military bases employ many residents, as do hotels and other facilities that serve nearly a million, mostly Japanese, tourists who visit Guam each year.

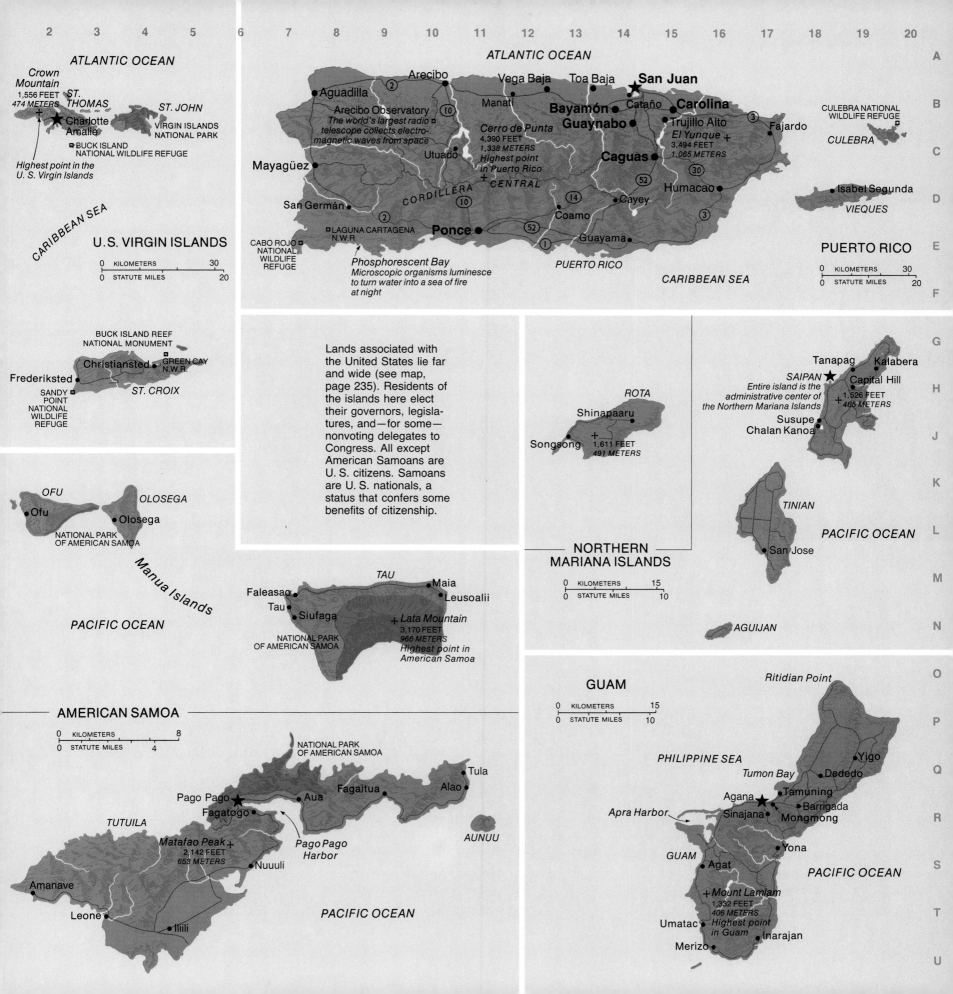

Column headers (top): 2 3 4 5 7 8 9 10 11 12 13 14 15 16 17 18 19 20

Row labels (right side): A B C D E F G H J K L M N O P Q R S T U

U.S. VIRGIN ISLANDS

ATLANTIC OCEAN

Crown Mountain
1,556 FEET
474 METERS
ST. THOMAS
ST. JOHN

+ Charlotte Amalie

VIRGIN ISLANDS NATIONAL PARK

BUCK ISLAND NATIONAL WILDLIFE REFUGE

Highest point in the U. S. Virgin Islands

CARIBBEAN SEA

0 KILOMETERS 30
0 STATUTE MILES 20

BUCK ISLAND REEF NATIONAL MONUMENT
GREEN CAY N.W.R.
Christiansted
Frederiksted
SANDY POINT NATIONAL WILDLIFE REFUGE
ST. CROIX

PUERTO RICO

ATLANTIC OCEAN

Arecibo
Vega Baja
Toa Baja
San Juan
Aguadilla
Manati
Bayamón
Cataño
Carolina
Arecibo Observatory
The world's largest radio telescope collects electro-magnetic waves from space
Guaynabo
Trujillo Alto
El Yunque
3,494 FEET
1,065 METERS
Cerro de Punta
4,390 FEET
1,338 METERS
Highest point in Puerto Rico
Utuado
Fajardo
Mayagüez
+ *CENTRAL*
Caguas
San Germán
CORDILLERA
Humacao
Cayey
Coamo
LAGUNA CARTAGENA N.W.R.
CABO ROJO NATIONAL WILDLIFE REFUGE
Ponce
Guayama
Phosphorescent Bay
Microscopic organisms luminesce to turn water into a sea of fire at night
PUERTO RICO
CARIBBEAN SEA

CULEBRA NATIONAL WILDLIFE REFUGE
CULEBRA
Isabel Segunda
VIEQUES

0 KILOMETERS 30
0 STATUTE MILES 20

Lands associated with the United States lie far and wide (see map, page 235). Residents of the islands here elect their governors, legislatures, and—for some—nonvoting delegates to Congress. All except American Samoans are U. S. citizens. Samoans are U. S. nationals, a status that confers some benefits of citizenship.

NORTHERN MARIANA ISLANDS

ROTA
Shinapaaru
Songsong
+ 1,611 FEET
491 METERS

Tanapag
Kalabera
SAIPAN
Entire island is the administrative center of the Northern Mariana Islands
Capital Hill
+ 1,526 FEET
465 METERS
Susupe
Chalan Kanoa

TINIAN
San Jose
PACIFIC OCEAN
AGUIJAN

0 KILOMETERS 15
0 STATUTE MILES 10

AMERICAN SAMOA

OFU
Ofu
OLOSEGA
Olosega
NATIONAL PARK OF AMERICAN SAMOA
Manua Islands
PACIFIC OCEAN

TAU
Maia
Faleasao
Leusoalii
Tau
Siufaga
+ *Lata Mountain*
3,170 FEET
966 METERS
Highest point in American Samoa
NATIONAL PARK OF AMERICAN SAMOA

0 KILOMETERS 8
0 STATUTE MILES 4

NATIONAL PARK OF AMERICAN SAMOA
Pago Pago
Fagatogo
Aua
Fagaitua
Tula
Alao
TUTUILA
+ *Matafao Peak*
2,142 FEET
653 METERS
Pago Pago Harbor
AUNUU
Amanave
Nuuuli
Leone
Iliili
PACIFIC OCEAN

GUAM

Ritidian Point
0 KILOMETERS 15
0 STATUTE MILES 10
PHILIPPINE SEA
Yigo
Tumon Bay
Dededo
Agana
Tamuning
Apra Harbor
Barrigada
Sinajana
Mongmong
Yona
GUAM
Agat
+ *Mount Lamlam*
1,332 FEET
406 METERS
Highest point in Guam
Umatac
Inarajan
Merizo
PACIFIC OCEAN

1 *Guam*

2 *American Samoa*

3 *Puerto Rico*

4 *U. S. Virgin Islands*

5 *Puerto Rico*

Guam

1 *Tourists cruise Tumon Bay in a double-hulled sight-seeing boat. Tourism, the island's fastest growing industry, helps give Guam a low unemployment rate.*

American Samoa

2 *Dinner by the bunch comes home at the end of the day with a Samoan villager. Rural Samoans live in large family groups, in which all resources are shared.*

Puerto Rico

3 *The guns of El Morro, the stout, 16th-century Spanish fortress, defended San Juan from attack by sea, including a 1595 attempt by an English pirate, Sir Francis Drake, to loot its treasure. Inside the walls are tunnels, barracks, and dungeons.*

U. S. Virgin Islands

4 *Closeup views of yellow tube sponges, sea fans, and yellow and orange reef sponges bring many divers to the Virgin Islands. Coral, sponge, and fish species abound in the warm, shallow waters.*

Puerto Rico

5 *Workers tend bins full of capsules at a pharmaceutical factory in Manatí. Industrialization brought to Puerto Rico dozens of companies that manufacture medicines.*

Facts at Your Fingertips

Populations of U.S. Cities

These pages list the largest legally incorporated cities in each state. Populations here and those given for cities in the state stories are from the 1990 census.

Alabama
Birmingham 265,968
Huntsville 159,789
Mobile 196,278
Montgomery 187,106
Tuscaloosa 77,759

Alaska
Anchorage 226,338

Arizona
Chandler 90,533
Glendale 148,134
Mesa 288,091
Phoenix 983,403
Scottsdale 130,069
Tempe 141,865
Tucson 405,390
Yuma 54,923

Arkansas
Fort Smith 72,798
Jonesboro 46,535
Little Rock 175,795
North Little Rock 61,741
Pine Bluff 57,140

California
Alameda 76,459
Alhambra 82,106
Anaheim 266,406
Antioch 62,195
Bakersfield 174,820
Baldwin Park 69,330
Bellflower 61,815
Berkeley 102,724
Buena Park 68,784
Burbank 93,643
Carlsbad 63,126
Carson 83,995
Chino 59,682
Chula Vista 135,163
Compton 90,454
Concord 111,348
Corona 76,095
Costa Mesa 96,357
Daly City 92,311
Downey 91,444
El Cajon 88,693
El Monte 106,209

Encinitas 55,386
Escondido 108,635
Fairfield 77,211
Fontana 87,535
Fremont 173,339
Fresno 354,202
Fullerton 114,144
Garden Grove 143,050
Glendale 180,038
Hawthorne 71,349
Hayward 111,498
Huntington Beach 181,519
Huntington Park 56,065
Inglewood 109,602
Irvine 110,330
Lakewood 73,557
Lancaster 97,291
Livermore 56,741
Long Beach 429,433
Los Angeles 3,485,398
Lynwood 61,945
Mission 72,820
Modesto 164,730
Montebello 59,564
Monterey 60,738
Moreno Valley 118,779
Mountain View 67,460
Napa 61,842
National City 54,249
Newport Beach 66,643
Norwalk 94,279
Oakland 372,242
Oceanside 128,398
Ontario 133,179
Orange 110,658
Oxnard 142,216
Palmdale 68,842
Palo Alto 55,900
Pasadena 131,591
Pico Rivera 59,177
Pomona 131,723
Rancho Cucamonga 101,409
Redding 66,462
Redlands 60,394
Redondo Beach 60,167
Redwood City 66,072
Rialto 72,388
Richmond 87,425
Riverside 226,505
Sacramento 369,365
Salinas 108,777
San Bernardino 164,164
San Diego 1,110,549
San Francisco 723,959
San Jose 782,248
San Leandro 68,223
San Mateo 85,486

Santa Ana 293,742
Santa Barbara 85,571
Santa Clara 93,613
Santa Clarita 110,642
Santa Maria 61,284
Santa Monica 86,905
Santa Rosa 113,313
Simi Valley 100,217
South Gate 86,284
South San Francisco 54,312
Stockton 210,943
Sunnyvale 117,229
Thousand Oaks 104,352
Torrance 133,107
Upland 63,374
Vacaville 71,479
Vallejo 109,199
Ventura 92,575
Visalia 75,636
Vista 71,872
Walnut Creek 60,569
West Covina 96,086
Westminster 78,118
Whittier 77,671

Colorado
Arvada 89,235
Aurora 222,103
Boulder 83,312
Colorado Springs 281,140
Denver 467,610
Fort Collins 87,758
Greeley 60,536
Lakewood 126,481
Pueblo 98,640
Thornton 55,031
Westminster 74,625

Connecticut
Bridgeport 141,686
Bristol 60,640
Danbury 65,585
Hartford 139,739
Meriden 59,479
New Britain 75,491
New Haven 130,474
Norwalk 78,331
Stamford 108,056
Waterbury 108,961
West Haven 54,021

Delaware
Wilmington 71,529

Florida
Boca Raton 61,492
Cape Coral 74,991

Clearwater 98,784
Coral Springs 79,443
Daytona Beach 61,921
Fort Lauderdale 149,377
Gainesville 84,770
Hialeah 188,004
Hollywood 121,697
Jacksonville 672,971
Lakeland 70,576
Largo 65,674
Melbourne 59,646
Miami 358,548
Miami Beach 92,639
Orlando 164,693
Palm Bay 62,632
Pembroke Pines 65,452
Pensacola 58,165
Plantation 66,692
Pompano Beach 72,411
Port St. Lucie 55,866
St. Petersburg 238,629
Sunrise 64,407
Tallahassee 124,773
Tampa 280,015
West Palm Beach 67,643

Georgia
Albany 78,122
Atlanta 394,017
Columbus 179,278
Macon 106,612
Savannah 137,560

Hawaii
Honolulu 365,272

Idaho
Boise City 125,738
Idaho Falls 43,929
Pocatello 46,080

Illinois
Arlington Heights Village 75,460
Aurora 99,581
Champaign 63,502
Chicago 2,783,726
Cicero 67,436
Decatur 83,885
Elgin 77,010
Evanston 73,233
Joliet 76,836
Naperville 85,351
Oak Lawn 56,182
Oak Park 53,648
Peoria 113,504
Rockford 139,426
Schaumburg 68,586

Skokie 59,432
Springfield 105,227
Waukegan 69,392

Indiana
Anderson 59,459
Bloomington 60,633
Evansville 126,272
Fort Wayne 173,072
Gary 116,646
Hammond 84,236
Indianapolis 731,327
Muncie 71,035
South Bend 105,511
Terre Haute 57,483

Iowa
Cedar Rapids 108,751
Council Bluffs 54,315
Davenport 95,333
Des Moines 193,187
Dubuque 57,546
Iowa City 59,738
Sioux City 80,505
Waterloo 66,467

Kansas
Kansas City 149,767
Lawrence 65,608
Olathe 63,352
Overland Park 111,790
Topeka 119,883
Wichita 304,011

Kentucky
Bowling Green 40,641
Covington 43,264
Lexington-Fayette 225,366
Louisville 269,063
Owensboro 53,549

Louisiana
Baton Rouge 219,531
Kenner 72,033
Lafayette 94,440
Lake Charles 70,580
Monroe 54,909
New Orleans 496,938
Shreveport 198,525

Maine
Lewiston 39,757
Portland 64,358

Maryland
Baltimore 736,014
Frederick 40,148

Gaithersburg 39,542
Rockville 44,835

Massachusetts
Boston 574,283
Brockton 92,788
Cambridge 95,802
Chicopee 56,632
Fall River 92,703
Lawrence 70,207
Lowell 103,439
Lynn 81,245
Malden 53,884
Medford 57,407
New Bedford 99,922
Newton 82,585
Quincy 84,985
Somerville 76,210
Springfield 156,983
Waltham 57,878
Worcester 169,759

Michigan
Ann Arbor 109,592
Dearborn 89,286
Dearborn Heights 60,838
Detroit 1,027,974
Farmington Hills 74,652
Flint 140,761
Grand Rapids 189,126
Kalamazoo 80,277
Lansing 127,321
Livonia 100,850
Pontiac 71,166
Rochester Hills 61,766
Royal Oak 65,410
Saginaw 69,512
St. Clair Shores 68,107
Southfield 75,728
Sterling Heights 117,810
Taylor 70,811
Troy 72,884
Warren 144,864
Westland 84,724
Wyoming 63,891

Minnesota
Bloomington 86,335
Brooklyn Park 56,381
Duluth 85,493
Minneapolis 368,383
Rochester 70,745
St. Paul 272,235

Mississippi
Biloxi 46,319
Greenville 45,226
Hattiesburg 41,882

Jackson 196,637
Meridian 41,036

Missouri
Columbia 69,101
Independence 112,301
Kansas City 435,146
St. Charles 54.555
St. Joseph 71,852
St. Louis 396,685
Springfield 140,494

Montana
Billings 81,151
Great Falls 55,097
Missoula 42,918

Nebraska
Grand Island 39,386
Lincoln 191,972
Omaha 335,795

Nevada
Henderson 64,942
Las Vegas 258,295
North Las Vegas 47,707
Reno 133,850
Sparks 53,367

New Hampshire
Manchester 99,567
Nashua 79,662

New Jersey
Bayonne 61,444
Camden 87,492
Clifton 71,742
East Orange 73,552
Elizabeth 110,002
Jersey City 228,537
Newark 275,221
Passaic 58,041
Paterson 140,891
Trenton 88,675
Union City 58,012
Vineland 54,780

New Mexico
Albuquerque 384,736
Las Cruces 62,126
Roswell 44,654
Santa Fe 55,859

New York
Albany 101,082
Binghamton 53,008
Buffalo 328,123
Mount Vernon 67,153

New Rochelle 67,265
New York 7,322,564
Niagara Falls 61,840
Rochester 231,636
Schenectady 65,566
Syracuse 163,860
Troy 54,269
Utica 68,637
Yonkers 188,082

North Carolina
Asheville 61,607
Charlotte 395,934
Durham 136,611
Fayetteville 75,695
Gastonia 54,732
Greensboro 183,521
High Point 69,496
Raleigh 207,951
Wilmington 55,530
Winston-Salem 143,485

North Dakota
Bismarck 49,256
Fargo 74,111
Grand Forks 49,425

Ohio
Akron 223,019
Canton 84,161
Cincinnati 364,040
Cleveland 505,616
Columbus 632,910
Dayton 182,044
Elyria 56,746
Euclid 54,875
Hamilton 61,368
Kettering 60,569
Lakewood 59,718
Lorain 71,245
Parma 87,876
Springfield 70,487
Toledo 332,943
Youngstown 95,732

Oklahoma
Broken Arrow 58,043
Lawton 80,561
Norman 80,071
Oklahoma City 444,719
Tulsa 367,302

Oregon
Beaverton 53,310
Eugene 112,669
Gresham 68,235
Portland 437,319
Salem 107,786

Pennsylvania
Allentown 105,090
Bethlehem 71,428
Erie 108,718
Lancaster 55,551
Philadelphia 1,585,577
Pittsburgh 369,879
Reading 78,380
Scranton 81,805

Rhode Island
Cranston 76,060
East Providence 50,380
Pawtucket 72,644
Providence 160,728
Warwick 85,427

South Carolina
Charleston 80,414
Columbia 98,052
Greenville 58,282
North Charleston 70,218
Spartanburg 43,467

South Dakota
Rapid City 54,523
Sioux Falls 100,814

Tennessee
Chattanooga 152,466
Clarksville 75,494

Knoxville 165,121
Memphis 610,337
Nashville-Davidson
   510,784

Texas
Abilene 106,654
Amarillo 157,615
Arlington 261,721
Austin 465,622
Baytown 63,850
Beaumont 114,323
Brownsville 98,962
Carrollton 82,169
Corpus Christi 257,453
Dallas 1,006,877
Denton 66,270
El Paso 515,342
Fort Worth 447,619
Galveston 59,070
Garland 180,650
Grand Prairie 99,616
Houston 1,630,553
Irving 155,037
Killeen 63,535
Laredo 122,899
Longview 70,311
Lubbock 186,206
McAllen 84,021
Mesquite 101,484
Midland 89,443

Odessa 89,699
Pasadena 119,363
Plano 128,713
Port Arthur 58,724
Richardson 74,840
San Angelo 84,474
San Antonio 935,933
Tyler 75,450
Victoria 55,076
Waco 103,590
Wichita Falls 96,259

Utah
Ogden 63,909
Orem 67,561
Provo 86,835
Salt Lake City 159,936
Sandy 75,058
West Valley City 86,976

Vermont
Burlington 39,127

Virginia
Alexandria 111,183
Chesapeake 151,976
Hampton 133,793
Lynchburg 66,049
Newport News 170,045
Norfolk 261,229
Portsmouth 103,907

Richmond 203,056
Roanoke 96,397
Virginia Beach 393,069

Washington
Bellevue 86,874
Everett 69,961
Seattle 516,259
Spokane 177,196
Tacoma 176,664
Yakima 54,827

West Virginia
Charleston 57,287
Huntington 54,844

Wisconsin
Appleton 65,695
Eau Claire 56,856
Green Bay 96,466
Kenosha 80,352
Madison 191,262
Milwaukee 628,088
Oshkosh 55,006
Racine 84,298
Waukesha 56,958
West Allis 63,221

Wyoming
Casper 46,742
Cheyenne 50,008

Largest U.S. Metropolitan Areas

What is a metropolitan area? It is a region that results when a city spreads beyond its limits, engulfing nearby communities and suburbs. The people in a metropolitan area become linked by jobs, schools, stores, and transportation systems such as subways. According to the 1990 census, 77.5% of the U. S. population lives in metropolitan areas of 56,000 or more people. And more than half of the nation lives in 39 metropolitan areas that have populations of over one million. Here are the ten largest.

Metropolitan Area	Location	Population
1. New York City	New York, New Jersey, Connecticut	18,087,251
2. Los Angeles	California	14,531,529
3. Chicago	Illinois, Indiana, Wisconsin	8,065,633
4. San Francisco	California	6,253,311
5. Philadelphia	Pennsylvania, New Jersey, Delaware, Maryland	5,899,345
6. Detroit	Michigan	4,665,236
7. Boston	Massachusetts, New Hampshire	4,171,643
8. Washington, D.C.	D.C., Maryland, Virginia	3,923,574
9. Dallas	Texas	3,885,415
10. Houston	Texas	3,711,043

250

More Facts at Your Fingertips

Top Products/Top States

Here, in order of their dollar value, are major farm products, fish, and minerals and the states that led in their production from 1987 through 1990. Nationwide leaders in each category are listed at right. Rank may change from year to year.

Farm Products | Leaders

1. *Cattle and calves*—Texas, Nebraska, Kansas, Colorado
2. *Dairy products*—Wisconsin, California, New York, Pennsylvania
3. *Soybeans*—Iowa, Illinois, Minnesota, Indiana
4. *Corn*—Illinois, Iowa, Nebraska, Indiana
5. *Hogs*—Iowa, Illinois, Minnesota, Indiana
6. *Broiler chickens*—Arkansas, Georgia, Alabama, North Carolina
7. *Greenhouse and nursery*—California, Florida, Ohio, New York
8. *Wheat*—Kansas, North Dakota, Oklahoma, Washington
9. *Cotton*—Texas, California, Mississippi, Arizona
10. *Eggs*—California, Georgia, Arkansas, Indiana
11. *Hay*—California, Arizona, Washington, Idaho
12. *Tobacco*—North Carolina, Kentucky, Virginia, South Carolina
13. *Turkeys*—Minnesota, North Carolina, California, Arkansas
14. *Oranges*—Florida, California, Texas, Arizona
15. *Potatoes*—Idaho, Maine, Washington, California
16. *Grapes*—California, Washington, New York, Arizona
17. *Tomatoes*—California, Florida, Ohio, New Jersey
18. *Rice*—Arkansas, California, Texas, Louisiana

Leaders
1. California
2. Texas
3. Iowa
4. Nebraska
5. Kansas
6. Illinois
7. Minnesota
8. Florida
9. Wisconsin
10. North Carolina

Fish

1. *Salmon*—Alaska, Washington, Oregon, California
2. *Shrimp*—Texas, Louisiana, Florida, Alabama
3. *Crabs*—Alaska, Florida, Maryland, Washington
4. *Cod*—Alaska, Massachusetts, Maine, New Hampshire
5. *Flounder*—Alaska, Massachusetts, Rhode Island, California

Leaders
1. Alaska
2. Massachusetts
3. Louisiana
4. Texas
5. Florida

Minerals

1. *Crude petroleum and natural gas*—Texas, Louisiana, Alaska, California
2. *Natural gas liquids*—Texas, Louisiana, Oklahoma, Kansas
3. *Coal and lignite surface mining*—Kentucky, West Virginia, Pennsylvania, Wyoming
4. *Coal underground mining*—West Virginia, Kentucky, Virginia, Pennsylvania
5. *Crushed stone*—Pennsylvania, Florida, Texas, Virginia
6. *Copper*—Arizona, New Mexico, Utah, Montana
7. *Cement*—California, Texas, Pennsylvania, Mississippi
8. *Construction sand and gravel*—Illinois, Michigan, California, New Jersey
9. *Gold*—Nevada, California, South Dakota, Utah
10. *Iron ore*—Minnesota, Michigan, Missouri, Utah
11. *Clay*—Georgia, Ohio, North Carolina, Texas
12. *Phosphate rock*—Florida, North Carolina, Idaho, Utah
13. *Lime*—Ohio, Missouri, Pennsylvania, Alabama
14. *Salt*—Louisiana, Texas, New York, Ohio
15. *Sodium carbonate*—Wyoming, California
16. *Magnesium*—Mississippi, California, Utah, Florida
17. *Sulfur*—Texas, Louisiana
18. *Boron*—California

Leaders
1. Texas
2. Louisiana
3. California
4. Alaska
5. Oklahoma
6. Kentucky
7. West Virginia
8. Wyoming
9. New Mexico
10. Pennsylvania

Superfacts

World's Rainiest Spot
Waialeale (mountain), Hawaii; annual average rainfall 661 inches (1,680 cm); rain falls 350 days a year

World's Strongest Surface Wind
231 mph (372 kmph), Mount Washington, New Hampshire; recorded April 12, 1934

World's Oldest Living Tree
Methuselah bristlecone pine, California; about 4,700 years old

World's Tallest Living Tree
Harry Cole redwood, California; 371 feet (113 m) tall

World's Largest Living Tree
General Sherman sequoia, California; 275 feet (84 m) tall, 82 feet (25 m) in circumference

World's Longest Cave System
Mammoth-Flint Ridge cave system, Kentucky; total mapped passageway length of more than 330 miles (531 km)

World's Largest Gorge
Grand Canyon, Colorado River, Arizona; 290 miles (466 km) long, 600 feet to 18 miles (183 m to 29 km) wide, 1 mile (1.6 km) deep

Driest Spot in U.S.
Death Valley, California; annual average rainfall 1.8 inches (4.6 cm)

Highest Temperature in U.S.
134°F (56.6°C), Death Valley, California; recorded July 10, 1913

Lowest Temperature in U.S.
Minus 80°F (−62.2°C) at Prospect Creek, Alaska; recorded January 23, 1971

Highest Point in U.S.
Mount McKinley, Alaska; 20,323 feet (6,194 m)

Lowest Point in U.S.
Death Valley, California; 282 feet (86 m) below sea level

Longest River System in U.S.
Mississippi-Missouri; 3,708 miles (5,971 km) long

Highest Town in U.S.
Climax, Colorado; 11,560 feet (3,526 m)

Lowest Town in U.S.
Calipatria, California; 185 feet (56 m) below sea level

Most Crowded State in U.S.
New Jersey; 992.7 people per sq mi (383.27 per sq km)

Least Crowded State in U.S.
Alaska; 0.93 people per sq mi (0.36 per sq km)

Illustrations Credits

Abbreviations for terms appearing below: (t)-top; (b)-bottom; (l)-left; (r)-right; (c)-center; NGP-National Geographic Photographer; NGS-National Geographic Staff; TIB-The Image Bank; LC-The Library of Congress; PA-Photographers/Aspen; WC-Woodfin Camp.

Cover and 2-3, Michel Tcherevkoff; eagle photograph, Tom and Pat Leeson.

America's Many Faces
9, Tom Bean. 10-11, Barry Lewis, Network. 12-13, Francisco Hidalgo, TIB. 14-15, Hank Morgan. 16-17, James A. Sugar.

The Maps in Your Atlas
18, William H. Bond, NGS.

The District of Columbia
20, LC. 22, (t) Larry Chapman; (b) Seny Norasingh. 23, (tl) Mark Avino, National Air & Space Museum; (tr) Olivier Martel, Black Star; (b) Adam Woolfitt, Susan Griggs Agency.

New England
24-25, William H. Bond, NGS. 26, Wills T. White, Images from the Past, Bennington, Vermont. 28, (t) Mike Clemmer; (b) Cynthia B. Foster. 29, (tl) (r) Michael Melford; (b) Nathan Benn, WC. 30, New Hampshire Hist. Soc. 32, (l) David Brownell, TIB; (t) Sandy Felsenthal. 32-33, Sandy Felsenthal. 33, (t) Sandy Felsenthal; (r) Sam Abell, NGP. 34, Joseph Coburn Smith. 36, (t) Michael Melford; (b) Kunio Owaki, The Stock Market. 37, (l) Phil Schermeister, PA; (t) Michael S. Yamashita; (b) Phil Schermeister. 38, Worthington Cornell, LC: Martin Sandler Productions. 40, (t) David Muench; (b) Peter Southwick, Stock Boston. 41, (t) Seth Resnick; (bl) Michael Carroll, New England Stock Photo; (br) Stephen J. Krasemann, Photo Researchers Inc. 42, Luis Marden. 44, (l) Gabe Palmer, The Stock Market; (r) Sarah Leen; (b) Robert Benson. 44-45, Tor Eigeland. 45, Randa Bishop. 46, Adler Art Associates. 48, (t) Robert D. Hagan; (b) Steve Dunwell, TIB; (r) Ira Block. 49, Steve Dunwell, TIB.

Mid-Atlantic States
50-51, William H. Bond, NGS. 52, LC. 54, (l) Bob Clemenz; (b) Lacrosse USA, Inc. 54-55, Jodi Cobb, NGP. 55, (b) Kenneth Garrett; (r) Ted Spiegel. 56, Lewis W. Hine, LC. 58-59, William T. Douthitt, NGS. 59, (tl) William T. Douthitt, NGS; (bl) J. Nettis, H. Armstrong Roberts; (tr) Russ Kennedy; (br) James L. Stanfield, NGP. 60, John E. Fletcher. 62, (t) David Muench; (b) Martha Cooper. 63, Bob Krist. 64, Hagerstown Chamber of Commerce. 66, (l) David Alan Harvey; (t) Lowell Georgia; (b) Greg Pease. 67, (l) Kevin Fleming; (r) Dan Dry. 68, E. I. du Pont de Nemours & Co. 70, Kevin Fleming. 70-71, Kevin Fleming. 71, (t) Kevin Fleming; (b) Stephen R. Brown.

Appalachian Highlands
72-73, William H. Bond, NGS. 74, B. Anthony Stewart. 76, (t) Bill Luster; (b) William Strode. 76-77, Bill Luster. 77, (b) Michael O'Brien; (r) Chip Clark. 78, Ben Shahn, LC. 80, (l) Michael O'Brien; (t) James P. Blair, NGP. 80-81, Sam Abell, NGP. 81, (t) Joseph H. Bailey, NGP; (r) James P. Blair, NGP. 82, Frances B. Johnston, The Mu-

seum of Modern Art, New York. 84, (l) D. Cary Jackson; (t) Nathan Benn. 84-85, Karen Kasmauski. 85, (t) Karen Kasmauski; (r) David Alan Harvey. 86, J. Baylor Roberts. 88, (l) David Muench; (b) Karen Kasmauski. 88-89, Joe Viesti. 89, (b) Karen Kasmauski; (r) Nathan Benn. 90, Lewis W. Hine, George Eastman House. 92, (tl) John Dominis; (bl) Joseph H. Bailey, NGP; (r) David Alan Harvey. 93, Bill Weems.

The Southeast
94-95, William H. Bond, NGS. 96, B. Anthony Stewart. 98, (t)(bl) Matt Bradley; (br) Charles O'Rear. 99, Garry McMichael, Root Resources. 100, Smithsonian Institution, National Museum of the American Indian. 102, Gail Mooney. 103, (tl) Gail Mooney; (tr) J. D. Schwalm, Stock South; (b) Nathan Benn, WC. 104, LC. 106, Ed Malles, Photo Options. 107, (t)(bc) Ed Malles, Photo Options; (bl) Charles O'Rear; (br) Randa Bishop. 108, Georgia Dept. of Archives and History. 110, (t) David Muench; (b) Jim Richardson. 111, (l) Jim Richardson, West Light; (tr) Bill Weems, WC; (br) Al Stepheson, WC. 112, LC. 114, (t) Tom Blagden Jr.; (b) David Dobbs, Photo Options. 114-115, Annie Griffiths Belt. 115, (t) Bill Curtsinger; (b) Annie Griffiths Belt. 116, Louisiana State Museum: Jan White Brantley. 118, (tl) C. C. Lockwood; (tr)(b) Nathan Benn. 119, (l) C. C. Lockwood; (r) Philip Gould. 120, Detroit Publishing Co., LC. 122, (t) Comstock; (bl) Nathan Benn; (br) James P. Blair, NGP. 123, (l) Roger Ressmeyer, Starlight; (r) Bill Curtsinger.

Great Lakes States
124-125, William H. Bond, NGS. 126, H. H. Bennett Studio Foundation. 128, (tl) Paul Damien; (tr) Jim Brandenburg; (b) Paul Damien. 128-129, Seny Norasingh. 129, Kenneth Garrett. 130, Michigan Dept. of State. 132, Michael S. Yamashita. 132-133, Robert M. Lightfoot III. 133, (tl) Phil Schermeister; (tr) Lowell Georgia; (b) Fred Ward, Black Star. 134, UPI, Bettmann Archive. 136, (t) Lynn Johnson; (bl) James L. Stanfield, NGP; (br) Ira Block. 137, (t) Louie Psihoyos; (b) Kevin Fleming. 138, J. C. Allen & Son. 140, (t) The Selmer Co., L.P.; (b) Sandy Felsenthal. 140-141, Karen Keeney. 141, (bl) Sandy Felsenthal; (r) Frank Cezus, Tony Stone Worldwide. 142, William H. Jenkins, Martin Sandler Productions. 144, (t) Jack Van Antwerp; (b) Dennis Barnes. 144-145, Richard Alexander Cooke III. 145, (t) Louie Psihoyos, Contact Stock Images, WC; (b) Joseph H. Bailey, NGP.

The Heartland
146-147, William H. Bond, NGS. 148, State Hist. Soc. of North Dakota. 150, (t) Richard Alexander Cooke III; (b) Annie Griffiths Belt. 151, Annie Griffiths Belt. 152, The Minnesota Hist. Soc. 154, (l) Raymond Gehman; (r) Richard Hamilton Smith. 155, (tl) Randall Hyman; (b) Annie Griffiths Belt; (r) Jim Brandenburg. 156, South Dakota State Hist. Soc. 158, (t) Jim Brandenburg; (b) Tom Nebbia. 158-159, Jim Brandenburg. 159, (t) Tom Nebbia; (b) Jim Brandenburg. 160, Nebraska State Hist. Soc. 162, (l) Terry Eiler; (t) Charles O'Rear. 162-163, Grant Heilman, Grant Heilman Photography Inc. 163, (t) David Muench; (r) James L. Amos. 164, Harold H. Jorgensen. 166, (l) Craig Aurness; (b) Tom Bean. 166-167, David Muench. 167, (t) Craig Aurness; (b) Scott Rutherford. 168, Grant Heilman Photography Inc. 170, Cotton Coulson. 171, (tl)(tr) Cotton Coulson, WC; (b) David Hornback. 172, Missouri Hist. Soc. 174, José Azel, Contact Press Images. 174-175, Annie Griffiths Belt. 175, (tl) Randy Olson; (tr) Nathan Benn; (b) Randall Hyman.

The Southwest
176-177, William H. Bond, NGS. 178, Bud DeWald. 180, Martha Cooper, Peter Arnold Inc. 180-181, Gordon Anderson. 181, (tl) Kerrick James; (bl) James A. Sugar; (r) Mike Clemmer. 182, Ben Wittick, Museum of New Mexi-

co. 184, (tl) Danny Lehman; (tr) Adam Woolfitt, WC; (b) Dan Budnik, WC. 185, (t) Danny Lehman; (b) Terry Eiler. 186, Arthur Rothstein, LC. 188, (tl) Annie Griffiths Belt; (b) Martin Rogers. 188-189, Chris Johns. 189, (t) Chris Johns; (b) Matt Bradley. 190, Fred A. Schell, American Petroleum Institute. 192, (l) Charles O'Rear; (c) Matt Bradley. 192-193, Dan Dry. 193, (bl) Steven C. Wilson, Entheos; (r) David Alan Harvey.

Mountain States
194-195, William H. Bond, NGS. 196, Idaho State Hist. Soc. 198, Chris Huskinson, F-Stock Photo Inc. 198-199, David R. Stoecklein. 199, (t) Dave Shippee; (bl) J. R. Simplot Co.; (br) Scott Rutherford. 200, Burlington Northern Railroad. 202, (tl) Scott Rutherford; (bl) Jeff Foott; (r) Dewitt Jones. 203, (t) Nicholas DeVore III, PA; (b) Paul Chesley. 204, B. Anthony Stewart. 206, (l) Raymond Gehman; (r) David Alan Harvey. 207, (tl) Jeremy Schmidt; (tr) Phil Schofield; (b) Tomasz Tomaszewski. 208, Maureen H. Wilson: Stanley Paher. 210, (tl) Tom Bean; (bl) Kerby Smith; (r) Jack Gucia, TIB. 211, (t) Phil Schermeister; (b) Phil Schofield. 212, Utah State Hist. Soc. 214, (t) Dennis Chamberlin; (b) Jim Richardson; (br) Dennis Chamberlin. 215, (l) George F. Mobley, NGP; (r) Floyd Holdman. 216, O. E. Aultman. 218, (t) Steve Raymer, NGS; (bl) Craig Aurness; (br) Paul Chesley. 218-219, David Muench. 219, Amy Deputy.

Pacific Coast States
220-221, William H. Bond, NGS. 222, News Tribune, Tacoma, Washington. 224, (t) Gary Braasch; (bl)(br) Sandy Felsenthal. 225, (l) Randy Wells, Allstock; (r) Robert W. Madden, NGS. 226, George M. Weister, Knight Library, University of Oregon. 228, (l) Annie Griffiths Belt; (r) David Muench. 229, (t) Ray Atkeson; (b) Robert W. Madden, NGS; (br) Harald Sund. 230, The Bancroft Library, University of California at Berkeley. 232, (t) Richard Alexander Cooke III; (b) Vince Streano. 233, (tl) Louie Psihoyos; (bl) Brent Bear, West Light; (r) Craig Aurness.

Alaska, Hawaii, and Distant Shores
234-235, William H. Bond, NGS. 236, Amos Burg. 238, (tl) John L. Hinderman; (tr) Cradoc Bagshaw, West Light; (bl) Jim Rearden; (br) David Alan Harvey. 239, Tom Bean. 240, Ray Jerome Baker, Bishop Museum. 242, Richard Alexander Cooke III. 243, (t) Paul Chesley; (bl) Steve Raymer, NGS; (bc) Paul Chesley, PA; (r) Paul Chesley. 244, Charles Allmon. 246, (tl) Ken Straiton, The Stock Market; (bl) Frederic Koehler Sutter, ASG. 246-247, Ira Block. 247, (t) Stephen Frink, The Waterhouse; (b) Stephanie Maze.

Acknowledgments

We wish to express our appreciation to the many individuals and organizations who helped in the preparation of the *National Geographic Picture Atlas of OUR FIFTY STATES*: Jim G. Rigby, Nevada Bureau of Mines and Geology; Whitney Smith, Flag Research Center; the Bureau of the Census; the Bureau of Indian Affairs; the National Marine Fishery Service; the National Park Service; Native American tribal associations; the United States Department of Agriculture; and the state divisions of forestry, geology, and tourism.

We are grateful to several divisions of the National Geographic Society: Valerie Mattingley and Jennifer Moseley of the United Kingdom Office; Administrative Services; Illustrations Library; the National Geographic Library, including its Map and News Collections; Messenger Center; Photographic Services; Production Services, Pre-Press Division; Records Library.

Index

Type composition by the Typographic section of National Geographic Production Services, Pre-Press Division. Color separations by Lanman Progressive Co., Washington, D.C.; Phototype Color Graphics, Pennsauken, N.J. Printed and bound by Ringier America, Inc., New Berlin, Wisc. Paper by Mead Paper Co., New York, N.Y.

Library of Congress CIP Data

National Geographic Society (U. S.). Book Division
    National Geographic picture atlas of our fifty states/prepared by National Geographic Book Division.
        p.   cm.
Includes index.
Summary: Includes maps and other pertinent information about the geography, industries, and population of each of the fifty states.
    ISBN 0-87044-859-5 (regular ed. : alk. paper). — ISBN 0-87044-860-9 (lib. ed. : alk. paper)
    1. United States—Maps.   [1. United States—Maps. 2. Atlases.]
    I. Title. II. Title: Our fifty states.
G1200.N33 1991 [G&M]
912.73—dc20   91-28084
                                        CIP
                                        MAP AC